CHILD DEVELOPMENT
IN
LIFE-SPAN PERSPECTIVE

CHILD DEVELOPMENT IN LIFE-SPAN PERSPECTIVE

Edited by

E. Mavis Hetherington
University of Virginia

Richard M. Lerner
Pennsylvania State University

Marion Perlmutter
University of Michigan

Sponsored by the Social Science Research Council

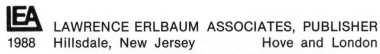 LAWRENCE ERLBAUM ASSOCIATES, PUBLISHER
1988   Hillsdale, New Jersey   Hove and London

Lawrence Erlbaum Associates, Inc., Publishers
365 Broadway
Hillsdale, New Jersey 07642

Library of Congress Cataloging-in-Publication Data

Child development in life-span perspective.

    Bibliography: p.
    Includes index.
    1. Child development.   2. Developmental psychology.
3. Life cycle, Human.   I. Hetherington, E. Mavis (Eileen
Mavis), 1926–   . II. Lerner, Richard M.
III] Perlmutter, Marion. IV] Social Science Research
Council (U.S.)
HQ767.9.C4445   1988   305.2′3   87–24355
ISBN 0-8058-0189-8
ISBN 0-8058–0190-1 (pbk.)

Printed in the United States of America
10 9 8 7 6 5 4 3 2 1

CONTENTS

| CONTRIBUTORS | xi |

| PREFACE | xiii |

1   **CHILD PSYCHOLOGY AND LIFE-SPAN DEVELOPMENT**   1
E. Mavis Hetherington and Paul B. Baltes

Introduction, *1*
Propositions in Life-Span Development, *3*
Intervention, *13*
Summary, *14*
References, *16*

2   **PERSONALITY DEVELOPMENT: A Life-Span Perspective**   21
Richard M. Lerner

Introduction: Definitional Debates
   About Personality, *22*
A Multilevel, Multiprocess Definition
   of Personality, *23*
A Life-Span Model of Personality Development, *32*
Conclusions, *41*
Acknowledgments, *42*
References, *42*

3   **THE SOCIAL CONSTRUCTION OF THE**   **47**
      PSYCHOLOGY OF CHILDHOOD
      Some Contemporary Processes
      John W. Meyer

      Introduction, *47*
      The Institutionalized Life Course, *50*
      Guiding the Ideas on the Institutional Character
        of the Individual, *52*
      Emergent Perspectives in Psychology, *55*
      Life-Span Ideas, *59*
      Normative and Social Structural Implications, *60*
      Conclusions: Some Implications for Research, *63*
      Acknowledgments, *64*
      References, *64*

4   **CLASS AND THE SOCIALIZATION**   **67**
      OF CHILDREN
      Constancy, Change, or Irrelevance?
      David L. Featherman, Kenneth I. Spenner,
      Naouki Tsunematsu

      Introduction, *67*
      Social Class as a Process Variable, *70*
      A Class Schema for Capitalist Economies, *74*
      Patterns of Class Mobility of Children
        in Two Settings, *76*
      Do Social Class and Class Mobility
        Influence Development? *80*
      Conclusions and Speculations Linking
        Class and Child Socialization in Life-Span
        Perspective, *85*
      Acknowledgments, *88*
      References, *88*

5   **EXPLANATORY STYLE**   **91**
      ACROSS THE LIFE SPAN:
      Achievement and Health
      Martin E. P. Seligman, Leslie P. Kamen,
      Susan Nolen-Hoeksema

      Introduction, *91*
      Explanatory Style: Link with Achievement, *92*

Explanatory Style: Link with Health, *93*
Measurement of Explanatory Style, *94*
Explanatory Style and Life-Span
   Development, *95*
Origins of Explanatory Style, *98*
Achievement, *101*
Health, *105*
Across the Life Span: Stability
   and Continuity of Explanatory Style, *109*
Summary, *110*
Acknowledgments, *110*
References, *110*

---

6 **CHILDHOOD PRECURSORS** 115
OF THE LIFE COURSE
Early Personality and Life Disorganization

Avshalom Caspi and Glen H. Elder, Jr.

Introduction, *116*
Studying the Coherence of Personality
   in the Life Course, *117*
Early Personality and Life Disorganization, *124*
How Early Personality Shapes
   the Life Course, *135*
Personality in the Life Course, *138*
References, *139*

---

7 **CHANGES IN CHILDREN'S SOCIAL LIVES** 143
AND THE DEVELOPMENT OF SOCIAL
UNDERSTANDING

Judy Dunn and Lonnie Sherrod

Introduction, *143*
The Arrival of a Sibling, *146*
Implications for the Study of Changes
   in Children's Social Lives, *149*
Developments in Social Understanding
   in the "Transition from Infancy
   to Childhood," *152*
Summary, *153*
References, *155*

8 **FAMILIES IN LIFE-SPAN PERSPECTIVE:** **159**
A Multilevel Developmental Approach
Ross D. Parke

Introduction, *159*
The Many Faces of Development, *160*
Historical Context: A Neglected Source
of Developmental Influence, *172*
Toward a Perspective of Multiple
Developmental Trajectories, *174*
The Timing of Parenthood: An Application
of the Multiple Developmental Trajectory
Perspective, *174*
Stressful Transitions
as Points of Intervention, *183*
Conclusions, *184*
References, *185*

9 **COGNITIVE DEVELOPMENT** **191**
IN LIFE-SPAN PERSPECTIVE:
From Description of Differences
to Explanation of Changes
Marion Perlmutter

Introduction, *191*
Questions to be Answered
by Cognitive Developmentalists, *192*
Major Approaches to the Study
of Cognitive Development, *197*
Integration of Research on Cognitive
Development, *205*
Conclusions, *212*
Acknowledgments, *214*
References, *214*

10 **INDIVIDUAL DIFFERENCES** **219**
IN COGNITIVE DEVELOPMENT:
Does Instruction Make a Difference?
Franz E. Weinert and Andreas Helmke

Introduction, *219*
Quality of Instruction, Learning, Progress,
and Achievement Differences, *224*

Quality of Instruction and Learning Outcomes, *227*
Concluding Remarks, *236*
References, *238*

---

11   CULTURE AND SCHOOLING: 241
Influences on Cognitive Development

Harold W. Stevenson

Introduction, *241*
Comparative Studies of Chinese, Japanese,
    and American Children, *242*
Comparative Studies
    of Quechua-Speaking Indian Children, *253*
Conclusion, *256*
Acknowledgments, *258*
References, *258*

---

12   LESSONS FROM THE LIFE-SPAN: 259
What Theorists of Intellectual Development
Among Children Can Learn from Their
Counterparts Studying Adults

Robert J. Sternberg

Introduction, *259*
Lesson #1: Intellectual Development
    Does Not End in Adolescence, *260*
Lesson #2: Adolescence Is Not the Pinnacle
    of Intelligence Either, *262*
Lesson #3: Intelligence Is Much More
    Multifaceted Than Traditionally Thought, *264*
Lesson #4: Informal Knowledge Can Be as Important
    to Intelligence as Is Formal Knowledge, *265*
Lesson #5: Intellectual Development Is Not
    a Subset of Cognitive Development Narrowly
    Defined, *266*
Lesson #6: The Traditional Evaluative Criteria
    for Theories and Tests of Intelligence
    Are too Narrow, *267*
Lesson #7: Intelligence Is in Part
    in the Eye of the Beholder, *268*

Lesson #8: What Is Novel or Familiar for Children in One Environment Is Not Necessarily Novel or Familiar for Those in Another Environment, *270*

Lesson #9: Intelligence Resides in the Interaction Between the Individual and the Environment, *271*

Lesson #10: Cohort Effects Apply to Children as Well as to Adults, *272*

Conclusion, *273*

Acknowledgment, *273*

References, *273*

13   THE LIFE-SPAN INTERVENTION CUBE   277

Orville G. Brim, Jr. and Deborah A. Phillips

Introduction, *277*

Life-Span Development Theory and Intervention, *280*

The Life-Span Intervention Cube, *282*

The Current Status of Social Policies for Children, *290*

Life-Span Development Theory and the Realities of Politics, *293*

Conclusions, *296*

References, *297*

AUTHOR INDEX   301

SUBJECT INDEX   311

CONTRIBUTORS

Paul B. Baltes, PhD Max-Planck Institute for Human Development and Education, Lentzeallee 94, 1000 Berlin 33, W. GERMANY

Orville G. Brim, Jr., PhD Van Zandt and Associates, 2140 Tenth Ave., Vero Beach, FL 32960

Avshalom Caspi, PhD Department of Psychology and Social Relations, Harvard University, Cambridge, MA 02138

Judith Dunn, PhD Department of Individual and Family Studies, College of Health and Human Development, Pennsylvania State University, University Park, PA 16802

Glen H. Elder, Jr., PhD Carolina Population Center, University of North Carolina, University Square 300A, Chapel Hill, NC 27514-3997

David L. Featherman, PhD Department of Sociology, 4434 Social Science Building, University of Wisconsin, Madison, WI 53706

Andreas Helmke, PhD Max-Planck Institute for Psychological Research, Leopoldstrasse 24, D-8000 Munich 40, W. GERMANY

E. Mavis Hetherington, PhD Department of Psychology, University of Virginia, Gilmer Hall, Charlottesville, VA 22901

Leslie P. Kamen Psychology Department, University of Pennsylvania, 3815 Walnut St., Philadelphia, PA 19104-6196

Richard M. Lerner, PhD Department of Individual and Family Studies, College of Health and Human Development, Pennsylvania State University, University Park, PA 16802

John W. Meyer, PhD Department of Sociology, Stanford University, Stanford, CA 94305

Susan Nolen-Hoeksema, PhD Psychology Department, Stanford University, Stanford, CA 94305

Ross D. Parke, PhD Department of Psychology, University of Illinois, Champaign, IL 61820

Marion Perlmutter, PhD Institute of Gerontology, University of Michigan, 300 North Ingalls, Ann Arbor, MI 48109-2007

Deborah Phillips, PhD Psychology Department, University of Virginia, Gilmer Hall, Charlottesville, VA 22901

Kenneth I. Spenner, PhD Department of Sociology, Duke University, Durham, NC 27706

Martin E. P. Seligman, PhD Psychology Department, University of Pennsylvania, 3815 Walnut St., Philadelphia, PA 19104-6196

Robert J. Sternberg, PhD Department of Psychology, Yale University, Box 11A Yale Station, New Haven, CT 06520

Harold W. Stevenson, PhD Department of Psychology, University of Michigan, Ann Arbor, MI 48109

Lonnie R. Sherrod, PhD Graduate Faculty, New School for Social Research, 65 Fifth Ave., Rm. 110, New York, NY 10003

M. Brewster Smith, PhD Stevenson College, University of California at Santa Cruz, Santa Cruz, CA 95064

Naouke Tsunematsu Department of Sociology, University of Wisconsin, Madison, WI 53706

PREFACE

Child development has always been a multidisciplinary field, one involving scholars from pediatrics and biology, from sociology and anthropology, and from education and psychology. Together, these fields have contributed to advancing the understanding of the bases of individual development, and of the implications of such change for child adjustment, health, pedagogy, and policy.

The life-span view of human development is also a multidisciplinary field. The perspective is associated with a theoretical conception of the life course as involving an integration of changes among variables from biological through sociocultural and historical levels of analysis. The study of these interrelations has aided life-span scholars' attempts at describing, explaining, and optimizing the several directions of intraindividual change that comprise the human condition.

There are, therefore, common intellectual interests found in the child development and life-span fields. However, these commonalities exist along with distinctions between the two areas. On the one hand, both fields are concerned with the embeddedness of human life in a complex and changing context; with the range of forms (i.e., with the plasticity) that development may take as a consequence of this link between the developing individual and a changing world. Thus, both perspectives are interested in the possibility—through either direct interventions or social policies—of enhancing the quality of individuals' lives.

On the other hand, until recently child development has emphasized the first decade of life, and has therefore understandably stressed the importance of early experience and/or maturation on later changes in development. This focus has led to a concern with general, developmental trajectories and with the more proximal contexts of human life such as the family, the peer group, or the school.

In turn, the life-span developmental perspective has evolved over the course of the last several decades through a focus on the study of adult development and aging and, more recently, on adolescence. These age period foci have resulted in an emphasis on normative and non-normative ontogenetic and contextual phenomena. Examples are the transitions to junior high school, marriage, parenthood, divorce, retirement, unexpected illness, death of a spouse, and wars or economic depressions. These phenomena may not have antecedents in earlier developmental periods; nevertheless, they may redirect the developmental trajectory of the individual. Thus, within the life-span perspective there has been an emphasis on individual differences, on later periods of life, on life transitions, and on the more distal sociocultural and historical contexts of life.

The commonalities and the differences between the child development and life-span fields make a synthesis of the theoretical and empirical traditions of the two areas a challenging, but nevertheless appropriate, and potentially mutually enriching, endeavor. Differences in perspective, even when they remain, can lead to a refinement in respective theoretical positions and to greater methodological precision. Commonality, when it is found, can result in a more holistic understanding of the course of human life.

For example, such integration may enhance the ability to articulate the conditions of continuity under which there are connections among all age periods of life, the bases of discontinuity in which age-period-specific phenomena occur, or the nature of transformations from one portion of life to another. In addition, such integration holds the promise of providing a stronger knowledge-base for decisions about the relative costs and benefits of either proximal or distal, and/or either concurrent or historical, interventions and policies aimed at fostering healthier development across the life span.

The present volume is one outcome of what was a relatively long-term commitment by child- and life-span-developmentalists to explore the limits of and possibilities for such integration. This volume is composed of contributions made by members of the Social Science Research Council Subcommittee on Child Development in Life-Span Perspective, a subgroup of the Committee on Life-Course Perspectives. Over the course of 6 years (1981–1986), this Committee, which was supported by funds from the Foundation for Child Development, sponsored several programs (conferences, workshops, a Summer Institute for young scholars at the Center for Advanced Study in the Behavioral Sciences), designed to explore the possibilities of, and uses for, a synthesis of the two fields. A final conference was held in June 1985 at the National Academy of Sciences Conference Center, in Woods Hole, Massachusetts. This meeting was designed to allow the members of the subcommittee to integrate what they learned from these programs, and to present their ideas, within their own specific areas of expertise, about the nature of the constraints on, and the potentials for, a synthesis of child development and the life-span perspective. The chapters in this book were derived in the main from the papers given at this conference.

We are indebted to several people and organizations for facilitating our work on this volume. Our most important intellectual debt is to our colleagues on the Child Development in Life-Span Perspective Subcommittee. It is their expertise and wisdom that fill the pages of this book, and it is their collaboration that made this book a reality. We are grateful also to the Social Science Research Council for the sponsorship and encouragement of the work of the Subcommittee. In particular we want to express our great appreciation to Dr. Lonnie R. Sherrod, now Dean at the New School for Social Research. In his former position as an SSRC staff member, he provided invaluable support and guidance for all of the Subcommittee's endeavors. We are deeply grateful also to the Foundation for Child Development for the awarding of a grant to the SSRC that enabled the Subcommittee to implement its programs.

Finally, each of us would like to express our gratitude to people at our respective institutions. E. Mavis Hetherington thanks Ann Gutterieg for secretarial support, and is grateful for grant support provided by the MacArthur Foundation during the period she worked on this book. Richard M. Lerner thanks Teri Charmbury for secretarial support, and is grateful to the William T. Grant Foundation and to the NIMH for grant support during the period in which he worked on this book. Marion Perlmutter thanks Patricia Blackman for secretarial support, and is grateful for grant support provided by the NIA, the Brookdale Foundation, and the Spencer Foundation during the period she worked on this book.

We believe this book provides a good representation of the current status of the relation between the child development and the life-span areas: There is evidence that there may be limits to the synthesis of these two fields; however, there is both conceptual and empirical evidence of current integration. Our hope is that our colleagues from the fields of child- and life-span-development will see this evidence in as positive a way as we do. If so, we believe that the book will underscore the potential of future attempts at collaborative cross-fertilization. Certainly the outcome of such future work will be a broadened theoretical and empirical understanding of the relations between the developing child and his/her changing world. Potentially, such work may provide new insight into the ways in which all scholars concerned with the child may work in concert to improve the quality of his or her development.

E. M. H.
R. M. L.
M.P.

ACKNOWLEDGMENT

The activities of the Council's Subcommittee on Child Development in Life-Span Perspective have been supported primarily by the Foundation for Child Development, a private foundation that makes grants to educational and charitable institutions. Its main interests are in research, social and economic indicators of childrens' lives, advocacy and public information projects, and service experiments that help translate theoretical knowledge about children into policies and practices that affect their daily lives.

1 CHILD PSYCHOLOGY AND LIFE-SPAN DEVELOPMENT

E. Mavis Hetherington
University of Virginia

Paul B. Baltes
Max Planck Institute for Human Development and
Education Berlin, F.R.G.

ABSTRACT

This chapter reviews the similarities and differences related to theory, methodology, and intervention in the perspectives of child psychologists and life-span developmentalists. The basic propositions underlying the life-span developmentalists and the basic propositions underlying the life-span developmental orientation are reviewed. These include the view of development as a life long process, issues of gains (growth) and losses (decline) in development, propositions related to age-graded, non-normative and history-graded influences on development, and the emphasis on organismic-contextualism. A brief review of advances in methodology addressed to issues of cohort effects and contextualism is presented as an exemplar of the intermeshing of theoretical and methodological concerns of life-span scholars. Finally possible applications of the life-span perspective to strategies in intervention are examined.

It is concluded that although there are more similarities than differences in the perspectives of child psychologists and life-span developmentalists there are mutual advantages to be gained by each field learning about the other. The advantages result primarily from (a) the differential emphases that child and life-span scholars place on the components contributing to the nature of developmental theory, and (b) the mutual need to develop a theory of interconnectedness of age periods.

INTRODUCTION

Life-span research exists in various forms. The first is the extension of developmental studies across the life course without a major effort at the construction of developmental metatheory that is unique to life-span work. The second form includes the specification of a family of metatheoretical propositions about the nature of developmental theory that emanate from life-span research. This second approach provides the framework for this chapter.

In recent years, proponents of life-span development from a variety of disciplines have expounded on the unique theoretical posture and possible advantages of a life-span perspective in the study of human development (Baltes, 1983; Baltes & Reese, 1984; Elder, 1985; Featherman, 1983; Lerner, 1984). In some cases, the life-span perspective has been presented as an alternative view to that of child and adolescent development. The response to this view by child psychologists has ranged from enthusiastic endorsement to bemusement or resentment of the proselytizing zeal of some of the life-span scholars. Thus, some child developmentalists have responded that there are few major differences between the underlying premises in child and adolescent development and in life-span development, that the differences are mainly those of emphasis. Moreover, it has been argued that in actuality, those who identify themselves as being in child development or in life-span development tend to be studying different parts of the life span. Child developmentalists study the early years, life-span developmentalists study the adult years or more commonly old age. Neither really are studying the life span. It is the old problem of the blind men feeling different parts of the elephant and describing its attributes. Finally, it has been argued that there is nothing new in the life-span perspective (Kaplan, 1983), that the basic life-span propositions have been accepted by most developmentalists and that many of these assumptions can be found in the work of early (Baldwin & Poulton, 1902) and contemporary child psychologists (Cairns & Hood, 1983; Scarr, 1982).

The current response by life-span scholars to this criticism of child developmentalists is two-fold. On the one hand, they emphasize that, in part, because of life-span work, child development has evolved increasingly in the direction of the conceptions and methodologies advanced by life-span scholars. On the other hand, they acknowledge similarities in approach but point to differences in the relative weighting of the components contributing to the nature of developmental theory. An example is Baltes' (1986) observation:

> The innovativeness lies in the gestalt and coordination of the perspectives into a patterned metatheoretical framework. Considering the whole complex of perspectives as a family and applying it with some degree of radicalism to the study of development, is what makes the difference. (p. 6)

The emphasis in this chapter on the contributions of life-span psychology to child development is not meant to imply that many other fields have not had as great or greater influence on the recent course of child development. Piagetian theory, information processing, family systems theory, cybernetics, and ecological theory have all had a profound influence on thinking and research in child development in the past 2 decades. However, this volume is the result of a series of meetings extending over a period of 4 years between a group of life-span researchers and child psychologists sponsored by the Social Science Research Council. The goal of these meetings was the mutual enhancement of each discipline by considering knowledge and perspectives from the other field and this is the focus of this volume.

PROPOSITIONS IN LIFE-SPAN DEVELOPMENT

Most life-span advocates work from a set of propositions or assumptions about the nature of human development and change. Table 1.1 summarizes some of the assumptions that many life-span scholars emphasize when specifying the uniqueness of their conceptual approach. In this opening chapter, these assumptions will be presented, and the congruence and disparities in the view held by life-span researchers and child psychologists will be discussed.

Development as a Life-Long Process

A key proposition in life-span development is that development is a life-long process, a process that one might say extends from sperm to worm. No one stage is most critical or salient in producing developmental change. Although child psychologists often have focused on infancy and the childhood years as the most important, formative, and rapid periods of development, life-span proponents assert that events and changes occurring after childhood and throughout the adult years have equally powerful effects on the direction and rate of human development.

Perhaps because of the past influence of psychodynamic and learning theory, most child psychologists believe that early experiences shape the responses to later experiences (Brim & Kagan, 1980a). However, child psychologists are not a homogeneous entity. A sizeable number would agree that development is being continuously modified across the life span. Many child psychologists are interested in the points in development when specific types of input will be most likely to be manifested in ontogeny. In fact, in contemporary child psychology, there is considerable controversy about the precise time periods in which certain social and cognitive experiences first become relevant and when they will be reflected in subsequent development. If we take the example of cognitive development, few significant relations have been found between parent–infant interaction and concurrent

TABLE 1.1
Summary of Family of Theoretical Propositions Characteristic
of Life-Span Developmental Psychology

Concepts	Propositions
Life-span development	• Ontogenetic development is a life-long process. No age period holds primacy in regulating the nature of development. During development and at all stages of the life span, both continuous (cumulative) and discontinuous (innovative) processes are at work.
Development at gain–loss	• The process of development in any given class of behavior is complex, and not a simple movement toward efficacy such as incremental growth. Rather, throughout life development is always constituted by the joint occurrence of gain (growth) and loss (decline).
Multidirectionality	• The direction of change varies by categories of behavior. In addition, during the same developmental periods, some systems of behavior show increases, whereas others evince decreases in level of functioning.
Plasticity	• Much intraindividual plasticity (within-person modifiability) is found in psychological development. Depending on the life conditions and experiences by a given individual, his or her developmental course can take many forms.
Historical embeddedness	• Ontogenetic development can also vary substantially in accordance with historical–cultural conditions. How ontogenetic (age-related) development proceeds is markedly influenced by the kind of sociocultural conditions existing in a given historical period, and by how these evolve over time.
Contextualism as paradigm	• Any particular course of individual development can be understood as the outcome of the interactions (dialectics) among three systems of developmental influences: age-graded, history-graded, and non-normative. These systems also show interindividual differentiation in conjunction with biological and social structure.
Field of development as multidisciplinary	• Psychological development needs to be seen in the interdisciplinary context provided by other disciplines (e.g., anthropology, biology, sociology) concerned with human development. The openness of the life-span perspective to interdisciplinary posture implies that a "purist" psychological view offers but a partial representation of behavioral development from conception to death.

Note: After Baltes (1986)

measures of infant cognitive development in the first 6 months of age although they emerge in the second year of life. Three hypotheses have been advanced to explain these nonsignificant early relationships. The scoop model advanced by McCall (1981) proposes that early intellectual development is largely controlled by genetic factors that lessen over the course of the first year and gradually allow environmental factors to become more influential (see, however, Plomin & Thompson, 1987). In contrast, the delayed impact hypothesis of Bradley and Caldwell (1984) assumes that there is a weak but consistent impact of early experience on development but that it needs to accumulate over time before it will be reflected in cognitive development. Finally, the environmental specificity hypothesis of Wachs and Gruen (1982) proposes that environmental stimulation will not equally influence all measures of cognitive performance in the same period of development. They suggested that most standard tests of early cognitive performance are heavily weighted with motor items. Because early motor development is strongly based on genetically programmed maturational factors (Murphy & Linden, 1982), Wachs and Gruen argue that early environment–cognitive relationships will be detected only on nonmotoric measures of early cognitive development.

It should be noted that none of these child psychologists proposed that there is one critical period in which the child is able to benefit cognitively from environmental stimulation, nor that the effects of early experience cannot be modified by later experience. Few child psychologists would accept the traditional notion of critical periods in social and cognitive development, however, many would accept the notion of sensitive periods in which the developing organism is particularly responsive to certain kinds of experiences or in which the solution of one set of developmental tasks is appropriate and prepares the individual to cope with subsequent developmental demands. Although disruptions in early mother–child attachment do not preclude the formation of later intimate relations, they may be associated with a higher probability of disruptions in subsequent interpersonal relations. Although a second language can be learned in the adult years, there is considerable evidence that such learning is easier in the childhood years. Although illiteracy in high school is reversible, it may increase the possibility of the individual encountering a series of experiences such as dropping out of school, unemployment or erratic employment, and antisocial behavior that is difficult to reverse even if the individual learns to read in adulthood. In the view of most child psychologists then, childhood and adolescent experiences do not result in a fixed developmental trajectory. Childhood experiences, however, may increase the probability of the occurrence of certain subsequent life experiences and influence the way in which the individual will respond to these experiences.

What then is unique about the argument of life-span scholars for a focus on life-long development? It seems consistent with much work in child development. Yet it is also true that the aftermath of child development typically is not always in the center of attention or the expertise of child researchers (Baltes, 1979). As child developmentalists begin to examine long-term consequences, they often are less informed about what should be studied in adulthood. Moreover, as child developmentalists have begun to study parents not as fixed persons, but as adults with their own developmental agenda, they are realizing that knowledge about the condition and course of adult and family development is important (Belsky, 1984; Cowan & Cowan, 1985; Hetherington, in press; Hetherington, Cox, & Cox, 1982). Thus it seems that the life-span-oriented study of children requires knowledge about the aftermath of childhood and of the adult social world (and its possible developmental course) in which children are embedded. The task of connecting age periods is not fully accomplished by putting together age-specific information. It includes the modification of age-specific approaches in light of factors and questions that emanate from the interage look espoused so strongly, but not only, by life-span researchers.

The Concept of Development

What about the concept of development itself? Life-span scholars claim, for example, that the concept of development means more than just aspects of growth or progression (Lerner, 1984). They have emphasized the many possibilities of newly emergent behaviors, discontinuities, and the idea that any developmental change is not only one of growth or progression but also always involves some loss in functional efficacy (Baltes, 1986).

Life-span researchers and child psychologists would agree that there is considerable variation in the course of development in different domains and in the development of components and attributes within domains. Moreover, they would concur that there is marked individual variation within these developmental trajectories. The same experiences may lead to different outcomes for different individuals and the same developmental ends may be reached through different developmental pathways. Thus, both the multidirectionality of behavior change and interindividual variability in development lead to pluralism in patterns of development.

Both child developmentalists and life-span researchers recognize that development is more than increases in frequency, size, complexity, or functional efficacy. For example, in some areas of psychometric intelligence, such as crystallized intelligence, development proceeds in an incremental fashion over the life span into late adulthood; in others, such as fluid intelligence, it declines beginning in early adulthood (Baltes, 1986; Horn, 1970). Similar phenomena exist in social development. Relationships with opposite-sex peers may show a discontinuous pattern with declines in the elementary school years and increases in adolescence and young adulthood (Hartup, 1983). Ontogeny therefore is a reflection of aspects of both growth and decline.

Development thus may be viewed as a gain–loss relationship. Both child development and life-span development have models involving such ideas (Baltes, 1986; Bower, 1976; McCall, 1979; Scarr & McCartney, 1983; Waddington, 1966). In research on adulthood and old age, Baltes (1986) has suggested that a basic process underlying this dynamic interplay between gains and losses over the course of development is selective optimization with compensation. As constraints in development or limitations in plasticity occur with age, individuals become more specialized and selective in adapting to situations and in solving problems. They develop substitutive skills to compensate for declining abilities. In confronting new tasks; the elderly draw selectively upon past experiences, existing knowledge and skills, and personal and social resources. The particular form of selective optimization or compensatory skills or strategies adopted will depend on the individual's past life conditions. Gains and losses may also exist in childhood development. For example, even in Piaget's theory there is evidence for loss (in perceptual accuracy) as children more toward a higher cognitive stage (Baltes, 1986). A more concerted effort by both child and life-span researchers to focus on gains and losses and multidirectionality in development could lead to enhanced and increasingly fruitful developmental models.

What about the question of openness or plasticity of development? Surely life-span developmentalists underscore multilinearity and plasticity in development. However, neither life-span scholars nor child psychologists believe that development is chaotic. Neither complete continuity nor complete change characterizes human development, rather the sequence or outcome of individual behavioral development is probable rather than certain (Gottlieb, 1970; Lerner, 1984). Thus, many child developmentalists see themselves as equally committed to openness and plasticity of development. In this view, Scarr (1982) proposed that:

> Development is a probablistic result of indeterminate combinations of genes and environments. Development is genetically guided but variable and probablistic because influential events in the life of every person can be neither predicted nor explained by general laws. . . . Human beings are made neither of glass that breaks in the slightest ill wind nor of steel that stands defiantly in the face of devastating hurricanes. Rather, in this view, humans are made of the newer plastics—they bend with environmental pressures, resume their shapes when the pressures are relieved and are unlikely to be permanently misshapen by transient experiences. When bad environments are improved, people's adaptations improve. Human beings are resilient and responsive to the advantages their environments provide. Even adults are

capable of improved adaptations through learning, although any individual's improvement depends on that person's responsiveness to learning opportunities. (pp. 852–853)

This probablistic–epigenetic view of human plasticity and adaptability and its relation to continuity and change then is found in the writing of both child psychologists and life-span researchers (Baldwin & Poulton, 1902; Baltes, 1986; Brim & Kagan, 1980a, 1980b; Lerner, 1984; Lerner & Kauffman, 1985; Werner, 1957). The difference between the perspectives of the two groups of scholars is one of theoretical argument and one of emphasis. The theoretical argument of some life-span proponents is to deduce from the empirical evidence on plasticity a need for meta-theoretical discourse about the nature of development (Lerner, 1984). This issue is discussed in more detail in the section that deals with contextualism as a metatheoretical paradigm. In terms of differences in emphasis, child psychologists recognize human plasticity but place relatively more emphasis in adapting to life events on constraints related to genetic and biological factors, previous experience, and the capacities, predispositions, and attributes of the individual.

In accordance with the previous quote by Scarr, child psychologists would emphasize the strong adaptive or righting responses of individuals who encounter temporary adverse experiences and the tendency to return to their previous normal developmental trajectory (Sameroff & Chandler, 1975; Werner & Smith, 1982). In contrast, life-span investigators (Brim & Kagan, 1980b) are more impressed with the possible nonexistence of a fundamentally fixed course of development especially for adulthood. They emphasize that there is little biological and cultural stabilization for the adult period of life. In this vein, they underscore the difficulty in anticipating what life experiences the individual is going to encounter during adulthood and how the person will respond to these life conditions. This interaction between unpredictable life events and interindividual variability in coping with these events contributes to problems in making long-term predictions about human development. Both child and life-span scholars have added the theoretical issue of paradigm to the questions of the extent of predictability and ontogenetic variability and both have advanced models of probabilistic contextualism. This topic is considered in more detail later.

As child developmentalists include more adults in their studies they need to be aware of these empirical and theoretical concerns of life-span scholars. Adult development may be more diverse and open than was once anticipated. One example is found in the dramatic changes in adults' and children's views of and experiences with marriage, divorce, and parenting. The traditional view of children developing in a nuclear family with two once-married parents does not hold true for many contemporary parents nor children. New and varied life styles and family forms have emerged that place children in less predictable and homogeneous households and family settings. Moreover, the complexity of generational relations has increased both in terms of the number of generations involved as well as the creation of new lineages through multiple marriages (Furstenberg, 1982; Hagestad, 1982; Hetherington, in press; Hetherington, Arnett, & Hollier, in press; Hetherington, Cox, & Cox, 1985). High rates of out-of-wedlock births to teenage mothers, divorce, and remarriage present multiple trajectories of marital and household arrangements to parents and children, and these impact on the psychological well-being of family members. For example, divorced women who do not remarry are more depressed and less satisfied with their lives than are never-married, once-married, or remarried women. Boys who remain in the custody of divorced mothers exhibit more behavior problems than do girls in such families or than do boys with nondivorced parents. In contrast, preadolescent boys may benefit from the introduction of a warm, competent stepfather, whereas girls are likely to show an increase in behavior problems in stepfamilies (Hetherington, in press; Hetherington, Arnett, & Hollier, in press; Hetherington, Cox, & Cox, 1985).

Age-Graded, Non-Normative, and History-Graded Influence on Development

The topic of contextual factors (Bronfenbrenner, 1979) is emphasized in general models of development proposed by life-span researchers. Life-span developmentalists propose that developmental trajectories and diversity in individual development will be influenced by age-graded, non-normative, and history-graded factors. The timing, duration, order, spacing, and patterning of such events will modify the course of development.

Two aspects are noteworthy. First, child developmentalists are likely not to give these sources of influence equal conceptual status. Rather, child psychologists are likely to postulate a "typical" course of ontogeny and to view non-normative and history-graded factors as modifiers, not as fundamental constituents, of development. This issue is discussed in a recent debate published in the American Sociological Review (Baltes & Nesselroade, 1984; Dannefer, 1984; Featherman & Lerner, 1986). Second, although both child and life-span developmentalists have focused more on age-graded and non-normative influences than on history-graded influences in their research, life-span developmentalists have been relatively more attentive to history-graded factors than have child developmentalists.

Certain experiences or events are age-graded. Within a given culture they are encountered at approximately the same chronological age. Some of these age-graded experiences such as pubescence, are based on biological or maturational factors, others, such as entrance and graduation from school or time of retirement, may be socially programmed. These age-graded events often are associated with specific social expectations, changing roles and task requirements, and altering patterns of privileges and responsibilities.

Sociologists have conceived of the life course as being composed of a set of interlocking careers such as education, work, marriage, and parenthood that involve socially proscribed roles (Elder & Rockwell, 1979; Riley, Johnson, & Foner, 1972). To a large extent, the developmental trajectories, role expectations, and relations among these careers are determined by age-graded events. However, if the timing, order, or duration of an event within one of these careers deviates from the expected age-graded progression, alterations in the developmental trajectory of multiple careers may occur. The birth of a child to an unwed teenaged girl may impact on her educational, occupational, and marriage career in addition to her parenthood career. The age at which military service is entered affects subsequent career and personality development (Elder, 1986).

Although many life events are age-graded, the occurrence of others such as divorce, mental or physical illness, accidents, or unemployment are non-normative, they are more unpredictable and can occur at almost any point in the life span. Although some static life events models tend to view these events as single points in time, they are best seen as life transitions involving multiple changes extending over time. Some of these non-normative events such as temporary physical illness, may lead to transitory deviations from a developmental pathway with a return to the same developmental trajectory after the event passes. Others such as divorce, chronic illness, or remarriage may result in long-lasting or permanent changes in roles, relationships, and individual development. Rutter (1983, 1985), in emphasizing the multiple impacts of such experiences, has referred to these events as *transactional events*.

Transactional events are events that increase the probability of a set of other events occurring. Thus an accident may involve enduring physical handicap, financial duress, career shifts, and alterations in social relations. Similarly, divorce may be associated with an increased probability of loss of income, shifts in residence, social isolation, task overload, disruptions in parenting behavior, and changes in self-concept for divorced custodial mothers (Hetherington, in press; Hetherington & Camara, 1984; Hetherington, Cox, & Cox, 1982). Of course, divorce may also result in freedom from conflict, a close mother–child relation, and increased independence and self-esteem.

Again, the great variability in response to non-normative life events must be underscored. The response to such life transitions depends on the timing of the event, the social and historical context in which it occurs, the past experiences and attributes of the individual, available personal and social resources, and the person's interpretation of the event. Thus the effects of loss of a spouse through death or divorce will likely differ in younger or in older couples, in couples with or without children, in economically affluent or deprived families, in individuals who are socially isolated or have strong support networks, and in couples who had a hostile, turbulent relationship or a close, satisfying marriage (Bloom, Asher, & White, 1978; Hetherington & Camara, 1984; Kurdek, 1983). Moreover, the response to loss of a family member may vary if the geographical, physical, or social setting, or historical times makes such loss commonplace or rare, accepted or deviant.

Finally, life-span developmentalists emphasize that history-graded influences shape the life course. The issue of history-graded factors emerged at about the same time in sociology (Riley et al., 1972; Ryder, 1965) and in developmental psychology (Baltes, 1968; Schaie, 1965). Riley, for example, has argued that cohorts age in different ways in response to social and historical change (Riley, 1979a, 1979b). The view of human development as that of a changing individual within a changing social–historical context has important implications not only for developmental theory, but, as is seen later, also for methodology in developmental research. Unless the effects of cohort, life stage, and normative and non-normative life events can be disentangled the results of some psychological research is uninterpretable. Even in areas where marked social changes have occurred such as in maternal employment, divorce, adolescent sexuality, and day care, child psychologists rarely attend to historical changes in the social context as a major factor of contributing to variations in development. However, it should be noted that the same is true for most of the research by life-span scholars. Even in the work of life-span developmentalists attention to historical change sometimes is found in theoretical writing but rarely is included in research studies.

Organismic–Contextualism

Both contemporary child psychologists and life-span developmentalists see human development as resulting from the interaction between an active, organized individual and an active, organized environment (Lerner, 1984; Lerner & Kauffman, 1985; Overton, 1985). Individuals act on their environments, evoke behavior from others, select settings, and discriminate among stimuli to which they respond. Moreover, the individual exists in multiple levels of embeddedness in his or her environment, for example at the individual psychological level, the dyadic level, the family level, the community level, the historical level, and so on. There is a dynamic interaction among these contextual levels and between the individual and the contextual levels. Development is a process of constant change based on the interaction between the changing individual and these changing contextual levels.

Although the ecological movement, led in child development by Bronfenbrenner (1979), has had a profound impact on theory in child development, much developmental research still presents a picture of the child developing within rather static ecosystems. Certainly more attention is focused on individual change than on contextual change. In addition, most studies investigate individual change within a single ecosystem such as the family or the school rather than the complex and changing relations between multiple contextual levels and the developing individual.

To some extent, this relative lack of emphasis on contextual factors in child development is the result of a lag between theory and manageable research paradigms and methods to study this complex dynamic interplay between the changing individual and a multiple-leveled context in constant flux. However, it is likely incorrect to assume that the matter is solely a matter of emphasis or lack of empirical scholarship. The difference also may be one of metatheory and world view.

The possible implications of the role of contextual factors for a metatheory of ontogenesis is illustrated in a study by Featherman and Lerner (1986) and an exchange between Lerner and Kendler (Kendler, 1986; Lerner & Kauffman, 1986) on child development? Are these historical influences fluctuant in the sense of temporary period effects or do they represent a fair degree of historical permanence? Are cohort effects transmitted to the next generation and how? Are the effects of historical changes more qualitative (affecting the nature of functioning) or more quantitative (resulting in differences in level rather than form)? Or, to give one more example: Are the effects of historical change widely spread or do they apply to particular societal clusters such as social classes or ethnic subgroups?

As the questions are posed in this manner, the theoretical meaning of cohort variation is specified in terms of the four prototypical conceptions previously mentioned. At the same time, research on cohort effects can be coordinated with available theories of child development without always arguing the case of complete historical relativism.

Similar views apply to the topic of metatheoretical paradigms. The earlier contributions on mechanism, organicism, dialectics, and contextualism argued for the exclusivity and irreconcilability of such paradigmatic views (Reese & Overton, 1970; Riegel, 1976). Current discussions seem less dogmatic. Recently it was proposed to consider the relative degree of usefulness of the respective paradigms of research and to move forward conceptions that permit an integrative consideration of each of the paradigms at different levels of analysis (Lerner & Kauffman, 1985).

INTERVENTION

What are the implications of the life-span emphasis on continued plasticity and contextual embeddedness for intervention programs? In chapter 13 (this volume) Brim and Phillips present a broadly based discussion of this topic. Thus, we restrict our comments to a few highlights.

First, in order to design a successful intervention program both the processes that constrain and those that promote change must be understood. Nevertheless, because the life-span view is that a system is never completely limited or constrained and that there is always a potential for change, successful interventions should be possible across the life span. Childhood is not a complete prologue to later life.

This has been taken by some child psychologists to mean that life-span scholars argue that early intervention is not warranted because later change is always possible. Life-span scholars, however, maintain that this distorts their perspective (Baltes, 1986; Lerner, 1984). There is not equal plasticity in all domains across the life span. In many domains there are fewer constraints in the ability to change in the childhood years. Moreover, it has been suggested that it is possible that accelerated child development may have negative consequences in adulthood. In fact, the late-life costs of early development form the essence of the so-called *counterpart* theory of aging (Birren & Cunningham, 1985).

However, the life-span view is less pessimistic than that of behavioral scientists who view the childhood years as the most formative in development (Brim & Kagan, 1980; see also Brim & Philipps, chapter 13, this volume). It holds that even in cases where early intervention or prevention might be preferable and more effective, changes can be affected in the adult years. This leads to a more optimistic and perhaps more humane response to undesirable attributes or conditions found or expected in adults and the aged. It views rehabilitation, and the reversal of undesired characteristics and the enhancement or development of positive attributes as possible in adulthood and old age. Recognizing the life-long capacity for change is important for another reason. Processes of historical change and the occurrence of non-normative life events challenge the aging organism to new tasks of adaptation.

Second, the perspective of contextual embeddedness implies that interventions should be focused on both the individual and the environment. Because the individual actively selects, modifies, and evokes responses from his or her environment, adaptive strategies appropriate for shaping the environment and eliciting desired responses from others should be promoted. Lerner (1984) has suggested that the goal of intervention should be to increase the persons ability for self-regulation so that the individual can both change his or her behavior to fit varying contexts and select or alter contexts to fit his or her needs. Such an approach is also implied in another life-span theory, that of selective optimization with compensation (Baltes, 1986).

Because the individual encounters varied situations, it may be that facilitating adaptive strategies or behaviors that will help him or her across multiple situations may be more advantageous than those that focus solely on specific contextual manipulation. However, intervention in the attitudes and behaviors of those who deal with the elderly, in the control adults have over their environment, and in the physical, social, and cognitive experiences available to adults, also have been found to be effective in altering adult development. Because organismic–contextualism suggests that the organism is constantly modifying and being modified by his or her environment, intervention that focuses on this interaction rather than solely on the individual or the context seems desirable.

Third, because processes in the multiple levels of context and in the multiple facets of the individual are inextricably enmeshed, intervening in one aspect of the environment or the individual may lead to unexpected or undesired changes in other parts of the system. Furthermore, recognizing the macrostructural embeddedness of human development leads to a focus on the importance of the opportunities and constraints for change provided by social structure and its interindividual differentiation (Featherman, 1983). As children of lower social classes engage in development enhancing activities, the general conditions of society may contain opposing forces. Understanding the continued operation of factors specific to later age periods is important. When child developmentalists understand and consider such processes they may be in a better position to appreciate that although child intervention programs may be effective when delivered, they may lose effectiveness because of factors specific to later age periods. Finally, there may be important cohort effects that preclude generalizing from the results of interventions conducted on one cohort to another.

SUMMARY

Life-span development is a perspective that integrates a number of interrelated propositions about the course of human development. The ideas are not new, however the weighting and combination of ideas have implications for theory, for research, for methodology, and for intervention. Both child psychologists and life-span developmental re-searchers have long histories of concern with many of these issues such as continuity and change in development, plasticity, and constraints in development, and the dynamic view of the actively changing individual shaping and being shaped by the changing contexts in which he or she lives. Moreover, in the past decade, since life-span scholars have moved away from notions of complete plasticity across development to one of plasticity within a set of constraints, and as child psychologists have moved away from a belief in the preeminence of early experiences, convergence between the two perspectives has occurred. Both believe in diverse and pluralistic origins of human development. However, perhaps because of their strong interdisciplinary orientation, life-span researchers continue to place more emphasis on history-graded factors in development than do child psychologists.

During recent years, then, there has been a growing convergence between the family of beliefs espoused by life-span developmentalists and child developmentalists. The result is that there seems to be an increasing number of researchers who feel comfortable wearing both labels. In our view, continued debates occur primarily because there is not enough exchange among scholars and, perhaps, because of differences in metatheoretical preferences. Furthermore, continued discrepancies occur more in the area of research than in theory, with each set of investigators focusing on the opposite extremes of the life span. In addressing most developmental questions, it is probably neither feasible nor desirable for a single investigation always to examine changes in development across the entire life span. Of more concern is the fact that some periods of development such as young adulthood and middle age receive less attention than do childhood, adolescence, and old age, and we have marked gaps in our knowledge about the degree and form of the interconnectedness of development across the life span.

We conclude that the theoretical and methodological similarities between child development and life-span development are greater than the differences. The main differences lie in the relative weighting and attention given to different factors in development and to the need for a new metatheory of development. What seems necessary is to recognize the mutual advantages to be gained in each field by informing itself about the other. For there is no complete account of child development unless we understand its aftermath and contributions to later life. Correspondingly, there can be no full account of life-span development unless the account includes knowledge about the ontogenetic beginnings. Collaboration seems desirable with due attention to and recognition of each partner's strengths. The time for open and honest courtship has come.

The chapters that follow reflect the shared and discrepant perspectives on development that remain after 4 years of discourse between a group of child psychologists and life-span researchers.

REFERENCES

Baldwin, J. M., & Poulton, E. B. (1902). Plasticity. In J. M. Baldwin (Ed.), *Dictionary of philosophy and psychology* (Vol. 2, pp. 302–303). New York: Peter Smith.

Baltes, P. B. (1968). Longitudinal and cross-sectional sequences in the study of age and generation effects. *Human Development, 11,* 145–171.

Baltes, P. B. (1979, Summer). On the potential and limits of child development: Life-span developmental perspectives. *Newsletter of the Society for Research in Child Development,* pp. 1–04.

Baltes, P. B. (1983). Life-span developmental psychology: Observations on history and theory revisited. In R. M. Lerner (Ed.), *Developmental psychology: Historical and philosophical perspectives* (pp. 79–111). Hillsdale, NJ: Lawrence Erlbaum Associates.

Baltes, P. B. (1986). *Theoretical propositions of life-span developmental psychology: On the dynamics between growth and decline.* Unpublished manuscript based on invited addresses to Division 7 of the American Psychological Association (Toronto, August 1984) and to the International Society for the Study of Behavioral Development (Tours, July 1985).

Baltes, P. B., & Nesselroade, J. R. (1984). Paradigm lost and paradigm regained: Critique of Dannefer's portrayal of life-span developmental psychology. *American Sociological Review, 49,* 841–847.

Baltes, P. B., & Reese, H. W. (1984). The life-span perspective in developmental psychology. In M. H. Bornstein & M. E. Lamb (Eds.), *Developmental psychology: An advanced textbook* (pp. 493–532). Hillsdale, NJ: Lawrence Erlbaum Associates.

Belsky, J. (1984). The determinants of parenting: A process model. *Child Development, 55,* 83–96.

Birren, J. E., & Cunningham, W. (1985). Research on the psychology of aging: Principles, concepts, theories. In J. E. Birren & K. W. Schaie (Eds.), *Handbook of the psychology of aging* (pp. 3–34). New York: Nostrand-Reinhold.

Bloom, B. L., Asher, S. J., & White, S. W. (1978). Marital disruption as a stressor: A review and analysis. *Psychological Bulletin, 85,* 867–894.

Bower, T. G. R. (1976). Repetitive processes in child development. *Scientific American, 235,* 38–47.

Bradley, R., & Caldwell, B. (1984). 174 children: A study of the relationship between home environment and cognitive development during the first 5 years. In A. Gottfried (Ed.), *Home environment and early cognitive development* (pp. 5–56). New York: Academic Press.

Brim, O. G., Jr., & Kagan, J. (Eds.). (1980a). *Handbook on constancy and change.* Cambridge: Harvard University Press.

Brim, O. G., Jr., & Kagan, J. (1980b). Constancy and change: A view of the issues. In O. G. Brim, Jr. & J. Kagan (Eds.), *Constancy and change in human development* (pp. 1–25). Cambridge, MA: Harvard University Press.

Bronfenbrenner, U. (1979). *The ecology of human development.* Cambridge: Harvard University Press.

Cairns, R. B., & Hood, K. E. (1983). Continuity in social development: A comparative perspective on individual difference prediction. In P. B. Baltes & O. G. Brim, Jr. (Eds.), *Life-span development and behavior* (Vol. 5, pp. 302–359). New York: Academic Press.

Cowan, C. P., & Cowan, P. A. (1985). A preventive intervention for couples becoming parents. In C. F. Z. Boukyokis (Ed.), *Research on support for parents and infants in the postnatal period.* Norwood, NJ: Ablex.

Dannefer, D. (1984). Adult development and socialization theory: A paradigmatic reappraisal.

American Sociological Review, 49, 100–116.

Elder, G. H., Jr. (1975). Age differentiation and the life course. *Annual review of sociology* (Vol. 1, pp. 165–190). Palo Alto, CA: Annual Reviews.

Elder, G. H., Jr. (1985, September). *Life course analysis in the 1980s: Some trends and reflections.* Paper presented at conference in "Trends in Sociology", Airline House, Washington, DC.

Elder, G. H., Jr. (1986). Military times and turning points in men's lives. *Developmental Psychology, 22,* 233–245.

Elder, G. H., & Rockwell, R. C. (1979). The life-course and human development: An ecological perspective. *International Journal of Behavioral Development, 2,* 1–21.

Featherman, D. L. (1983). The life-span perspective in social science research. In P. B. Baltes & O. G. Brim, Jr. (Eds.), *Life-span development and behavior* (Vol. 5, pp. 1–59). New York: Academic Press.

Featherman, D. L., & Lerner, R. M. (1986). Ontogenesis and sociogenesis: Problematics for theory and research about development and socialization across the life span. *American Sociological Review, 10,* 659–676.

Furstenberg, F. (1982). Conjugal succession: Reentering marriage after divorce. In P. B. Baltes & O. B. Brim, Jr. (Eds.), *Life-span development and behavior* (Vol. 4, pp. 108–148). New York: Academic Press.

Gottlieb, G. (1970). Conceptions of prenatal behavior. In L. R. Aronson, E. Tobach, D. S. Lehrman, & J. S. Rosenblatt (Eds.), *Development and evolution of behavior* (pp. 231–237). San Francisco: Freeman.

Hagestad, G. O. (1982). Parent and child: Generations in the family. In T. Field, A. Huston, H. C. Quay, L. Troll, & G. E. Finley (Eds.), *Review of human development* (pp. 485–499). New York: Wiley.

Hartup, W. W. (1983). Peer relation. In E. M. Hetherington (Ed.), *Socialization, personality and social development. Vol. 3: Handbook of child psychology* (pp. 103–195). New York: Wiley.

Hetherington, E. M. (in press). Family relations six years after divorce. In K. Paysley & M. Ihinger-Tollman (Eds.), *Remarriage and stepparenting today: Research and theory.* New York: Garland Press.

Hetherington, E. M., Arnett, J., & Hollier, A. (in press). The effects of remarriage on children and families. In P. Karoly & S. Wolchick (Eds.), *Family transition.* New York: Garland Press.

Hetherington, E. M., & Camara, K. A. (1984). Families in transition: The process of dissolution and reconstitution. In R. D. Parke (Ed.), *Review of child development research: The family* (Vol. 7, pp. 398–439). Chicago: University of Chicago Press.

Hetherington, E. M., Cox, M., & Cox, R. (1982). Effects of divorce on parents and children. In M. E. Lamb (Ed.), *Nontraditional families: Parenting and child development* (pp. 233–288). Hillsdale, NJ: Lawrence Erlbaum Associates.

Hetherington, E. M., Cox, M., & Cox, R. (1985). Long-term effects of divorce and remarriage on the adjustment of children. *Journal of the American Academy of Child Psychiatry, 24*(5), 518–530.

Horn, J. L. (1970). Organization of data on life-span development of human abilities. In L. R. Goulet & P. B. Baltes (Eds.), *Life span developmental psychology: Research and theory* (pp. 423–466). New York: Academic Press.

Kaplan, B. (1983). A trio of trials. In R. M. Lerner (Ed.), *Developmental psychology: Historical and philosophical perspectives* (pp. 185–228). Hillsdale, NJ: Lawrence Erlbaum Associates.

Kendler, T. S. (1986). World views and the concept of development: A reply to Lerner and

Kauffman. *Developmental Review, 6,* 80–95.

Kurdek, L. A. (Ed.). (1983). *Children and divorce.* San Francisco: Jossey-Bass.

Lerner, R. M. (1984). *On the nature of human plasticity.* New York: Cambridge University Press.

Lerner, R. M., & Kauffman, M. B. (1985). The concept of development in contextualism. *Developmental Review, 5,* 309–333.

Lerner, R. M., & Kauffman, M. B. (1986). On the metatheoretical relativism of analyses and metatheoretical analyses: A critique of Kendler's comments. *Developmental Review, 6,* 96–106.

McCall, R. B. (1979). *Infants.* Cambridge, MA: Harvard University Press.

McCall, R. B. (1981). Nature–nurture and the two realms of development. *Child Development, 52,* 1–12.

Murphy, T., & Linden, C. (1982, March). *The relationship of neurological maturation and cognitive development in infants.* Paper presented to the International Conference on Infant Studies, Austin, TX.

Overton, W. F. (1985). World views and their influence on scientific research: Kuhn, Lakatos, Lauden. In H. W. Reese (Ed.), *Advances in child development and behavior* (pp. 194–226). New York: Academic Press.

Plomin, R., & Thompson, L. (1987). Life-span developmental behavioral genetics. In P. B. Baltes, D. L. Featherman, & R. M. Lerner (Eds.), *Life-span development and behavior* (Vol. 8, pp. 1–31). Hillsdale, NJ: Lawrence Erlbaum Associates.

Reese, H. W., & Overton, W. F. (1970). Models and theories of development. In C. R. Goulet & P. B. Baltes (Eds.), *Life-span developmental psychology: Theory and research* (pp. 115–145). New York: Academic Press.

Riegel, K. F. (1976). The dialectics of human development. *American Psychologist, 31,* 689–700.

Riley, M. W. (1979a). Introduction: Life-course perspectives. In M. W. Riley (Ed.), *Aging from birth to death* (pp. 3–13). Washington, DC: American Association for the Advancement of Science.

Riley, M. W. (1979b). Aging, social change, and social policy. In M. W. Riley (Ed.), *Aging from birth to death* (pp. 109–120). Washington, DC: American Association for the Advancement of Science.

Riley, M. W., Johnson, M., & Foner, A. (Eds.). (1972). *Aging and society. Vol. 3: A sociology of age stratification.* New York: Russell Sage.

Rosow, I. (1978). What is a cohort and why? *Human Development, 21,* 65–76.

Rutter, M. (1983). Stress, coping, and development: Some issues and some questions. In N. Garmezy & M. Rutter (Eds.), *Stress, coping and development in children (pp. 25–44).* New York: McGraw-Hill.

Rutter, M. (1985). *Meyerian psychobiology, personality development and the role of life experiences.* Paper presented at the annual meeting of the American Psychiatric Association, Dallas, TX.

Ryder, N. B. (1965). The cohort as a concept in the study of social change. *American Sociological Review, 30,* 843–861.

Sameroff, A. J., & Chandler, M. J. (1975). Reproductive risk and the continuum of caretaking causality. In F. Horowitz (Ed.), *Review of child development research* (Vol. 4, pp. 187–244). Chicago: University of Chicago Press.

Scarr, S. (1982). Development is internally guided, not determined. *Contemporary Psychology, 27,* 852–853.

Scarr, S., & McCartney, K. (1983). How people make their own environments: A theory of genotype environment effects. *Child Development, 54,* 424–435.

Schaie, K. W. (1965). A general model for the study of developmental problems. *Psychological Bulletin, 64,* 92–107.

Wachs, T. D., & Gruen, G. (1982). *Early experience and human development.* New York: Plenum.

Waddington, C. H. (1966). *Principles of development and differentiation.* New York: MacMillan.

Werner, E. E., Smith, R. S. (1982). *Vulnerable but invincible: A longitudinal study of resilient children and youth.* New York: McGraw-Hill.

Werner, H. (1957). The concept of development from a comparative and organismic point of view. In D. B. Harris (Ed.), *The concept of development* (pp. 125–148). Minneapolis: University of Minnesota Press.

2 PERSONALITY DEVELOPMENT:

A Life-Span Perspective

Richard M. Lerner
The Pennsylvania State University

ABSTRACT

This chapter presents a model of the development of personality structure across life. The goal of the model is to facilitate the understanding of issues of organism–context relations and of continuity–discontinuity. I argue that individuals possess structural and functional characteristics which are: universal (nomothetic-generic); common to some but not all others (nomothetic-differential); and unique (ipsative-idiographic). The two nomothetic components of personality structure assure interindividual commonality; however, even these features of the person, as well as of course the third one, function to assure basic, lawful intraindividual distinctiveness. An integrated understanding of the contribution of these three components of personality involves the idea that humans are relatively plastic across life, a plasticity which derives from the evolution of delayed development and is ontogenetically based in humans' genetic, neuroanatomical, and neurochemical attributes. These attributes constitute the basis of humans' responsivity to the particular sets of groups, events, and roles to which they are exposed. It is this responsivity that promotes development across life along dimensions of commonality-singularity and constancy–change. Assets and limitations of the model for developmental research are noted, and the use of the model is illustrated by reference to the literature linking the timing of pubertal maturation and the social context with early adolescents' psychosocial functioning.

INTRODUCTION:
DEFINITIONAL DEBATES ABOUT PERSONALITY

Definitions of *constructs* provide the link between theory and research. The definition of a construct derives from metatheoretical and theoretical considerations and shapes the selection of research designs, observational methods, and approaches to statistical analysis (Baltes, Reese, & Nesselroade, 1977; R. M. Lerner, 1976, 1986). Within the field of personality, definitional issues have been of central concern. Indeed, in Wiggins' *Annual Review of Psychology* (1968) chapter the definition of *personality* itself appeared as one of the major issues dividing the field. Several dimensions of definitional difference were presented. One involved a structuralist orientation, emphasizing multivariate measurement, versus a processes orientation, emphasizing typically a laboratory–experimental approach. Wiggins decried the fact that across the field one-shot studies predominated. Little if any evidence existed for concern with long-term multivariate assessment of the processes by which structures change within the context of their ecologically prototypic milieus. No conceptual models legitimating such foci were prominent.

Today, there is evidence of both consistency and change in relation to the field of personality in 1968. For example, in his introduction to the special issue of the *Journal of Personality* on methodological developments in personality research, West (1986, p. 3) noted that "Personality research is still dominated by the traditional designs, measurement strategies, and analyses available" in 1968. However, definitions are derived from theory, and theory prescribes and proscribes: levels and units of analysis, variables admitted into explanatory systems, and positions about the openness to change of these variables. As such, other issues related to the definitional one have arisen. One is the source or determinant of personality structures and/or functions; the second is the course of personality development, its continuity and/or its discontinuity (e.g., Block, 1981; Brim & Kagan, 1980; Costa & McCrae, 1980; Epstein, 1983; Mischel, 1968; Mischel & Peake, 1982; Moss & Susman, 1980). Although with few exceptions (e.g., Brim & Kagan, 1980; R. M. Lerner, 1984; Magnusson & Allen, 1983), the role of theory-based definitional differences in these two other debates typically has not been emphasized, most contemporary discussions of these issues take "middle-grounds," or "compromises" between the extreme alternatives. Both organismic and situational, or contextual, factors are held to be interactive, codeterminants of personality and, in turn, personality is held to reflect both continuous and discontinuous features (e.g., Lerner, 1984; Magnusson & Allen, 1983). However, these compromises fall short of fully resolving these two issues. Insufficiently present is an appropriate conceptual model linking organism and context and depicting the conditions for continuity and discontinuity. One reason for the relative neglect of such a model is that personality typically has not been defined in a manner affording the requisite conceptual integrations. In this chapter I suggest such an integrative definition and present a model aimed at resolving these issues.

A MULTILEVEL, MULTIPROCESS DEFINITION OF PERSONALITY

Several excellent reviews of the personality literature have appeared recently (e.g., Bengtson, Reedy, & Gordon, 1985; Houts, Cook, & Shadish, 1986; Moss & Susman, 1980; Snyder & Ickes, 1985). These reviews, especially those that take a developmental perspective encompassing the life span (Moss & Susman, 1980) or life course (Bengtson et al., 1985), provide useful descriptions of constancies and changes in the affective, cognitive, ego, and motivational contents of personality. However, in addition to its content, personality may be discussed in regard to its *function* and, most important for this chapter, its *structure*. As reviewed by both Emmerich (1968) and R. M. Lerner (1976, 1986), there are at least three different theoretical approaches to the conceptualization of the development of personality structure: First, there are nomothetic-generic or -universal approaches, exemplified most prominently by the stage theories of Freud (1949) and of Erikson (1959); second, there are nomothetic-differential approaches, exemplified by trait-theoretical (Cattell, 1957) and/or social learning (e.g., Kagan & Moss, 1962) perspectives; third, there are ipsative-idiographic analyses, exemplified classically by Allport (1937) and, more recently, by Nesselroade's (1988; Nesselroade & Ford, 1985) intensive measurement studies of the factorial structure of intraindividual change.

These three approaches to the development of personality structure were identified by Kluckhohn and Murray (1948). They noted that each person is like all other people, that each person is like some other people, and that each person is like no other person. What we may take from this observation is that each person possesses universal (generic) components of structure and function; that each person has commonalities with particular subgroups, but not others; and that there are idiographic, individual difference features present in each person. Accordingly, from a perspective emphasizing the simultaneous contribution to personality structure associated with each approach to development, we may define *personality* as the specific set of generic, subgroup and idiographic biological, psychological, behavioral, and sociocultural attributes possessed by an individual. In my view, these components involve variables from bioevolutionary through sociocultural evolutionary levels of analysis. As such, one must understand personality as involving multiple processes from across this range of levels.

Previous discussions of the personality development literature have rarely included such a multilevel, multiprocess definitional perspective (however, see Murphy, 1947). It is certainly the case that within each type of approach to personality development statements exist about structure, function, and content (Hall & Lindzey, 1978); however, little cross-approach integration has been evident in either theoretical and/or research reviews. As such, previous reviews have not specified, across the three approaches, content-general structural or functional features of personality development. As a consequence, the ideas about structure found within each theoretical approach have not been evaluated in the service of devising an integrative model of personality development, one that facilitates the understanding of issues of organism–context relations and of continuity–discontinuity. Such a specification is the goal of this chapter.

In order to present a general model of the structural and functional features of personality development, I consider not the already well-reviewed features of the content of personality development, but rather what may be taken from a revised and integrated understanding of each of the three major types of personality theory (Emmerich, 1968; Kluckhohn & Murray, 1948; R. M. Lerner, 1976, 1986): the nomothetic-generic, the nomothetic-differential, and the ipsative-idiographic. I stress that an appropriate understanding of both nomothetic-universal and nomothetic-differential features of personality involves a recognition of how they provide bases of each person's lawful individuality. In addition, I stress that an idiographic analysis of the person affords a partitioning of personality structure not only into potentially singular components but also into nomothetic, and possibly species invariant, components as well (Nesselroade, 1987). Finally, I stress that both individual and general structures of personality derive from the nature of person-context relations, relations that set the conditions for continuity and/or discontinuity in personality.

Universal (Generic) Components

In previous reviews, both Emmerich (1968) and I (R. M. Lerner, 1976, 1986) have discussed the classical, stage approaches to the development of personality structure and function (e.g., Erikson, 1959; Freud, 1949). These positions posit universal structures of personality and generic and invariant stage progressions, characteristics believed to provide adaptive means for people to meet the culturally and/or societally textured demands of reality. Little interest in, or room for, individual differences exists in these approaches, given the interpretation of adaptation as requiring all people to develop the same structures in an invariant sequence.

These classic stage theories are to be applauded for their placement of personality within a biosocial evolutionary framework, and as such, for their stress on features of personality common to the species. However, because of when they were devised, these approaches have not profitted from recent studies of human's evolutionary heritage; as a consequence, the views of classical stage theory regarding structure, function, and individuality are not adequate.

It is indeed the case that all people share a common evolutionary heritage. However, what is most important for understanding the implications of evolution for personality development is that a key feature of human evolution has been that, relative to other current, nonhuman species and to human ancestral species, humans have the slowest, the most retarded, rate of development. This delayed development is termed *neoteny* (Gould, 1977). As a consequence of this slowness, human development extends well into the adult years of life. This extended period of development means that humans retain juvenile features – of growth and development – into relatively advanced portions of ontogeny. This retention is termed *paedomorphy*.

The general evolutionary retardation of human development and the retention into adulthood of juvenile features of growth has meant that human evolution has involved not only prolonged postnatal development, but as a consequence, greater social dependency, smaller family sizes (to give adequate care to more immature organisms), greater opportunity for learning and socialization, increased brain development, and the development of the family unit. That is, as Gould (1977) noted:

> Delayed development, particularly as expressed in late instruction and extended childhood . . . reacted synergistically with other hallmarks of hominization – with intelligence (by enlarging the brain through prolongation of fetal growth tendencies and by providing a longer period of childhood learning) and with socialization (by cementing family units through increased parental care of slowly developing offspring). (p. 400)

In summary, our evolutionary heritage has embedded us necessarily in a social context, one having a requisite set of institutional features interacting dynamically with our biology (Featherman, 1985; Featherman & Lerner, 1985). The extended period of dependent childhood seems to have led to the evolution of features of adult human behavior (e.g., parental behavior). The presence of young and dependent children requires adults to be organized in their adult–adult and adult–child interactions in order to support and guide the children effectively. Furthermore, because the period of childhood dependency is so long, it appears that human history tended to involve the appearance of later born children before earlier born ones achieved full independence (Gould, 1977). Gould sees such an occurrence as facilitating the emergence of pair bonding, and contends that there exists "in delayed development a primary impetus for the origin of the human family" (p. 403). The set of biological-social context relations involved in this evolutionary heritage is illustrated in Figure 2.1.

Human's delayed development and their retention into adulthood of juvenile features of growth have at least two important implications for personality development. First, humans remain open to influence by their world, and as a consequence they may change across much, if not all, of life (Featherman & Lerner, 1985; R. M. Lerner, 1984). Such flexibility in functioning is influenced by the relative plasticity of humans' neuroanatomy. Comparative developmental research (e.g., Greenough & Green, 1981) demonstrates that within selective portions of the mammalian (i.e., rodent) cortex new dendritic connections can be developed, and Nordeen, Nordeen, Sengelaub, and Arnold (1985) found that such changes can be induced: Dendritic number and size were altered in rats by exogenous

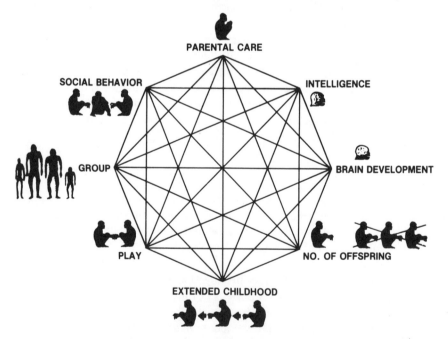

FIGURE 2.1   Components of the system of reciprocal influences believed to be involved in the evolution of human neoteny and social embeddedness. *Note.* Figures 2.1 and 2.2 (based on Johansen and Edey, 1981) are from *Concepts and Theories of Human Development* (p. 151, 176) by R. M. Lerner, 1986, New York: Random House. Reprinted by permission.

steroid administration. Similarly, new dendritic growth has been found within healthy human adults in their seventh and eighth decades of life (Buell & Coleman, 1979). Simply, responsiveness to one's context throughout life means that changes in structure and/or function may occur in at least some, if not all, domains of behavior.

This relative openness leads to a second point. Humans' delayed development and their retention into adulthood of juvenile features of growth constitute a generic "developmental function" (Wohlwill, 1973) of humans. However, the openness to experience that is a result of this developmental function assures significant individual variation around the function. Across life, humans are exposed to increasingly more individually distinct sets of contexts and events. These sets accrue as a consequence of new ecological niches being encountered, selected, or imposed (Brim, in preparation), and through the person's experiencing a potentially unique array of life events. These contextual and event arrays may continue to have functional significance because the person remains relatively plastic as a consequence of the possession of a potential for growth throughout adulthood (Featherman & Lerner, 1985). Thus, these person-specific arrays may continue across life to result in "trace effects" (Schneirla, 1957) — organismic changes resulting from experience, which affect future experiences; the individual's history of these effects serves to establish him or her as a unique organism.

It is, then, a universal feature of development that a generic characteristic of humans — a developmental function involving delayed development — serves to insure individuality, and potentially increasing individuality, across life.

The Nomothetic-Differential Approach and Subgroup Commonalities

The assorting of humans into subgroups having commonality by virtue of shared status and behavioral attributes has been the domain of the differential approach to personality development (Emmerich, 1968; R. M. Lerner, 1976). People's constancy or change within the differential dimensions specified in a given theoretical (e.g., Erikson, 1959) or empirical (e.g., Kagan & Moss, 1962) instance of this approach are held to subserve presses for adaption imposed by one's biology (Erikson, 1959) and/or one's social learning environment (Kagan & Moss, 1962). The content of personality is represented by the particular differential dimensions used in a given instance of this approach and *individual structure* is defined as a person's location in multidimensional space.

As with the nomothetic-universal approach, there is merit in this nongeneric but nonetheless nomothetic orientation. Although it is the case that in its specifics the array of contexts and events experienced by each person is unique, this does not preclude that some clusterings across individuals exist as well. People are not ordinarily exposed to a random sequence of contexts and, in turn, events may be age- or history-graded (Baltes, Reese, & Lipsitt, 1980). Thus, common, cross-person experiences exist because of social class, cultural, and historical groupings. Consequently, although each person has unique trace effects he or she has, as well, trace effects that are isomorphic with others of his or her age, sex, race, social class, religion, school, vocation, culture, and historical epoch (Featherman, 1985).

However, in their combination across life a person's set of subgroup-common trace effects continues to assure his or her uniqueness. As people age they acquire a unique historical chain of familial, neighborhood, civic, professional, and other groups to which they belong for various lengths of time. Thus, although the embeddedness of each of us in a social context assures some commonality with others, the net effect of this embeddedness is an individual history, a unique biography. It is this relation between the common and the unique that makes biographies inherently fascinating as literature and that, in addition, makes biographical analysis a potentially rich tool for social science research.

The social embeddedness that produces both common and unique attributes of personality relates also to continuity and discontinuity in personality development. For example, the premise of Blocks' (1971) work in *Lives Through Time* was that personality development is not solely a homogeneous, generic process characterized by a single developmental function. Instead, people's personality development becomes differentiated on the basis of organismic and contextual factors marked, for instance, by sex-group membership. However, differentiation even within sex group occurs as a consequence of people's specific history of organism-context interactions. Thus, between the early adolescent and the adulthood periods Block (1971) reported five distinct personality trajectories for males and six distinct trajectories for females. Some of these trajectories are marked by continuity across these years, others by discontinuity. In some instances continuity involves constancy of a relatively unhealthy trajectory (e.g., as occurred with the male "unsettled undercontrolers" and with the female "vulnerable undercontrolers"); in other cases continuity of healthy functioning is seen (e.g., in regard to male "ego resilients" and to the group labeled "female prototypes"). In turn, discontinuity can involve people falling off the track of healthy development (e.g., as occurred with the male "anomic extroverts" and with the female "lonely independents"); in addition, what may be labeled a self-righting trajectory toward healthy development is evidenced (e.g., as occurred with the male "belated adjusters" and the female "cognitive copers"). In each case, a particular array of contexts and events, in interaction with a set of individual resources present in a person, were implicated in the specific trajectory that was seen.

Other evidence that the social categories and contexts of life promote both continuity and discontinuity derives from the research of Chess and Thomas (1984) with the New York Longitudinal Study sample. Particular constellations of temperamental attributes in combination with the demands and expectations of parents lead some children to be categorized as "difficult" and others as "easy." A generalization in the temperament literature is that a difficult temperament affords maladaptive development, whereas an easy temperament affords adaptive development (Bates, 1980). Although the personality developments of some difficult and easy children are consistent with this generalization, its strength is limited by the sequence of roles and contexts within which each type of child develops. Some difficult children enter into particular vocational roles or careers, such as professional musicians, where their particular behavioral styles are reinterpreted by others, for example, as "artistic" temperaments; the revised meaning attached to their behaviors seems sufficient to alter the functional import of their temperament (Chess & Thomas, 1984). Discontinuity in the functional significance of an easy temperament can occur too. For instance, the marked tendency to accommodate to contextual demands that are present in such a person may be used by others to either impose an oppressive context and/or press the person into behavior not optimal for him or her (Chess & Thomas, 1984).

Thus, the particular groups to which one belongs can override the influence on personality development of other potentially potent variables, for example, those marked by age (Featherman, 1985). The time of measurement effects found by Nesselroade and Baltes (1974) and the cohort effects identified by Elder (1974) illustrate that historical era can present to people a set of events and contexts that not only may outweigh age-associated variation, in the former case, but, in the latter one, can lead people to have personality changes different from people developing in other historical periods.

In summary, subgroup membership assures some commonality of experience and of personality development. Yet, because of the relative plasticity of humans, the unique temporal array of roles, events, and groups to which each person will inevitably be exposed assures his or her uniqueness. To introduce an oxymoron, then, this sequence constitutes a person's *social genotype*—the unique time-ordered set of contexts and events that an individual accrues over the life course. As with the universal components of personality, this still nomothetic, but nongeneric, subgroup component of personality leads necessarily to individual distinctiveness. Such individuality is brought to the fore when we consider—to use a redundancy—one's biological genotype. This concept is discussed in relation to the ipsative-idiographic approach to personality development.

The Ipsative Approach and Idiographic Components

Ipsative analyses aimed at identifying idiographic components of human personality have been the least used of the three major approaches to personality development (Emmerich, 1968; R. M. Lerner, 1976, 1986). I argue here that this approach represents a powerful tool for identifying both singular and more general, and potentially species invariant, structural developments. Moreover, the focus on individuality within the idiographic approach has a strong empirical basis in human biology.

As previously noted, the biological heritage that provides common features of human ontogeny provides also that this ontogeny occur in respect to a genotypically unique organism. For example, Hirsch (1970) estimates there are over 70 trillion potential human genotypes; in effect, this means that "the likelihood of anyone ever—in the past, present, or future—having the same genotype as anyone else (excepting multiple identical births, of course) becomes dismissably small" (McClearn, 1981, p. 19).

Moreover, human genetic individuality is enhanced by its developmental character. *Genetic* does not mean *congenital*. The "total genome is not functioning at fertilization, or at birth, or at any other time of life" (McClearn, 1981, p. 26). Different genes come into play at various times during life, making the expression of any individual human genotype a developmental phenomenon. The turning on and/or off of genes is influenced by endogenous biological variables and by exogenous components of the individual's genotype-environment interaction history (McClearn, 1981).

If exogenous components of the organism's context can turn genes on and off, then, in effect, the context may produce a different functional genotype at different times in the life span. Indeed, exogenous effects may alter the very nature of the genotype itself. Uphouse and Bonner (1975) assessed the transcription of DNA by RNA from the brains or livers of rats exposed to high environmental enrichment, low environmental enrichment, or isolation. The RNA from the brains of the environmentally enriched rats showed a level of transcription of DNA significantly greater than that of the other groups. No significant differences were found with liver RNA. Grouse, Schrier, Bennett, Rosenzweig, and Nelson (1978) also found significant differences between the brain RNA of rats reared in environmentally rich versus environmentally impoverished contexts. In addition, Grouse, Schrier, and Nelson (1979) found that the total complexity of brain RNA was greater for normally sighted kittens than for kittens who had both eyelids sutured at birth. However, the RNAs from the nonvisual cortices and from subcortical structures were not different for the two groups.

Even if genotypes were not so individually distinct, that is, even if—and in the case of monozygotic twins, when—comparability exists, the responsiveness of genotypes to contextual influences would assure the individuality of each human. Given the openness to influence of genes, a particular genetic inheritance can eventuate in a vast, indeed an infinite (Hirsch, 1970), array of possible "outcomes," of possible phenotypes, given of course the limitless possibilities of contextual variation to which a genotype may be exposed. The range of phenotypes which may derive from a given genotype is termed the *norm of reaction* (Hirsch, 1970). Although it is obvious that at the human level the norm of reaction cannot be determined, and the number of functionally distinct phenotypes associated with any one genotype is certainly likely to be less than the number of possible phenotypes, the norm of reaction concept underscores the truly vast material basis of human individuality and of the human species' plasticity.

In summary, the molecular biological characteristics of organisms interact with contextually textured experiences to produce a singular organism. Said another way, one's biological genotype exists in reciprocal relation with one's social genotype and, as such, produces a phenotypically unique individual. Indeed, even monozygotic twins reared in the same home do not completely share the same environments (Plomin, 1986); as such, they may be phenotypically unique.

The basic, lawful character of the person and his or her life span make requisite developmental analyses focusing on the individual and on the role of individuality in development. Emphasis should be placed on how individuals evoke and/or select features of the context with which they interact, and on how they construct relations with their contexts; indeed, these are foci that have become increasingly prominent in personality (Snyder & Ickes, 1985) and developmental (R.M. Lerner, 1982; Scarr & McCartncy, 1983) theory and research. The import of these foci is that study needs to be made of the person–context exchanges involved in the development of fits (Windle & Lerner, 1986) or correlations (Plomin, 1986; Scarr & McCartney, 1983) between people and their settings. Here, intensive measurement designs coupled with data analytic methods, such as time series analysis or P-technique factor analysis, which are especially useful for assessing intraindividual and contextual constancy and change, seem desirable (Nesselroade & Ford, 1985).

When ipsative strategies, such as intensive intraindividual measurement designs and P-technique factor analysis are replicated across individuals both idiographic change factors and invariant, perhaps species general, ones may be identified. As suggested in earlier reviews by both Emmerich

(1968) and Lerner (1976), at an item or surface-trait level people may show distinct change factors. However, at a higher level of abstraction, for instance, in respect to source-traits, an invariant pattern of change, for example, one involving orthogenesis, may occur. Thus, the study of intraindividual change structures may afford the identification of both singularities and, as well, invariances, in human development (Nesselroade, 1987).

In summary, whether one starts from the nomothetic or from the idiographic, the reciprocal embeddedness of people in their contexts provides the basis of both constancies and change in the shared and unique structures comprising the individual. A model of this perspective is presented in the next section.

A LIFE-SPAN MODEL OF PERSONALITY DEVELOPMENT

I have argued that individuals possess structural and functional characteristics that are universal, are common to some but not all others, and are unique. However, even the nomothetic features of the person function to assure his or her basic, lawful individuality: humans' relative plasticity across life derives from the evolution of delayed development; plasticity is materially enabled ontogenetically by the nature of humans' genetic, neuroanatomical, and neurochemical attributes; these attributes constitute the basis of human responsivity to the particular sets of groups, events, and roles to which they are exposed; it is this responsivity which promotes development across life along dimensions of both commonality-singularity and constancy-change.

A model of these relations is presented in Figure 2.2. In this figure the term *maturation* (abbreviated as "mat." in the figure) represents endogenous organism changes, and the term *experience* (abbreviated as "exp." in the figure) denotes all stimulative influences acting on the organism over the course of its life. A conception of interaction levels is used in the figure. The organism's individual developmental history of maturation-experience interactions (termed Level 1 development) provides a basis of differential organism–environment interactions; in turn, differential experiences accruing from the individual developmental history of organism-environment interactions, or Level 2 development, provide a further basis of Level 1 developmental individuality.

As illustrated in the figure, endogenous maturation-experience relations are not discontinuous with exogenous organism–environment ones. As a consequence, a basis of an organism's individual distinctiveness is provided by: (a) the timing of the interactions among the specific variables involved in an organism's maturation-experience relations; and (b) the rate of these interactions; these may differ across developmental periods involving, for

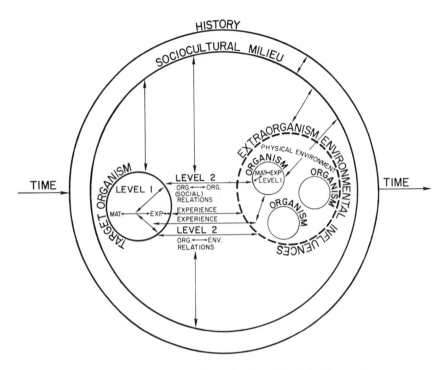

FIGURE 2.2   A dynamic interactional model of development.

instance, relative stasis versus major biological changes (e.g., menarche, menopause) or significant contextual alterations (e.g., school or family transitions). This distinct organism interacts differently with its environment as a consequence of its individuality. In turn, these new interactions are a component of the organism's further experience and thus serve to promote further its individuality. Endogenous maturation-experience relations provide a basis of organism individuality, and as a consequence differential organism-environment (exogenous) relations develop.

Thus, the role of the individually distinct organism is central in the model of development I propose (R. M. Lerner, 1982). This concept of an active organism, one whose activity (or, in more basic biological terms, *irritability*) is a defining feature of living tissue, has been a central idea in at least some versions of organismic developmental theory (Schneirla, 1957). In recent years, this concept has become increasingly popular (Brim, in preparation; Lerner & Busch-Rossnagel, 1981; Lewis & Rosenblum, 1974; Scarr & McCartney, 1983); it is consistent as well with parental belief systems about the nature of child development, that is, attitudes and values that may lead to parent–child relations allowing children to act as agents in their own development (Parke, 1978). This scientific and popular emphasis on children as producers of their development has led to developmental and experimental social psychological research (e.g., Bell & Harper, 1977; Snyder, 1981) verifying that children can indeed act as shapers of the social situations within which they act, and as agents of their own development. Thus, the individuality of the organism influences its own development by shaping feedback from the context in which it interacts and, as well, organisms choose and generate their own contexts (Snyder & Ickes, 1985; Wachtel, 1973). Indeed, experimental personality research has demonstrated that when individuals are allowed to select or modify the situation in which they will interact, a substantial increase in the predictability of behavior occurs (Snyder & Ickes, 1985; West, 1986).

In summary, then, the target organism in Figure 2.2 is unique because of the quality and timing of endogenous Level 1 maturation-experience relations; but the experiences that provide a basis of Level 1 development are not discontinuous with other, extraorganism experiences influencing the target individual. The target interacts with environmental influences composed of other organisms (themselves having intraindividual Level 1 developmental distinctiveness) and of physical variables, which also show individual change over time. Indeed, all tiers of Level 2 — the extraorganism (social), the physical–environmental, the sociocultural, and the historical — change over time. The timing of interactions among variables within and across all tiers not only provides a distinct experiential context impacting on the developing organism, but this distinctiveness is itself shaped by the individually distinct organism. In short, in the model shown in Figure 2.2 I attempt to illustrate the character of what I term *probabilistic epigenetic development* (R. M. Lerner, 1986; Lerner & Kauffman, 1985).

A "translation" of this model into one focusing specifically on child and parent development is presented in Figure 2.3. Here, I try to illustrate the complex nature of intraindividual, interindividual, and contextual relations. As previously discussed, children and adults — as parents — have evolved to exist in a reciprocal relationship (Gould, 1977). At the same time, both members of the dyad are not only interacting; they are also both developing. And the development of each is, at least in part, both a product and a producer of the development of the other. Moreover, both parents and children are embedded in other social networks with which they interact. This exists because both child and parent are much more than just unirole or undifferentiated organisms. The child may also be a sibling, a peer, and a student; the parent may also be a spouse, a worker, a peer, and an adult child. In addition, both parent and child have temperaments, cognitions, emotions, interests, attitudes, values, demands, and physical and health characteristics. Each of these attributes may be influenced by the intraindividual developmental status of the remaining attributes, and by the developmental status of one or all of the other dyad member's attributes.

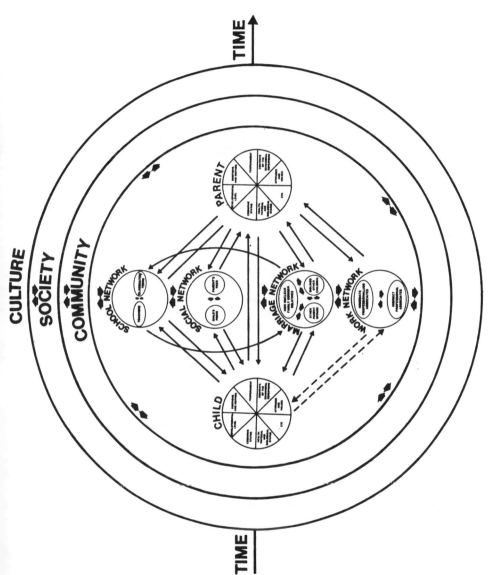

FIGURE 2.3 A dynamic interactional model of child and parent development.

The bidirectional relations depicted in Figures 2.2 and 2.3 may be seen to be akin to those presented earlier in Figure 2.1. Indeed, in my view Figures 2.2 and 2.3 are just translations of the earlier figure into ones stressing ontogenetic, as opposed to evolutionary, relations.

Several points about Figure 2.3 should be emphasized. First, the figure is only *descriptive* of the relations specified in theory and research (e.g., Baltes et al., 1980; Bronfenbrenner, 1979; Chess & Thomas, 1984; Schneirla, 1957; Tobach & Schneirla, 1968) to be involved in person–context relations. Indeed, the bidirectional arrows in the figure correspond to relations identified in various portions of the child, adolescent, or adult development empirical literatures (e.g., Bronfenbrenner, 1979; Lerner & Lerner, 1983).

Second, it would not be useful or even possible to test the figure as a whole within a single study. Instead, the use of this or similar representations (e.g., Baltes et al., 1980) of person–context relations is to provide parameters about the generalizability to one's findings, and to guide the selection of individual and ecological variables in one's research. That is, the model represented in the figure prescribes that variables from two or more levels of analysis need to be studied in order to gain some understanding of the interactive bases of personality development; however, the particular variables selected need to be derived from a separate theory, one about which variables from which levels are involved in a particular feature of development (e.g., see Lerner, 1984).

To illustrate, then, how the model of Figure 2.3 may be used as a guide for the theoretically-based selection of variables from the individual and "contextual" levels depicted in the model, let me note how some of my own research is based on selected components of the model. In Figure 2.4, I show the "restricted" or "reduced" model used in my research on child temperament–social context relations. *Temperament* in this research is defined as the style of behavior, that is, the "how" of personality, as compared to the contents of behavior (the "what" of personality) or to the motivation of behavior (the "why" of personality) (Thomas & Chess, 1977). In the studies that my collaborators and I have conducted, we have adopted a theory that emphasizes that the functional significance of temperament derives from the degree to which a given temperament attribute is congruent, matched, or provides a "goodness of fit," with the demands or expectations regarding that attribute present in a person's social context. We have focused on how the demands regarding temperament held by a child's parents, teachers, or peers are associated with adjustment among children with different repertoires of temperamental individuality (e.g., J. V. Lerner, 1983; Lerner, Lerner, & Zabski, 1985; Windle & Lerner, 1984; Windle et al., 1986). In addition, we have contrasted the relation between parent demands and child temperament with the relation between teacher or peer demands and child temperament. The contrasts have occurred in

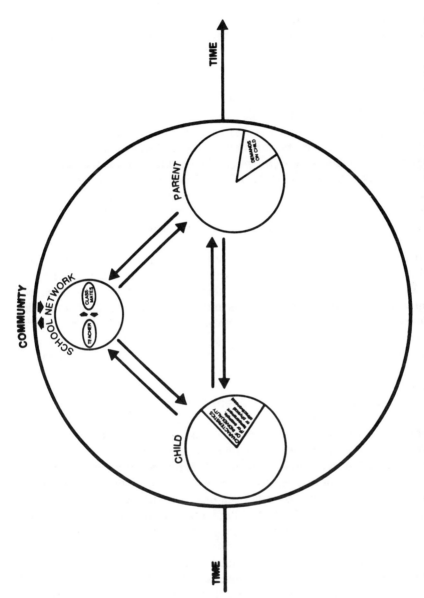

FIGURE 2.4 The variables and levels of analysis studied in the child temperament-social context research of Lerner and Lerner.

studies appraising how a child's temperament at one time of measurement may lead at another time of measurement either to changes in parents' demands and/or to altered implications for the child's adjustment when he or she moves from the home to another context (cf. Thomas, Chess, Sillen, & Mendez, 1974).

To illustrate, as part of the Pennsylvania Early Adolescent Transitions Study (PEATS; Lenerz, Kucher, East, Lerner, & Lerner, 1987) a group of about 100 early adolescents, studied at the beginning, middle, and end of the sixth grade, were assessed in respect to their temperament, their peer group relations, and their personal and social adjustment. In addition, we assessed the demands of the peers regarding the temperamental character-istics they desired in the early adolescents. Although there were no systematic significant relations between temperament, measured alone, and either peer relations or adjustment, as expected the goodness of fit—between temperament and peer demands—predicted peer relations; peer relations in turn predicted early adolescent adjustment (East, Lerner, & Lerner, in press). More specifically, the results of several path analyses indicated that across time early adolescents whose temperaments afforded a good fit with peers' temperamental preferences received significantly more positive peer sociometric nominations and fewer negative peer sociometric nominations than did youth whose temperaments did not provide a good fit with the peer group. In addition, although subjects' fit with peer preferences had little direct effect on their adjustment, across time fit influenced adjustment indirectly through the quality of subjects peer relations (East et al., in press).

The support found for the goodness of fit model within the PEATS data set is not limited only to measures of organismic individuality in regard to temperament. Consistent with their degree to fit with a "what is beautiful is good" physical attractiveness stereotype (Langlois & Stephan, 1981), dif-ferences in the subjects' physical attractiveness related to teachers' ratings of their scholastic competence, to subjects' self-perceptions of scholastic competence, and to subjects' actual academic competence, as measured by grade point average (R. M. Lerner, in press). Specifically, as predicted by the goodness of fit model, the results of path analyses indicated that across the sixth grade the more physically attractive PEATS subjects (i.e., those subjects who best fit the "what is beautiful is good" stereotype) received higher ratings of scholastic competence, perceived themselves as more competent, and achieved more than did their less attractive schoolmates. The direct effects, however, between physical attractiveness and actual academic competence were small and, in addition, the teachers' appraisals of the competence of adolescents who differed in attractiveness could not be totally accounted for by aptitude differences among the youth.

My own research is of course neither the only nor the best example of the usefulness of the model of personality development I have proposed. In fact, findings from developmental psychology and sociology pertinent to the timing of pubertal maturation also illustrate the use of several key features of the model.

An Empirical Illustration: Timing of Pubertal Maturation, Social Context, and Early Adolescents' Psychosocial Functioning

When, and under what conditions, do biological changes, such as those associated with puberty, have specific influences on personality development? Said another way, why do particular biological changes sometimes influence personality development in one way and, at other times, influence personality in another manner? A growing body of evidence indicates that biology's influences on personality development are moderated by the social context within which the influence is expressed (cf. Petersen & Taylor, 1980). Simmons, Carlton-Ford, and Blyth (1987) assessed how a child will cope with the transition from elementary school (sixth grade) to junior high school (seventh grade). They found that some variables, for example, perceived physical attractiveness, predicted the self-esteem of early adolescents across this transition in a manner that is generalizable across gender. However, they find also that in respect to some other variables the world of the junior high school differs substantially for boys and girls. One variable differentiating boys from girls in this setting is the timing of pubertal maturation. In seventh grade, late-developing boys have higher grades, but lower self-esteems, than do early maturing boys. Among girls, however, late maturation relates to positive self-esteem. Early maturation in girls is related to a higher incidence of problem behaviors that, in turn, predicts lower levels of self-esteem.

Findings from the longitudinal research of Magnusson, Stattin, and Allen (1986) suggest that the link among girls between early maturation and problem behaviors may be moderated by the girls' particular peer context. Magnusson et al. differentiated early maturing girls on the basis of whether they had older friends. Early maturing girls with older friends expected fewer sanctions from friends for norm-breaking behavior and, in fact, broke more norms than was the case for early maturing girls without older friends.

The longitudinal research of Hetherington (in press-a, in press-b) provides additional data indicating that the influence of pubertal maturation on the development of problem behavior is mediated by particular features of the early adolescent's social world. Hetherington finds that early pubescence in girls in divorced, mother-custody families is associated with the emergence of externalizing behavior, sexual acting-out behavior, and substance abuse at levels that are even higher than the increased ones found in nondivorced families. Moreover, as do Magnusson et al., Hetherington (in press-a, in press-b) finds that these high levels of problem behaviors among early maturing girls in divorced, mother-custody homes is associated also with their relations with older peers.

Brooks-Gunn (1987) also provided data indicating that the effects of timing of pubertal maturation are moderated by social context. Studying a group of female adolescents enrolled in prestigious and competitive ballet companies and a comparison group of noncompetitively dancing female adolescents, Brooks-Gunn assessed the relation of on-time versus late maturation on body image and on problem behaviors, for instance, regarding eating. The dancers were embedded in a rather unique social context, one requiring intense physical stamina, motivation, self-discipline, and competitiveness. Pressures existed in this setting to remain slim and, in fact, to possess a prepubertal body build. As such lower weight and later maturation might be expected to be advantagious in this setting; in turn on-time maturing dancers might be at a competitive and personal disadvantage, although no general disadvantage for on-time maturation has been identified in the literature (Brooks-Gunn, 1987).

Dancers, as would be expected, weighed less than the comparison girls; as also expected, late maturers weighed less than on-time maturers. Although there was no interaction between maturational timing and activity group status, there was, as predicted on the basis of knowledge of the dancers' social context, an interaction between activity group status and maturational timing in respect to body image. The body image of the comparison group of girls was virtually identical in respect to both on-time and late development. However, the on-time girls within the dancer group had significantly lower (more negative) body image scores than the late-maturing dancers. Similar findings were obtained in respect to the incidence of problematic eating behaviors (Brooks-Gunn, 1987).

The nature of the later life implications of these early adolescent maturation-social context relations illustrates another facet of the model of personality development I am forwarding. Figure 2.3 illustrates that the developing individual continues across life to be embedded in, and therefore interactive with, his or her social context; thus, either individual or context may change across life. The potential plasticity of this person-context relation means that its functional implications may change as well. Not only is this idea the cornerstone of the optimism within the life-span perspective regarding the possibility of successful intervention across life (Baltes et al., 1980; Brim & Kagan, 1980; Brim & Phillips, this volume; R. M. Lerner, 1984), but it is also the central idea in life-span thinking that legitimates the view that there is a potential for change in each period of life (Hetherington & Baltes, this volume).

Although of the studies reviewed in this section only the Magnusson et al. (1986) study has data about the implications in adulthood of early adolescent maturation-social context relations, these data are consistent with those of other investigations (see Lerner & Spanier, 1980, for a review) in underscoring the point that relations at one time in life may be altered by later individual and/or contextual changes; however, and consistent with the model I have been forwarding, whether constancy or change is seen depends on the specific facet of behavioral development in question and the specific features of the context within which the person is embedded. For example, Magnusson et al. found that relations in early adolescence between menarche and alcohol drinking virtually disappear by middle adolescence (by age 15 years 10 months); similarly, by young adulthood (age 26), no effects of maturational timing on alcohol habits are seen. Moreover, at best, only a very weak relation exists between early adolescent maturation and adult norm-breaking behavior. However, in regard to education, a long-term effect of timing of menarche is found. Magnusson et al. reported that early maturing girls have a significantly lower level of educational attainment in adulthood than do their later maturing peers.

Why one behavioral covariate of biological maturation is continuous while there is change in respect to another cannot be determined unequivocally from either the Magnusson et al. (1986) data or from those of other studies of long-term implications of maturational timing (e.g., Ames, 1957; Jones, 1957, 1965; Jones & Mussen, 1958; Shipman, 1964). Such longitudinal research will need to move beyond the description of relations to the advancing and testing of causal models of constancy and change. Nevertheless, at the present time, the aforementioned data linking maturational timing, social context, and early adolescent personality, as well as other findings in this literature (e.g., Crockett & Petersen, 1987) are consistent with a "mediated effects" model (Petersen, 1987; Petersen & Taylor, 1980) of the links between biology and personality. Consistent with the model I have presented, biology, individual functioning, and social context must be understood in an integrative manner in order to understand the conditions under which particular features of personality will develop and/or change. This view leads to some concluding observations.

CONCLUSIONS

The position taken in this chapter is that an adequate conception of personality involves universal, subgroup, and idiographic components of the person. Separately and in combination each of these components assures the lawful individuality of the person, his or her reciprocal embeddedness in a social context across life and, as well, his or her relative plasticity and openness to this context across life. This model, and the data presented to illustrate it, suggest that it is the conditions of organism-context relations that shape the course of features of personality development as continuous or discontinuous.

The model implicitly proscribes unilevel conceptions of, and research approaches to, personality. Instead, longitudinal, change sensitive, multilevel, and therefore multivariate, research, ideally in ecologically meaningful settings, is promoted. The demonstrated use of the proposed model is its ability to integrate a broad range of phenomena pertinent to a multilevel, multiprocess view of personality. The aspired to potential of the model is that it be richly generative, and ideally uniquely so, of a new set of empirical findings linking individuals to their contexts across their lives.

ACKNOWLEDGMENTS

A previous version of this chapter was presented at the Social Science Research Council conference on "Child Development in Life-Span Perspective," National Academy of Sciences Conference Center, Woods Hole, MA, June 20–24, 1985. Work on this chapter was supported in part by a grant from the William T. Grant Foundation. In addition to my colleagues on the SSRC Subcommittee on Child Development in Life-Span Perspective, whose ideas and feedback were seminal in influencing my thinking, I thank E. Mavis Hetherington, Karen Hooker, Jacqueline V. Lerner, John R. Nesselroade, Anne C. Petersen, Robert Plomin, Elizabeth J. Susman, Alexander von Eye, and Michael Windle for critical readings of earlier versions of this chapter.

REFERENCES

Allport, G. W. (1937). *Personality: A psychological interpretation.* New York: Holt.
Ames, R. (1957). Physical maturing among boys as related to adult social behavior: A longitudinal study. *California Journal of Educational Research, 8,* 69–75.
Baltes, P. B., Reese, H. W., & Lipsitt, L. P. (1980). Life-span developmental psychology. *Annual Review of Psychology, 31,* 65–110.
Baltes, P. B., Reese, H. W., & Nesselroade, J. R. (1977). *Life-span developmental psychology: Introduction to research methods.* Monterey, CA: Brooks/Cole.
Bates, J. E. (1980). The concept of difficult temperament. *Merrill-Palmer Quarterly, 26,* 299–319.
Bell, R. Q., & Harper, L. V. (1977). *Child effects on adults.* Hillsdale, NJ: Lawrence Erlbaum Associates.
Bengtson, V. L., Reedy, M. N., & Gordon, C. (1985). Aging and self-conceptions: Personality processes and social contexts. In J. E. Birren & K. W. Schaie (Eds.), *Handbook of the psychology of aging* (2nd ed., pp. 544–593). New York: Van Nostrand Reinhold.
Block, J. (1971). *Lives through time.* Berkeley, CA: Bancroft.

Block, J. (1981). The many faces of continuity. *Contemporary Psychology, 26,* 748–750.

Brim, O. G., Jr. (in preparation). *Losing and winning.*

Brim, O. G., Jr., & Kagan, J. (1980). Constancy and change: A view of the issues. In O. G. Brim, Jr., & J. Kagan (Eds.), *Constancy and change in human development* (pp. 1–25). Cambridge, MA: Harvard University Press.

Bronfenbrenner, U. (1979). *The ecology of human development.* Cambridge, MA: Harvard University Press.

Brooks-Gunn, J. (1987). Pubertal processes and girls' psychological adaptation. In R. M. Lerner & T. T. Foch (Eds.), *Biological-psychosocial interactions in early adolescence: A life-span perspective* (pp. 125–153). Hillsdale, NJ: Lawrence Erlbaum Associates.

Buell, S. J., & Coleman, P. D. (1979). Dendritic growth in the aged human brain and failure of growth in senile dementia. *Science, 206,* 854–856.

Cattell, R. B. (1957). *Personality and motivation: Structure and measurement.* New York: World.

Chess, S., & Thomas, A. (1984). *Origins and evolution of behavior disorders.* New York: Brunner/Mazel.

Costa, P. T., & McCrae, R. R. (1980). Still stable after all these years: Personality as a key to some issues in aging. In P. B. Baltes & O. G. Brim, Jr. (Eds.), *Life-span development and behavior* (Vol. 3, pp. 65–102). New York: Academic Press.

Crockett, L. J., & Petersen, A. C. (1987). Pubertal status and psychosocial development: Findings from the Early Adolescence Study. In R. M. Lerner & T. T. Foch (Eds.), *Biological-psychosocial interactions in early adolescence: A life-span perspective* (pp. 173–188). Hillsdale, NJ: Lawrence Erlbaum Associates.

East, P., Lerner, R. M., & Lerner, J. V. (in press). Early adolescent-peer group fit, peer relations, and adjustment. *Journal of Youth and Adolescence.*

Elder, G. H., Jr. (1974). *Children of the great depression.* Chicago: University of Chicago Press.

Emmerich, W. (1968). Personality development and concepts of structure. *Child Development, 39,* 671–690.

Epstein, S. (1983). The stability of confusion: A reply to Mischel and Peake. *Psychological Review, 90,* 179–184.

Erikson, E. H. (1959). Identity and the life cycle. *Psychological Issues, 1,* 18–171.

Featherman, D. L. (1985). Individual development and aging as a population process. In J. R. Nesselroade & A. von Eye (Eds.), *Individual development and social change: Explanatory analysis* (pp. 213–241). New York: Academic Press.

Featherman, D. L., & Lerner, R. M. (1985). Ontogenesis and sociogenesis: Problematics for theory about development across the lifespan. *American Sociological Review, 50,* 659–676.

Freud, S. (1949). *Outline of psychoanalysis.* New York: Norton.

Gould, S. J. (1977). *Ontogeny and phylogeny.* Cambridge, MA: Harvard University Press.

Greenough, W. T., & Green, E. J. (1981). Experience and the changing brain. In J. L. McGaugh, J. G. March, & S. B. Kiesler (Eds.), *Aging: Biology and behavior* (pp. 159–200). New York: Academic Press.

Grouse, L. D., Schrier, B. K., Bennett, E. L., Rosenzweig, M. R., & Nelson, P. G. (1978). Sequence diversity studies of rat brain RNA: Effects of environmental complexity and rat brain RNA diversity. *Journal of Neurochemistry, 30,* 191–203.

Grouse, L. D., Schrier, B. K., & Nelson, P. G. (1979). Effect of visual experience on gene expression during the development of stimulus specificity in cat brain. *Experimental Neurology, 64,* 354–364.

Hall, C. S., & Lindzey, G. (1978). *Theories of personality* (3rd ed.). New York: Wiley.

Hetherington, E. M. (in press-a). Family relations six years after divorce. In K. Pasley & M. Ihinger-Tollman (Eds.), *Remarriage and step-parenting today: Research and theory.* New York: Guilford.

Hetherington, E M. (in press-b). The impact of divorce and remarriage on early adolescents and their families. In M. D. Levine & E. R. McArarney (Eds.), *Early adolescent transitions.* Lexington, MA: D. C. Heath.

Hirsch, J. (1970). Behavior-genetic analysis and its biosocial consequences. *Seminars in Psychiatry, 2,* 89–105.

Houts, A. C., Cook, T. D., & Shadish, W. R. (1986). The person-situation debate: A critical multiplist perspective. *Journal of Personality, 54,* 52–105.

Johanson, D. C., & Edey, M. A. (1981). *Lucy: The beginnings of humankind.* New York: Simon & Schuster.

Jones, M. C. (1957). The later careers of boys who were early- or late-maturing. *Child Development, 28,* 133–138.

Jones, M. C. (1965). Psychological correlates of somatic development. *Child Development, 36,* 899–911.

Jones, M. C., & Mussen, P. H. (1958). Self-conceptions, motivations, and inter-personal attitudes of early and late-maturing girls. *Child Development, 29,* 491–501.

Kagan, J., & Moss, H. (1962). *Birth to maturity.* New York: Wiley.

Kluckhohn, C., & Murray, H. (1948). Personality formation: The determinants. In C. Kluckhohn & H. Murray (Eds.), *Personality in nature, society, and culture* (pp. 35–48). New York: Knopf.

Langlois, J. H., & Stephan, C. W. (1981). Beauty and the beast: The role of physical attraction in peer relationships and social behavior. In S. S. Brehm, S. M. Kassin, & S. X. Gibbons (Eds.), *Developmental social psychology: Theory and research* (pp. 152–168). New York: Oxford University Press.

Lenerz, K., Kucher, J. S., East, P. L., Lerner, J. V., & Lerner, R. M. (1987). Early adolescents' organismic physical characteristics and psychosocial functioning: Findings from the Pennsylvania Early Adolescent Transitions Study (PEATS). In R. M. Lerner & T. T. Foch (Eds.), *Biological-psychosocial interactions in early adolescence: A life-span perspecitve* (pp. 225–247). Hillsdale, NJ: Lawrence Erlbaum Associates.

Lerner, J. V. (1983). A "goodness of fit" model of the role of temperament in psychosocial adaptation in early adolescents. *Journal of Genetic Psychology, 143,* 149–157.

Lerner, J. V., & Lerner, R. M. (1983). Temperament and adaptation across life: Theoretical and empirical issues. In P. B. Baltes, & O. G. Brim, Jr. (Eds.), *Life-span development and behavior* (Vol. 5, pp. 197–231). New York: Academic Press.

Lerner, J. V., Lerner, R. M., & Zabski, S. (1985). Temperament and elementary school children's actual and rated academic performance: A test of a "goodness of fit" model. *The Journal of Child Psychology and Psychiatry, 26,* 125–136.

Lerner, R. M. (1976). *Concepts and theories of human development.* Reading, MA: Addison-Wesley.

Lerner, R. M. (1979). A dynamic interactional concept of individual and social relationship development. In R. L. Burgess & T. L. Huston (Eds.), *Social exchange in developing relationships* (pp. 271–305). New York: Academic Press.

Lerner, R. M. (1982). Children and adolescents as producers of their own development. *Developmental Review, 2,* 342–370.

Lerner, R. M. (1984). *On the nature of human plasticity.* New York: Cambridge University Press.

Lerner, R. M. (1986). *Concepts and theories of human development* (2nd ed.). New York: Random House.

Lerner, R. M. (in press). Individual development and the family system: A life-span perspective. In K. Kreppner & R. M. Lerner (Eds.), *Family systems and life-span development.* Hillsdale, NJ: Lawrence Erlbaum Associates.

Lerner, R. M., & Busch-Rossnagel, N. A. (1981). Individuals as producers of their develop *ment: Conceptual and empirical bases. In R. M. Lerner & N. A. Busch-Rossnagel (Eds.), Individuals as producers of their development: A life-span perspective* (pp. 1–36). New York: Academic Press.

Lerner, R. M., & Kauffman, M. B. (1985). The concept of development in contextualism. *Developmental Review, 5,* 309–333.

Lerner, R. M., & Spanier, G. B. (1980). *Adolescent development: A life-span perspective.* New York: McGraw-Hill.

Lewis, M., & Rosenblum, L. A. (Eds.). (1974). *The effect of the infant on its caregiver.* New York: Wiley.

Magnusson, D., & Allen, V. L. (Eds.). (1983). *Human development: An interactional perspective.* New York: Academic Press.

Magnusson, D., Stattin, H., & Allen, V. L. (1986). Differential maturation among girls and its relations to social adjustment: A longitudinal perspective. In P. B. Baltes, D. L. Featherman, & R. M. Lerner (Eds.), *Life-span development and behavior* (Vol. 7, pp. 135–172). Hillsdale, NJ: Lawrence Erlbaum Associates.

McClearn, G. E. (1981). Evolution and genetic variability. In E. S. Golin (Ed.), *Developmental plasticity: Behavioral and biological aspects of variations in development* (pp. 3–31). New York: Academic Press.

Mischel, W. (1968). *Personality and assessment.* New York: Wiley.

Mischel, W., & Peake, P. K. (1982). Beyond deja vu in the search for cross-situational consistency. *Psychological Review, 89,* 730–755.

Moss, H. A., & Susman, E. J. (1980). Longitudinal study of personality development. In O. G. Brim, Jr. & J. Kagan (Eds.), *Constancy and change in human development* (pp. 530–595). Cambridge, MA: Harvard University Press.

Murphy, G. (1947). *Personality: A biosocial approach to origins and structure.* New York: Harper.

Nesselroade, J. R. (1988). Some implications of the state-trait distinction for the study of development over the life span: The case of personality. In P. B. Baltes, D. L. Featherman, & R. M. Lerner (Eds.), *Life-span development and behavior* (Vol. 8, pp. 163–189). Hillsdale, NJ: Lawrence Erlbaum Associates.

Nesselroade, J. R., & Baltes, P. B. (1974). Adolescent personality development and historical changes: 1970–72. *Monographs of the Society for Research in Child Development, 39,*(154).

Nesselroade, J. R., & Ford, D. H. (1985). P-technique comes of age: Multivariate, replicated, single-subject designs for studying older adults. *Research on Aging, 7,* 46–80.

Nordeen, E. J., Nordeen, K. W., Sengelaub, D. R., & Arnold, A. P. (1985). Androgens prevent normally occurring cell death in a sexually dimorphic spinal nucleus. *Science, 229,* 671–673.

Parke, R. D. (1978). Parent-infant interaction: Progress, paradigms and problems. In G. P. Sackett (Ed.), *Observing behavior. Vol. 1: Theory and applications in mental retardation* (pp. 69–95). Baltimore, MD: University Park Press.

Petersen, A. C. (1987). The nature of biological-psychosocial interactions: The sample case of early adolescence. In R. M. Lerner & T. T. Foch (Eds.), *Biological-psychosocial interactions in early adolescence: A life-span perspective* (pp. 35–61). Hillsdale, NJ: Lawrence Erlbaum Associates.

Petersen, A. C., & Taylor, B. (1980). The biological approach to adolescence. In J. Adelson (Ed.), *Handbook of adolescent psychology* (pp. 117–155). New York: Wiley.

Plomin, R. (1986). *Genetics, development, and psychology.* Hillsdale, NJ: Lawrence Erlbaum Associates.

Scarr, S., & McCartney, K. (1983). How people make their own environments: A theory of genotype— — >environment effects. *Child Development, 54,* 424–435.

Schneirla, T. C. (1957). The concept of development in comparative psychology. In D. B.

Harris (Ed.), *The concept of development.* Minneapolis: University of Minnesota Press.

Shipman, W. G. (1964). Age of menarche and adult personality. *Archives of General Psychiatry, 10,* 155–159.

Simmons, R. G., Carlton-Ford, S. L., & Blyth, D. A. (1987). Predicting how a child will cope with the transition to junior high school. In R. M. Lerner & T. T. Foch (Eds.), *Biological-psychosocial interactions in early adolescence: A life-span perspective* (pp. 325–375). Hillsdale, NJ: Lawrence Erlbaum Associates.

Snyder, M. (1981). On the influence of individuals on situations. In N. Cantor & J. F. Kihlstrom (Eds.), *Personality, Cognition, and social interaction* (pp. 309–329). Hillsdale, NJ: Lawrence Erlbaum Associates.

Snyder, M., & Ickes, W. (1985). Personality and social behavior. In G. Lindzey & E. Aronson (Eds.), *Handbook of social psychology* (3rd ed., Vol. 2, pp. 883–947). New York: Random House.

Thomas, A., & Chess, S. (1977). *Temperament and development.* New York: Brunner/Mazel.

Thomas, A., Chess, S., Sillen, J., & Mendez, O. (1974). Cross-cultural study of behavior in children with special vulnerabilities to stress. In D. F. Ricks, A. Thomas, & M. Roff (Eds.), *Life history research in psychopathology* (pp. 53–67). Minneapolis: University of Minnesota Press.

Tobach, E., & Schneirla, T. C. (1968). The biopsychology of social behavior of animals. In R. E. Cooke & S. Levin (Eds.), *Biologic basis of pediatric practice* (pp. 68–82). New York: McGraw-Hill.

Uphouse, L. L., & Bonner, J. (1975). Preliminary evidence for the effects of environmental complexity on hybridization of rat brain RNA to rat unique DNA. *Developmental Psychobiology, 8,* 171–178.

Watchel, P. (1973). Psychodynamics, behavior, therapy, and the implacable experimenter: An inquiry into the consistency of personality. *Journal of Abnormal Psychology, 83,* 324–334.

West, S. G. (1986). Methodological developments in personality research: An introduction. *Journal of Personality, 54,* 1–17.

Wiggins, J. S. (1968). Personality structure. *Annual Review of Psychology, 19,* 293–350.

Windle, M., Hooker, K., Lenerz, K., East, P. L., Lerner, J. V., & Lerner, R. M. (1986). Temperament, perceived competence, and depression in early- and late-adolescents. *Developmental Psychology, 22,* 384–392.

Windle, M., & Lerner, R. M. (1984). The role of temperament in dating relationships among young adults. *Merrill-Palmer Quarterly, 30,* 163–175.

Windle, M., & Lerner, R. M. (1986). The "goodness of fit" model of temperament-context relations: Interaction or correlation? In J. V. Lerner & R. M. Lerner (Eds.), Temperament and social interaction during infancy and childhood. *New Directions for Child Development* (Vol. 31, pp. 109–120). San Francisco: Jossey-Bass.

Wohlwill, J. F. (1973). *The study of behavioral development.* New York: Academic Press.

3 THE SOCIAL CONSTRUCTION OF THE PSYCHOLOGY OF CHILDHOOD:

Some Contemporary Processes

John W. Meyer
Stanford University

In modern societies, ideas about the individual person in the life course and about the individual as a subjective self are institutions with histories and logics of their own, as well as reflections of individual experience. The agendas of lay and professional psychologies indicate these institutional perspectives on the individual; these agendas change over time with changes in social structure and with alterations in models of this structure. The earlier psychologies of market society constructed general notions of an integrated personality; the more contemporary social structuring of the individual life course, in such areas as education and occupation, differentiates the theory of the individual (and thus psychologies) into socially structured attainment processes and into distinct and enhanced notions of free individual subjectivity (the more modern idea of the self). The notion of the self involved in these later perspectives becomes disconnected from narrower ideas about development as linked to social progress and takes a more subjectivist form. Implications of these changes for the kinds of issues and variables to which psychologists attend and for changed explanatory models are discussed, with special attention to the life-span movement in contemporary psychology.

INTRODUCTION

Public attention to psychological conceptions and issues is a notable feature of contemporary society. Such matters are discussed in mass media as well as in specialized media, and by technical professionals as well as by many sorts of amateurs. Exotic specialists and common members of society are involved. The intensity and extensity of this public discussion clearly distinguishes modern societies — especially more individualist ones — from others. Further, the attention involved goes not only or especially to adult members of society but reaches back into infancy and childhood, which are main foci of professional and lay psychologies.

The agendas of the public psychological discussions clearly change over time. There is obviously an expansion, but issues and problems change too. Empirical studies of changes in psychological discourse over time (and across societal settings) would be of great interest. In this chapter, we offer some speculations about what such studies might find, and why. We see the agendas of the psychologies, like those of any other social science, as indicative of the sociocultural context and as in part changing in response to changes in that context.

One can take a number of different perspectives on the evolution of public psychological attention and discourse. First, one can see it as simply reflecting technically developing changes in the scientific field itself. From this narrower point of view — given little emphasis here — psychological theory and research have their own autonomous scientific histories, some of which may flow out into public attention. Psychological agendas may affect public life, but not be penetrated by it on a short-term basis.

Second, one can see psychological agendas as indicating the state and problematics of the individual persons making up modern society. There is a well-developed line of sociological thought, built up in the 19th century and still very much alive, tracing the creation of the modern psychological individual to great social changes of recent centuries. The argument was best formalized by Simmel (1955; see the more recent literature overview by Kornhauser, 1959). Complex large-scale societies — the sociological word is differentiation — build up huge specialized systems of social life. Markets and bureaucracies, distinctive systems of schooling, family life, and medical care, and specialized political and legal systems develop. A rationalized and carefully sequenced life-course trajectory for individuals is produced (Mayer & Mueller, 1986; Meyer, 1986), fitting them into this system. This institutional differentiation creates individuation: People have multiple roles, and unique combinations of them in the differentiated institutional system (see Lerner, this volume). And they have their own individuated life course over time, structured and sequenced in terms of the individual's own properties, rights, and choices. In this context, the modern psychological individual develops (Inkeles & Smith, 1974) through the mechanisms classically discussed by Mead (1934). Given a society of highly psychologized individuals, it is natural and necessary that cultural observations prominently include psychological theories and ideologies. They reflect the social facts of life in such a society, and also attend to the needs and problems that arise, issues that inevitably take on a psychological character. The social individuation extends into childhood (through the machinery of life-course organization), and so do the psychologies. Thus, this model social differentation generates more elaborated psychological individuals, whose properties receive the expanded cultural attention indicated by psychological thinking. The agendas of the psychological discussions reflect not only the technical evolution of the sciences involved but also the state of individualistic society.

Third, psychological agendas reflect not only the evolution of a science and of the developing realities of individual life and mind, but also macrosociological forces built into legal and other institutions. The Western economic, cultural and political systems are all built up around—and are justified or legitimated by—expanded and expanding notions of individual personhood. Economies create and require enlarged notions of individual market choice, politics require citizen competence, and cultural systems depend on ideologies of the morally endowed and responsible individual.

The expansion of this whole institutional system in recent centuries produces a great expansion in the ideologies of individualism—the rules allocating rights and duties to the individual, socially entitling and often legally requiring this individual to assume them, as with compulsory education (Boli-Bennett, 1981; Ramirez & Boli, 1982). The culture changes to become more psychological, then, because the modern institutional system culturally requires and creates the psychologized individual as a matter of cultural (and political or legal) theory and legitimation (Bell, 1976). The causal link between the differentiated modern institutions and the rise of the psychologies is direct, not necessarily mediated by changes in the nature of typical individual persons.

Fourth, this line of reasoning can be carried one step further. The great cultural history of the West is not only economic and political, but has had important protoindividualist religious and cultural properties from the start. These properties are more than responses to changes in other institutions; they play a causal role in the development of the whole system. This theme, developed in Weber's (1930) arguments about the causal role of the Protestant Reformation in the rise of the modern economy, has been re-emphasized in the recent literature (Anderson, 1974; Hall, 1986; Mann, 1986). From this point of view, Western psychological thought is a direct secularized reflection of earlier forms of relatively individualist religious ideology, as opposed to a result of the technical history of psychology, or of putatively changed individuals, or of ideological adaption to an evolving differentiated political and economic system. The inclination to cultural psychologization is a causal force in its own right, not simply an adaptation to other forces.

The latter two lines of argument, stressing the autonomous importance of psychologies as ideology, have gained a good deal of prominence in current "institutionalist" thinking in sociology (Thomas, Meyer, Ramirez, & Boli, 1987). They provide a useful perspective for our discussion here, and suggest lines of interpretation of the rise and change in psychological agendas. Modern systems develop and change their embedded theories of the individual in ways that both drive and reflect other aspects of *institutional* structure. The ideologies involved are likely to be linked closely to the themes of both professional and lay psychologies.

THE INSTITUTIONALIZED LIFE COURSE

Historical Western reality has posed a continuing series of surprises to those theorists who saw it as primarily an evolving political and economic Leviathan dominating individual life (e.g., on the left, Marx; on the right Ortega y Gasset). A number of these surprises have to do with the emergence and evolution of much social structure organizing and sequencing the individual life course, under all sorts of norms of justice and of individual and social development. Early in life there are the institutions and ideologies emphasizing childhood and its distinct stages (Aries, 1962), developing into an elaborately sequenced, regulated, and universal system of mass education, and also reconstructing the earlier states of childhood as themselves making up a socially controlled developmental process: The educational parts of this are now worldwide (Boli, Ramirez, & Meyer, 1985). This childhood system is linked by rules and organizations to a system of work roles with its own stages and rules of sequencing — more loosely regulated than childhood, but still a recognizable normative system with elaborate rhetorical standards of fairness and career development. This system, in turn, links up to the social rights of retirement, with still more (although rather loosely structured) definitions of stages, of rights, and of developmental progressions.

Why is all this in place, and so widely institutionalized in socio-political systems around the world? Lame arguments that it is somehow in the interests of expanding political bureaucracies and economic organizations or classes to create so elaborate a system of rights and protections have fared ill empirically: The system appears in too many politically unlikely countries (e.g., the United States) and economically implausible places (e.g., the entire Third World). It makes more sense to see this system as a result of the institutionalization of the individual as a building block of the whole system, as in our more institutional lines of argument just presented. If the primacy of the perspective of the individual is treated as a central factor in Western history, or as a necessary cultural element in the emerging political and economic expansions of this system, the rapid expansion of the institutionalized life-course system makes more sense (Boli et al., 1985).

From this point of view, the regulated modern life-course system—the object of continuing public scrutiny and management, from our concerns with fetal rights through childrearing, education, and career sequences and retirement to our intensified concern with the management of death—is a sort of organized treaty between the two great legitimated value perspectives in the Western world system, perspectives that have always been in a tension that many analysts see as at the root of the expansive potential of the system. On the one side is the primacy of the self (earlier, soul) of the individual. On the other side is the good society as a project in progress and of justice. The two sets of values are always in tension, and in Western theory may never be entirely reduced to each other (e.g., the value of human personhood may not be reduced to the individual's contribution to the Gross National Product). The life-course system can be seen as providing rules of integration by which the individual self and the social good are aligned in rules regulating both equality and inequality, and both individual and social development.

But this means that we have institutionalized in an increasingly intensive way (Bell, 1976; Meyer, 1986) two distinct aspects of individual personhood: the individual as an element in a rationalized career line and the individual as a free subjective being. As has been noted often, the modern system generates both an extreme subjectivity and an extreme rationalization of the individual life perspective. Both of these perspectives, we argue, appear and gain strength on contemporary psychological agendas.

There is clearly a sharp distinction to be made between the institutionalized life course—the individual as a productive and protected career line, normatively tied together over time and with a complex set of social roles and activities—and what we have called the *subjective side* of the individual's life course. But definitions of the latter tend to be unclear.

Discussions of modern subjectivity sometimes take it with excessive romanticism, as unique to each individual, and ignore its social content. In fact, the modern subjective self is a highly socially shared phenomenon, not a radically individuated one: The Thoreaus alone at their Waldens go there taking positions from society and return to write and sell books for everyone else to read. In fact, many of the most discussed expressions of modern subjectivity occur in such social media as the high arts of literature, painting, and music: created to be shared. Similarly, there is much professionalized psychological discourse on subjectivity in the mass media. There are socially standardized and technically rule-like discussions of how to experience uniquely individual subjectivity—how to "get in touch with" one's feelings and perceptions, and how to express these to others in approved formats.

GUIDING IDEAS ON THE INSTITUTIONAL CHARACTER OF THE INDIVIDUAL

The previous discussion suggests three main ideas that are useful for our subsequent speculations on long-term changes in psychological agendas. First, the subjective perspective of the individual, the structures of the life course, and the macrosociological system in which these located, are all institutions operating at very general levels. They are highly theorized and ideologized, built into law and culture, and have histories of their own; they are not simply summaries of the changing accidents of microsocial experience. The psychologies that account for the subjective self have histories and logics of their own.

Second, at the institutional level, there has been increasing differentiation in the organization of the rules of individualism, between the social structures and rules attending to and legitimating individual subjectivity and choice, and those psychologies and ideologies accounting for the individual life career that is socially regulated as an exercise in development and equity. This, we suppose, is linked to the differentiation in psychological theories and ideologies discussed (and criticized) as embodying contradictions by Bell (1976) and Lasch (1983), among many others.

Third, the cultural theories involved operate in continuing balance, deriving from their roots in both the value of the good society and the ultimate value of the individual. As economies and polities (and their ideologies) expand and intensity, so do the theories and rights celebrating the individual subject. And so do the rules and ideologies standardizing and regularizing the life course as in the interests of both the sacred individual and the virtuous society. Thus, as new elements of the individual's life are regularized in the institutional system, new elements of subjectivity arise, and are adapted to, but exist distinct from life-course regularization.

In practice, then, our independent variables become the changes in recent decades in the public normative and organizational structuring of the legitimate life course. These operate in a context of continuing pressure to elaborate and theorize a subjective perspective. Thus, social changes expanding the life-course system should be accompanied by new psychological emphases that transcend them, retaining a subjective individuality independent of them. We therefore list some of the changes in recent decades in explicit social ordering of the life course (our immediate independent variable):

1. There has been a continued expansion of the organized and sequenced educational system, and much attention to its proper role in creating legitimate social membership, equality, and stratification (Boli et al., 1985).

2. There has been much extension of similar logics into adult life: (a) the continued increases in regularization of career lines, and the discovery of psychological stages, sequences, and crises appropriate to them; and (b) the extension of similar considerations to retirement and aging and death, with a socially organized expansion in rules, ideas of justice, and rights, and with psychologically organized discussions of appropriate perspectives (Meyer, 1986).

3. There is an increase in the public penetration of preschool life, with expanded organizations and facilities worldwide (O'Connor, in press) and with an expansion of public control and concern over the rights, proper development, and equality of children (e.g., with regard to issues of child abuse and neglect, of medical attention, and of the problems of poverty).

4. In all these areas, there has been a radical delegitimation of the primordial authority of "natural" or ascriptive identities in the life course: (a) a narrowing of the general legitimacy of gender and sexual identities throughout the life course; (b) delegitimations of the use of ethnic, racial, class, or regional distinctions as basic identities; and (c) even though the institutionalized life course is organized around age distinctions, there has been a sharp reduction in the legitimacy of age as a general identity distinction, and as in other areas an increased concern with justice and equality. Age is used constantly but in a rationalized way, as a set of steps in the properly sequenced life course. As identity elements, the old and the young are equal to the main identities of adults.

5. The organizational changes involved have normative and institutional aspects. Each step of the life course is tied more closely to concepts of the collective good: Social progress and justice are seen to depend on, more and more heavily (both in definition and in consequence), the proper organization of life courses. Child abuse, or gender discrimination, or the mistreatment of the old, indicate defects in collective life and are societal responsibilities; but it is believed they will also produce collective failure resulting from the poor performance or dissatisfaction of the mistreated groups. The failures involved are seen as very general—both societal (violations of citizenship rights) and worldwide (violations of human rights).

The Resulting Self.   Thus, both birth and death become foci of societal scrutiny, along with each step in between. The life course is to be a regularized project for the individual, and not in principle distinct for different genders, ethnic groups, and so on. The individuals are all in some ultimate sense the same over each step of the process, with similar standing and rights.

Much that was once considered the individual self is now absorbed in a regularized social system. But this system is itself organized around the rights and capabilities of the individual as a self: We argue that this derives from Western ideologies about such rights. Clearly, new and changed elements of the self need to be constructed, legitimated, and given attention. But what kind of self is involved?

The ground rules are fairly clear—the Western self must always be conceived as some sort of actor, on which all of society rests. Three primitive elements are involved in the construction of an actor, in this sense. First, there is the economy of the self: the *motives* and goals, from which society is produced; and the *resource* or *satisfaction* payoffs that society must provide. Second, there is the technological capability structure of the self: *perceptions* and *competencies* to see, think, and act. And third, there is the polity of the self: the construction of a *bounded control* system. In each of these areas previous elements have been partially absorbed by society, and removed from the primary agenda of the self. What does the emergent theorized self look like?

1. *Motives.* Long-run motives—goal and aspirations—are in some measure removed from individual responsibility and located in a sequenced life course. Subjective (and theoretical) attention should be found to shift to motives related to proper participation in this system (not so much to managing individual progress in it)—to social satisfaction and self-esteem and good relationships. Motives should be less and less distinct to gender, ethnicity, class, or even age, and should be increasingly abstractly individual.

2. *Satisfactions.* These should shift, similarly, away from long-term life-course progress, but also from the uniqueness of gender, age group, ethnicity, and so on. Satisfaction with self and situation becomes more important than food, sex, and status.

3. *Perception.* Educated knowledge is built into the institutional system and is a main focus within the system. The business of the modern self is to see things in ways that fit its own needs, not mainly in ways that are true (that is, part of the objectified system). Subjective vision is connected to private purpose more and public purpose less. One should see the surrounding world in ways that fit the subjective self as a project: The good self, like a good artist, should do so in highly selective ways, in some measure ignoring realities, the recognition of which might hamper perceived efficacy.

4. *Competence.* In judging thought and action, standards relative to the subjective self and its needs are appropriate for the self—other forms of competence are regulated in the institutionalized life course. There are many kinds of good thought and good action: the only things that are really

wrong are those that undercut the self (or the legitimacy of the selves of others).

5. *Boundaries.*   In the institutional system, the individual is immersed in socially controlled identities (student, worker, retiree). The subjective boundary should, correspondingly, be clear and large. The individual should see many activities and choices as internally controlled, with a rich and voluntaristic model of private action in consumption and of the personal aspects of production. This should involve an elaborate private analysis of the individual's relation to public life-course roles.

6. *Control.*   The public system has its own controls. The private emergent one should have elaborated pictures of its own internal control over not only private action but also over much personal activity in the public sphere (autonomous aspects of work, study, and so on). One can let it all hang out, and should, but it is all also supposed to be under one's own control and responsibility.

All of this applies not only to action in some sort of private social space. It is also the proper perspective of the individual on much life in the standardized system. The individual should have a rich subjective analysis of his or her motives and satisfactions and competences in work places, in school life, in family and sexual relationships, and even vis-á-vis such formerly communal identities as ethnicity and religion. The modern individual should even be able to articulate ideas about god whose primary function is to be satisfying to him or herself, or to work out his or her own satisfying and competent sexual life.

All these changes in models of the person are on modern cultural agendas: Their effects can be found in law, religion, and political ideology. They appear prominently, we argue, in changes in agendas and domains of the psychologies, which are of course special repositories of models of the individual person. We examine them here.

EMERGENT PERSPECTIVES IN PSYCHOLOGY

It is central to our argument that the developments we discuss — whatever their role in individual experience and its problematics — are institutional and ideological matters. It is the business of *society* to construct the proper perspective of the self, not simply the enterprise of individual humans suffering in the coils of the rationalized life. In looking at the official and institutional side, one can find many loci — in law, religion, culture, and so on — in which these matters are worked out. But a central place, given Western individualism, is in the academic field of psychology, whose emergence and change is at every point linked to the development of the theory of the individual in modern history. Psychology in its modern form arises with such theory, and its form and focus change with changes in such theory. Although a detailed history is beyond the present frame and competence, some comments are in order.

Clearly, in much psychological thinking of the 18th and early 19th centuries, the individual is a rather simple and natural structure lying mainly outside the social system or at least its more modern dimensions. In Lockeian liberal thought, or later utilitarianism, the individual is variously a material and biological or a moral and ideal entity, entering into society as a small point in social space—a collection of a few natural interests and capabilities. (German thought included a natural social community, not just individuals.) Because in all modern ideologies, individuals have a biological as well as moral primordial quality (qualities of some importance to the legitimation of many aspects of society, including its inequality), this theme remains alive today. It is stronger at some times than others, and in some social systems more than others. One could envision useful comparative and time-series analyses of the matter.

The great social organizational changes of the late 19th century, involving the creation of large scale political and economic organizations and their penetration of society, produced a new and much more social theory of the individual. Just as society became a more substantively specified structure, so did the basic models of the individual, and thus a number of new branches of psychology developed. In the work of Freud, Hall, James, Dewey, and Mead, a more social psychology arose, but also new and more social reassertions of the autonomy of the individual: A theory of personality (the individual as much richer and more complex) embodying some consistency over time; and theories of development, with great attempts at synthesizing these ideas about personality. In all these perspectives, some common elements appeared, which now come to be seen as a little archaic (given the evolution of the modern system): There is a social, but subjective, point of view (the self); this self has continuity and is a carrier of the whole (now institutionalized) life project; thus there is great emphasis both on notions of long-term motivation and long-term capacity (as with intelligence); and most important, there is a simultaneous logic of both social progress and individual development. Especially in its American versions, this emergent ideology seems highly progressive, in the several senses of that term. Smarter, more committed, and better self-controlled individuals are better ones (then, as now), but all of this was to be seen in terms of objective social progress and its requirements—in each great area, there is one general high standard. Better people, in terms of these standards, will create social progress. The whole project rests on better people, and betterness has a general evolutionary standard.

As noted at the outset, this project has been institutionalized in the rules of the life course, most nakedly in those pertaining to childhood. Capacity is built into the rules of educational attainment, and into the commonly used general measures (IQ, SAT, GRE, MCAT, and so on), and the whole stratification system and its doctrines of development and fairness rest on such an impersonal competition. Social commitment is built into the ideology and practice of progressive education, with its emphasis on social participation, citizenship, and social relations. Social commitment is also found in American notions of good childrearing. So also with self-control, which is built into the structure of both education and family life; responsible choice, rather than authority, is emphasized. Fiala and Lanford (in press) find, in coding world educational ideologies of the 1950s, that both *individual development* and *national progress* are defined as central goals, with little sense of much inconsistency between them (a distinct aspect of the modern system, and very illustrative of the perceived significance of individual development in terms of social progress).

But, returning to the main theme of our discussion, if all of this material that is constitutive of the proper individual self comes to be institutionalized, taken as a societal responsibility, and increasingly brought under organizational control, it is no longer the autonomous core of the individual self. The institutional success of personality, social, and developmental psychologies in the first part of the 20th century changes the psychological conception of what is uniquely the self of the individual in the contemporary period. The subjective individual is no longer primarily defined in terms of educational and occupational aspirations or expectations, or in terms of intellectual capacity or in terms of social responsibility and control.

Some elements of the definition of the *self* drop out or become problematic, while new themes now gain prominence. The elements that weaken are those that have been most absorbed in the institutional project:

1. The idea of general laws of individual development clearly weaken. They remain as metaphors and conceptions at a very abstract level, but the idea that there is one general process—an idea now absorbed by the educational system which has just this character—leading to one virtuous outcome, is weakened. There is much interest in looking for multiple pathways, unique sequences, individuated patterns, and so on, and a disavowal of setting up one general desired outcome as successful;

2. Trait theories of personality, and associated emphases on continuity over time, are clearly weakened (Kagan, 1983; Mischel, 1971). There is an emphasis on adaptability, on multiplicity, and on variability over time; exactly the opposite properties, of course, characterize the rules of the educational system;

3. Faith in the tight linkage between individual personality and social progress weakens (Bowles & Gintis, 1976; Kohn & Schooler, 1983) — although it is axiomatic in the main rules of childrearing and education.

4. The notion of the tight linkage between personality and social action also weakens — a notion that is again educationally axiomatic (Epstein, 1979, 1980; Mischel, 1971).

What is clearly strengthened in the emergent system of psychology? Notions of motivation and satisfaction that are more transitory, disconnected from the main axes of the stratification system, situational, and unique to the individual. These are often put together in a kind of metatheory emphasizing the value of the self to itself as a subjective entity, independent of social or stratificational success (for example, see Perlmuter, this volume). As a consequence, therefore, we have notions of perception and cognition that are similarly self-referential and subjective, and which are in some measure cut off from the criterion of "objective reality" or accuracy. Again, these are often abstract, and unrelated to the standard of social progress. Finally, there emerge notions of control and boundedness that dramatically emphasize a subjective side, and a side independent of social authority.

Strong normative elements remain in the more modern psychologies. There is still some stress on the individual virtues of extended motivation and satisfactions, of enhanced perceptual and cognitive complexity, and of the extension of self-control and efficacy. But these are no longer resolutely tied to a theory of life as a personal project in a social career, or to a theory of the expanded and improved subjective self as linked closely to the definition of social progress. As a result, the psychology that remains seems a bit fragmented — in the earlier period, it was held together by a general theory of persons in society that is now institutionalized.

Proper research on these questions would examine empirically the types of variables on which psychologists focus, and how these have changed over time. The older variables remain — intelligence, and educational and career choices — but it seems clear that newer emphases in professionally differentiated subspecialties arise. There is much interest, motivationally, in all sorts of satisfaction and self-esteem (in the work place, in school, in retirement, and so on) independent of actual stratificational success; in perception and cognition independent of an evolutionary notion of intelligence; and in such matters as internal control and efficacy independent of actual social responsibility and authority. Empirical research on changes in the themes of psychological thinking and research, along these lines, would be most useful.

One main current locus of the changes in focus we previously discussed is in the emergence of the life-span movement in psychology, with its altered notions of both personhood and development, and with its more complex view of the relations between self and society. We note some prominent themes, which appear among other places in the work reported in this volume.

LIFE-SPAN IDEAS

The life-span movement in psychology, and to some extent sociology, provides a good place to look at contemporary trends. Many of its emerging themes, we argue, reflect the larger social processes just discussed.

1. With the institutionalization of the life course as a socially managed project, conceptions of the stages of subjective individual life primarily in terms of their role in this developmental project are undercut. Childhood as a project leading to school and work becomes less important, and it becomes easier to think of childhood as containing present individuality in its own right. Thus, there can be more emphasis on the child as creating his or her own environment, on the satisfactions and dissatisfaction of the child qua child, or on the motivations and cognitions of the child vis-á-vis activities that may have little to do with progress toward educational and occupational attainment.

On the other side, metaphors of development, at a very abstract level, can be extended to other stages of life — adulthood and retirement, for instance. Again, interest in motivation and cognition can be pursued independent of aspects of life related to the main career system, or in ways unrelated to a theory of success in this system.

2. Similarly, emphases on continuity are weaker. With a highly abstract and metaphorical notion of development, the individual can be seen as a series of subjective projects disconnected over time and roles. Interest in individual adaptation to life events and discontinuities increases, as development and personality are conceived abstractly as adaptations to contexts rather than as project-shaping enterprises.

3. There are the general shifts in dependent varable foci that were noted previously: from those aspects of motivation, cognition, and control that are linked to ideas of unilinear individual and societal evolutionary process to much more subjectivist variables. Motivation and satisfaction are more personal than stratificational (self-esteem, not sex and money), perception becomes attribution, and cognition becomes wisdom. Control becomes a personal myth of efficacy. Interest in education and work lowers, in contrast to other older psychologies.

4. There is an almost doctrinaire rejection of the older notion of development in several senses: (a) First, the idea that life is a project in

irreversible time is rejected. This means, first, that psychological characteristics can be seen in their own right, not only in terms of their significance for an unfolding future; second, changes can reasonably be thought to go in more than one direction; and, third, there is not necessarily one direction of virtuous change. (b) Second, the idea—tied to a simple theory of social progress—that developmental patterns are or should be the same for everybody is rejected. There are many sorts of development, directions of adaptation, and so on. Different patterns may be useful in different contexts or periods, or for different groups, or for people facing different personal and historical events. (The peculiar affection of modern psychologists for interaction effects of any sort seems to arise because such effects are thought to show the freedom of humans from rigid and homogeneous developmental patterns.) (c) It is even held that developmental patterns may look different—go at different paces, lead to different outcomes, have inconsistent properties—in different aspects of life, and as a normal phenomenon. Development in different roles is seen contextually, (d) At the more general and normative level, there is a tendency to reject—or treat as metaphoric—any normative notation of development at all, at least as a general or universal standard (see Lerner, this volume). But there is much uncertainty here, and the matter deserves more attention.

NORMATIVE AND SOCIAL STRUCTURAL IMPLICATIONS

Beyond technical and scientific aspects, any developed psychology is likely to be linked to implied models of society, with a good many normative implications. We have already noted the linkage between progressive psychologies and progressive politics—these were in fact American versions of phenomena going on elsewhere in the world system too. In contrast to a laissez-faire picture of progress as working out from the natural rules of human action, the turn-of-the-century idea was to tame and organize this evolution, with better developed people (through purposive mechanisms) functioning for social progress in rational organization. It was organized individualism, rather than natural selection in markets. A substantive psychology, linked to a substantive theory of organizational rationality, was required (Hamilton & Sutton, 1987).

What kinds of parallel normative models are implied by psychologies that relinquish past notions of development and straightforward ideas of social progress? What kind of good society is implied by modern subjectivism?

Obviously, the specialized character of the modern psychologies (for instance, their separation from the institutionalized structures of education and career sequencing) increases the likelihood that general normative imagery will be rejected, either in favor of more narrowly scientific postures or of highly situational normative perspectives. But there seems to be a reluctance to let go of larger normative visions embracing general models of the good society and of some sort of social progress.

What happens when the subjectivist vision of the individual, cut off from the aspects of life institutionalized as the educational and occupational career, is turned into a general normative vision (or model of society)? The idea of development then tends to simply look like self-expansion, and on subjectivist terms — more motives and satisfactions in more activity, a wider and wider arena of perceived competence and control and efficacy, a stronger sense of mastery over everything, and so on. And a society that reinforces such visions in the individual is envisioned. One can see this as the ethic of the self (and of consumption) described by Lasch (1983), Bell (1976), and many others (Bellah, Madsen, Sullivan, Swidler, & Tipton, 1985). It seems a prescription for self-centeredness, unrealism, and rejection of social interdependence.

It makes more sense to see the modern psychological vision as a very partial, not a complete, normative theory of society. The subjectivist conception of the self is not so anarchic, and for two main reasons. First, as we have stressed throughout, it is culturally interdependent with another more institutional conception of the individual (and of psychologies that go with it). The older psychologies are still there, embedded in the institutional matrices of education and of the organized occupational system. They seem less interesting now, because their ideas are built into the rules of the system itself — the professional aspects center mainly on counseling individuals to work their way properly through the structure.

Second, the ideology of the subjective self is not really all that naricissistic. The general idea is still a universalistic social one, not a celebration of the relation of the individual to an entirely unique perceived natural and supernatural environment. There is a social grammar to it: In expanding motives and satisfactions, a core issue is self-esteem derived from others — from the reciprocal exchange of unrealistic subjective admiration. The motives and satisfactions are to be located in some sort of participatory activity — not necessarily work or school, but something social. So also with perceptions and cognitions: There seems an idea that these, although less subject to the realistic constraints of the main stratification system, are still to be subject to some sort of social judgment of other subjects. Communication, now widely emphasized, is a main test rather than viridicality, but also rather than a completely privatized cognitive and perceptual structure. And the sense of internal control is carefully bounded from any glorification of feelings of dominance: The actor is to feel autonomy, but is also to treat others so that their feelings of autonomy are enhanced.

The larger society involved in this conception is a classically American one. It involves highly participatory and active individuals operating in a network of equal status relationships all with enhanced senses of self and satisfactions, and with strong perceptions of choice and autonomy. Constraining, zero-sum aspects of horizontal exchange and vertical authority are to be transcended, presumably by the constant creation of new, free arenas for free activity.

The institutional aspects of this system as ideology seem to legitimate very high levels of associational activity—the formation of new arenas of valued activity in which each individual can find subjective satisfaction, esteem, and a sense of control. This has certainly been and continues to be, a main historical outcome in the United States—perhaps our discussion defines one of the motors for this, and for its high legitimacy in this society (Bellah et al., 1985).

But there is a dialectic side here—the American system tends also to institutionalize such activities, and the life-career patterns associated with them, into general rules of stratification and achievement. It tends, in other words, to absorb the social content of free subjectivity into organized systems. The standardization of the subjective in objective forms institutionalizes it in a new control system. Exactly this, we have argued, has gone on with education and the occupational system—the notion of autonomy of the capable and motivated individual is partly absorbed in institutional rules of the life course. There is no reason to believe this process stops.

So we have to add a notion of a dynamic to the process. American students and workers are organized in long and controlled career chains. These are legitimated in terms of individuality, but the legitimate subjective side of this individuality must be located outside the "9-to-5" framework. To express this individuality Americans are all encouraged to find a free, but still social, arena. For example, skiing: They all go skiing as free subjects, learning to properly enjoy, feel capable, assume a posture of internal control over their downhill slide, and so on. They are free subjects, all mixed up by age, sex, and status.

Our point is that this subjectively focused arena is a highly social one (Hochschild, 1983). Standards quickly emerge. And so do controls and sequences of progression in terms of competence—a mini version of the institutionalized life course, with standards of performance, of dress, attitude and style, of postskiing skill, and so on. Now our free actor, although increasingly able to participate in an expanding arena, is not quite so subjective and so free. Motives and satisfactions come to be linked to standards of performance—one is better if one can slide downhill faster, with fewer mistakes, or around more obstacles, and not everyone is as good as everyone else. Perceptions and cognitions of the performance of oneself are no longer quite so free. Control again becomes relative: One can no longer feel quite so much in control if sliding downhill on one's rump is a *mistake.*

The same story can be told in a hundred areas—societies for the enjoyment and admiration of dogs become quite objectified in their cultures, and so do groups producing and consuming all sorts of music (including random music). The social processes that create new areas for subjectivity also operate to build new institutions of the life course. And at their bases, given the individualism of West, new forms of schooling arise—ski schools, dog showing schools, and of course, schooling in the performance and appreciation of random noise.

CONCLUSIONS: SOME IMPLICATIONS FOR RESEARCH

We take the stance of observers trying to account for some of the cultural and intellectual emphases on the child and the subjective person. The posture is an external one, but not particularly critical. On one theme, however, a more critical remark may be useful.

The ready acceptance of the culturally established differentiation between the more subjective person and the now-objectified career line seems too limiting, and the informal division of labor between the psychologies and psychologists involved seems too restricting. It would be good to give more recognition to the interdependence between the two sides of the distinction. Two central points may make the idea clearer.

First, subjective actors (with satisfaction, senses of mastery and control, and so on) are constantly forming themselves under quite restrictive and objective life-course conditions involving specified pasts, presents, and futures. These conditions constitute the taken-for-granted conditions and frames within which persons are to find their satisfactions and senses of control. Researchers might better understand how actors do this differently in varying contexts by taking institutional frames into account. For instance, the high satisfaction, sense of competence, and sense of control of children in school can best be understood if one understand that they take for granted that they are students and that this has a valued logic of its own. So also with the similar perceptions common in even quite objectively limiting roles in the workplace. Obviously, comparative research would be useful; and such research should be built on some theories about what is institutionalized in the actor's identity (that is, the aspects of the past, present, and future that are taken for granted).

Second, researchers in more traditional psychological veins dealing with the institutionalized life course can make more sense out of their work if they recognize the high legitimacy of the individual subjective point of view in the constitution of the system and in the individual's own reaction to it. The institutionalization of the career helps explain why individuals are often so strikingly uncareerist in constructing their senses of subjective self.

Again, comparative work—across contexts that vary in the degree to which the legitimacy of the individual is built in—would be most useful. Analyses of childrearing for instance, that do not take into account the extraordinary modern emphasis on the development of the self seem too limited: It is normative and cultural phenomenon, not simply an interactional and situational one.

ACKNOWLEDGMENTS

Work on this chapter was supported by the Youth Development Center at Stanford University, with funds from the Boys Town Foundation. The chapter benefitted greatly from comments from Center colleagues, and also from colleagues on the SSRC Subcommittee. In particular, Richard Lerner gave many comments and suggestions that have been most useful.

REFERENCES

Anderson, P. (1974). *Lineages of the absolutist state.* London: Verso.

Aries, P. (1962). *Centuries of childhood.* New York: Random House.

Bell, D. (1976). *The cultural contradictions of capitalism.* New York: Basic Books.

Bellah, R., Madsen, R., Sullivan, W., Swidler, A., & Tipton, S. (1985). *Habits of the heart; Individualism and commitment in American life.* Berkeley: University of California Press.

Boli, J., Ramirez, F., & Meyer, J. (1985). Explaining the origins and expansion of mass education. *Comparative Education Review, 29,* 145–170.

Boli-Bennett, J. (1981). Human rights or state expansion? Cross-national definitions of constitutional rights, 1870–1970. In V. Nanda, J. Scarritt, & G. Shepard (Eds.), *Global human rights* (pp. 173–193). Boulder, CO: Westview, 173–193.

Bowles, S., & Gintis, H. (1976). *Schooling in capitalist America.* New York: Basic Books.

Epstein, S. (1979). The stability of behavior: I. On predicting most of the people much of the time. *Journal of Personality and Social Psychology, 37,* 1097–1126.

Epstein, S. (1980). The stability of behavior II. Implications for psychological research. *American Psychologist, 35,* 790–806.

Fiala, R., & Lanford, A. (in press). Educational ideology and the world educational revolution, 1950–70. *Sociology of education.*

Hall, J. (1986). *Powers and liberties: The causes and consequences of the rise of the West.* Pelican: New York.

Hamilton, G., & Sutton, J. (1987). *The problem of control in the weak state: Domination in the U.S., 1880–1920.* Davis, CA: Department of Sociology, University of California.

Hochschild, A. (1983). *The managed heart: Commercialization of American feeling.* Berkeley: University of California Press.

Inkeles, A., & Smith, D. (1974). *Becoming modern.* Cambridge, MA: Harvard University Press.

Kagan, J. (1983). The premise of connectivity. In R. M. Lerner (Ed.), *Developmental psychology.* Hillsdale, NJ: Lawrence Erlbaum Associates.

Kohn, M., & Schooler, C. (1983). *Work and personality: An inquiry into the impact of social stratification.* Norwood, NJ: Ablex.

Kornhauser, W. (1959). *The politics of mass society*. Glencoe, IL: The Free Press.

Lasch, C. (1983). *The culture of narcissism*. New York: Warner Books.

Mann, M. (1986). *The sources of social power*. New York: Cambridge University Press.

Mayer, K., & Mueller, W. (1986). The state and the structure of the life course. In A. Sorensen, F. Weinert, & L. Sherrod (Eds.), *Human development and the life course* (pp. 217–245). Hillsdale, NJ: Lawrence Erlbaum Associates.

Mead, G. (1934). *Mind, self and society*. Chicago: University of Chicago Press.

Meyer, J. (1986). The self and the life course: Institutionalization and its effects. In A. Sorenson, F. Weinert, & L. Sherrod (Eds.), Human development and life course (pp. 199–216). Hillsdale, NJ: Lawrence Erlbaum Associates.

Mischel, W. (1971). *Introduction to personality*. New York: Holt.

O'Connor, S. (in press). The expansion of preschool education. *Sociology of Education*.

Ramirez, F., & Boli, J. (1982). Global patterns of educational institutionalization. In P. Altbach, R. Arnove, & G. Kelley (Eds.), *Comparative Education* (pp. 15–38). New York: Macmillan.

Simmel, G. (1955). *The web of group-affiliations*. (Trans. Reinhard Bendix). New York: The Free Press.

Thomas, G., Meyer, J., Ramirez, F., & Boli, J. (1987). *Institutional structure*. Beverly Hills, CA: Sage.

Weber, M. (1930). *The Protestant ethic and the spirit of capitalism*. (Trans. Talcott Parsons) New York: Scribner.

4 CLASS AND THE SOCIALIZATION OF CHILDREN:

Constancy, Change, Or Irrelevance?

David L. Featherman
University of Wisconsin at Madison

Kenneth I. Spenner
Duke University

with the assistance of Naouki Tsunematsu
University of Wisconsin at Madison

ABSTRACT

Studies of the psychological development and socialization of children that link these outcomes with the concurrent developmental histories of their parents or care-givers exemplify the richness of a life-span approach to child development. We illustrate such an intergenerational relationship in address-ing the pattern of social class mobility of parents and its relation to children's socialization context. Our aim is to emphasize the need for dynamic ap-proaches to class as a context for child development and the need for bringing changing socioeconomic contexts into the study of the changing child. We speculate on the degree of influence that social class and social status may have on socialization and development of parents and children in modern industrial societies.

INTRODUCTION

Studies of socialization and development during childhood have overlooked a potentially important influence on patterns of constancy and change in mind and behavior among children. The missing information represents a link between the child's developmental context within the familial house-hold and the household head's occupational and economic history. Namely, we contend that conventional representations of social class, both as it applies to the household setting of socialization and to the family head's career, fail to reflect with fidelity the dynamic fluctuations in a family's social class that occur over the duration of the child's years in the family.

This oversight misrepresents the impact of class as a source of both constancy and change within the child and of time-dependent developmental outcomes among children, both between siblings born of different pregnancies but also among children from different families as they mature. Specifically, if it can be shown that the social class context of childhood is rather impermanent, especially for some class categories, then we must question the significance attributed to class per se as a major developmental influence during socialization (Kohn, 1969). Should many children experience multiple class contexts, then analysts of the role of a child's social world in his or her development might look to other, more abiding, attributes of family and household (e.g., life style emanating from parental education) to explain differences among children from different families (e.g., Alwin, in press).

We do not provide a review of the class socialization and psychological development literatures (e.g., Alwin, in press; Gecas, 1979; Hernandez, 1986; Sewell, 1961). However, we think it is useful to characterize its main tendencies. First, the concept of class lacks a conceptual and theoretical base. In many psychological studies, class represents some ill-defined variation among families (or their children) by economic life style or social prestige. These variations more accurately capture features of social status then class. Nevertheless, measures of class usually are applied as control variables so that within-class processes of development can be studied with greater precision. Without a theoretical basis and appropriate measures for interpreting the observed and expected impact of class categories on children's development, psychological studies often focus on typical, middle-class families; how these settings and children might differ from non-middle-class subpopulations is not the theoretical burden of such research. Ironically, when comparisons are made by some measure of class background, the influences of class often are regarded as notable, if not profound (e.g., Kagan, 1984). But what these effects mean is an open question, especially without the benefits of conceptual grounding.

For example, psychologists (and many sociologists) might view class as a nuisance variable to be controlled, much like the concept of birth cohort. It is not interpreted as a "theoretical process variable" (as in Baltes, Cornelius, & Nesselroade, 1979, on the treatment of cohort). In that view, social class is a proxy variable for unmeasured, proximate variables in the socialization process—for example, parental childrearing practices or values. If these proximate variables had been measured, then it follows that the analyst would not need any measure of social class per se (Bronfenbrenner, 1958). We believe that this view, although defensible in part, overlooks aspects of social class as a theoretical process variable that are not capture by reductionistic logic.

Second, and related, measures of social class background are ad hoc, opportunistic, and inconsistently applied (Mueller & Parcell, 1981). Categories such as manual and nonmanual, working class and middle class, white-collar and blue-collar abound in the developmental literature. *Class* and *status* are terms used interchangeably. How they relate to specific operational indicators, such as family head's occupation, education, and income, has little consistency from study to study. There is little reason to care whether on the several available scales of "status" (i.e., Hollingshead, Duncan's socioeconomic scale, NORC prestige scale), a family would be similarly classified by "class." Whether the phenomenon of social class has the same biocultural and social structural significance in one time period or societal setting as another is rarely considered; findings reported for manual workers are taken as equivalent, as if there were a well-understood constancy of contextual meaning across time and place (as provided in part by Kohn, 1969 and Pearlin & Kohn, 1966).

Finally, a third characteristic is the assumption of stability or consistency of class for a given child's developmental origins. This is a curious assumption, for it seems inconsistent with the realities of substantial occupational and class mobility in the work histories of male family heads, at least up through ages 35–45 in many industrial societies (e.g., Featherman, 1980). Kohn et al. (1983) have proposed and replicated a model of occupational socialization for adult workers and their offspring. Their model supports the conclusion of considerable change in adult (parental) personality as a function of changing job conditions over a decade of work experience. For example, parental goals of self-direction in their children (a childrearing goal), as well as their own intellectual flexibility, varied over the decade in proportion to the degree of change in job conditions like complexity, routinzation, and closeness of supervision (Kohn et al., 1983, p. 172). These effects, although correlated with measures of "occupational position," like occupational prestige (status) and job income, prevailed even after controls for occupational changes in status and income were applied.

To be sure, studies of child development have identified several aspects of household and family structure and functioning having profound effects when they change. Some of these, such as income loss and loss of one parent, are at least correlated with social class in America (e.g., Elder, 1974; Hetherington, Camara, & Featherman, 1982). Nevertheless, in studies that take change in socioeconomic characteristics into account, measurements of social class per se typically assume that the content and meaning of class will remain stable across the course of childhood.

This chapter examines the empirical basis for the later assumption of constancy of class as a socialization experience. We take advantage of rather unique data, representing a complete working history of fathers in Norway and the United States, to assess constancy and change in the class backgrounds of children during the first 18 years of their lives. We focus on the extent of change in class background and the ensuing changes in the more proximate characteristics of jobs (e.g., occupational self-direction) that have been shown to affect socialization (e.g., in the Kohn et al., 1983, research).

SOCIAL CLASS AS A PROCESS VARIABLE

Sociologists distinguish between the concept of social class and that of *social status*, although both concepts refer to different but correlated dimensions of a society's system of social stratification. *Status* includes elements like the prestige or standing in the community, based on gender, race, ethnicity, and a family's reputation. It also reflects standards or tastes for life style and consumption, that is, how persons and families spend the money and leisure time they have. *Class* refers to position in the market-place, usually based on the kinds of jobs and industries of persons' work. Although status and class are related, they are not equivalent in theoretical meaning or in their bearing for how a person is evaluated by peers (e.g., the Black surgeon whose tastes in music are classical and who vacations in the Bahamas versus the White lawyer who dresses in jeans, listens to hard rock, and vacations in her canoe).

Although distinguishing clearly between individual differences that reflect status or prestige and those that reflect social class, sociologists are to blame for the lack of theoretical clarity and substantive richness in these terms when applied to socialization research. It is no wonder that the developmental literature outside sociology might reflect a misspecification of what class (vs. status) is and how it might affect children.

At the level of empirical observations, sociologists disagree about the existence and significance of social class as an efficacious domain for individual behavior in the United States (Blau & Duncan, 1967; Jackman & Jackman, 1982; Wright, 1985). That is, sociologists disagree not only over what class is — a statistical category of persons who share some common statuses of income, education, and occupation versus a socially conscious and self-identified group based on its position in the capitalist market-place — but also about the prevalence of class actions — for example whether class has greater structural articulation and behavioral impact in capitalist Britain than in capitalist America (e.g., Giddens, 1973).

Sociologists may be blamed, as well, for the tendency to view class in static terms. Surely, one legacy of the socialist era in American sociology and the community studies of social class that it spawned (e.g., Warner & Lunt, 1941) was the provenance of Marxist thought about class structure and formation in capitalism. Namely, it was anticipated that the internal logic of capitalism would lead, through class actions promoting exclusion and solidarity, into an essentially bifurcated structure of proletariat and capitalists. The working class would grow in size and consciousness, and despite appearances of intergenerational class mobility—appearances that would be used by capitalists to fragment and deflect the inexorable forces of proletarianization—the eventual state of society would be a well-articulated class structure with essentially closed membership. Intergenerational mobility would be an interim historical phenomenon; and intragenerational (career) mobility, would be a virtual impossibility outside a given class of entry.

Sorokin's (1959) empirical assessment of social mobility in the United States belied this idealized notion of stabilizing (if not stabilized) class stratification in America. Like Parkin (1971) in Britain, Sorokin argued that the political and social order of industrial societies were linked to their capacities for social fluidity. Both Sorokin and Parkin viewed class categories as dynamic units of dynamic social structure. That is, classes as structural units can be differentiated by size, demographic composition (of their incumbents), and turnover (rates of changing incumbents), among other features. Rather than seeing them as idealized, typological entities, Sorokin and Parkin put forward the idea that classes and the class system were constantly in the throes of transformation. One studies this transformation with data about social mobility, looking for the potentials for class formation (classes as self-interested groups with a collective agenda of action) that are implied by the size, demographic composition, and turnover rates of structural class categories. Sorokin concluded that the extent and pattern of social mobility in America was counteracting any major tendencies for class formation in that country. (See Blau & Duncan, 1967, for a similar assessment based on a more thorough study in a later decade.)

Despite the empirical study of class transformation and formation from a dynamic point of view, the intellectual appeal of the more structuralist, Marxist perspective remains a strong influence in the thinking about social class in America and Europe (Wright, 1985). One effort to synthesize the two perspectives arises in work by Goldthorpe and his associates (Erikson, Goldthorpe, & Portocarero, 1979; Goldthorpe, 1980). We adopt this framework for our exposition of class as a dynamic context for socialization.

From a structural, although not necessarily Marxian, point of view, class categories can be defined by at least two relationships: *market forces* and *work relations* (e.g., Lockwood, 1958). Market forces refer to an ecological relationship between a given occupational grouping and its command over employment security, income from labor and other sources, and chances for economic advancement with the constraints of existing demand for labor and skills. That is, class refers to a distinctive pattern of economic adaptation within a niche of the market economy. By inference of this language, one might expect class categories so defined to be fluid historically to the extent that the overall pattern of economic activity and competition for the same niche remains in flux. Structural analysis of class rarely takes such an ecological view, however, and settles instead for a static snapshot under assumptions of equilibrium conditions. (This often forces class analysts to define "transitional" categories, or "contradictory" class positions that do not fit the orthodox Marxian model of a capitalistic class system: e.g., Wright, 1979.)

Similarly, work relations can be defined in ecological terms, albeit with reference to patterns of authority and control over the amount and pace of production within a given employment grouping, occupation, or firm. These, too, are subject to change in connection with forces like unionization, bureaucratization, professionalization, and technological change. In modern industrial economies where work is organized by bureaucratic principles, these factors of control and authority over the process of production are just as significant for class definition, perhaps even more so, as the orthodox Marxian desiderata of ownership of physical capital itself versus the ownership of merely human or cultural capital (Bourdieu, 1977; Parkin, 1971).

Thus, if functionally defined occupations (i.e., the division of labor) are the basic atoms that constitute classes, then the classes themselves are constituted by grouping occupations that have quite similar relationships in the capitalist marketplace and within which work relationships on the job show similar kinds of control over the process of what is produced or offered as service.

Our structural definition of class already reflects a dynamic or ecological dimension. Yet we wish to go farther and address the matter of class transformation, under assumed conditions of stable market and work ecology. That is, let us suppose that the classes as previously defined are relatively enduring "empty places" in some steady-state socioeconomic structure. It is still possible that the class system, as a total sociological phenomenon, might be changing in a significant dimension. This possibility is captured by Giddens' (1973) rather awkward term, *class structuration*. Put simply, "the rate and pattern of mobility . . . will determine the extent to which classes may be recognized as collectivities of individuals or families occupying similar locations with the social division of labor over time" (Goldthorpe, 1980, p. 40). In other words, flows among class categories and changes in the rates of such flows might transform the class system.

For example, a flow of individuals and families among classes, that is, social mobility, alters the demographic identity or composition of structural categories. From the point of view of their cumulative life histories, the same structural category takes on a vastly different sociological character if it is composed of a very heterogeneous rather than a homogeneous set of individuals. Likewise, if over some fixed interval of history the membership in a given category is very fluid, because of average short durations of membership in this class, then this is quite a different situation from one in which the class is an "absorbing state" of life-long incumbency once it is entered. Then, too, a small class whose members live close together (e.g., urban working class) has a different potential for collective action than a large but dispersed one (e.g., farmers).

The relevance of social mobility for the structuration of class hangs on the difference between class as a nominal or structural category versus class as a social collectivity poised for class action. The distinction, of course, can be traced to Marx, but the implications for the study of class have divided sociological inquiries into essentially static versus dynamic perspectives on what a class "is" and how it is defined.

This distinction is quite important for this analysis. We view the socialization of children within class categories as being influenced by both structural and dynamic properties of the class structure. First, growing up in a household with the following characteristics has a substantially different bearing on the child's development than one with contrasting features: With a secure economic base in uninterrupted employment; where the head has good prospects for gains in income over the life course through a well-organized career line; where on-the-job training reconfirms the value of familial investments in the education and skills of their offspring; where control over one's rate and quality of work generalizes to a sense of personal control and competence, among other self-related outcomes (e.g., Kohn et al., 1983).

In addition to these structural dimensions of class, the dynamics also play a part. Duration of exposure to homogeneous versus heterogeneous classes should affect the socialization process and introduce variance into the impact of any given class of birth (or of later assumption) on the child. With regard to the process of class transformation, if children are socialized in structurally homogeneous classes for extensive durations of childhood, there would be a greater probability of a high stability of class structuration from generation to generation. Children of an unskilled manual class (vs. service/professional class) would more readily drop out of school early, assume jobs in the periphery of the economy, marry younger, be subject to repeated "squeezes" in their income-consumption ratios over the life course (Oppenheimer, 1982), have wives working at dead-end jobs, and would be at greater risk for divorce. Their children would be at high risk to reproduce this cycle and to episodes of behavioral deviance (e.g., Rutter, 1979), especially if the peer network is organized by residentially segregated (by class) neighborhoods and schools. These are the core ingredients for galvanizing nominal classes into social classes through a congruent process of socialization over the life course and from generation to generation (e.g., Bowles & Gintis, 1976).

By contrast, if the child experiences a high degree of class mobility during the pre-adult years and/or remains in a single class that is composed of highly class-mobile and impermanent families, the forces for class transformation are very high. In turn, the tendencies for class formation are mitigated by the discontinuities in the class context of childhood and the lack of congruence in socialization over the life course (Spenner, in press).

Contemporary studies of child socialization rarely consider the dynamic features of class formation and transformation. Our analysis addresses this facet of dynamic social structure, its impacts on children's developmental contexts, and, reciprocally, the implications of child socialization for the persistence and change in class as cohorts of children flow through society and into their adulthood (Riley, 1985).

A CLASS SCHEMA FOR CAPITALIST ECONOMIES

Goldthorpe and colleagues (Erikson, Goldthorpe, & Portocarero, 1979; Goldthorpe, 1980, pp. 40–42) have proposed a class schema for western industrial nations that incorporates the twin dimensions of market forces and work relations that define categories of social structure within capitalist economies (Table 4.1). This schema has proven useful in making across nation comparisons in order to detect similarities and differences in social (class) mobility (see Erikson & Goldthorpe, 1985; Erikson, Goldthorpe, & Portocarero, 1982, for a discussion of United States and Scandinavian data according to this schema).

We have employed this class schema in a study of constancy and change in children's class contexts in both Norway and the United States (Featherman & Spenner, 1987). Here we summarize our results and comment on their implications for the study of child development from the life-span perspective.

Our data were drawn from two separate studies in which continuous records of parental employment were obtained through extensive retrospective interviews. These data enabled us to reconstruct class histories, based on the categories in Table 4.1, for each child born into the household where an adult respondent had provided both the employment history and a fertility history. Because the histories of parental employment (we used the data for male family heads) were continuous, we knew the exact duration of each class a given child encountered from birth. Our own and others' efforts to validate the accuracy of the employment data from which the class designations were made are cited in our analytical paper (Featherman &

TABLE 4.1
A Class Schema for Capitalist Economies

Class	Name	Description
I	Service Class, I	High-grade professionals, both self-employed and salaried; higher grade administrators and officials in government and the private sector; managers in large industrial firms; and large proprietors.
II	Service Class, II	Lower grade professionals, high-grade technicians; lower grade administrators and officials; managers of small businesses, industrial firms, and service enterprises; supervisors of nonmanual employees.
III	Routine Nonmanual	Mainly clerical employees in administration and commerce, sales personnel, and other rank and file in service firms.
IV	Petite Bourgeoisie (with employees)	Small proprietors, self-employed crafts; all other self-employed other than professionals and farmers.
V	Petite Bourgeoisie (without employees)	Same as class IV.
VI	Farmers	Self-employed farmers, fishers, and timbermen.
VII	Technicians	Lower grade technicians of highly manual work and supervisors of manual laborers.
VIII	Skilled Wage Labor	Skilled manual labor, including apprentices.
IX	Unskilled Labor	Manual labor of semi- and unskilled kinds.
X	Farm Labor	Agricultural workers and similar wage labor in fishing and lumber industries.

Spenner, 1987; suffice it to say here that recall errors are not a major factor in our analysis of change.

From the Norway study (Featherman, Hogan, & Sørensen, 1984; Featherman & Sørensen, 1983; Ramsøy, 1977), we summarize data based on a 1921 birth cohort of men who fathered 1,412 children, born between 1935–1953, and who survived for 17 years prior to the interview in 1971. For the United States we use a state-level high-school sample, born in the State of Washington between 1948–1950; no equivalent national data for the Norway comparison are available. From this United States study, which followed up men as young fathers (ages 23–25) in 1979 (Otto, Call, & Spenner, 1981), we report histories for 876 children who survived for 6 years from birth and had fathers with recordable class (e.g., the fathers were not students).

We are not comparing the two countries, for the data are not comparable in population coverage or in the social and historical milieux to which they pertain (see Featherman & Spenner, 1987). Rather, our purpose is to illustrate patterns of constancy and change in class context in ways hitherto not possible, using the respective strengths and representations of the two unique sources of information.

Our summary of the extent and pattern of change in class during childhood (up to age 17 in Norway and age 7 in the United States) reflects a different level of class detail in the two countries. For Norway, we used the full 10 categories in Table 4.1. Because in the United States, data of the absence of sufficient detail about employment necessary for making a class assignment (e.g., information about size of employing firm), we were forced to collapse the 10 categories in Table 4.1 into 5 larger classes. Thus, in the United States, Class I combines I and II; Class II is equivalent to Class III; Class III combines Classes IV, V, and VI; Class IV combines Classes VII and VIII; and Class V is equivalent to Classes IX and X. Obviously, the wider boundaries of the class categories in the United States also adds to the lack of precise comparability between the data for the two countries.

PATTERNS OF CLASS MOBILITY
OF CHILDREN IN TWO SETTINGS

How much class mobility do children experience? Are most children mobile from their classes of birth or do most remain stationary? We find evidence for extensive and prevalent change in the class of socialization in both Norway and the United States. For example, in their first 17 years of life, 51% of Norwegian children moved between two and five classes, and 11% experienced six or more classes; Only a large minority (38%) remained continuously in their class of birth.

Much of this class mobility occurs early in children's lives. Table 4.2 calculates mobility during the preschool years (prior to age 7) for both countries. Forty percent of Norwegian preschoolers and over 50% of American children experienced at least one class change prior to entering school. If a developmentalist studying first graders was to measure social class based on information collected at enrollment, the data would contain large errors for substantial fractions of children. That is, the social class at enrollment is not an accurate portrayal of children's class histories since birth.

Another way to view the rate of class mobility is by focusing on the pace of leaving the class of birth (Table 4.3). In Norway, 11.3% change class during the first year of life. Of those who remain, 7.5% leave in the second year and so on until by age 10 over 50% no longer remain in the class of birth. Rates of experiencing one or more changes in any year are highest through ages 6 to 8 (ranging between 10% and 12% of children in each of those ages). In the United States, the pattern during the ages of overlapping coverage (up to age 7) with the Norway data is very similar, but more children exit class of birth more quickly. For example, 50% no longer remain in the class of birth by age 5, but 34% had moved from birth class

TABLE 4.2
Number of Social Classes Occupied by Norwegian (A)
and United States (B) Children During First 6 Years of Life[a]

No. Classes	No. Children	Percent	Cumulative %
		(A) Norway	
1	850	60.2	60.2
2	316	22.4	82.6
3	132	9.3	91.9
4	39	2.8 $\}$ 35.8	94.7
5	18	1.3	96.0
6+	57	4.0	100.0
		(B) United States	
1	399	45.6	45.6
2	284	32.4	78.0
3	122	14.0	92.0
4	47	5.4	97.4
5	16	1.8	99.2
6+	8	.9	100.1

[a]Featherman and Spenner (1987).

by age 3. In the United States as well, rates of having one or more class changes in any year are highest in the youngest ages.

Life-span views of child development are wont to question the merit of research that dwells on infancy and early childhood, and by implication, that suggests a greater significance of maturational and environmental events in the early years. These data on class changes during early childhood in two societies with markedly different social and economic histories are noteworthy from this perspective. They suggest that marked and rapid environmental changes may be occurring in the first 6 to 8 years — a rate of change that is not specific to the period of very rapid post war industrial expansion in Norway or to the mobility proneness of American society. Whether the biological program for maturation that infants and young children share overrides the individual differences arising from unique and prevalent class mobility histories in early life is beyond our knowledge. Yet these data suggest that early class history may be an unexplored basis of individual differences in child development, one that may perhaps extend into adulthood, to the extent that social class per se (and not elements of social prestige or life style) represents a set of strong developmental influences. (See Featherman, 1980, for a review of how parental social class affects attainments of children in school and later in the world of work.)

However, not all children experience rapid mobility even at the young ages when the likelihood of parents changing social class is highest. In both Norway and the United States, the chances of exiting class of birth are lowest in the services classes (upper middle class) and the working class

TABLE 4.3
Percent Who Remain in Class of Birth by End of Each Age,
and Age-Specific Rate of One or More Changes, Norwegian
(A) and United States (B) Children

Age	Percent	Percent Who Leave by Age	Rate of One or More Changes
		(A) Norway	
1	88.7	11.3	11.3
2	81.2	7.5	11.8
3	73.4	7.8	12.5
4	67.6	5.8	12.3
5	63.7	3.9	10.1
6	60.2	3.5	10.4
7	56.8	3.4	10.3
8	53.6	3.2	10.7
9	51.6	2.0	9.0
10	48.9	2.7	9.8
11	47.6	1.3	8.4
12	46.2	1.4	7.7
13	44.5	1.7	7.6
14	43.1	1.4	7.7
15	41.9	1.2	6.7
16	41.1	.8	6.1
17	39.9	1.2	6.4
		(B) United States	
1	77.6	22.4	22.4
2	66.8	11.8	15.1
3	60.0	5.8	8.8
4	54.1	5.9	9.9
5	49.8	4.3	8.0
6	45.6	4.2	8.5

aristocracy of technicians and foremen; they are greatest outside the echelons of the middleclass, broadly construed. These differentials in class immobility are illustrated in Figure 4.1, representing the rates of survivorship of Norwegian children in their classes of birth.

Over 60% from the services classes (upper white-collar) and about 50% from the technicians and foremen class (upper blue-collar) remain stationary from birth. By contrast, only 25%–33% of children from unskilled labor, farm, and entrepreneurial families remain in their classes of birth for the full 18 years. In similar computations for the United States (but only to the seventh birthday), the same pattern appears. Namely, 50% or more of the children from service and blue-collar aristocratic families have not changed classes by age 7, but only 22% from routine nonmanuals (clerical and retail sales), 32% from small business, and 45% from unskilled and farm labor families are stationary.

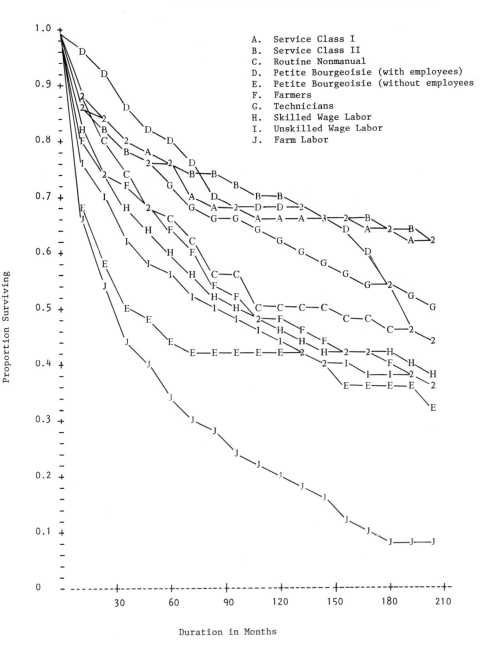

FIGURE 4.1 Survival curves for social classes at birth. Norwegian children through age 17. *Note:* Those children who experienced six or more class changes in their first 6 years of life, which accounts for 4% of all children, are excluded.

At the same time, in each class in the United States over a 25% of the children leave their class of birth by their second birthday. Those from clerical and retail sales families are the earliest to leave (prior to age 1); those from service classes, the latest (at age 2). For Norway, the pattern is rather similar, although the ages by which 25% leave the class of birth range from 1 to 4, except for the service class where fewer than 25% have left by very late adolescence.

Thus, each social class has its distinctive pattern of early exits, subsequent rates of attrition from class of birth, and patterns of ultimate immobility. These patterns are roughly similar in the two countries, despite widely different historical and economic circumstances. We emphasize here the major difference between the relative stability of class background for the broad middle class (upper white-collar and upper blue-collar) when contrasted to other class categories, although even in these classes in the United States a large minority has changed class by age 7.

This pattern in the two societies suggests a major implication for developmental research that draws its samples so frequently from middle-class samples. Namely, the typical assumption that children born into an occupational class remain of that class during socialization is valid only for the middle class and especially for professional families of that class. Yet even within this relatively stable category, many children experience class mobility within their preschool years. Therefore, if social class is an important context for developmental influences on the child, then a child's history of class membership is part of the individual differences in development. Measuring social class as a static feature at birth or at some particular age will not capture this history, this dynamic feature of socialization.

Finally, geographically localized, middle-class samples of children, including those with upper blue- and white-collar families (e.g., Block, 1971), are not accurate cross-sectional representatives of the experiences of families from the total population. At least, their mobility experiences underreport the volume and range of change in social class that the largest volume of families encounter. When one carefully defines the concept of social class and distinguishes it from measures of life style, parental education, income, and social prestige that constitute the concept of status, most children do change class and do so rather early in their lives.

DO SOCIAL CLASS AND CLASS MOBILITY INFLUENCE DEVELOPMENT?

Does all this mobility from class of birth and subsequent class change during childhood have any bearing on the development of children? We cannot answer this important question; neither can it be answered definitively from available longitudinal studies. We know of no study that collects detailed information both about the psychological changes in children and the histories of class attributes of the families in which these children reside (so that conceptually valid measures of class and status can be constructed for dynamic analysis in the fashion of the analysis of psychological changes).

Reviewers of research suggest that changes in work settings and class-related factors like market position and work relations do influence adult development (Mortimer & Simmons, 1978; Spenner, in press), even though these differences among parents and their patterns of adult development that arise from their working lives may not affect their children directly (Bronfenbrenner, 1979). Because we do not have the requisite data to probe these complexities with precision, the question about the bearing of class and class changes on child development remains largely unanswered.

However, our data from the United States study do permit some inferences about the range of effects of class change on parental development and on those adult variables such as conception of self, intellectual flexibility, and values for childrearing that are part of the parent–child relationship during socialization (Kohn, 1969; Kohn et al., 1983; Spenner, in press). We assume that the effects of these variables and changes in them do affect children's development.

In our continuing research program we are interested in the question: Is the range of change in social class environments we have reported for the childhood years large enough to produce change in the parental variables like intellectual flexibility, self-concept, and childrearing values during the socialization of a child? If the answer to this question is negative, then there is little point to pursuing the developmental implications of class change for children's development. We summarize some provisional findings that suggest a nontrivial impact of class mobility on the parental variables that children encounter during socialization (see Featherman & Spenner, 1987, for greater detail).

In illustrating the general tenor of our findings, we focus on three measures of job characteristics that are related to cross-sectional differences in parental values for socialization and to changes in such beliefs and values (among a wider set of adult developmental outcomes); these relationships have been replicated in structural equation models estimated for the United States, Poland, and Japan by Kohn, Schooler, and collaborators (Kohn & Schooler, 1982; Kohn et al., 1983; Slomczynski, Miller, & Kohn, 1981). *Substantive complexity* refers to the degree and extent of involvement on the job with people, data, and things; and, to the amount of specific and general education required to perform the job well. *Closeness of supervision* measures the performance of jobs under direct, specific instructions and without the latitude for independent judgments when problems arise. *Routinization* in jobs involves short and repetitive cycles of standardized procedures and sequences. All three variables are components of a latent construct, *occupational self-direction*, by which the several thousand different jobs and occupations in the American labor force can be characterized (see Spenner, 1980).

In addition, we include a measure of occupational prestige or socioeconomic status (SES). Duncan's socioeconomic index (Duncan, 1961; Hauser & Featherman, 1977). This index for the several thousand occupational titles recognized by the United States census is a widely used indicator of global educational and income characteristics of the incumbents of these jobs. It is highly correlated with a variety of attitudinal and behavioral differences and developmental changes in adults (Featherman, 1980; Spenner, in press).

Our interests in these characteristics is in comparing their variation across social classes in cross-section with the range of change in them that ensues from patterns of class change during childhood. In this comparison we get some purchase, provisionally and inferentially, on the question, "does class change during childhood matter for socialization?" We know that the cross-sectional differences in these variables are correlated with over-time changes in parental psychological variables; we know that changes in these occupational self-directions are correlated with changes in intellectual flexibility and values for childrearing. Therefore, the change in occupational self-direction (and occupation-based prestige or status) that ensues from class mobility provides insight, albeit inferential, into the probable impact of mobility on developmental outcomes.

Table 4.4 compares cross-sectional differences in the three job characteristics and the SES index (typifying employed males in their full-time work after completing their educations) with variations in these measures for class-mobile and class-immobile children during their first 6 years of life. We have computed individual averages for each child on each measure, taking the scores for each job of the father during the 6-years period. Table 4.4 summarizes these individual histories as class-specific means and standard deviations of the individual averages, partitioning them on the basis of whether or not the child had experienced mobility out of the class of birth by age 7.

Preschool children of class-mobile fathers are subject to variation in socioeconomic status, and the three components of their fathers' occupational self-direction range from 75% to 85% of the respective standard deviations in the cross-section of all jobs in the economy at the time the fathers began full-time careers. For example, the standard deviation in social status (17.9) and in substantive complexity (5.3) are over 80% of the cross-sectional values (21.4 and 6.4, respectively). By contrast, children who

TABLE 4.4

Variability During First 6 Years in Job Dimensions and Status, by Class Mobile–Immobile, Within United States Social Classes at Birth[a]

Job Dimension	Class Mobile–Class of Birth					Class Immobile–Class of Birth				Cross Sectional Differences in Father's First Job
	I	II	IV	V	All	I	IV	V	All	
Socioeconomic Status										
Mean of individual averages	49.7	43.3	34.2	30.1	36.1	67.1	30.8	16.4	33.4	31.2
Standard deviation	18.9	15.5	15.4	19.4	17.9	5.5	3.3	5.1	5.1	21.4
Substantive Complexity										
Mean of individual averages	12.9	11.3	8.6	7.5	9.2	17.0	8.3	2.8	8.0	7.5
Standard deviation	5.2	4.0	4.2	6.2	5.3	2.0	.5	1.6	1.6	6.4
Routinization										
Mean of individual averages	.19	.32	.23	.37	.30	.03	.09	.59	.33	.37
Standard deviation	.22	.26	.24	.33	.28	.02	.04	.18	.10	.35
Closeness of Supervision										
Mean of individual averages	.13	.22	.18	.32	.25	.01	.05	.52	.27	.31
Standard deviation	.16	.21	.21	.32	.25	.01	.03	.21	.11	.33
N	75	69	91	225	477	95	93	183	399	876

[a]All estimates are 6-year individual averages computed on each change in job or status during the 6-year period for each person. Only class of origin by class mobile–immobile categories with more than 20 cases are shown; class N's do not add to mobile–immobile subtotals.

83

remain in their class of birth apparently experience comparatively little change in status and occupational self-direction as their fathers change jobs within that class—about 25% to 33% of the cross-sectional variation. The latter contrast is not surprising, and had the outcome been otherwise we might have questioned whether we had constructed class categories that were too heterogeneous with respect to the status and work characteristics that comprise them.

If we accept the structural equation estimates of Kohn, Schooler and their various collaborators in modeling the effects of change in substantive complexity (for example, controlling for other variables in their model) on change in paternal intellectual flexibility or self-concept or values for childrearing (e.g., Kohn et al., 1983), we can assay the likely effects of change in class categories on the socialization predispositions of fathers during the first 6 years of their children's lives. In brief (see Featherman & Spenner, 1987, for fuller exposition), a 6-year variation in substantive complexity that is equivalent to 80% of a standard deviation translates into about one-fifth of a standard deviation of change in childrearing values or in paternal self-concept (as measured by the Kohn–Schooler model). This is roughly equivalent to the father moving from the 50th percentile to the 58th percentile (or down to the 42nd) in the dependent variable (childrearing values of self-concept that putatively affect socialization).

What is even more striking in its implications for the Kohn–Schooler research program, is the magnitude of change in especially the substantive complexity index during these 6 years. The 5.3-point standard deviation for the class mobile is roughly the same as the cross-sectional difference between skilled crafts jobs (a blue-collar group from Class IV) and sales jobs (a white-collar group from Class II). This means that the typical child, whose family is class mobile during the first 6 years of its life, experiences as much change in the input to parental socialization values as separates the differences in beliefs and goals for childrearing between families from white-collar and blue-collar groups. Because the replicated finding from the Kohn–Schooler research is that white-collar and blue-collar households differ in the balance of emphasis on conformity versus self-direction in their children (Kohn et al., 1983), our finding about change within a family raises real questions about the enduring significance of such class differences in socialization.

When viewed longitudinally, the short-term class-mobility experiences of large segments of American children apparently encompass nearly as much change in the work-related influences on their father's (and mother's) predispositions for socialization as separate major occupational and social class groupings of families. Of course, some classes are more likely to provide this wide range of contextual influences on parents and, we assume, their young children. Table 4.4 reconfirms the lesser consistency in the status and job characteristics for Class V families, which experience the greatest mobility during the 6-year period of socialization we are describing for each mobile child. Interestingly, it is also this class that has the greatest instability in two of the four measures of socialization context (routinization and closeness of supervision) even among those families who remain in Class V (unskilled and farm labor) during the 6 years after the birth of each child. The latter finding may warrant our redefining this class to achieve greater homogeneity.

Nevertheless, we believe there is presumptive evidence for the hypothesis that children's early lives are marked by comparatively large changes in the work-related environments of their parents, in the course of class mobility of their families. These changes within families are manifest across a range of status and job characteristics that have been shown to produce significant differences between families in parental predispositons and socialization, such as childrearing values, intellectual functioning, and self-concept. Indeed, the changes during the first 6 years of children's lives encompass nearly the full range of difference that separates major occupational groups of white- and blue-collar families. As such, we close with some speculations about the significance of these findings for child development research.

CONCLUSIONS AND SPECULATIONS LINKING CLASS AND CHILD SOCIALIZATION IN LIFE-SPAN PERSPECTIVE

There is little doubt that the changing economic fortunes of families that arise from severe economic depressions (Elder, 1974) or from disruptions of marital bonds and the formation of female-headed households (Hetherington, Camara, & Featherman, 1982, 1983) have large impacts on the development of children. Whether less sudden and perhaps less unpredictable changes in a family's social and economic circumstances, as are entailed by class mobility, have similar impacts remains unknown, but there is reason to discount the developmental significance of the predictable (e.g., Brim & Ryff, 1980).

It is presumption of major socialization studies that the social class histories of parents alter the developmental courses of adults as agents of children's socialization (e.g., Kohn et al., 1983). This is a life-span orientation, linking changes in the parental with changes in the filial generations through the mediating mechanism of occupation- and class-based experiences. Yet all too often, research that examines the details of children's psychological development fails to acknowledge the dynamics of class mobility that form part of the social context of childhood and that might introduce patterns of individual differences in developmental outcomes. Research that selects its samples to restrict the range of class at birth (or at any fixed age) also restricts and selects the types and rates of class mobility, and resulting developmental differences, that enter the data. Studies that presume a rather stable class history for the duration of childhood, or that select those families that are mobile only within a particular social class, present an incomplete, perhaps distorted, picture of childhood in the United States and apparently in other industrial societies.

We have reported evidence for substantial and early mobility from the social class of birth, together with continuing mobility for the duration of childhood for most United States children and a large minority of Norwegian children. Class immobility is quite class-specific, being relative prevalent for professional, lower technical/skilled craft, foreman, and other occupations that make up the service and technical classes. These are the groups that comprise the broad middle class, the target of generalization for much developmental research. Other classes, particularly those containing farmers and other entrepreneurs, or unskilled labor, have many out-mobile children after birth.

There is an important methodological implication of this rate and pattern of mobility that we have not mentioned. Namely, the prevalence and pattern of class mobility can affect the accuracy of class assignments in studies of children at different ages. For example, studies of infant as that index social class at birth and presume that children remain in that class from birth will have made a rather accurate assumption if the children are from professional families and the service class generally. This is because there is little out-mobility from the service class but much greater rates of exit from other classes of birth. Or, if one is studying late adolescents and taking their social classes at that time as indicative of their class histories, the assumptions of constancy would be correct for the highly mobile class categories such as unskilled labor and farm groups. This is because those who remain in this class in adolescence must be the immobile, because little mobility into these classes from a different class at birth is observed (Featherman & Spenner, 1987). Otherwise, there are many errors encountered in classifying a given child on the basis of one measurement of class membership that is assumed to reflect the context of socialization for the entire duration of childhood. This is most notably the case when samples of middle-class adolescents are drawn and classified by class, because there is a high inflow into these classes from other birth classes.

Substantively, our research raises some fundamental questions about the significance of social class for child development. If class membership is not very enduring, if many children exit their classes of birth by age 6, how shall we interpret cross-sectional class differences in socialization practices and developmental trajectories? On the one hand, what is reported as class differences may really be differences stemming from purely economic, educational, or life-style variations rather than from class per se. Alwin (in press) finds a smaller significance of occupation (relative to the net effect of education) in explaining beliefs and values for childrearing among Americans since 1950. Kohn in 1969, and more recently in unpublished papers, shifts the emphasis from occupation status and class to the effects of stable educational differences among adults in setting and reshaping adult personality. In short, despite the reality of substantial class mobility, what creates the stable differences between families in socialization may not be social class as such. Instead it may be the consequences of educational differences in the form of core values, life-style goals, and mobility aspirations and other motivations for self and children. In this case, our findings warrant the ending of research into the effects of class (rather than of status) on child development, because there may be none to find.

On the other hand, we might come to the opposite conclusion. Namely it may be precisely because class histories rather than class membership at some point in time is the life-course phenomenon of interest, present data and findings linking class with development and socialization variables are not the adequate basis for sealing the fate of class and socialization research. Consider Alwin's (in press) conclusion that education, rather than occupational class or status, may be the relatively greater influence on the socialization values of Americans since the 1950s. His careful analysis of intercohort trends could not illuminate the issue of within-family, within-career, or intraindividual change in values and their association with career mobility by occupational status or class. (He is very careful to indicate that his results refer to occupation-based prestige or social status and not to social class.) Is it possible that if Alwin and other analysts could estimate predictive equations for socialization values and other parental variables that included multiple observations of class membership, that the mobility history would be more predictive than just one point from it?

Of course, the Kohn–Schooler model introduces some of this information by including occupational status and job characteristics at two points in time, separated by 10 years for a cross-sectional panel of adults. Here, again, the predictive power of occupational details that reference class-like concepts is lower than of educational differences. However, although structural equation models such as theirs (Kohn et al., 1983) are useful in illuminating interindividual differences and changes in them over time, they do not necessarily reproduce the same results as models for intraindividual change and between-person differences in these changes (e.g., Rogosa, 1980). However, to engage in detailed analysis of intraindividual change requires more data organized more nearly as event histories (Featherman, 1985, 1986; Tuma & Hannan, 1984), so that the nature of time trajectories of career events can enter the analysis in a fully diachronic fashion.

In summary, we do not believe that the genre of research that inquires into the social class and social status correlates and causes of parental and child socialization has reached a dead end. We do emphasize that prior research in both psychology and sociology that assumes a static class context for socialization, that confuses the measurement of class with that of status, and that models only one or two points of data rather than individual event histories, has not analyzed the phenomenon appropriately. A life-course approach that links class- and status-based changes in the social world of parents with the socialization of children still remains to be implemented in current longitudinal projects.

ACKNOWLEDGMENTS

An earlier version of this chapter was presented at an SSRC Conference on Child Development in Life-Span Perspective, Woods Hole, MA, June 19–24, 1986. We wish to thank Professor Tom Colbjørnsen for guidance with these preliminary constructions of class categories for Norway; final errors and discrepancies are entirely ours. Ms. Julia Gray prepared the data file for the children of Norway. Support for this research was provided by a grant from the National Institute on Aging (PO1 AG04877-02), the National Science Foundation (SES 8520088), and the John Simon Guggenheim Foundation. The Career Development Study data were collected by Luther B. Otto, Project Director, and Vaughn R. A. Call and Kenneth I. Spenner, Project Associates, with support provided by the U.S. Office of Education and Washington State University (Wave I); and support provided by the Boys Town Center and the National Institute of Education (NIE-G-79-0046) (Wave II).

REFERENCES

Alwin, D. (in press). Education, occupation and parental values. In N. Eisenberg, J. Reykowski, & E. Staub (Eds.), *Social and moral values.* Hillsdale, NJ: Lawrence Erlbaum Associates.

Baltes, P. B., Cornelius, S. W., & Nesselroade, J. R. (1979). Cohort effects in developmental psychology. In J. R. Nesselroade & P. Baltes (Eds.), *Longitudinal research in the study of behavior and development* (pp. 61–88). New York: Academic Press.

Blau, P. M., & Duncan, O. D. (1967). *The American occupational structure.* New York: Wiley.

Block, J. (1971). *Lives through time.* Berkeley, CA: Bancroft.

Bourdieu, P. (1977). Cultural and social reproduction. In J. Karabel & A. H. Halsey (Eds.), *Power and ideology in education* (pp. 487–511). New York: Oxford.

Bowles, S., & Gintis, H. (1976). *Schooling in capitalist America.* New York: Basic Books.

Brim, O. G., Jr., & Ryff, C. (1980). On the properties of life events. In P. B. Baltes & O. G. Brim, Jr. (Eds.), *Life-span development and behavior (Vol. 3, pp. 368–338). New York: Academic Press.*

Bronfenbrenner, U. (1958). Socialization and social class through time and space. In E. E.

Maccoby, T. M. Newcomb, & E. L. Hartley (Eds.), *Readings in social psychology* (pp. 400–425). New York: Holt, Rinehart & Winston.

Bronfenbrenner, U. (1979). *The ecology of human development.* Cambridge, MA: Harvard University Press.

Duncan, G. (1961). A socioeconomic index for all occupations. In A. J. Reiss, Jr. (Ed.), *Occupations and social status* (pp. 109–129). Glencoe, IL: The Free Press.

Elder, G. (1974). *Children of the great depression.* Chicago, IL: University of Chicago Press.

Erikson, R., & Goldthorpe, J. H. (1985). Are American rates of social mobility exceptionally high? New Evidence on an old issue. *European Sociological Review, 1,* 1–22.

Erikson, R., Goldthorpe, J. H., & Portocarero, L. (1979). Intergenerational class mobility in three Western European societies. *British Journal of Sociology, 30,* 415–441.

Featherman, D. L. (1980). Schooling and occupational careers: Constancy and change in worldly success. In O. G. Brim Jr., & J. Kagan (Eds.), *Constancy and change in human development* (pp. 675–738). Cambridge, MA: Harvard University Press.

Featherman, D. L. (1985). Individual development and aging as a population process. In J. R. Nesselroade & A. von Eye (Eds.), *Individual development and social change: Explanatory analysis* (pp. 213–242).

Featherman, D. L. (1986). Biography, society, and history: Individual development as a population process. In A. B. Sórensen, F. E. Weinert, & L. R. Sherrod (Eds.), *Human development and the life course: Multidisciplinary perspectivse* (pp. 99–152). Hillsdale, NJ: Lawrence Erlbaum Associates.

Featherman, D. L., Hogan, D. P., & Sórensen, A. B. (1984). Entry into adulthood: Profiles of young men in the 1950s. *Life-span development and behavior* (Vol. 6, pp. 159–202). New York: Academic Press.

Featherman, D. L., & Sórensen, A. B. (1983). Societal transformation in Norway and change in the life course transition into adulthood. *Acta Sociologica, 26*(2), 105–126.

Featherman, D. L., & Spenner, K. I. (1987, August). *Comparative impacts of social class as a context for childhood in Norway and the U.S.* Paper presented at the 1987 Annual Meetings of the American Sociological Association, Chicago, IL.

Gecas, V. (1979). The influence of social class on socialization. In W. R. Burr, R. Hill, F. I. Nye, & I. L. Reiss (Eds.), *Contemporary theories about the family* (pp. 365–404). New York: The Free Press.

Giddens, A. (1973). *The class structure of the advanced societies.* London: Hutchinson.

Goldthorpe, J. H. (1980). *Social mobility and class structure in modern Britain.* Oxford: Clarendon Press.

Hauser, R. M., & Featherman, D. L. (1977). *The process of stratification: Trends and analysis.* New York: Academic Press.

Hernandez, D. (1986). Childhood in a sociodermographic perspective. In R. Turner (Ed.), *Annual review of sociology* (Vol. 12, pp. 159–180). Palo Alto, CA: Annual Reviewers.

Hetherington, E. M., Camara, C., & Featherman, D. L. (1982). *Intellectual functioning and achievement of children in one-parent households.* Washington, DC: National Institute of Education.

Hetherington, E. M., Camara, C., & Featherman, D. L. (1983). Achievement and intellectual functioning of children in one-parent households. In J. T. Spence (Ed.), *Achievement and achievement motives* (pp. 205–284). San Francisco: Freeman.

Jackman, M., & Jackman, R. (1982). *Social class awareness in the United States.* Berkeley, CA: University of California Press.

Kagan, J. (1984). *On the nature of the child.* New York: Basic Books.

Kohn, M. L. (1969). *Class and conformity: A study in values.* Homewood, IL: Dorsey.

Kohn, M. L., & Schooler, C. (1982). Job conditions and personality: A longitudinal assessment of their reciprocal effects. *American Journal of Sociology, 87,* 1257–1286.

Kohn, M. L., Schooler, C., Miller, J., Miller, K. A., Schoenbach, C., & Schoenberg, R.

(1983). *Work and personality: An inquiry into the impact of social stratification.* Norwood, NJ: Ablex.

Lockwood, D. (1958). *The black-coated worker.* London: Allen & Urwin.

Mortimer, J. T., & Simmons, R. G. (1978). Adult socialization. In R. Turner, J. Coleman, & R. Fox (Eds.), *Annual Review of Sociology* (Vol. 4, pp. 421–454). Palo Alto, CA: Annual Reviewers.

Mueller, C. W., & Parcell, T. L. (1981). Measures of socioeconomic status: Alternatives and recommendations. *Child Development, 52,* 13–30.

Oppenheimer, R. (1982). *Work and the family: A study in social demography.* New York: Academic Press.

Otto, L. B., Call, V., & Spenner, K. I. (1981). *Design for a study of entry careers* (Vol. 1). Lexington, MA: Lexington Books.

Parkin, F. (1971). *Class inequality and political order.* New York: Praeger.

Pearlin, L. I., & Kohn, M. L. (1966). Social class, occupation, and parental values: A cross-national study. *American Sociological Review, 31,* 446–479.

Ramsøy, N. R. (1977). *Sosial mobilitet i Norge* [Social Mobility in Norway]. Oslo: Tilden Norsk.

Riley, M. W. (1985). Age strata in social systems. In R. H. Binstock & E. Shanas (Eds.), *Handbook on aging and the social sciences* (pp. 369–414). New York: Van Nostrand Reinhold.

Rogosa, D. (1980). Time and time again: Some analysis problems in longitudinal research. In C. Bidwell & D. M. Windham (Eds.), *The analysis of educational productivity* (Vol. 2, pp. 153–201). Cambridge, MA: Ballinger.

Rutter, M. (1979). Protective factors in children's responses to stress and disadvantage. In M. W. Kent & J. E. Rolf (Eds.), *Primary prevention of psychopathology: Social competence in children* (Vol. 3, pp. 49–74). Hanover, NH: University of New England.

Sewell, W. H. (1961). Social class and childhood personality. *Sociometry, 24,* 340–356.

Slomczynski, K. M., Miller, J., & Kohn, M. L. (1981). Stratification, work and values: A Polish-United States comparison. *American Sociological Review, 46,* 720–744.

Sorokin, P. A. (1959). *Social and cultural mobility.* New York: The Free Press.

Spenner, K. I. (1980). Occupational characteristics and classification system: New uses for the Dictionary of Occupational Titles in social research. *Sociological Methods and Research, 9,* 239–264.

Spenner, K. I. (in press). Occupations, work settings and the course of adult development: Tracing the implications of select historical change. In P. B. Baltes, D. L. Featherman, & R. M. Lerner (Eds.), *Life-Span Development and Behavior* (Vol. 8). Hillsdale, NJ: Lawrence Erlbaum Associates.

Tuma, N. B., & Hannan, M. T. (1984). *Social dynamics: Models and methods.* New York: Academic.

Warner, W. L., & Lunt, P. S. (1941). *The social life of a modern community.* New Haven, CT: Yale University Press.

Wright, E. O. (1979). *Class, crisis and the state.* London: Verso.

Wright, E. O. (1985). *Classes.* London: NLB/Verso.

5 EXPLANATORY STYLE ACROSS THE LIFE SPAN:

Achievement and Health

Martin E. P. Seligman
Leslie P. Kamen
Susan Nolen-Hoeksema
University of Pennsylvania

ABSTRACT

The purpose of this chapter is to describe empirically and theoretically the influence and structure of explanatory style across the life span. We use cross-sectional and longitudinal data to trace how the types of causal explanations one makes can affect subsequent achievement and psychological and physical health. We examine also the influence of explanatory style at several developmental periods from childhood to older adulthood.

INTRODUCTION

Throughout the life span, people are constantly exposed to good and bad events; but the way they respond to these events varies. Some will bounce back when a bad event happens; others will give up. Likewise, certain people will become invigorated following a good event, whereas others will remain unaffected.

What may account for these different reactions to good and bad events? We have proposed that individuals are by nature information seekers; that is, when a good or bad event occurs, people search for a cause. The way individuals assess this cause is not via some haphazard process; rather, people have a consistent style for explaining such events. Attributional style or alternatively explanatory style can be thought of as a tendency to explain good and bad events in a characteristic way (Abramson, Seligman, & Teasdale, 1978; Peterson & Seligman, 1984).

The theory that guides our investigation of explanatory style is the reformulated learned helplessness theory (Abramson et al., 1978). According to the reformulation, the explanations people give for good and bad outcomes influence their expectations about future outcomes, and thereby determine their reactions to outcomes. Three dimensions along which explanations can vary influence the helplessness deficits individuals experience following an event. First, causes can be stable in time or they can be unstable. If the person explains a bad event by a cause that is stable rather than unstable in time, he or she will expect bad events to recur in the future and will show chronic helplessness deficits. Second, causes can affect many areas of an individual's life or they can affect only one area. If a person explains a bad event by a cause that has global effects instead of a cause that influences only that specific event, he or she will expect bad events to occur in multiple domains and helplessness deficits will generalize across domains. Third, causes can be internal to the individual or external. If a person explains a bad event by a cause internal, rather than external to him or herself, he or she will be more likely to show lowered self-esteem.

Abramson et al. (1978) explained the individual differences in vulnerability to helplessness by arguing that people who habitually explain bad events by internal, stable, and global causes and explain good events by external, unstable, and specific causes (the maladaptive explanatory style) will be more likely to experience general and lasting symptoms of helplessness than will people with the opposite style. The original application of the reformulation was to explain depression, but the relationship between explanatory style and depression has been extensively reviewed elsewhere (Peterson & Seligman, 1984). As a consequence, our major focus is on how explanatory style affects achievement and health.

EXPLANATORY STYLE: LINK WITH ACHIEVEMENT

Performance in achievement settings can be strongly influenced by motivation (Atkinson, 1957; McClelland, Atkinson, Clark, & Lowell, 1953; Moulton, 1965; see Dweck & Wortman, 1982 for a review). Thus, individuals with similar ability frequently differ in how they actually perform. Some remain persistent when faced with challenge; others give up. For some, success will engender greater creativity and risk-taking on future tasks, whereas for others, it will have little or no effect.

The theoretical and empirical link between learned helplessness and achievement has been clearly demonstrated in the work of Dweck and her associates (Diener & Dweck, 1978, 1980; Dweck, 1975; Dweck & Goetz, 1978; Dweck & Licht, 1980; Dweck & Reppucci, 1973). In a series of experiments, they found that the way in which children explain their performance strongly influences whether they will, following failure, either give up ("helpless" children) or persist ("mastery-oriented" children). Specifically, helpless children, as identified by the Internal Achievement Responsibility Scale (Crandall, Katkovsky, & Crandall, 1965), believe their failures are caused by a lack of ability, whereas mastery-oriented children explain their failures by a lack of effort (see Dweck & Wortman, 1982). Moreover, helpless children do not benefit from successful performance (e.g., in terms of increased expectations for future performance) to the degree that mastery-oriented children do (Diener & Dweck, 1980).

Consider how explanatory style should operate in achievement situations. Individuals who habitually provide internal, stable, and global explanations for failure should be less likely to persist, take chances, or rise above their potential in achievement settings than those who explain failure in external, unstable, or specific terms. Likewise, underachievement should be more likely in those who make external, unstable, and specific explanations for successful outcomes than for those who make internal, stable, and global explanations for positive events.

EXPLANATORY STYLE: LINK WITH HEALTH

There is a growing body of research that indicates psychological factors can and do interact with biological factors in determining the onset and course of disease (Fox, 1981; Jemmott & Locke, 1984). In particular, helplessness has been reliably associated with immunosuppression and increased susceptibility to cancer in animals. (Laudenslager, Ryan, Drugan, Hyson, & Maier, 1983; Seligman & Visintainer, 1985; Sklar & Anisman, 1979; Visintainer, Volpicelli, & Seligman, 1982; see Levy, 1986). Recent evidence also suggests that stressful life events such as bereavement, academic pressure, and family-related pressures may produce increased vulnerability to infection in humans (Bartrop, Lazarus, Luckhurst, Kilch, & Penny, 1977; Jemmott et al., 1983; Kasl, Evans, & Niederman, 1979; Meyer & Haggarty, 1962; Schleifer, Keller, & Stein, 1984).

Although *stress* per se may be a risk factor for hypersensitivity to certain diseases, there are tremendous individual differences with regard to actual onset and growth of illness. Thus, how one perceives, interprets, and reacts to a particular stressor will impact on his or her susceptibility to developing certain illnesses (e.g., cancer; Canter, Cluff, & Imboden, 1972; Levy, 1984; McClelland, 1979).

A common theme throughout the literature linking psychological factors and disease is that experience with uncontrollable events (or stressors) may have a deleterious effect on health. In particular, reactions of helplessness and hopelessness may be a significant underlying factor with regard to physical vulnerability (LeShan, 1966; Levy, 1984, 1986; Schmale & Iker, 1966a, 1966b; Seligman & Elder, 1986). Because explanatory style provides an index of helplessness and hopelessness, it allows us to evaluate the process by which helplessness and hopelessness influence health. Specifically, we predict that people with the maladaptive explanatory style should be more prone to ill health in both the short and long term.

Conclusions

In highlighting how explanatory style might influence two areas of primary concern to life-span developmental psychology—achievement and physical health—we have suggested that a maladaptive explanatory style can put one at risk for two types of problems: underachievement and illness. Because the reformulated learned helplessness model specifies a theory for predicting our reactions to important events throughout development, it should be a useful tool for life-span psychology. Following a discussion of the measurement of explanatory style, we examine how it relates to achievement and health over the life span.

MEASUREMENT OF EXPLANATORY STYLE

There are two techniques for measuring explanatory style: The Attributional Style Questionnaire, and the Content Analysis of Verbatim Explanations. Each is described here.

The Attributional Style Questionnaire

The first technique for assessing explanatory style consists of a 48-item self-report instrument: The Attributional Style Questionnaire (ASQ; Peterson et al., 1982; Seligman, Abramson, Semmel, & von Baeyer, 1979). The questionnaire was designed to measure an individual's characteristic explanatory style across a variety of situations rather than his or her explanation for a particular outcome (Peterson & Seligman, 1984). As such, the ASQ consists of 12 hypothetical events. Six describe positive outcomes (e.g, "You become very rich") and 6 describe negative outcomes (e.g., "You have been looking for a job unsuccessfully for some time").

The ASQ has three subscales (internal, stable, and global) for both positive and negative outcomes. In addition, the three subscales can be combined to yield a composite score for positive events (Composite Positive or CP) and a composite score for negative events (Composite Negative or CN). Finally, an overall composite score that takes ratings for both positive and negative events into account can be formed by subtracting the composite negative score from the composite positive score (CP-CN).

Reliability, consistency, and validity of the ASQ are reviewed in detail elsewhere (e.g., Peterson & Seligman, 1984).

Content Analysis of Verbatim Explanations (CAVE)

The second technique for assessing explanatory style is via the content analysis of verbatim explanations—the CAVE technique. This method allows us to go back in time (i.e, to an earlier time of the subject's life) and in a sense to carry out retrospective studies prospectively.

Using this technique to measure an individual's explanatory style, we would need, first, a sample (generally about 500–1000 words) of some verbatim material (e.g., a diary, letter, newspaper quote, therapy transcript). Second, a trained judge would extract form this sample all statements describing an event for which a causal explanation was provided. For example, "I got fired from my job *because* I will never be able to learn to type." Third, three independent raters would rate this event-explanation unit on a 7-point scale (following the ASQ) for each of the explanatory dimensions. Thus, for the example regarding job loss, the ratings might be: Internality: 7, Stability: 7, Globality: 2 (Peterson & Seligman, 1986; see Schulman & Castellon, 1986, for guidelines of the CAVE technique).

The CAVE technique has been used in a variety of studies, has high interrater reliability, is easily trainable, and has accumulated considerable validity data, some of which we review in this chapter (e.g., Peterson, Luborksy, & Seligman, 1983; Peterson & Seligman, 1986). Further, the CAVE procedure is a completely blind one; that is, the raters see only one statement when they make their rating and they do not know who the person quoted is or what else the person said. This means that the CAVE technique is useful in doing retrospective studies because it removes one major methodological difficulty: knowing the outcome during the rating. Thus, CAVE offers us a method of undertaking longitudinal studies retrospectively and provides us with the exciting possibility of going back in time to obtain postdictive data.

EXPLANATORY STYLE AND LIFE-SPAN DEVELOPMENT

"Life-span developmental psychology is concerned with the description, explanation, and modification (optimization) of developmental processes in the human life from conception to death" (Baltes, Reese, & Lipsitt, 1980, p. 2). Life-span theorists argue that three influences impact on these developmental processes. The first are normative age-graded influences that include behavioral and environmental events encountered by all members of a particular culture and that correspond to chronological age (e.g., starting school). The second are normative history-graded (evolutionary) influences. These are historical events that affect most of the members of particular cohort in a similar way (Schaie, 1984). Historical events can include discrete events such as the Great Depression (Elder & Liker, 1982) or continuous processes such as industrialization (Neugarten & Datan, 1973). Finally, development is influenced by non-normative life events. These include individual-specific life events that do not follow an age-graded or predictable developmental pattern, for example, death of a parent (Baltes & Nesselroade, 1979; Baltes et al., 1980; Brim & Ryff, 1980).

An important life-span consideration is how events that take place at an earlier age affect and influence later development. Often, longitudinal research focuses on a single variable (e.g., age of first words) and examines its influence on some aspect of later life (e.g., intelligence). But this approach leaves out or ignores a whole host of intervening events that might link the earlier variable of interest to later development. Moreover, what happens early in life will not perfectly predict what will happen later in life because "later life is based in part on factors and experiences that are unique to the later periods" (Baltes et al., 1980, p. 50). A life-span theory of development thus requires a framework that specifies the link between early development and later life. Explanatory style provides one such link.

Consider first how normative age-graded events might influence explanatory style. One such event is starting school. The school setting provides a child with a series of experiences in which he or she is likely to encounter failure: A peer might reject him or her, the teacher might scold him or her, the test might be too difficult. Such failure can lay the groundwork for helplessness symptoms and for the emergence of a particular explanatory style. In addition, the types of feedback teachers give to students can have a profound influence on how well they perform and how long they persist on certain tasks (Dweck & Licht, 1980; Raber & Weisz, 1981; Weisz, 1981). We examine how exposure to adult evaluations can lead to the development of a depressive explanatory style in the section on Origins of Explanatory Style.

Here, however, consider how history-graded events might influence explanatory style. Elder and Liker (1982) conducted a study examining how the tremendous economic hardship and loss experienced by individuals during the Great Depression affected their emotional health (well-being) 40 years later. The most salient finding was that for middle-class women, those who endured a major financial loss (35% or more of income) in the 1930s showed higher degrees of emotional health (self-assuredness, cheerfulness, and freedom from worry) 40 years later than those who did not suffer a large monetary loss. Conversely, for those in the working class, material deprivation was associated with helplessness and passivity in later life.

One interpretation of how early economic hardship might be linked to emotional well-being in later years focuses on the role of explanatory style. As noted previously, working-class women had few available resources to deal effectively with their economic loss. For them, the Depression provided a tremendous hardship that was unsurpassable and uncontrollable. Moreover, the financial difficulties represented a stable and global loss that was likely to engender a sense of personal helplessness. For those in the working class, there was no end in sight, that is, they had great reason to expect that future events would be uncontrollable as well. Further, such long-term hardship might foster and support a depressive explanatory style through which losses encountered in old age (e.g., death of a friend) would be interpreted. Thus, the decreased emotional well-being found in working-class women 40 years after the Depression might indicate a depressive explanatory style generated by global financial loss and reinforced by continued hardship (see Elder, Liker, & Jaworski, 1984).

In contrast, middle-class women who suffered deprivation in the 1930s were more resilient when challenged with the losses of old age. For them, dealing effectively with the strain encountered by the Depression provided a training ground for coping with future hardship and loss (Elder & Liker, 1982). Nondeprived middle-class women, however, did not undergo the mastery experience of overcoming a major financial loss—they also did not rank as high in measures of emotional well-being as their economically deprived peers 40 years later. This result suggests that early mastery experience will tend to produce the nondepressive explanatory style (external, unstable, and specific). As one Berkeley woman put it "it's only when you have lived through experiences and digested them that you come to acquire enough sense to know how to deal with them" (Elder & Liker, 1982, p. 267).

Finally, consider the influence of non-normative events on explanatory style. Baltes et al. (1980) suggested that over the course of the life-span the influence of non-normative events increases. This may occur because the strength of evolutionary-based genetic control lessens with age and because, as each individual experiences a lengthening history of distinct experiences, chronological age weakens as a predictor of developmental differences in adulthood.

Another reason why non-normative events may have a significant impact as we grow older concerns the role of explanatory style. In older adulthood, a large number of the non-normative events we face involves losses over which we have no control (Schultz, 1980). Such losses are likely to promote a helpless outlook in some but not all individuals. One buffer against developing this outlook is having a nondepressive explanatory style—that is, being able to regard these losses as isolated, transient setbacks that can be overcome. Thus, with increasing age, there is more room for non-normative events to foster developmental differences and interindividual variability (Baltes et al., 1980), and the expression of these differences may well be mediated by explanatory style.

ORIGINS OF EXPLANATORY STYLE

Where does our explanatory style originate? We identify four possible sources that might shape explanatory style. It should first be mentioned that young children (up to about 8) do not seem to suffer much from helplessness deficits when they fail. They also maintain high expectancies for future performance following experience with failure (Parsons & Ruble, 1977), overestimate their attainment (Nicholls, 1978, 1979; Weisz, 1983), and do not tend to show negative affect when they fail (Ruble, Parsons, & Ross, 1976).

It is possible that young children do not suffer helplessness deficits following failure because they tend to explain bad events in external, unstable, and specific terms. Three experiments with young children suggest this.

Rholes and Ruble (1984) examined young children's understanding of the globality of personality traits and abilities. They found a developmental trend such that older children (9–10 years old) expected traits and abilities of videotaped actors to operate in a variety of situations whereas younger children (5–6 years old) did not perceive the global implications of dispositions. The differences between older and younger children were more pronounced when the predictions involved negative traits or low abilities. Thus, young children may be shielded from helplessness deficits because they do not believe negative characteristics will affect a wide range of situations.

Rotenberg (1982) tested young children's beliefs about the stability of personality characteristics. He asked kindergarteners, first, second, and third graders to judge whether a character portrayed as kind or mean would still have these qualities 1 day later, 2 days later, on up to 7 days later. Older children believed the characteristics to persist longer than younger children. The developmental differences were sharper when judging negative traits as opposed to positive ones; younger children were less likely to regard meanness as stable than kindness (19% of kindergarteners believed meanness to be stable whereas 56% believed kindness to be a persistent trait).

Finally, Nolen-Hoeksema (1986) performed the most direct test of developmental differences in explanatory style. In a cross-sectional study, she interviewed 94 children from 4 to 8 years of age, asking them to talk about why each of six hypothetical events (e.g., "A friend says he doesn't want to play with you anymore") might happen to him or her. The causal explanations the children provided for these events were subjected to CAVE analysis. Nolen-Hoeksema found that the youngest children (4–5 years old) were significantly less likely than the older children to explain bad events by internal and global causes. For example the 4- and 5-year-olds tended to say that a friend might not want to play with them because the friend simply wanted to play with another child. The 7- and 8-year-olds tended to explain such an event in more internal and global terms such as "Maybe I was mean." No age differences in the stability dimension were found. Taken together, these three studies suggest that young children may not readily make internal, stable, and global explanations for bad events.

As children grow older, they may show a greater tendency to make internal, stable, and global explanations for bad events. But not all children do. Why might one child develop a maladaptive explanatory style whereas another child might not? We suggest four possibilities.

The Role of Adult Feedback

There is a fair amount of evidence suggesting that girls tend to exhibit more helpless behavior than boys when interacting with adult evaluators in achievement settings (see Dweck & Licht, 1980). Specifically, girls are less likely to persist following failure and are more likely to explain their failures by a lack of ability (stable and global) than are boys. Boys on the other hand tend to explain their failures by lack of effort (unstable and specific). Moreover, girls have lower expectations for future performance when challenged with failure (Dweck & Busch, 1976; Dweck & Gilliard, 1975; Dweck & Reppucci, 1973). These sex differences remain even though elementary-school girls receive better grades and less criticism than boys (Dweck & Goetz, 1978; McCandless, Roberts, & Starnes, 1972).

Dweck argues that the focus of the adult feedback provided to boys and girls can explain their divergent reactions to failure. Specifically, Dweck and Gilliard (1975) found that when boys receive negative evaluations, the criticisms they were given were diffuse and centered on nonintellectual aspects of their behavior such as conduct. The opposite pattern of evaluative feedback was provided to girls. For them, the negative evaluations they received specifically focused on their lack of intellectual abilities.

In summary, entrance into the evaluative setting of the classroom is a normative age-graded event that can directly impact on how children come to explain their failures and begin to develop expectations for future performance. To the extent that children receive failure feedback indicating they lack ability, they will begin to explain their failures as caused by internal, stable, and global factors. In other words, the foundation for a maladaptive explanatory style will be laid. In the section on Academic Achievement, we examine how such a maladaptive explanatory style affects actual performance.

Intergenerational Transmission

A second major source that may shape explanatory style is one's parents (or primary caregivers). Children spend a great deal of time with their parents and are therefore continually exposed to the ways parents explain good and bad events. It seems plausible that they might imitate and adopt a similar explanatory style.

Seligman et al. (1984) found evidence for the intergenerational transmission of explanatory style in a study that looked at the correlations between explanatory style of children and their parents. The way mothers and children explained negative events (CN score) was significantly correlated at $r(45) = .39$, $p < .01$ although there was no reliable relationship between explanatory style of fathers and their children. Even in very young children (4- to 8-year-olds) this relationship holds: Mothers and children's explanatory style for negative events correlated at $r(22) = .58$, $p < .01$ (Nolen-Hoeksema, 1986). This correlation is compatible with either the child's explanatory style leading to the mother's style or the mother's style leading to the child's. A longitudinal study is needed to determine which has causal priority.

First Major Trauma

The third major influence on the development of explanatory style might be the timing and reality of one's first major trauma or loss. Brown and Harris (1978) measured onset of depression in a large-scale study of working- and middle-class women in Camberwell, London. They found that depression was significantly more common if loss of their mother occurred before age 11.

What might account for the relationship between early loss of mother and later depression when challenged with a major life difficulty? The loss of one's mother at a young age is a significant negative event with stable and global implications; that is, the mother will never return, and a large part of the child's overall routine (daily events, social interaction, emotional support) is suddenly drastically altered. Moreover, young children (especially kindergarten age) tend to blame themselves as opposed to others when bad events occur (Keasy, 1977). Thus, the reality of a mother's death represents a stable, global, and possibly internally caused loss for a young child that may set the pattern for which future losses or major difficulties are interpreted (Peterson & Seligman, 1984). In other words, when loss is encountered as an adult, it might trigger an internal, stable, and global explanation that might in turn lead to the onset of depression.

When Solutions Do Not Work

The last possibility for the origins of explanatory style lies in the cognitive work the child does when routine solutions to problems fail. Peirce (1955) suggested that the function of thought is to allay doubt. When does a young child begin to analyze the causal texture of the world? Perhaps when the child encounters major failures of accustomed solutions.

Nolen-Hoeksema (1986) has found an intriguing cross-sectional trend among children of different ages for a solution-explanation trade-off in answers to "why?" questions. At 4 and 5 years old, 25% of youngsters answer "why?" questions, not with an explanation, but with the solution. So that when asked why a playmate might be mean to them in the playground, a 4-year-old might say, "I'd call the teacher." By age 6, all the solution answers have dropped out, and all why questions are answered with explanations.

This suggests that solution precedes explanation developmentally. As such, children may first seek to find out what works and do not or cannot engage in causal searches. When old solutions fail, children need to develop a more abstract theory that leads to new solutions. The particular causal theory to which the child comes may mold his or her explanatory style. This suggests that explanatory style may start to emerge in times of first childhood troubles and take on the characteristics of those troubles.

Having speculated on four possible origins of explanatory style in childhood, the remainder of this chapter discusses how explanatory style works: (a) we examine the relationship between explanatory style and achievement over the life span, (b) we look at how explanatory style can influence health in the short and long term, and (c) we examine the continuities and changes in explanatory style over the life span.

ACHIEVEMENT

The relation between explanatory style and achievement has been investigated in respect to several age groups. We consider three of these: children, young adults, and adults.

Children

Learned helplessness theory has been used to explain deficits in achievement-oriented behaviors (Dweck, 1975; Dweck & Reppucci, 1973; for a review, see Dweck & Wortman, 1982). Dweck and others have found that some children tend to explain academic failure in terms of stable and global causes, such as stupidity, and success in terms of unstable, specific causes, such as luck. As predicted, these explanatory patterns correlated with decreased persistence, decreased initiation of tasks, lowered quality of problem-solving strategies, and lowered expectations for future success. Most studies on the relationship between causal explanations and achievement behaviors have focused only on ability versus effort explanations for success and failure and have used only performance on laboratory tasks as dependent measures of achievement behaviors.

Nolen-Hoeksema, Gergus, and Seligman (1986) tested the predictions of the reformulated helplessness model regarding achievement directly. Toward this end, they gave third, fourth, and fifth graders the Children's Attributional Style Questionnaire (CASQ), a 48-item forced choice inventory that presents subjects with a hypothetical event and asks them to choose one of two explanations for why the event might happen to them. They compared the children's explanatory style with their scores on a standardized achievement test, the California Achievement Test (CAT; 1983) and with teachers' ratings of the children's helpless behaviors in the classroom.

Children who explained bad events in internal, stable, and global terms and good events in external, unstable, and specific terms (i.e., children who had a maladaptive explanatory style) tended to have lower achievement test scores and to show more helpless behaviors than those with an adaptive explanatory style. Specifically, Composite Positive minus Composite Negative (CP-CN) scores measured 1 month before administration of the CAT correlated with CAT scores ($r(166) = .26, p < .05$). In addition, there was a significant correlation betwen the children's CP-CN scores and teachers ratings of concurrent helplessness ($r(166) = -.51, p < .001$ and mastery-oriented behavior ($r(166) = .56, p < .001$). These findings suggest that explanatory style correlates synchronously with actual achievement and helpless behavior in children. The authors are presently engaged in a 5-year longitudinal study of this population to test whether explanatory style is causal.

Young Adults in College

At present, the majority of American universities almost exclusively depend on aptitude test scores (Scholastic Aptitude Test, or SAT, and achievement test scores) and high-school grade point average (GPA) in selecting candidates for admission (College Entrance Examination Board, 1980). Despite the wide use of these measures, their ability to predict college performance is limited. On the average, SAT scores and high-school grades and/or rank in class account for only 34% of the variance in college grades (Educational

Research Service, 1981). This still leaves a large gap between measured aptitude and actual performance.

In attempting to close this gap, Kamen and Seligman (1987) carried out two longitudinal studies at the University of Pennsylvania to examine the relationship between explanatory style and college GPA. They were interested in two specific questions: (a) Does explanatory style predict college GPA above and beyond traditional measures of talent (SAT scores, achievement test scores, and high-school rank in class)? At the University of Pennsylvania, these three measures form the Predictive Index (PI), which the Admissions Committee uses to forecast college GPA; and (b) Do those who do better than expected in college differ on explanatory style from those who do not?

Freshmen.   Upon entering the University of Pennsylvania, 289 freshmen completed the ASQ. The Admissions Committee provided the PI for each student. This measure is based on a 0 to 4-point scale and hence is readily comparable to an actual GPA (see Kamen & Seligman, 1987, for discussion of the empirical development of the PI). For the purpose of these studies, the PI served as a measure of aptitude. Fall term GPA was the dependent variable.

The results of this study support the reformulated learned helplessness theory. Explanatory style predicted college GPA above and beyond measures of ability (PI). Specifically, three regression analyses were performed using each of the three composite explanatory style variables (CP, CN, and CP − CN). The basic model for each analyses was: Fall GPA = PI + Explanatory Style + PI × Explanatory Style, entered in that order.

Controlling for the influence of the PI, there was a signficant PI × CP interaction $F(1, 285) = 5.37$, $p < .02$. Those with a low to mid-range PI (less than or equal to 3.1) obtained higher GPAs if they had good scores on the CP scale. This trend, however, did not hold for those with a high PI. A plausible reason for this finding is that those with a high PI do not have much room for improvement.

The results of this study also showed that those who exceeded their PI ($N=83$) had a significantly better explanatory style for positive events than those who dropped below ($N=17$) $t(98) = 2.82$, $p < .006$. This relationship held for the variable CP − CN as well $t(98) = 2.28$, $p < .02$. Thus, students who believe their successes are internal, stable, and global subsequently get better grades than expected.

Upperclassmen.   One hundred and seventy-five upperclassmen in an abnormal psychology course at the University of Pennsylvania completed the ASQ at the beginning of the fall, 1983 semester. GPA at the end of the semester was the target variable. Predictions from the helplessness reformulation again received support. Explanatory style predicted college GPA over and above the PI, and these results held for all three explanatory style variables.

Three regression analyses were performed as in the freshman study. In the first analyses, we found a significant PI $\times$ CP interaction $F(1, 166) = 4.39$, $p < .04$). Thus, for those with a low to mid-range PI, higher GPAs were obtained with higher scores on the CP scale. Explanatory style for negative events (CN) was also a significant predictor of GPA controlling for the influence of the PI $F(1, 166) = 8.11$, $p < .005$. Finally, $CP - CN$ predicted GPA as well $F(1, 166) = 8.28$, $p < .005$.

Taken together, these two studies show a significant prediction by explanatory style of performance in college. Specifically, when measures of ability are controlled, a tendency to explain good events (successes) in internal, stable, and global terms and bad events (failures) in external, unstable, and specific terms predicts higher GPAs and a greater likelihood of doing better than expected by aptitude measures.

Adults in the Workplace

Following school, the next achievement setting the adult enters is the workplace. Does explanatory style predict performance in occupational settings? Seligman and Schulman (1986) investigated this question in a longitudinal field study using life insurance agents as subjects. Because sales agents have repeated encounters with failures and rejections, they are a particularly appropriate group for examining the relationship between explanatory style and performance. Seligman and Schulman measured explanatory style by the ASQ and operationalized performance in two ways: (a) survival of the sales agents (the likelihood of quitting or remaining on the job), and (b) productivity (the amount of commission earned by the agents).

Explanatory style was measured upon hiring of 101 agents and the target variable was performance (survival and productivity) during the first year of work.

With regard to survival, 42 out of 101 agents were still working for the insurance company at the end of the year. Agents in the top half of the $CP - CN$ distribution were twice as likely to survive than those in the bottom half. Specifically, 67% ($N=28$) of the survivors had $CP - CN$ scores in the optimistic half, whereas only 33% ($N=14$) of the survivors had scores in the pessimistic half $X(1) = 6.63$, $p < .005$. When upper versus lower 25% of the $CP - CN$ distribution are compared, the differences in survival rate are even more marked (see Table 5.1)

Having an adaptive explanatory style also predicted higher productivity in the survivors for the second half of the year. There was a significant

TABLE 5.1
Prospective Study Survival Rates

	Percent Survivors	Percent Drop-Outs	X	P
Distribution of Survivors by Top Half vs. Botom Half of CPCN[a]				
Good CPCN[a] > = 6.33	67 (28/42)	41 (24/59)	6.63	.05
Bad CPCN[a] < = 6.17	33 (14/42)	59 (35/590)		
	100%	100%		
Distribution of Survivors by Top Quartile vs. Bottom Quartile of CPCN				
Good CPCN > = 8.17	74 (14/19)	31 (9/29)	8.37	.002
Bad CPCN < = 4.00	26 (5/19)	69 (20/29)		
	100%	100%		

[a]From Seligman and Schulman (1986).

correlation between CP – CN scores and productivity [$r(66) = .27, p < .03$] and agents in the upper half of the CP – CN distribution sold 25% more insurance than agents in the bottom half $t(66) = 1.55, p < .06$ (see Table 5.2 for productivity comparisons for those in upper vs. lower 25% of the CP – CN distribution).

In summary, the results of this study indicate that agents with an adaptive explanatory style are less likely to quit and more likely to achieve greater productivity than those with a depressive explanatory style. These findings suggest that the way one reacts to failure in the workplace can powerfully affect his or her overall performance and likelihood of success on the job and this reaction can be predicted by explanatory style.

HEALTH

Evidence from animal and human studies indicate that the way one perceives and reacts to undesirable life events can profoundly influence susceptibility to disease (see Levy, 1986 for a review). Because explanatory style is a major potentiator of helplessness, we focus on this link between psychological variables and illness in humans (for a review of the animal literature, see Sklar & Anisman, 1981). Specifically, we argue that when an individual perceives events as uncontrollable and reacts to these events with helplessness (passivity) and hopelessness, he or she will show an increased vulnerability to developing certain illnesses. Further, we propose that the biological process through which this increased vulnerability occurs results from suppressed activity of the immune system. We present some new longitudinal data that support these claims.

TABLE 5.2
Prospective Study

	n	Quarterly Production Average	T	P	Percent Superiority in Production
Top Half vs. Bottom Half of Sales Force on CPCN and Their Productivity (Excluding Drop-Outs' Production)					
Production—First Year					
Good CPCN > = 6.33	47	2268	1.06	ns	14%
Bad CPCN < = 6.17	45	1993			
Production—First Six Months					
Good CPCN > = 6.33	47	2295	.65	ns	9%
Bad CPCN < = 6.17	45	2109			
Production—Second Six Months					
Good CPCN > = 6.33	35	2617	1.55	.06	25%
Bad CPCN < = 6.17	33	2096			
Top Quartile vs. Bottom Quartile of Sales Force on CPCN and Their Productivity (Excluding Drop-Outs' Production)					
Production—First Year					
Good CPCN > = 8.17	21	2689	1.92	.03	40%
Bad CPCN < = 4.00	23	1915			
Production—First Six Months					
Good CPCN > = 8.17	21	2659	1.53	.07	33%
Bad CPCN < = 4.00	23	2004			
Production—Second Six Months					
Good CPCN > = 8.17	16	3024	2.05	.02	57%
Bad CPCN < = 4.00	17	1929			

(From Seligman & Schulman, 1986)

Helplessness, Hopelessness, and Health

The inability to display a fighting spirit in the face of adversity can be thought of as helplessness. In one investigation, Greer, Morris, and Pettingale (1979) carried out a prospective study of 69 women who underwent surgery (simple mastectomy) for early breast cancer. Three months following the operation, the women were interviewed and asked about how they perceived "the nature and seriousness of the disease and how their lives had been affected by it." The results showed a significant relationship between reactions to the diagnosis and 5-year outcome. Specifically, 75% of the women who reacted to the diagnosis with denial and fighting spirit were alive with no recurrence at follow-up, whereas only 35% of the women who showed stoic acceptance and helplessness/hopelessness had this favorable outcome at follow-up. Moreover, 88% of the women who subsequently died showed initial reactions of helplessness/hopelessness and stoic acceptance, whereas only 12.5% of the women who were dead at follow-up reacted with denial and a fighting spirit. Thus, responding to illness (cancer) with helplessness/hopelessness can have a deleterious effect on the ability to combat the disease. Our studies of explanatory style and illness are an attempt to illuminate the psychological and immunological mechanisms of findings such as this.

Explanatory Style and Health

Explanatory style provides an empirical measure of the relationship between having a pessimistic outlook and subsequent susceptibility to illness. The central prediction is that people who have a maladaptive explanatory style and thus perceive the events in their lives as uncontrollable (e.g., "It's my fault that I have cancer. I'm never going to be cured and the rest of my life will be ruined") should be more likely to show impaired health than those with an optimistic outlook (e.g., "I can overcome the cancer, and I'm not going to let it affect the other areas of my life").

Immune function is a good candidate for assessing such susceptibility to illness because it serves as the body's defense mechanism for fighting disease. In 1980, Judith Rodin at Yale University began a large-scale study examining the role of psychosocial factors on nutritional intake and health in older adults (mean age = 71.97 years). She interviewed subjects nine times over the course of 2 years and information regarding life changes, stressors, and health states was obtained during each interview. In addition, she obtained a sample of blood from a subsample of the subjects. Subjects were ineligible to provide blood if they were taking medications known to affect the immune or endocrine systems or had any medical conditions that might affect immune function (e.g., neoplastic disease). Further, subjects who had undergone a major life stressor in the 2-year period preceding the first interview were also ineligible to provide blood.

Kamen, Seligman, Dwyer, and Rodin (1987) submitted the interview closest to before the blood draw to analysis by the CAVE technique. They were interested in whether explanatory style was associated with one measure of immune status: the T-helper cell/T-suppressor cell ratio (T4/T8 ratio). Proper functioning of the immune system requires that these two subpopulations of T-lymphocytes be in balance; therefore, a low ratio implies immunosuppression. Preliminary results of this study indicate that CN is negatively correlated with the T4/T8 ratio suggesting that a pessimistic outlook is associated with increased immunosuppression.

Although a maladaptive explanatory style may be associated with immunosuppression, is there any evidence that a pessimistic, hopeless outlook also predicts actual illness? Peterson & Seligman (1987) addressed this question in a study of 172 undergraduates. They measured explanatory style at an initial time and reports of illness (number of different days that at least one symptom was present) at a later time (1 month later) and doctor visits at a still later period (1 year later).

The results of this study indicate that a hopeless explanatory style is significantly associated with subsequent illness; that is, there was a significant correlation between hopelessness at the first time and illness at the second [$r(170) = .27, p < .05$]. In addition, hopelessness predicted illness at the second time even when illness at the first time was controlled ($p < .04$). Similarly hopelessness at the initial time predicted the number of doctor visits 1 year later, controlling for illness at the initial time.

Taken together, these two studies provide evidence that a maladaptive or hopeless explanatory style is associated with an increased vulnerability to illness at least in the short run. Does this relationships hold over the long run? Specifically, does explanatory style early in life predict health later in life?

Seligman, in collaboration with George Vaillant, addressed this question using a randomly chosen subsample ($N = 18$) of male subjects from the Grant Study, a longitudinal investigation of psychological variables (defenses) and future life course of members of the Harvard classes of 1939–1942. In 1946, the men responded to open-ended questionnaires regarding their experiences in World War II. Seligman submitted the responses to analysis by the CAVE technique to see if explanatory style for negative events (CN) could predict physical health later in life. In 1980, health ratings were obtained (1 = healthy to 5 = dead) for each subject. The results of this study show that explanatory style is reliably associated with health status 36 years later [$r(16)$ for CN and health $= .40, p < .05$]. These findings are preliminary (the number of subjects is small and the influence of other variables has not yet been examined) and we are presently replicating them on the entire Grant study sample.

Seligman and Peterson (1987) ask a similar question using the members of the Baseball Hall of Fame. Does explanatory style extracted from sports page quotes while a young, healthy, and successful player predict length of life?

There are 94 members of the Hall of Fame who meet the following two criteria: (a) not managers, and (b) began their career between 1900 and 1950 (to insure that they are now dead or in the last third of life). They read the entire sports pages of the *New York Times* and the *Philadelphia Inquirer* for all of September and early October from 1900 to 1950. Of these men, 24 were quoted enough to extract 2 or more event-explanation units for bad events and 30 for good events. They correlated the CAVE explanatory style profile with the age at death (in the case of the dead) or their age currently (in the case of the living). About half are dead now.

Both measures yielded suggestive results. For good events, optimistic explanatory style correlated with longevity ($r(22) = .45$, $p < .01$); those in the upper versus lower quartile of optimism for good events significantly differed on longevity ($U = 6$, $p < .01$). For bad events, optimism also correlated marginally with longevity ($r(22) = .26$, $p < .08$); those in the upper versus lower quartile of optimism also significantly differed on longevity ($U = 16$, $p < .05$).

Taken together, these four studies suggest that a pessimistic explanatory style puts one at risk for lowered immune status and for later illness both in the short and in the long run.

ACROSS THE LIFE SPAN: STABILITY AND CONTINUITY OF EXPLANATORY STYLE

We have shown that explanatory style organizes and predicts both achievement and health data across the life span. But is it stable?

First, the evidence suggests that explanatory style is stable in the short term in both children and adults. Seligman et al. (1984) found that over a 6-month interval the test–retest correlations for CP and CN in children were .71 and .66 respectively ($p < .001$, $N = 96$). Similar levels of stability were found in adults over a 5-week period (test–retest correlation for CP = .70 and for CN = .64, $p < .05$, $N = 100$) and for time periods of up to 1 year (see Seligman & Elder, 1986).

We are currently investigating the longer term stability of explanatory style. Preliminary data using small numbers of men and women from the Berkeley–Oakland Growth Study showed significant stability for negative events across a span of 27 years, but not for positive events (in fact, explanatory style was significantly reversed for good events). In addition, Burns (1986) is in the process of investigating (via the CAVE technique) the stability of explanatory style across a span of 40 years in a larger sample of individuals who have kept diaries throughout their lives.

We believe that explanatory style is somewhat plastic. Indeed, we have argued that age-graded, history-graded, and non-normative events all can change explanatory style (Seligman & Elder, 1986). In addition, we have suggested that explanatory style predicts such later events as depression, achievement, and health. But how do these events influence later explanatory style? There is evidence from several studies of psychiatric inpatients that as depression improved, explanatory style changed for the better (e.g., Hamilton & Abramson, 1983; Persons & Rao, 1985). In addition, among school children, depression influenced later explanatory style even more than explanatory style influenced later depression (Nolen-Hoeksema et al., 1986). Thus, it seems that there is a bidirectional influence between explanatory style and depression. Similarly, it is likely that reciprocal influences occur between explanatory style and outcomes relating to achievement and health and we plan to investigate such reciprocal influences.

SUMMARY

We have presented theory and data that suggest that explanatory style may play an important role in predicting achievement and health across the life span. We argued that the helplessness reformulation provides a useful theoretical framework for addressing the concerns of the life-span perspective, and speculated about how normative age-graded, history-graded, and non-normative events might influence the development, maintenance, and change of explanatory style. We are presently conducting further research to determine how explanatory style develops, under what conditions it will remain stable, and when it will change.

ACKNOWLEDGMENTS

Supported by the U.S. Public Health Service Grant MH-19064 and by National Institute of Aging Grant AG05590 to Martin E. P. Seligman; U.S. Public Health Service Grant MH40142-01A1 to Martin E. P. Seligman, Joan S. Girgus, and Susan Nolen-Hoeksema; National Science Foundation Graduate Fellowship to Leslie P. Kamen; National Science Foundation Doctoral Dissertation Grant BNS8512551 to Susan Nolen-Hoeksema; National Science Foundation Graduate Fellowship to Susan Nolen-Hoeksema. Supported in part by the MacArthur Foundation Research Network on Determinants and Consequences of Health-Promoting and Health-Damaging Behavior.

REFERENCES

Abramson, L. Y., Seligman, M. E. P., & Teasdale, J. D. (1978). Learned helplessness in humans: Critique and reformulation. *Journal of Abnormal Psychology, 87,* 49–74.
Atkinson, J. W. (1957). Motivational determinants of risk-taking behavior. *Psychological Review, 64,* 359–372.
Baltes, P. B., & Nesselroade, J. R. (1979). History and rationale of longitudinal research. In J. R. Nesselroade & P. B. Baltes (Eds.), *Longitudinal research in the study of behavior and development* (pp. 1–39). New York: Academic Press.

Baltes, P. B., Reese, H. W., & Lipsitt, L. P. (1980). Life span developmental psychology. *Annual Review of Psychology, 31,* 65–110.

Bartrop, R. W., Lazarus, L., Luckhurst, C., Kiloh, L. G., & Penny, R. (1977). Depressed lymphocyte function after bereavement. *Lancet I,* 834.

Brim, O. G., & Ryff, C. D. (1980). On the properties of life events. In P. B. Baltes & O. G. Brim (Eds.), *Life span development and behavior* (Vol. 3, pp. 367–388). New York: Academic Press.

Brown, G. H., & Harris, T. J. (1978). *Social origins of depression.* London: Tavistock.

Burns, M. (1986). [Unpublished data, University of Pennsylvania].

California Achievement Test. (1982). Monterey, CA: McGraw-Hill.

Canter, A., Cluff, L. E., & Imboden, J. B. (1972). Hypersensitive reactions to immunization innoculations and antecedent vulnerability. *Journal of Psychomatic Research, 16,* 91–101.

College Entrance Examination Board (1980). *Undergraduate admissions: The realities of institutional policies, practices, and procedures.* New York: Author.

Crandall, V. C., Katkovsky, W., & Crandall, V. J. (1965). Children's belief in their own control of reinforcements in intellectual-academic achievement situations. *Child Development, 36,* 91–109.

Diener, C. I., & Dweck, C. S. (1978). An analysis of learned helplessness: Continuous changes in performance, strategy, and achievement conditions following failure. *Journal of Personality and Social Psychology, 36,* 451–462.

Diener, C. I., & Dweck, C. S. (1980). An analysis of learned helplessness: II. The processing of success. *Journal of Personality and Social Psychology, 39,* 940–952.

Dweck, C. S. (1975). The role of expectations and attributions in the alleviation of learned helplessness. *Journal of Personality and Social Psychology, 31,* 674–685.

Dweck, C. S., & Bush, E. S. (1976). Sex differences in learned helplessness: I. Differential debilitation with peer and adult evaluators. *Developmental Psychology, 12,* 147–156.

Dweck, C. S., & Gilliard, D. (1975). Expectancy statements as determinants of reactions to failure: Sex differences in persistence and expectancy change. *Journal of Personality and Social Psychology, 32,* 1077–1084.

Dweck, C. S., & Goetz, T. E. (1978). Attributions and learned helplessness. In J. H. Harvey, W. Ickes, & R. F. Kidd (Eds.), *New directions in attribution research* (Vol. 2, pp. 157–179). Hillsdale.

Dweck, C. S., & Licht, B. (1980). Learned helplessness and intellectual achievement. In J. Garber & M. E. P. Seligman (Eds.), *Human helplessness* (pp. 197–221). New York: Academic Press.

Dweck, C. S., & Reppucci, N. D. (1973). Learned helplessness and reinforcement responsibility in children. *Journal of Personality and Social Psychology, 25,* 109–116.

Dweck, C. S., & Wortman, C. B. (1982). Learned helplessness, anxiety, and achievement motivation. In H. W. Krohne & I. Laux (Eds.), *Achievement, stress, and anxiety* (pp. 93–125). New York: Hemisphere.

Educational Research Service. (1981). *Testing for college admissions: Trends and issues.* Arlington, VA: author.

Elder, G. H., & Liker, J. K. (1982). Hard times in women's lives: Historical influences across forty years. *American Journal of Sociology, 88,* 241–269.

Elder, G. H., Liker, J. K., & Jaworski, B. J. (1984). Hardship in lives: Depression influences. In K. A. McCluskey & H. W. Reese (Eds.), *Life-span developmental psychology: Historical and generational effects* (pp. 161–201). Orlando, FL: Academic Press.

Fox, B. H. (1981). Psychological factors in the immune system in human cancer. In R. Ader (Ed.), *Psychoneuroimmunology* (pp. 103–158). New York: Academic Press.

Greer, S., Morris, T., & Pettingale, K. W. (1979). Psychological response to breast cancer: Effect on outcome. *Lancet, 2,* 785–787.

Hamilton, E. W., & Abramson, L. Y. (1983). Cognitive patterns and major depressive disorders: A longitudinal study in a hospital setting. *Journal of Abnormal Psychology, 92,* 173–184.

Jemmott, J. B., III, Borysenko, J. Z., Borysenko, M., McClelland, D. C., Chapman, R., Meyer, D., & Benson, H. (1983). Academic stress, power motivation, and decrease in secretory immunoglobulin A secretion rate. *Lancet, I,* 1400–1402.

Jemmott, J. B., III, & Locke, S. E. (1984). Psychological factors, immunologic mediation and human susceptibility to infectious diseases: How much do we know? *Psychological Bulletin, 95,* 78–108.

Kamen, L. P., & Seligman, M. E. P. (1987). *Explanatory style predicts college grade point average.* Unpublished manuscript, University of Pennsylvania.

Kamen, L. P., Seligman, M. E. P., Dwyer, J., & Rodin, J. (1987). Pessimism and cell-mediated immunity. Unpublished manuscript, University of Pennsylvania.

Kasl, S. V., Evans, A. S., & Neiderman, J. C. (1979). Psychosocial risk factors in the development of infectious mononucleosis. *Psychosomatic Medicine, 41,* 445–466.

Keasy, D. B. (1977). Young children's attributions of intentionality to themselves and others. *Child Development, 48,* 261–264.

Laudenslager, M. L., Ryan, S. M., Drugan, R. C., Hyson, R. L., & Maier, S. F. (1983). Coping and immunosuppression: Inescapable but not escapable shock suppresses lymphocyte proliferation. *Science, 221,* 568–570.

LeShan, L. (1966). An emotional life-history pattern associated with neoplastic disease. *Annals of the New York Academy of Sciences, 125,* 780–793.

Levy, S. M. (1984). The expression of affect and its biological correlates: Mediating mechanisms of behavior and disease. In C. VanDyke, L. Temoshok, & L. S. Zegans (Eds.), *Emotions in health and illness: Applications to clinical practice* (pp. 1–18). Orlando, FLA: Grune & Stratton.

Levy, S. M. (1986). Behavior as a biological response modifier: The psychoimmuno-endocrine network and tumor immunology. *Behavioral Medicine Abstracts, 6,* 1–5.

McCandless, B., Roberts, A., & Starnes, T. (1972). Teachers marks, achievement test scores, and aptitude relations with respect to social class, race, and sex. *Journal of Educational Psychology, 63,* 153–159.

McClelland, D. C. (1979). Inhibited power motivation and high blood pressure in man. *Journal of Abnormal Psychology, 88,* 182–190.

McClelland, D. C., Atkinson, J. W., Clark, R. W., & Lowell, E. L. (1953). *The achievement motive.* New York: Appleton-Century-Crofts.

Meyer, R. J., & Haggarty, R. J. (1962). Streptococcal infections in families. *Pediatrics, 29,* 539–549.

Moulton, R. W. (1965). Effects of success and failure on level of aspiration as related to achievement motives. *Journal of Personality and Social Psychology, 1,* 399–406.

Neugarten, B. L., & Datan, N. (1973). Sociological perspectives on the life cycle. In P. B. Baltes & K. W. Schaie (Eds.). *Life-span developmental psychology: Personality and socialization.* New York: Academic Press.

Nicholls, J. G. (1978). The development of the concepts of effort and ability, perception of academic attainment, and the understanding that difficult tasks require more ability. *Child Development, 49,* 800–814.

Nicholls, J. G. (1979). The development of our attainment and causal attribution for success and failure on reading. *Journal of Educational Psychology, 71,* 192–197.

Nolen-Hoeksema, S. (1986). *Developmental differences in explanatory style and its relationship to learned helplessness.* Unpublished dissertation, University of Pennsylvania.

Nolen-Hoeksema, S., Girgus, J. S., & Seligman, M. E. P. (1986). Learned helplessness in children: A longitudinal study of depression, achievement, and explanatory style. *Journal of Personality and Social Psychology, 51,* 435–442.

Parsons, J. E., & Ruble, D. N. (1977). The development of achievement-related expectancies. Child Development, 48, 1075-1079.

Peirce, C. S. (1955). The fixation of belief. In J. Buchler (Ed.), *Philosophical writings of Pierce* (pp. 5-22). New York: Dover.

Persons, J. B., & Rao, P. A. (1981). *Cognitions and depression in psychiatric inpatients.* Unpublished manuscript, University of Pennsylvania, University Park.

Peterson, C., Luborsky, L., & Seligman, M. E. P. (1983). Attributions and depressive mood shifts: A case study using the symptom-context method. *Journal of Abnormal Psychology, 92,* 96-103.

Peterson, C., & Seligman, M. E. P. (1984). Causal explanations as a risk factor for depression: Theory and evidence. *Psychological Review, 91,* 347-374.

Peterson, C., & Seligman, M. E. P. (1986). *Content analysis of verbatim explanations: The CAVE technique for assessing explanatory style.* Unpublished manuscript, University of Pennsylvania.

Peterson, C., & Seligman, M. E. P. (1987). Explanatory Style and Illness. *Journal of Personality, 55,* 237-265.

Peterson, C., Semmel, A., von Baeyer, C., Abramson, L. Y., Metalsky, G. I., & Seligman, M. E. P. (1982). The attributional style questionnaire. *Cognitive Therapy and Research, 6,* 287-299.

Raber, S. M., & Weisz, J. R. (1981). Teacher feedback to mentally retarded and nonretarded children. *American Journal of Mental Deficiencies, 86,* 148-156.

Rholes, W. S., & Ruble, D. N. (1984). Children's understanding of dispositional characteristics of others. *Child Development, 55,* 550-560.

Rotenberg, K. J. (1982). Development of character constancy of self and other. *Child Development, 53,* 505-515.

Ruble, D. N., Parsons, J. E., & Ross, J. (1976). Self-evaluative responses of children in an achievement setting. *Child Development, 47,* 990-997.

Schaie, K. W. (1984). Historical time and cohort effects. In K. A. McCluskey & H. W. Reese (Eds.), *Life-span developmental psychology: Historical and generational effects* (pp. 1-15). Orlando, FLA: Academic Press.

Schleifer, S. J., Keller, S. E., & Stein, M. (1985). Stress effects on immunity. *The Psychiatric Journal of the University of Ottawa, 10,* 125-131.

Schmale, A. H., & Iker, H. P. (1966a). The effect of hopelessness and the development of cancer. I. Identification of uterine cervical cancer in women with a typical cytology. *Psychosomatic Medicine, 28,* 714-721.

Schmale, A. H., & Iker, H. P. (1966b). The psychological setting of uterine cervical cancer. *Annals of the New York Academy of Sciences, 125,* 807-813.

Schulman, P., & Castellon, C. (1986). *Guidelines for extracting and rating spontaneous explanations.* Unpublished manuscript, University of Pennsylvania.

Schultz, R. (1980). Aging and control. In J. Garber & M. E. P. Seligman (Eds.), *Human helplessness: Theory and applications* (pp. 291-277). New York: Academic Press.

Seligman, M. E. P., Abramson, L. Y., Semmel, A., & von Baeyer, C. (1979). Depressive attributional style. *Journal of Abnormal Psychology, 88,* 242-247.

Seligman, M. E. P., & Elder, G. H. (1986). Learned helplessness and life-span development. In A. Sorenson, F. Weinert, & L. Sherrod (Eds.), *Human development and the life course: Multidisciplinary perspectives* (pp. 377-427). Hillsdale, NJ: Lawrence Erlbaum Associates.

Seligman, M. E. P., & Peterson, C. (1987). *Explanatory style and longevity.* Unpublished Data, University of Pennsylvania, University Park.

Seligman, M. E. P., Peterson, C., Kaslow, N. J., Tanenbaum, R. L., Alloy, L. B., & Abramson, L. Y. (1984). Explanatory style and depressive symptoms among children. *Journal of Abnormal Psychology, 93,* 235-238.

Seligman, M. E. P., & Schulman, P. (1986). Explanatory style as a predictor of productivity and quitting among life insurance sales agents. *Journal of Personality and Social Psychology, 50,* 832–838.

Seligman, M. E. P., & Visintainer, M. A. (1985). Tumor rejection and early experience of uncontrollable shock in the rat. In F. R. Brush & J. B. Overmier (Eds.), *Affect, conditioning, and cognition: Essays on the determinants of behavior* (pp. 203–210). Hillsdale, NJ: Lawrence Erlbaum Associates.

Sklar, L. S,., & Anisman, H. (1979). Stress and coping factors influence tumor growth. *Science, 205,* 513–515.

Sklar, L. S., & Anisman, H. (1981). Stress and cancer. *Psychological Bulletin, 89,* 369–406.

Visintainer, M. A., Volpicelli, J. R., & Seligman, M. E. P. (1982). Tumor rejection in rats after inescapable versus escapable shock. *Science, 216,* 437–439.

Weisz, J. R. (1981). Effects of the "mentally retarded" label on adult judgments about child failure. *Journal of Abnormal Psychology, 90,* 371–374.

Weisz, J. R. (1983). Can I control it? The pursuit of veridical answers across the life span. In P. B. Baltes & O. G. Brim (Eds.), *Life-span development and behavior* (Vol. 5, pp. 233–300). New York: Academic Press.

6 CHILDHOOD PRECURSORS OF THE LIFE COURSE:

Early Personality and Life Disorganization

Avshalom Caspi
Harvard University

Glen H. Elder, Jr.
University of North Carolina at Chapel Hill

ABSTRACT

How does personality shape the life course? In particular, why do mal-adaptive behaviors persist? What are the processes that sustain them across time, in new situations, and in diverse relationships? These are ancient and enduring questions and we believe that a purely psychological framework cannot address them adequately. A more satisfactory view calls for a joint psychological and sociological framework, a framework that not only takes account of the person but also of the person's engagement in society. In this chapter we provide details of such a framework and document its usefulness for understanding the sources of continuity of problem behavior. Two empirical demonstrations are reported. Using the Berkeley Guidance Study, we identified a group of undercontrolled, explosive children and a group of withdrawn, inhibited children (ages 8–10). We then traced their life-course trajectories across 30 years and multiple situations, seeking both the recurring expressions of these behavioral styles and their cumulative consequences in the adult roles of work, marriage, and parenting. Explosive behavior was recreated in new roles and settings, especially in relation to subordination — in education, military, and work settings — and in situations that required negotiating interpersonal conflicts, in marriage and parenting. Withdrawn behavior was recreated in new situations that required initiating action, in mate selection and vocational decision-making. Maladaptiave behaviors appear to be sustained across the life course through the progressive accumulation of their own consequences (cumulative continuity) and by evoking maintaining responses from others in reciprocal social interactions (interactional continuity).

INTRODUCTION

How does personality shape the course of lives? Our thinking in addressing this question views personality in the life course. Using this perspective, we explore some continuities and consequences of two maladaptive childhood behaviors: the inability to modulate impulses—a behavior pattern that threatens the stability and quality of relationships—and behavioral inhibition—a pattern that may limit initiative and action in the later years. Our aim here is to offer a framework for the study of personality in the life course and to document its usefulness for understanding the sources of continuity of problem behavior.

As a sociologically minded psychologist and a psychologically minded sociologist, respectively, we hold a causal view of personality asserting that personality dimensions can be usefully construed as causes of life outcomes and that personality influences the state of the individual at any given stage in the life course (McCrae & Costa, 1984). Personality explains, in part, the choices individuals make at various age-related transition points, the maintenance of life styles across different contexts, and the level of adaptation in new settings.

Moreover, we assume that the expression of personality is culture-bound and socially defined, and that predictions from early personality must be concerned with behavior in relation to a changing or stable social structure and culture pattern in historical time (LeVine, 1982). Indeed, we consider behavior to be adaptive to the social and physical environments of individuals only when it is appropriate or confers advantage in relation to a given context or occasion.

Our thinking is thus rooted in theorizing relevant to social structure, culture, and personality. We follow the lead of W. I. Thomas in our view of personality development as a

> struggle between the individual and society—a struggle for self-expression on the part of the individual, for his subjection on the part of society . . . [For] it is in the total course of this struggle that the personality—not as a static "essence" but as a dynamic, continually evolving set of activities—manifests and constructs itself. (Thomas & Znaniecki, 1918–1920, pp. 1861–1862)

And we agree also with Murray that the functions of personality are to "reduce conflicts between needs by following schedules which result in an harmonious way of life" and to "design serial programs for the attainments of distant goals" (Murray & Kluckhohn, 1953, p. 49). Our corresponding research agenda is aimed at the exploration of individual personalities as "coherent ways of being and doing" (Scarr, in press) that develop across the life span.

What do we mean by studying personality in the life course? How does this differ from other modes of personality study? Before getting into the empirical facts of adult continuities from childhood maladaptive behavior, we provide some details of an outline for investigating the coherence of personality in the life course.

STUDYING THE COHERENCE OF PERSONALITY IN THE LIFE COURSE

A purely psychological framework is inadequate for the study of personality in the life course. A more satisfactory view calls for a joint psychological and sociological framework, a framework that not only takes account of the person, but also of the person's engagement in society. A developmental perspective on personality in the life course thus requires information not only about processes of internal differentiation but also about the institutional nexus of roles through which individuals pass and the manner in which these roles are patterned by the social meanings of age.

Indeed, the interactional framework toward which personality psychology aspires is best conceived of as a sequence of interactions of personality with age-graded roles and social transitions. For it is in these circumstances that individuals bring their unique characteristics to bear on the interpretation and enactment of roles they are required to play. And by tracing personality development through the individual's participation in increasingly diverse and complex social roles we may be assured of discerning the meaningful patterns that reflect the enduring components of personality.

A Prescriptive Framework

The essential strategem for research on personality development is to trace personality variables through a succession of changes while simultaneously keeping track of their continuities. This tactic, however, is seldom taken in actual research. Most often, subjects are randomly selected and assigned to contrived situations that severely limit the stimulus context and the range of responses available to them. The strategy we advocate is to identify people who differ along a fundamental behavioral dimension and allow them to select environments and choose experiences (Scarr, in press). Indeed, the burden of proof for falsifying Mischel's (1968) thesis that personality traits show little generalizability or consistency across situations lies not with psychologists and constrained laboratory paradigms but with people and their freedom to select and construct their environments over time.

This strategy implies that both situational and temporal distinctions must be simultaneously included in personality assessment across the life course.

The artificial separation of cross-situational consistency and temporal stability obscures development and adaptation; people do not move across time without also moving across situations. Indeed, this distinction is a contrivance of research (Conley, 1984). On the one hand, longitudinal studies that cover extensive time periods usually neglect situational parameters (e.g., Block, 1971; Costa & McCrae, 1980). On the other hand, consistency research (e.g., Mischel & Peake, 1982) typically embraces severely limited time periods (weeks, hours, minutes, even seconds); moreover, the selection of situations in consistency research is not informed by temporal distinctions and the choice of situations itself is frequently impoverished and trivial. This state of affairs has given birth to personality psychology's latest paradox: stable traits and inconsistent behavior (Epstein, 1984).

Figure 6.1 (adapted from Labouvie, 1982) shows four possible ways of

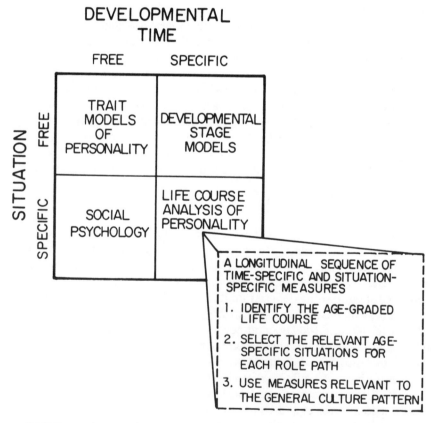

FIGURE 6.1 Personality in the life course: Ways of organizing measurements across time and situations.

organizing measurements across time and situations, but only one of these is useful for the study of personality in the life course.

Both Time- and Situation-Free Measures. The use of measures that are both time-free — in the sense that they represent central tendencies over relatively large time frames — and situation-free — in the sense that they have a high degree of generality with regard to the situation dimension — is illustrated by longitudinal research on individual difference stability (Costa & McCrae, 1980). In this strategy, however, an attribution is made to the person without reference to a setting and with reference to a chronological period whose meaning, especially beyond childhood, is often poorly understood.

Situation-Free but Time-Specific Measures. The use of measures that are situation-free, thus representing central tendencies across many different situations, although not across points in time, is especially appealing to developmentalists because it allows for a distinction between developmental and nondevelopmental phenomena (Wohlwill, 1973). This position is illustrated by the theoretical framework of Erikson (1950). Situation-free measures, however, foreclose the possibility of detecting situation-related variance.

Situation-Specific but Time-Free Measures. Social psychology exemplifies this approach. It answers the question of how people change their behavior under specific conditions, but it is of limited use in describing and explaining long-term changes. Indeed, the situations investigated in such research have a diffuse temporal boundary and are of only temporary psychological significance to the individual. Moreover, by overlooking the longitudinal aspect of situations we cannot understand the adaptation of individuals over time to a particular setting.

Both Time- and Situation-Specific Measures. This, the most desirable strategy, focuses on units of behavior in specific situations that are relevant to specific time periods (or developmental phases). Such a strategy enables us to study what people do in specific situations at specific points in the developmental process. But the strategy is also very cumbersome. In order to make time- and situation-specific measures useful in the description and explanation of long-term change, a longitudinal sequence of such measures must be constructed. We require some organizing principle or data reduction strategy to grapple with the voluminous data generated by this strategy. As the following discussion makes clear, we favor a conceptual rather than a statistical approach to the organization of measurements across time and situations.

The Life Course Analysis of Personality

As shown in the inset of Figure 6.1, three issues are involved in the study of personality in the life course (Caspi, 1987).

1. The Structure and Pattern of the Life Course. To study personality in the life course we must first have a way of thinking about the course of lives and a way of assessing how adaptational processes are patterned over time in a changing society. Our approach to the study of personality development centers on the life course of age-graded transitions and social roles as influenced by historical change. This conception of the life course is borrowed from the sociology of age-stratification that emphasizes the social and historical meanings of age in the ordering of life transitions and roles by age-linked expectations, sanctions, and options (Elder, 1975; Kertzer & Keith, 1984; Riley, Johnson, & Foner, 1972).

As socially recognized divisions of the life course, age-grades are defined by norms that specify appropriate behaviors, roles, and time schedules that constitute a basis for self-definitions (Hagestad & Neugarten, 1985). Studies that have explored regularities in age-expectations among adults suggest that there exists a shared system of social age definitions that provides a frame of reference for evaluating life experience. For example, shared social judgments about age expectations define appropriate times for major life evens and transitions, such as leaving home, marriage, and child bearing (Neugarten, Moore, & Lowe, 1965).

As individuals move through the age structure they are made cognizant of being early, on time, or late in role performance and accomplishments by an informal, consensual system of rewards and negative sanctions. Such awareness of the relations between age and status has received ample documentation in research on organization careers and worklives (Sofer, 1970). Concepts about the proper phasing of the life course, however, are not only expressed in normative prescriptions. They may be registered also as cognitive descriptions or predictions of what will happen (Elder, 1975). In particular, ethnographic accounts of the life course have shown that self-evaluations drawn vis-á-vis collective standards—shared expectancies about how lives are lived—play a central role in regulating an individual's sense of personal worth throughout life (LeVine, 1980).

An emphasis on the age-related life schedules of individuals in particular societies and cohorts organizes the study of lives in terms of patterned movements into, along, and out of multiple role paths such as education, work, marriage, and parenthood (Helson, Mitchell, & Moane, 1984). In this fashion, the life course can be charted as a sequence of social positions or trajectories of social roles that are enacted over time. According to this framework, successful transitions and adjustments to age-graded roles are the core developmental tasks faced by the individual across the life course. The corresponding agenda for personality psychology is to examine how individuals confront, adapt, and make adjustments to age-graded roles and transitions.

2. Situations in the Life Course.   In what types of situations will personality dispositions predict individuals' behavior (Snyder & Ickes, 1985)? Behavior occurs in a variety of social and physical situations that themselves evolve and change over time. Thus, to study personality in the life course we must trace not only people but also situations across time. This requires selecting age-relevant situations, each of which demands a range of behavior patterns that is more or less adaptive for a given age period.

We know of no attempt to describe the situations in which personalities act over the course of time. Consider the treatment of situations in contemporary psychology. A conceptual distinction is usually drawn between the situation as it is perceived and the situation as it is defined by objective characteristics (Pervin, 1978). The perceived or functional situation refers to the demand qualities of behavior settings as they are perceived and cognitively construed by the individual. The basic assumption of research on the functional situation is that behaviors can best be understood and explained in terms of the individual's perception and interpretation of situational cues. Knowing how individuals perceive situations makes it possible to understand and predict their actual behavior in those situations (Magnusson, 1981). What perceptions measure, however, remains unclear: a personal characteristic, a situational feature, maybe a holistic person–situation unit? Moreover, behavioral predictions based on perceptual schemata can be tautological: we can know a person only by watching him or her behave in a situation, but we know the situation only by watching the person behave in it.

An alternative procedure focuses on the objectively defined environment and favors situational attributes that can be defined independently of the individual. Barker (1968), for example, conceives of behavior settings in terms of defined boundaries and physical properties that regulate and control behavior. This approach, however, fails to express both the prescriptive and proscriptive significance of situations to the individual (Block & Block, 1981).

Neither the perceptual nor the physicalistic approach to the assessment of situations represents an adequate method for investigating the coherence of personality. Indeed, both approaches neglect two essential facts. First, situations are embedded in the context of a social institution with its own norms and roles. For example, the test-taking situation in the classroom has little meaning outside of the superordinate context of the educational system. Second, situations are extended temporally. Every situation is implicitly connected with the past and the future. Indeed, what observers of behavior delimit as a situation does not exist for the individual in an atemporal vacuum. The test-taking situation, for example, represents but a momentary contact on a time-continuum in which teachers and schoolmates change, and in which other experiences, successes and failures, are registered.

Thus, we must have a way of thinking about situations that accords attention to their institutional as well as their temporal contexts. Here we focus on given, inclusive social situations (Green, 1942). These situations represent the *faits accomplis* individuals encounter in life — the adolescent-in-school, the young man-on-the-job — over whose origins the individual has no control and that exist independently of the individual. Each such situation comprises a set of role expectations and offers certain options and choices that must be met by a series of reactions in order for the individual to achieve a measure of control in obtaining a socially and individually desired effect.

An emphasis on social situations, given and inclusive, focuses attention on a third feature of situations: their psychologically normative, consensual meaning. Indeed, consensual agreement about psychologically normative features of situations has been shown at very different levels of analysis. For example, Arsenian and Arsenian (1948) have shown that it is possible to define the formal properties of *tough* and *easy* cultures. The *Dictionary of Occupational Titles* (1982) describes *demand* qualities that underlie most occupations in our culture. And Block and Block (1981) have been able to describe problem-solving and cognition-demanding situations in terms of their normative meaning.

Thus, any assessment of personality in the life course must attend to the stimulus context of each situation as it is "generally understood and as it should register on the individual" (Block & Block, 1981, p. 88). For it is primarily around normative, consensually defined action parameters that behavior is forged and it is in a circumscribed world of norms, roles, and expectations that individuals strive toward the achievement of an effect.

3. Measuring Behavior in the Life Course.   How does the individual relate to the patterned sequence of age-graded roles and social settings in the life course? What type of data are needed to trace the implications of personality in the life course?

In the final analysis, we are concerned with the acts of the individual and, most importantly, with role enactment, what he or she does given a set of expectations. Not all behavior, of course, qualifies as role enactment. Role enactment consists of all those expectation-related acts that normally validate one's occupancy of a social position.

Consider the role of parenting. What one should and should not do in enacting the role of parent is not specified in minute detail. There are many forms of appropriate parenting. It does not matter whether the child is held in the left or right arm as long as he or she is nurtured. The dominant content of roles is thus prescriptive and consists of activities that the role occupant is expected to perform. There is also a proscriptive component that consists of activities from which the role occupant is expected to refrain. Acts that exceed the latitude of acceptable behavior (e.g., inconsistent discipline, child abuse) will result in the evaluation of unacceptable role enactment. Of course, role enactment is not taken to mean merely high conformity to role expectations (Turner, 1962). Rather, role expectations generally imply behavioral limits beyond which negative sanctions will be forthcoming. Within the latitude of acceptable behavior, however, many different responses will satisfy role expectations.

Failure to appreciate this conceptual (not only methodological, see Epstein, 1983) distinction has trivialized the functions of personality. For example, it does not matter much if on occasion the college student is late for class. But the student who is habitually late and often neglects to submit his or her work on time is likely to incur the wrath of teachers. Personality dispositions should be most predictive of adherence to or deviations from generally acceptable behavior in the enactment of roles.

Thus, the predictive threads of personality in the life course will be best detected in the highly comprehensive sampling of behavior from the life-record domain (Cattell, 1957). Indeed, of the various kinds of data available, personality should relate most importantly to L-data, to observations that are made in situ, and that are embedded in history and the group culture pattern. There are sound methodological grounds for this claim. For example, rather than measure behavior at a given moment, L-observation is usually spread over longer periods and is thus relatively free of unreliability (e.g., Block, 1977). There are, however, equally compelling theoretical reasons for emphasizing L-data. Insofar as behavior in the life course involves interaction with institutions, mores, and the general culture pattern, the natural-history mapping of human behavior as expressed in L-data is most promising. For L-data are ultimately concerned with inclination and volition—with how, whether, and when a person chooses to perform.

Cattell (1957), of course, expressed some reservations about the use of L-data—actual records of the person's behavior in society—because of their cultural and historical relativity. We view this as a strength: An adequate theory of personality must attend to the sociocultural context of behavior. Although social change may produce change in particular manifestations of a disposition, this need not preclude abstracting principles about the functions and processes of personality in the life course.

Up to this point we have discussed a number of issues that bear upon a framework for the study of personality in the life course. These include a concept of the life course structured by age-grading and historical forces, the temporal measurement of personality and situations, and suitable types of data. With key features of this framework in mind, we turn now to some life-course implications of explosive, undercontrolled behavior and social withdrawal (see Caspi, Elder, & Bem, 1987, 1988).

EARLY PERSONALITY AND LIFE DISORGANIZATION

We have been using the framework just outlined to study the life-course continuities of two maladaptive behaviors: undercontrolled, explosive patterns and withdrawn, inhibited reaction patterns. This work has its origins in a program of research on social change and human development where we first observed these adjustment problems in relation to family hardship (Elder & Caspi, in press). Our efforts to understand the family dynamics that gave rise to and sustained these behavior problems inevitably led us to think about the processes by which problem behaviors might persist and shape the life course, and also about the conditions that could minimize the chances of problem children becoming problem adults. As Robins (1978) notes, most problem children do not become problem adults. But the fact that many do is puzzling. Why should maladaptive behaviors persist? What are the processes that sustain them across time and circumstance?

One process refers to the reciprocal, dynamic transaction between the person and the environment: the person acts, the environment reacts, and the person reacts back. For example, Patterson's (1982) work with aggressive boys has shown in elegant detail how family interactions can create and sustain destructive and aversive patterns of behavior. By extension, we suggest that children who coerce others into providing short-term payoffs in the immediate situation may thereby learn a behavioral style that continues to "work" in similar ways in later years. The immediate situation short-circuits the learning of more appropriate interactional styles that might have greater adaptability in the long term. We call continuity of this kind *interactional continuity*.

Another process refers to the case in which the individual's dispositions systematically select him or her into particular environments, environments that, in turn, might reinforce and sustain those dispositions (e.g., Scarr & McCartney, 1983; Wachtel, 1977). For example, when extraverts preferentially seek out social situations they thereby select themselves into environments that further nourish and sustain their sociability. Maladaptive behaviors can similarly select individuals into environments, albeit more coercively and not always intentionally (Rutter, 1983). For example, the ill-tempered boy who flunks out of school may thereby limit his future career opportunities and "select" himself into frustrating life circumstances that evoke a pattern of striking out explosively against the world. His maladaptive behaviors increasingly channel him into environments that perpetuate those behaviors; they are sustained by the progressive accumulation of their own consequences. We call continuity of this kind *cumulative continuity*.

To examine these processes and the maintenance of problem dispositions in the life course, we turned to the archival resources of the Berkeley Guidance Study, a longitudinal study that spans 40 years and multiple situations. The study was begun in 1928 with approximately 200 children sampled from every third birth in Berkeley, CA. Initially these children were followed on an annual basis, and from late adolescence until today they have been followed at intervals of 10 years (see Eichorn, 1981).

Life-Course Patterns of Explosive Children

A child who becomes highly skilled and effective in using temper tantrums to alter his or her environment may continue with similar efforts to alter ongoing social interactions. Children who get their way by screaming, hitting, or smashing things may be learning a relational style that could persist across their life course and may prove critical in the formation of new relationships.

We identified a group of explosive, undercontrolled children on the basis of clinical interviews with their mothers (Macfarlane, Allen, & Honzik, 1954). This explosive style is based on annual ratings at ages 8, 9, and 10 of the severity and frequency of temper tantrums. Severe tantrums involved biting, kicking, striking, and throwing things, as well as screaming and shouting that were accompanied by marked emotional reactions. Tantrum frequency ranged from one per month to several times a day. From other analyses we know that explosive girls and boys were significantly more likely to express hostility directly, to be unpredictable, and to push the limits of social encounters. Interactional continuity suggests that these styles of approach and response should be replicated when individuals enter new relationships and assume new roles. Indeed, the most relevant questions for personality psychology concern the pervasive and perhaps invariant ways that people manage changes in their environment.

To document this process we rely on our prescriptive framework for studying personality in the life course. Figure 6.2 shows the organization of life-course trajectories in terms of military, education, work, marital, and parenting roles. For each role there exists a normative, prescribed timetable that defines the appropriate age for engaging in particular behaviors and

← YOUNG ADULTHOOD ———→ MIDDLE ADULTHOOD ———→

	Education	Military	Work	Marriage	Parenting
AGE-GRADED ROLES A sequence of social positions enacted over time					
SITUATIONS settings that encourage the recreation of interaction patterns	institutions that require students to modulate emotional expression	regimented and authoritarian context	supervision and subordination to authority esp. lower-status jobs, blue-collar jobs characterized by high supervision	situations that may strain the usual limits of self-control situations that require gaining control and attention	
BEHAVIORAL OUTCOMES Example of behavioral outcomes as expressed in data from the life-record domain (L-data)	educational attainment	military rank	unemployment, shifts between functionally unrelated lines of work (disorderly career lines)	divorce	inadequate parenting

Figure 6.2 Personality in the age-graded life course: Charting the expression of an explosive childhood.

making critical choices. In addition, each role encompasses situations in which the individual is engaged in significant social interactions that may evoke previously established relational styles. In terms of impulse control, these phenotypically diverse situations represent periods in which behavior should be brought under the governance of the "reality principle." Each demands modulating impulsive needs and determining the appropriate modes and timing of their fulfillment. Furthermore, our strategy calls for measures of adjustment, behavior, and performance in these situations that are relevant to specific time periods or developmental phases in the life course. In this type of analysis we should be able to see what specific people do in specific situations at specific points in the developmental process.

Educational settings are an especially suitable starting point for charting the life course of explosive children because they demand that children and, later, adolescents modulate emotional expression. Whether expressed in the number of schooled years, the number of educational degrees, or the status of degrees, we have found that men with a history of childhood tantrums lose out in formal education, in part because, as teacher reports indicate, problems of subordination burdened explosive children with a series of disadvantages in educational advancement. In fact, an undercontrolled expressive style matches IQ in predicting their educational attainment.

Similar outcomes are expressed in novel settings that evoke a patterned response to authority. The prototype is the military setting, largely because the authoritarian and regimented context of military life creates an inter- actional context in which the suppression of impulses is highly valued. The military also figured prominently in the lives of men who were born in the late 1920s and over 70% of the Berkeley men served in the army. In keeping with the interactional continuity model, there is a significant negative correlation between childhood tantrums and military rank, the most reasonable volitional and performance outcome in this setting.

Yet another illustration of interactional continuity is to be found in work settings. Specifically, we hypothesized that exposure to close and perhaps authoritarian supervision in the work setting would make the disorderly work manifestations of childhood tantrums more likely. We sought evi- dence for this process by dividing men into those with a history of childhood tantrums and those with no such history. We further divided the men into those who held high-status jobs characterized by relative auton- omy and into those who held lower status jobs characterized by close supervision.

Some illustrative findings from our analyses are shown in Figure 6.3. The first table shows the number of jobs held by men over a 10-year period during middle adulthood. The results show a marginally significant effect of childhood tantrums on the number of jobs held. More interesting is the clear interaction of early personality—a way of approaching the world—

Dependent Variable: Number of jobs

	ADULT JOB CONDITIONS	
TEMPER TANTRUMS	Low Job Status	High Job Status
Low	2.55	2.11
High	(5.07)	1.92

Number of jobs by childhood tantrums and adult job conditions.

Dependent Variable: Number of functional breaks

	ADULT JOB CONDITIONS	
TEMPER TANTRUMS	Low Job Status	High Job Status
Low	.80	.87
High	(2.13)	.33

Number of functional breaks in line of work by childhood tantrums and adult job conditions.

Dependent Variable: Number of months unemployed

	ADULT JOB CONDITIONS	
TEMPER TANTRUMS	Low Job Status	High Job Status
Low	.71	.61
High	(2.59)	1.76

Number of months unemployed by childhood tantrums and adult job conditions.

FIGURE 6.3 Erratic worklives by childhood tantrums and adult job conditions.

with select environmental conditions. A tantrum history coupled with jobs characterized by close supervision significantly increased the likelihood of changing jobs more often. This pattern obtains for other worklife variables, as well. The dependent variable in the second table refers to switches between functionally unrelated lines of work. Once again, a childhood disposition coupled with supervisory settings significantly increased the likelihood of an erratic worklife. This general pattern obtains even when the statistical interactions are not significant. The third table in this sequence shows that explosive boys who in adulthood held jobs characterized by close supervision were unemployed four times longer than nonexplosive boys who, in adulthood, held jobs characterized by greater autonomy.

The adult careers of explosive children are punctuated by disorganization and instability, but their behavior remains coherent throughout. We believe this is partly a function of characteristic responses and expectations that are brought to bear on the interpretation and enactment of behavior in new roles and settings in the life course. In addition, the coherent trajectories of explosive children derive from a cumulative dynamic, illustrated in Figure 6.4, in which the consequences (e.g., truncated education) of an early disposition accumulate over time, frustrating culturally and personally desirable outcomes (e.g., occupational status) and thereby resulting in additional difficulties (e.g., erratic work lives).

The occupational role was less salient to Berkeley women within the historical period studied, and we find few direct connections between childhood tantrums and women's achievements. However, the implications of an explosive behavioral style for women's status achievements can be traced through their husbands. Women with a childhood history of tantrums paid an ever-increasing price for their undercontrolled behavior — whatever the underlying process may be. They married men who were significantly less well-positioned in the post war economy, and these achievement differentials through marriage persisted into mid-life.

These sex differences in the continuity of explosive, undercontrolled behavior must, of course, be viewed in cultural and historical perspective. For example, recent sex-role changes in our society will probably be expressed in life-course consequences of childhood tantrums that are more

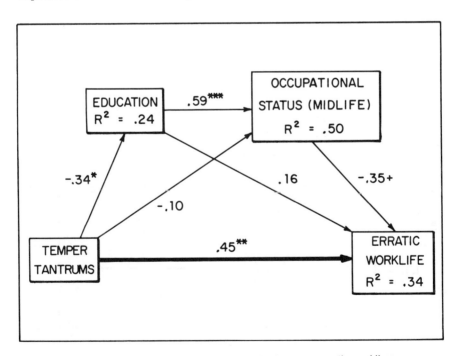

FIGURE 6.4 Effects of childhood temper tantrums on erratic worklives.

similar for men and women in the future. As we pointed out in the beginning of the chapter, particular life-course patterns depend not only on the individual's pattern of approach and response, but also on the structure of the environment in any given historical period. But although social change may produce change in particular manifestations of a disposition in the life course, we can still hope to abstract the general principles of personality functioning that produce these manifestations.

Because new relationships are often approached in terms of their similarity to earlier ones, they often evoke responses similar to those in previous settings. Explosive styles of relating to people should thus be replicated in new relationships, and this should be especially evident as children move from their family of orientation to their family of procreation.

Indeed, Figure 6.5 suggests that children who have trouble controlling their impulses are likely to become adults who have trouble sustaining a marriage. When contacted in 1970, men with a childhood history of tantrums were significantly less likely to have had an intact first marriage. Almost half of the men with a tantrum history divorced. In contrast, only 22% of their even-tempered counterparts divorced. A similar pattern obtains for women in our sample. Women with a tantrum history were twice as likely to divorce by mid-life.

Parental situations are also emotion-laden and can strain the usual limits

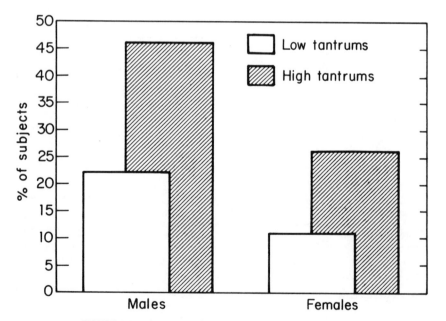

FIGURE 6.5   Marital dissolution by childhood temper tantrums.

of self-control. Under the pressures of the moment, will a parent's response take the form of an emotional outburst without regard to the incident in question? Interactional continuity suggests that adults who learned the effectiveness of rage reactions in gaining control and attention in childhood may well be inclined to use this response in their own parent–child confrontations.

Independent reports from the Berkeley subjects' spouses and children confirm the replication of explosive interactions in the parenting domain. The most reliable etiological clue concerning the ill-tempered behavior of mothers is their own undercontrolled childhood history. The connection for men is more elusive but nevertheless coherent. Men with a childhood history of tantrums become inadequate parents through a self-perpetuating dynamic in which accumulated work difficulties spill over into parenting difficulties.

An explosive childhood pattern has clearly shaped the life course. The initial tendency toward explosive, undercontrolled behavior, observed here in late childhood, was recreated in new roles and settings, especially in problems with subordination — in educational, military, and work settings — and in situations that required negotiating interpersonal conflicts, such as marriage and parenting. We have hinted also about the self-perpetuating nature of early personality in the life course; the accumulation of consequences, each building upon the other, that stem from an initial disposition. This cumulative dynamic is documented further in our analysis of socially withdrawn boys.

Life-Course Patterns of Withdrawn Children

The initial tendency toward withdrawal probably has a partial base in the child's biology (Buss & Plomin, 1984; Garcia, Kagan, & Reznick, 1984). A biological tendency toward inhibition or withdrawal may then be strengthened by interactions with the social environment. In every day life, many moments are punctuated by interactions with other people that require a decision to withdraw or to participate. Each time the child chooses either course, the relevant habit is strengthened, thus making the initial disposition an increasingly salient component of the developing child's character. At a more molar level, the life course is similarly punctuated by transition points that require the individual to initiate action (i.e., to enter new roles and to organize behavior around a normatively defined set of tasks). Moreover, each decision made in the transition period has consequences for subsequent development and tends to channel behavior into particular directions. In this sequence, initial individual differences that affect behavior during transition events are further maintained and strengthened by the consequences of the transition event.

We identified a group of withdrawn boys on the basis of clinical interviews with their mothers (Macfarlane, Allen, & Honzik, 1954). The index of social withdrawal is based on annual ratings at ages 8, 9, and 10 of two behaviors: shyness and excessive reserve. Extremely shy children experienced acute discomfort to the point of panic in social situations. In interpersonal settings they would often hang their head and not look at people. Often these children were not at ease even with people they had known for a long time. The shyness rating was supplemented by a rating of reserve that at its extreme gets at children who characteristically produced feelings of strain and awkwardness in those around them.

From other analyses we know that withdrawn boys experience greater difficulty initiating action and they tend also to avoid potentially difficult situations. In young adulthood, symptoms of withdrawal and related difficulties are most likely to be expressed again when men are called upon to make critical choices and decisions about adult roles, such as family and work. In particular, withdrawn, inhibited reaction patterns may impair the transition of boys to adulthood, especially through delayed and off-time choices and actions.

The results in Figure 6.6 show striking differences between withdrawn and nonwithdrawn children in the timing of transition events in early

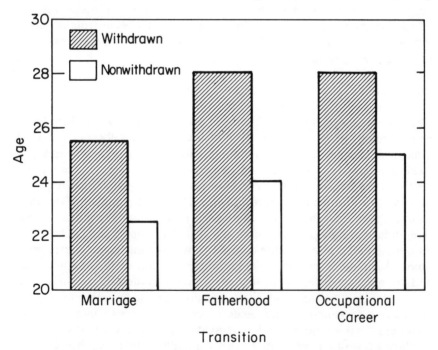

FIGURE 6.6 Timing of life transitions by withdrawn behavior in childhood.

adulthood. Men with a childhood history of social withdrawal marry at a significantly older age than adults with no such behavioral history. The difference between the groups is 3 years. Not surprisingly, delayed age at marriage corresponds also with delayed parenthood. Men with a childhood history of social withdrawal became fathers at a significantly older age than men with no such behavioral history. Finally—and most interesting—withdrawn behavior in late childhood hindered men's transition into an occupational career. Figure 6.6 shows that men with a childhood history of withdrawn behavior assumed a work career 3 years after the majority of their peers were already established in an occupation. Intracohort variations in the age-graded life course clearly depend on dispositions that are brought to transition events.

The timing of transitions in young adulthood is not a benign event. It represents an important contingency in the life course, one that has critical implications for achievements and subsequent behavior (Hogan, 1981). Indeed, delays in social transitions often generate conflicting obligations and options that may enhance stress and the risk of social pathology (Elder, 1985). It is this cumulative process—from withdrawn behavior to delayed transitions—that represents the connection between withdrawn behavior in late childhood and life disorganization at mid-life.

Elsewhere we have documented this sequence more fully (Caspi et al., 1988). Here we should like to be more case-analytic. We selected the 7 most withdrawn boys in the Berkeley Guidance Study and matched them on social class origin, adolescent IQ, and educational level with 7 non-withdrawn children. The analysis in Figure 6.7 shows how the effects of withdrawn behavior accumulate over time in the life course.

The first box in Figure 6.7 refers to the transition into an occupational career, coded as on-time or off-time. Off-time behavior is operationalized as 2 years above the median age for this transition. The second box refers to achievement level, coded as high or low. The group of high achievers includes men whose occupational status at mid-life (age 40) equalled or surpassed their expected attainment level given what we know about their adolescent IQ, adolescent aspirations, senior high-school grade point average (GPA) and educational level. The group of low achievers includes men whose occupational status fell below their predicted attainment level. The third box refers to marital status at mid-life—whether men's first marriages are intact or not.

We have shown already that withdrawn children are more prone to difficulties in adhering to on-time transition schedules in early adulthood. Indeed, of the 7 withdrawn children, 5 are off-time in establishing a career. The opposite pattern obtains in the matched control group: of the 7 nonwithdrawn children, 5 are on-time and only 2 are delayed in career entry.

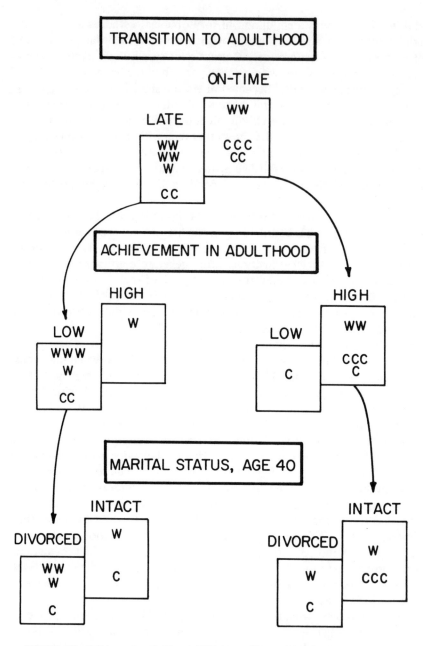

FIGURE 6.7 Pathways to adulthood: Withdrawn (W) vs. Control (C) children.

As we move forward in time, the selection of environments and roles further elaborates and maintains initial individual differences between the two groups. Of the 5 withdrawn children who are off-time, 4 are now low achievers. Again, the opposite pattern obtains in the matched control group: of the 5 nonwithdrawn children who are on-time, 4 are high achievers.

Achievement levels in adulthood have much to do with disadvantages that stem from nonadherence to normative schedules. But it is critical to recognize that attributing adult outcomes to proximal events—such as the timing of transitions—is spurious because these effects derive from the attributes of individuals, already evident in late childhood, who self-select particular experiences and events.

The final sequence in Figure 6.7 shows that mid-life problems in family management arise also in response to problems in coordinating transition events and new roles earlier in adulthood. Divorce is overrepresented among men with a history of social withdrawal who delayed career entry and who are low achievers. Intact marriages are concentrated among men without a history of social withdrawal who entered careers on time and who are high achievers. The key process here is role strain. By mid-life, withdrawn children faced a structurally incompatible nexus of roles because they delayed both careers and marriage, and family establishment often occurred prior to establishment in a work career. Faced with such strain— and, importantly, an age-atypic strain—the risk of marital instability increased significantly among men with a childhood history of social withdrawal.

A childhood pattern of social withdrawal has clearly shaped the life course. The initial tendency toward inhibition or withdrawal, observed here in late childhood, was recreated in new settings that required initiating action, as in mate selection and vocational decision making. The data suggest that withdrawn children exert different selective efforts than nonwithdrawn children and respond differently to similar social demands. Moreover, the consequences of withdrawn children's behavior during critical transition periods appear to "pile-on" or "snowball," and, in the course of this cumulative process, the effects of an early disposition are expanded and elaborated in new behavioral domains that are not directly bound to the initial disposition.

HOW EARLY PERSONALITY SHAPES THE LIFE COURSE

The two studies we have summarized suggest that the ways individuals deal with experiences in early life strongly influence other experiences they will encounter and how they deal with them. We have demonstrated this by tracing early personality through the age-graded life course, across time and in diverse circumstances. Moreover, we have proposed that the long-term continuities of personality are to be found in interactional styles that are sustained by their contemporary consequences in reciprocal social interaction (interactional continuity) and/or by the progressive accumulation of their own consequences over time (cumulative continuity).

Interactional Continuity

Early behavior patterns may persist because the individual's pattern of interacting with others tends to recreate the same conditions over and again. Indeed, relational styles that are learned in one situation and that bring about certain kinds of rewards are likely to be evoked in similar situations for new rewards. Moreover, when relational patterns are carried into new situations they will elicit responses from others that "support and validate" that pattern (Wachtel, 1977).

In the life course, we do not find situations exactly similar to past situations; we must define every situation as similar to certain past situations in order to apply solutions to new situations and encounters. The tendency to find in new experiences older elements that enable the individual to react to them in an old way is the key process in interactional continuity.

This process is well illustrated by Piagetian dynamics in a social world (Piaget, 1970). Viewed sequentially, the dynamics of assimilation and accommodation suggest that individuals will seek to equilibrate first via assimilation, and only when assimilative efforts cannot achieve integration of regnant elements requiring understanding will they move on to accommodative efforts (Block, 1983). Given nonreactive sources of stimulation, accommodation should continue apace until optimal, adaptive organism-environment interactions are achieved. But in personality development accommodative efforts are more rare than is generally acknowledged, because in a social world individuals rarely deal with passive, nonreactive sources of stimulation.

Consider Piaget's concept of a schema—implying that not only do we assimilate new experiences to familiar ways of viewing events around us, but that we do eventually accommodate to new sources of stimulation—in relation to the behavior of highly explosive children. The motive systems of highly explosive children (and perhaps of withdrawn children, though evidence is lacking) often involve biased perceptions of the environment and expectations of hostility from others (Dodge, 1986). Given nonreactive sources of environmental stimulation, a highly explosive child should eventually adopt a more accurate, perhaps more benign, view of the social world. But the child's social world is not passive. In fact, the child's biased view of other people may eventually depict an accurate view, partly because intitial expectations will elicit confirming behavior from the environment, as when expectations of hostility evoke hostile behavior from others.

The assimilative tendency may thus explain also why individuals retain schemes, scripts, and behavior patterns in new settings even when these prove maladaptive: Existing structures are often supported by the actions of others and affirmed by the reactions we bring about. There is often little need to accommodate new experiences; familiar ways of viewing others and the self will find constant affirmation in a reactive social world. In addition, assimilation is cognitively more economical. The route to achieve accommodation—to construct or invent new schemes to process experience—is arduous, protracted, and often more difficult for the individual who must remain in an unstructured state for extended periods. The common goal of most therapeutic interventions is, after all, to encourage the patient to abandon existing structures in favor of new, more adaptive, motive systems. This process, as therapists and patients would agree, is far more taxing.

Cumulative Continuity

A related process that generates connections between early and later behavior is cumulative continuity. Cumulative continuity refers to dispositional continuity that is maintained through the progressive accumulation of its own consequences. For example, early withdrawn behavior may preclude experiencing role and rule negotiations that are important in the growth of social knowledge (Rubin, 1982) and the resultant social cognitive deficits may lead to involuntary social isolation. In this scenario, initial individual differences have been amplified into larger differences in a similar domain. Moreover, initial differences in one domain often will produce amplified manifestations in additional domains. Involuntary social isolation may lead initially withdrawn children to develop behavioral repertoires that are inappropriate for the mastery of adult demands and roles, leading initial differences in a childhood behavioral style to snowball into extensive differences in various competencies later in life. Cumulative continuity is thus similar to the process of divergent causality in which differences between individuals become amplified and extended over time, producing larger differences between individuals in similar domains as well as in additional behavioral domains (Gangestad & Snyder, 1985).

We believe that Scarr (in press; Scarr & McCartney, 1983) has correctly identified the causal contribution of personality: The individual's genotype both influences the impact that environments have on him or her, and increasingly during the course of development, drives the individual's own selection of environments and experiences. In accounting for the persistence of individual differences we emphasize, in addition, the contribution of these environments and experiences to the course of later behavior, especially in expanding and elaborating the course of individual differences in social development that are not directly related or bound to the initial disposition or genotype.

The cumulative effects of early personality thus resemble Smith's (1968) observation on benign and vicious cycles of life-span development:

> Launched on the right trajectory, the person is likely to accumulate successes that strengthen the effectiveness of his orientation toward the world while at the same time he acquires the knowledge and skills to make his further success more probable. His environmental involvements generally lead to gratification and to increased competence and favorable development. Off to a bad start, on the other hand, he soon encounters failures that make him hesitant to try. What to others are challenges appear to him as threats; he becomes preoccupied with defense of his small claims on life at the expense of energies to invest in constructive coping. And he falls increasingly behind his fellows in acquiring the knowledge and skill that are needed for success on those occasions when he does try. (p. 277)

Evidence of this sustaining process suggests that to understand how personality shapes the life course we must trace the path by which earlier dispositions affect behavior in new settings and how the outcomes of these interactions influence subsequent behavior in related as well as in novel situations. Indeed, one possible view of the inadequacy of previous developmental predictions from early personality sees their source not in the absence of lawful relations but in our inability to locate the critical links in the causal chain connecting earlier and later modes of adaptation (Hinde & Bateson, 1984). For this reason, an adequate conceptualization of life-span personality development must be complemented by a social theory that identifies periods in the life course that are critical for the organization of behavior.

PERSONALITY IN THE LIFE COURSE

The idea of continuity in development implies that early personality has lawful implications for later personality:

> What is contended is that how experience registers, how environments are selected or modified, and how the stages of life are negotiated depends importantly and coherently on what the individual brings to these new encounters—the resources, the premises, the intentions, the awareness, the

fears and the hopes, the forethoughts and the afterthoughts that are subsumed by what we call personality. (Block, 1981, pp. 40–41)

This contention is borne out by our findings.

Rather than seek behavioral identities across the life span, we have focused on the coherence of personality across social transformations in the age-graded life course; on how individuals meet developmental challenges, adapt to new settings, and on the long-term consequences of these adaptational strategies (cf. Sroufe, 1979). We have accomplished this by combining the longitudinal assessment of personality with the longitudinal assessment of situations, showing how early personality shapes the achievements and relationships of men and women in diverse situations at different ages.

The exploration of individual personalities across the life course is a hard task, and our prescription makes the task twice as hard. If we are to account for how personality — ways of approaching and responding to the world — shapes individual lives, we must be psychologically and sociologically minded; we must have a way of thinking about individual personalities in their changing environmental contexts. The search for personality continuities in the life course should thus prove less elusive but much more demanding.

ACKNOWLEDGMENTS

This work was also supported in part by grants from the National Institute of Mental Health (MH-34712, MH-37809 and MH-41827). Glen H. Elder, Jr. was supported by a NIMH Senior Scientist Fellowship (MH00567). We are indebted to the Institute of Human Development, University of California, Berkeley, for permission to use archival data from the Berkeley Guidance Study. Our thanks to Daryl Bem, Steven Cornelius, Karen Hooker, and Jaan Valsiner for their insights and suggestions.

REFERENCES

Arsenian, J., & Arsenian, J. M. (1948). Tough and easy cultures. *Psychiatry,* 11, 377–385.
Barker, R. G. (1968). *Ecological psychology.* Stanford: Stanford University Press.
Block, J. (1971). *Lives through time.* Berkeley, CA: Bancroft.
Block, J. (1977). Advancing the psychology of personality: Paradigmatic shift or improving the quality of research. In D. Magnusson & N. S. Endler (Eds.), *Personality at the crossroads: Current issues in interactional psychology* (pp. 37–63). Hillsdale, NJ: Lawrence Erlbaum Associates.
Block, J. (1981). Some enduring and consequential structures of personality. In A. I. Rabin,

J. Aronoff, A. Barclay, & R. Zucker (Eds.), *Further explorations in personality* (pp. 27–43). New York: Wiley.

Block, J. (1983). Assimilation, accommodation, and the dynamics of personality development. *Child Development, 53,* 281–295.

Block, J., & Block, J. H. (1981). Studying situational dimensions: A grand perspective and some limited empiricism. In D. Magnusson (Ed.), *Toward a psychology of situations* (pp. 85–102). Hillsdale, NJ: Lawrence Erlbaum Associates.

Buss, A. H., & Plomin, R. (1984). *Temperament: Early developing personality traits.* Hillsdale, NJ: Lawrence Erlbaum Associates.

Caspi, A. (1987). Personality in the life course. *Journal of Personality and Social Psychology, 53,* 1203–1213.

Caspi, A., Elder, G. H., Jr., & Bem, D. J. (1988). Moving away from the world: Life-course patterns of withdrawn children. In review.

Cattell, R. B. (1957). *Personality and motivation structure and measurement.* New York: World Books.

Conley, J. J. (1984). Relation of temporal stability and cross-situational consistency in personality: Comment on the Mischel-Epstein debate. *Psychological Review, 91,* 491–496.

Costa, P. T., & McCrae, R. R. (1980). Still stable after all these years: Personality as a key to some issues in adulthood and old age. In P. B. Baltes & O. G. Brim, Jr. (Eds.), *Life span development and behavior* (Vol. 3, pp. 65–102). New York: Academic Press.

Dictionary of occupational titles. (1982). Washington, DC: U.S. Department of Labor, Employment, and Training Administration (4th ed. supplement).

Dodge, K. (1986). A social-information processing model of social competence in children. In M. Perlmutter (Ed.), *Minnesota symposia on child psychology* (Vol. 18, pp. 77–125). Hillsdale, NJ: Lawrence Erlbaum Associates.

Eichorn, D. H. (1981). Samples and procedures. In D. H. Eichorn, J. A. Clausen, N. Haan, M. P. Honzik, & P. H. Mussen (Eds.), *Present and past in middle life* (pp. 33–51). New York: Academic Press.

Elder, G. H., Jr. (1975). Age differentiation and the life course. In A. Inkeles, J. Coleman, & N. Smelser (Eds.), *Annual review of sociology* (Vol. 1, pp. 165–190). Palo Alto: Annual Review.

Elder, G. H., Jr. (1985). Perspectives on the life course. In G. H. Elder, Jr. (Ed.), *Life course dynamics: Trajectories and transitions* (pp. 23–49). Ithaca, NY: Cornell University Press.

Elder, G. H., Jr., & Caspi, A. (in press). Social change and human development: An emerging perspective on the life course. In N. Bolger, A. Caspi, G. Downey, & M. Moorehouse (Eds.), *Persons in context: Developmental processes.* Cambridge University Press.

Epstein, S. (1983). Aggregation and beyond,: Some basic issues in the prediction of behavior. *Journal of Personality, 51,* 360–392.

Epstein, S. (1984). The stability of behavior across time and situations. In R. Zucker, J. Aronoff, & A. I. Rabin (Eds.), *Personality and the prediction of behavior* (pp. 209–268). New York: Wiley.

Erikson, E. (1950). *Childhood and society.* New York: Norton.

Gangestad, S., & Snyder, M. (1985). "To carve nature at its joints": On the existence of discrete classes in personality. *Psychological Review, 92,* 317–349.

Garcia, C., Kagan, J., & Reznick, J. S. (1984). Behavioral inhibition in young children. *Child Development, 55,* 1005–1019.

Green, A. W. (1942). The social situation in personality theory. *American Sociological Review, 7,* 388–393.

Hagestad, G. O., & Neugarten, B. (1985). Age and the life course. In R. H. Binstock & E. Shanas (Eds.), *Handbook of aging and the social sciences* (pp. 35–61). New York: Van Nostrand Reinhold.

Helson, R., Mitchell, V., & Moane, G. (1984). Personality and patterns of adherence and nonadherence to the social clock. *Journal of Personality and Social Psychology, 46,* 1079–1096.

Hinde, R. A., & Bateson, P. (1984). Discontinuities versus continuities in behavioral development and the neglect of process. *International Journal of Behavioral Development, 7,* 129–143.

Hogan, D. P. (1981). *Transitions and social change.* New York: Academic Press.

Kertzer, D., & Keith, J. (Eds.). (1984). *Age and anthropological theory.* Ithaca, NY: Cornell University Press.

Labouvie, E. (1982). Life-span development. In B. Wolman (Ed.), *Handbook of developmental Psychology* (pp. 54–62). New York: Wiley.

LeVine, R. A. (1980). Adulthood among the Gusii of Kenya. In N. J. Smelser & E. Erikson (Eds.), *Themes of work and love in adulthood* (pp. 77–104). Cambridge, MA: Harvard University Press.

LeVine, R. A. (1982). *Culture, behavior, and personality.* New York: Aldine.

Macfarlane, J. W., Allen, L., & Honzik, M. P. (1954). *A developmental study of the behavioral problems of children between twenty-one months and fourteen years.* Berkeley, CA: University of California Press.

Magnusson, D. (1981). Wanted: A psychology of situations. In D. Magnusson (Ed.), *Toward a psychology of situations* (pp. 9–32). Hillsdale, NJ: Lawrence Erlbaum Associates.

McCrae, R. R., & Costa, P. C., Jr. (1984). *Emerging lives, enduring dispositions.* Boston, MA: Little, Brown.

Mischel, W. (1968). *Personality and assessment.* New York: Wiley.

Mischel, W., & Peake, P. (1982). Beyond déjà-vu in the search for cross-situational consistency. *Psychological Review, 89,* 730–755.

Murray, H. A., & Kluckhohn, C. (1953). Outline of a conception of personality. In C. Kluckhohn & H. A. Murray (Eds.), *Personality in nature, society, and culture* (pp. 3–49). New York: Knopf.

Neugarten, B., Moore, J., Lowe, J. W. (1965). Age norms, age constraints and adult socialization. *American Journal of Sociology, 70,* 710–717.

Patterson, G. R. (1982). *Coercive family process.* Eugene, OR: Castallia.

Pervin, L. A. (1978). Definitions, measurements, and classifications of stimuli, situations, and environments. *Human Ecology, 6,* 71–105.

Piaget, J. (1970). Piaget's theory. In P. H. Mussen (Ed.), *Carmichael's manual of child psychology* (Vol. 1, pp. 703–732). New York: Wiley.

Riley, M. W., Johnson, M., & Foner, A. (1972). *Aging and society: A sociology of age stratification.* New York: Russell Sage.

Robins, L. N. (1978). Sturdy predictors of adult antisocial behavior: Replications from longitudinal studies. *Psychological Medicine, 6,* 611–622.

Rubin, K. H. (1982). Social and social-cognitive developmental characteristics of young isolate, normal, and sociable children. In K. H. Rubin & H. S. Ross (Eds.), *Peer relationships and social skills in childhood.* New York: Springer.

Rutter, M. (1983). Statistical and personal interactions: Facets and perspectives. In D. Magnusson (Ed.), *Human development: An interactional perspective* (pp. 296–320). New York: Academic Press.

Scarr, S. (in press). Personality and experience: Individual encounters with the world. In J. Aronoff, A. I. Rabin, & R. Zucker (Eds.), *Emergence of Personality.* New York: Springer.

Scarr, S. (in press). How genotypes and environments combine: Development and individual differences. In N. Bolger, A. Caspi, G. Downey, & M. Moorehouse (Eds.), *Persons in context: Developmental processes.* New York: Cambridge University Press.

Scarr, S., & McCartney, K. (1983). How people make their own environments: A theory of genotype-environment correlations. *Child Development, 54,* 424–435.

Smith, M. B. (1968). Competence and socialization. In J. A. Clausen (Ed.), *Socialization and society* (pp. 270–320). Boston, MA: Little, Brown.

Snyder, M., & Ickes, W. (1985). Personality and social behavior. In G. Lindsey & E. Aronson (Eds.), *Handbook of social psychology* (pp. 883–947). New York: Random House.

Sofer, C. (1970). *Men in mid-career: A study of British managers and technical specialists.* New York: Cambridge University Press.

Sroufe, L. A. (1979). The coherence of individual development. *American Psychologist, 34,* 834–841.

Thomas, W. I., & Znaniecki, F. (1918–20). *The Polish peasant in Europe and America* (2 vols.). Chicago, IL: University of Chicago Press.

Turner, R. H. (1962). Role-taking: Process vs. conformity. In A. M. Rose (Ed.), *Human behavior and social processes* (pp. 20–40). Boston, MA: Houghton Mifflin.

Wachtel, P. L. (1977). *Psychoanalysis and behavior therapy.* New York: Basic.

Wohlwill, J. (1973). *The study of behavioral development.* New York: Academic Press.

7 CHANGES IN CHILDREN'S SOCIAL LIVES AND THE DEVELOPMENT OF SOCIAL UNDERSTANDING

Judy Dunn
Pennsylvania State University

Lonnie Sherrod
New School for Social Research

ABSTRACT

This chapter explores the impact of the birth of a sibling on social under-standing in a first-born child during the second and third year of life. It examines the mechanisms and changes in childrens' social lives that affect social cognitive development. Finally it discusses implications for long-term development of early life events such as the birth of a sibling.

INTRODUCTION

By the time that children in Europe and the United States are 5 years old, a high proportion of them have had to cope with major and potentially stressful changes in their world: divorce and separation of parents; change in family structure such as the birth of a sibling; the experience of separation from parents in the form of group care, illness, and accidents, periods of hospitalization or residential care; or physical or mental illnesses of family members. Even relatively routine or normal experiences of moving between houses or neighborhoods or starting or changing schools may involve major changes in the lives of children. Research on children's perceptions and experiences of routine events such as being graded in class, nightmares, or minor illnesses such as chicken pox has shown that such events carry some significance for children (Dunn, 1987; Elizur, 1986; Field, 1984; Hughes, Pinkerton, & Plewis, 1979; Yamamoto, 1979; Yamamoto & Davis, 1982), comparable to the adult experiences of critical life events, or turning points, that life-span-oriented research has demonstrated to have significant effects on adult development (Callahan & McCluskey, 1983; Dohrenwend & Dohrenwend, 1974).

Research on child development is increasingly focusing on the effects of such changes, but it has been primarily concerned with the more extreme stresses. There is, for instance, a wealth of research on the consequences of perinatal trauma and of adverse early experiences and a growing literature on the effects of events such as maternal employment, parental separation and divorce, hospitalization, maternal illness, and change in family structure (Hetherington, Cox, & Cox, 1982, 1985; Hoffman, 1979; Hurme, 1978, 1983; Paykel, 1978; Rutter, 1983; Sherrod, 1983).

The literature on adults' experiences of life events is voluminous and it is reasonable to inquire about the developmental significance of parallel experiences for children. There are, however, serious issues of definition and research strategy involved in incorporating concepts that grew out of research on adulthood into child developmental theory and research. It is beyond the scope of this chapter to review this work on adults; it is partly handled in other chapters of this volume (e.g., Caspi and Elder, and Parke) and also summarized elsewhere (Coddington, 1972a, 1972b; Herzog, 1984; Sherrod & Brim, 1986). From this literature, three approaches to research on adults' experiences of events can be delineated: (a) the study of individuals' coping with the stress of multiple changes or events, (b) the study of changes in the structuring of life by changes in social roles or statuses, and (c) the detailed case study of the individuals' experiences of a single event. In the bulk of the work on children's experience of events, however, the concern has been to assess the clinical risks or problems associated with these experiences, or to paint in broad strokes the picture of children's outcome after such events. That is, most childhood research on life events is concerned with stress and coping, subsuming the first and third of the approaches described previously. This research on stress and coping is summarized and evaluated in the chapter by Parke (this volume). In the most careful work such as that on divorce (Hetherington, Cox, & Cox, 1982, 1985) and on hospitalizations (Rutter, 1983), the interest of researchers has been to document the changes in children's lives in detail in order to understand how the effects of the life events are mediated. Nonetheless, as Hetherington and Baltes note in the introductory chapter to this volume, those studying child development have tended to see events as modifiers not as constituents of developmental transitions. They have not, as have life-span researchers of adult development, given events or changes in the child's social and physical environment equal conceptual status to organism-based change.

Moreover, although most childhood studies of obviously negative or stressful life changes have included a consideration of individual differences in the responses of children, the few existing studies of age-related changes in social life, such as starting school, have been concerned with "normative" changes in children irrespective of individual differences. As with research into stressful events, these studies have primarily reported prevalence rates of problems following the event. Rarely has there been serious attention to the causes and consequences of individual differences in response to such life changes, including positive as well as negative outcomes. That is, again as Hetherington and Baltes argue in chapter 1 of this volume, those studying child development have tended to postulate typical courses of development, and have emphasized constraints related to the child's developmental level in the individual's response to events. It is an approach that focuses on how the event intrudes on the typical course of development.

In contrast, this chapter examines the characterization of the child's experience of events as a mediator or modifier of development. What aspects of the child's development, of the event, and of the context are important to the child's experience? We focus on potential positive outcomes as well as on negative consequences. That is, we do not necessarily view the event as a stressor. To undertake such an examination, we focus specifically on one event, the birth of a sibling, and examine its interaction with the developments in one relevant domain, social understanding as it blossoms during the second and third years of life, a period during which many first born children experience the arrival of a sibling. The idea that life changes affect children's social cognition has been explored, at a speculative level, by Higgins and Parsons (1983). They relate, in broad terms, the changes in children's social lives during different age phases to developments in social cognition. They emphasize that "social life phases have received, at best, benign neglect by developmental psychologists" (p. 54) and their concern is to draw broad parallels rather than to explore possible mechanisms that might link the changes in social life with the changes in modes of social thought.

We wish to do a bit of both—to explore mechanisms and processes by which social changes may affect social cognitive development in our particular chosen example and to draw some broader implications. In particular, in regard to the latter, we view the efforts in this chapter as one tentative step toward a more ambitious goal of examining the respective child developmental and life-span developmental views of the role of life events across the life course. Should those who study child development consider life events in more formative terms than solely as modifiers in development? Experiences of life events in early childhood, and the research strategies for examining these events in childhood carry implications for research on critical life events during other periods of life such as adulthood?

We begin by summarizing some key features of the changes within a sample of families in which a second child is born, and explore the possible significance of these events for changes in the children's behavior and development, emphasizing individual variability in children's responses and considering how the analysis of this one change in children's lives may illuminate the significance of other life changes. We turn then to the normative changes in social understanding that take place over the second and third year, arguing that the same features that stood out as important in mediating the changes in children's behavior that followed the sibling birth may also be important in these normative developmental changes. Finally, we place these observations in a broader framework of research on social cognition in early childhood and suggest some implications for research on adult's experiences of events.

THE ARRIVAL OF A SIBLING

Immediate Impact

For the sample of 40 families that Dunn and colleagues studied in Cambridge, England (for a detailed account see Dunn & Kendrick, 1982), the arrival of a second child meant major changes, at every level examined, in the lives of the first-born children, who were aged on average 23 months. These changes were evident during the first days after the sibling's birth.

First, the children were for a brief period in the care of someone other than their mother, who was for these children their usual caregiver. This entailed modifications in the children's usual routine that the mothers, interviewed a few days later, considered of real significance in accounting for the alterations in the children's behavior after the birth.

The children's relationship with their mothers also changed after the birth. Mothers became more restrictive, controlling, and punitive, whereas all indices of sensitive maternal attention showed decreases. Children took a greater responsibility for initiating communicative exchange and play; many also became more demanding of their mothers, as well as assertive and naughty.

There were, in fact, many other shifts in the children's behavior — both changes in bodily function such as sleeping problems and breakdown in toilet training and alterations in patterns of play and social relationships. These changes highlighted the emotional impact on the children of the constellation of events surrounding the sibling birth. The individual differences were marked: Some children became miserable, clinging, and tearful, whereas others became aggressive and demanding.

Most notably, about half the children studied also showed developmental advances over the few days following the sibling birth that seemed to reflect new signs of independence and maturity.

The children also began to talk differently about themselves and others in their world. For the first time in the children's lives, someone other than themselves was frequently the topic of conversation between child and mother. In some families the new baby was often discussed as a person with needs, wishes, and feelings. For some children, new categories of self-hood were now evident in their conversation. Now she was a sister, the big girl not the little, the older not the younger, the girl not the baby, the good one who did not cry, and so on.

Changes Over the Longer Term

These Cambridge families were followed over the next year in some detail by Dunn and colleagues, and a subsample was seen again 3 years later (Stillwell & Dunn, 1985). Four additional points should be noted from this followup data.

First, the mother–child relationship was never reestablished as it had been before. In particular, maternal attention and play never regained the levels found before the birth of the second child. Dunn and colleagues do not have directly comparable data on mother–child interaction in families with only or second-born children, thus it cannot be determined whether these new levels of maternal attention are systematically related to birth order. However, the point to which we want to draw attention is the potential significance of the dramatic change in the experiences of the first-born children.

Second, a new relationship, that between sibling and child, developed. Complex patterns of mutual influence between the different family relationships, between mother and child, sibling and child, and mother and sibling were evident. Although some of the disturbances in behavior shown by the first-born children immediately following the birth disappeared over the next few months, for some children, there were increasingly marked problems such as anxiety, fearfulness, or mildly neurotic behavior. In addition, the developmental advances observed during the first 2 weeks after the sibling birth that were not related to the incidence of disturbance did not disappear.

Just as the individual differences found in the immediate responses of the children to the sibling birth were marked, so too were the individual differences in the persistence of their problem behaviors found in the children's relationships with the sibling that developed over the next years, and in the features of sociocognitive development associated with differences in that relationship. A serious consideration of these individual differences is of central importance in any attempt to evaluate the developmental significance of social changes in the lives of young children.

Individual Differences

It was clear from the analysis of the children's immediate responses to the sibling birth that a simple index of disturbance applied to the first-born child would have been misleading. Not only did the children respond very differently in terms of the frequency and intensity of different forms of disturbed behavior, but there was no simple relation between different aspects of disturbance and the positive interest the children showed in the new baby. The signs of disturbed behavior demonstrated unequivocally that the constellation of effects surrounding the sibling birth was of profound emotional importance to most children. However, to understand the impact of that experience on the children's social behavior and understanding, and its relation to the children's growing relationship with the new sibling, a more detailed analysis than a simple summary in terms of the prevalance of disturbed behavior was required.

Such an extended analysis highlighted three points. First, differences in the immediate response of the children were related to individual differences in the quality of the mother–child and father–child relationships before the arrival of the sibling. Second, they were related to temperamental differences between the children, assessed before the sibling birth; temperament and the parent–child relationship were more important in accounting for differences in the immediate response than were the gap in age between the siblings or the separation experiences at the time of the birth. Third, the quality of the relationship that developed between the siblings was related to differences in their mothers' conversation about others, specifically in the extent to which mothers discussed the motives, intentions, and feelings of others. In those families in which the mother discussed the new baby as a person with feelings, wishes, and intentions the children behaved with far more friendliness toward their siblings a year later than did the children in those families in which such discussion had not taken place. The quality of the sibling relationship over the next 4 years showed considerable stability. Continuity was found between assessments of the relationship in the first months and those made 4 years later, and most strikingly between these later assessments and the first-born child's positive behavior toward the baby sibling 4 years earlier during the first weeks after the birth (Stillwell & Dunn, 1985).

So, to summarize the short-term and longer terms effects on a first child of the birth of a sibling: Age-related factors were of relatively little importance across the age range of 17 to 43 months in accounting for the differential responses observed following the birth of a sibling. Rather, a constellation of non-age-related factors such as the child's temperament, the parent–child relationship prior to the event, and the nature of the communication between mother and child about the event determined the short- and long-term impact on the children of this major change in social and emotional lives. However, the significance of the changes in communication between mother and child about the social world may well have been age-related, a point that we take up in the following section.

IMPLICATIONS FOR THE STUDY
OF CHANGES IN CHILDREN'S SOCIAL LIVES

What are the implications of these findings for a general inquiry into the significance of changes in children's social lives for the development of their social understanding? We suggest that there are a number of points highlighted by the data that should be considered.

First, the marked changes in the children's behavior and relationships were precipitated by the birth of the sibling, but their form and developmental significance depended on individual differences in the children and in their family relationships before the birth. Clinical studies of the effects on children of other life events such as hospitalization and divorce echo this finding (Hetherington, 1986; Rutter, 1983): (a) temperamental differences affect children's immediate response; (b) previous experiences of related events and the quality of family relationships account for differences in whether there are long-term links between early childhood, experiences of such events, and problems in adolescence and early adulthood. Thus, analyses of "average" or "typical" responses are probably not useful.

Second, a sharp change in the children's world led to rapid effects, including developmental advance for some. Why? What processes could link the environmental event to the new maturity in the children's behavior? The changes in the children's social lives that accompanied the birth could well have contributed to these developmental advances:

It is certainly plausible that a shift in the routine of the child, and in what is expected of him by the caregiver, might lead the child to discover for himself that he can do certain things, and that such achievement is enjoyable, whether it be mastering a difficult task like putting on a shoe, or conquering his fear of going to the toilet alone, or discovering that he has resources for play within himself.

There are three different possibilities here that need to be distinguished. The first is that with a different caregiver different requirements are placed on the child: the second is that the new caregiver has different expectations and beliefs concerning the child. He or she attributes intentions and interprets the child's behavior differently than the mother does. With both these interpretations, the explanation for the changed behaviour lies in the molding by the adults of the child's actions. A third possibility is to view the altered behavior as essentially a response by the child to an altered environment: if you greatly change the world of a child (or indeed of an adult), the chances are that you will not only draw his attention to new possibilities in that world, but also to new possibilities in himself as an actor in that world. It may be that with a change in caregiver both the first two effects are operative. With either kind of change in the caregiver, though, the consequence is likely to be a change in the child's feelings, beliefs, and ways of acting in the world. (Dunn & Kendrick, 1982, p. 56)

Similar processes could mediate the effects on children of other social life changes such as starting school, or changing from junior to high school. Naturalistic, fine-grained analyses are needed if we are to understand the processes by which social interaction may influence the impact of such experiences.

Third, in any attempt to understand the developmental changes that followed the sibling birth, the emotional impact of the events should be carefully considered. Research on child development is, in fact, increasingly demonstrating the importance of affective factors, especially in the area of social cognitions (Dunn, 1988). Although the quality of the affective relationship between parent and child is clearly of general developmental importance, the nature of the specific affect that accompanies a particular communication seems also to be of particular importance in relation to the kind of developmental outcome. The work of Radke-Yarrow and her colleagues on the development of prosocial and altruistic behavior demonstrates this particularly clearly (Radke-Yarrow, Zahn-Waxler, & Chapman, 1983). It seems very likely that this point about the importance of affect and the need for a fine-grained analysis of the interaction between affect and communication holds equally well for research on adolescents' and adults' experiences of events. Yet it is rarely emphasized in adult research on the consequences of life events that both cognitive and affective components are involved in such experiences.

Fourth, changes in family relationships accompanied the changes in the children's behavior. It is argued elsewhere that it may be very misleading to regard "stressful life events" as single short-term events (Dunn, 1985). It may well be that what links the initial environmental change with long-term behavioral, affective, or cognitive changes in development is a more enduring change in family interaction. Many stressful changes in children's lives, such as parental separation or divorce, are likely to involve marked and sustained changes in the interaction between parent and child (see

Hetherington, Cox, & Cox, 1982). Studies of attempted suicide have also shown that the link between early loss of parent and suicidal ideation is through the long-term consequences of the loss for family organization (Adam, 1982). Even in Hinde's experiments on the effects on rhesus monkeys of separation from the mother, every independent variable that affected infant rhesus monkey depression also affected mother–infant interaction (Hinde & McGinnis, 1977).

Fifth, there were changes in conversations about the social world; such discussion was linked over time to the quality of the relationshp that developed between the siblings. This was a particularly striking finding, given how young the children were. It raises three points concerning the mechanisms by which this event may influence children's social awareness. The first point concerns the children's reflection on their social world. We would not want to draw a simple cause–effect inference from the association, because families in which mothers discuss feelings and intentions of others could well differ in many other ways from families in which mothers did not discuss the social world in this way. In fact, the analyses of Dunn and colleagues showed that the families did indeed differ in the nature of maternal discussion of people, motives, and intentions. However, one implication that must be considered is that children as young as 2 years old are interested in and discuss their social world, and may refer to the feelings and intentions of others. In addition, events that precipitate or foster such discussion may have a developmental significance previously not considered with such children. This point is considered further, in the discussion on normative changes of the second year.

The second point is that it should be remembered that children of around 2 years are just at the stage of developing a sense of self. They could, therefore, be regarded as at a "stage of proximal development" for self-hood (Vygotsky, 1978). What this means is that events that precipitate discussion of issues of relevance to the child's developing notions of self are of particular salience to the child and may have a special importance for development in that domain. This point of potential match/mismatch between social change and developmental status has also been made in regard to parental separation, divorce, and remarriage. Hetherington and colleagues, (Hetherington, Cox, & Cox, 1985) for example, discussed the significance of interactions between the child's pubertal status and changes in the status of the family, and in this volume, Parke considered interactions between developmental status and life events more generally.

Third, it seems plausible that changes in communication about the self and others are a particularly important feature of social life changes at other phases of the life span, adolescence for instance. Given what is known of the significance of attributional style in later childhood, adolescence, and adulthood for individuals' mental health (Seligman, this volume), it appears that research into the links between changes in styles of communication about self and other may well be an important area for future research in these stages of the life span.

DEVELOPMENTS IN SOCIAL UNDERSTANDING IN THE "TRANSITION FROM INFANCY TO CHILDHOOD"

We have argued, from a consideration of one particular life event, that changes in social relationships, in discourse about the social world, and in emotional experiences with other family members following life events may be importantly related to developmental change in children, and have suggested that these principles may be equally important in individuals' experiences of life events later in life. It is also useful to consider these principles in thinking about normal developmental changes. We take as an illustrative case, the development of social understanding in the second and third year of life, a period sometimes referred to as the *transition from infancy to childhood*. It is not a sharp transition in the sense of the changes in experience or development that accompany a sibling birth, yet it is a period in which children change rapidly from month to month in their ability to "read" the feelings and goals of other family members, and in their understanding of the social rules and roles of the family. These changes have been beautifully documented in the work of Radke-Yarrow and her colleagues (Radke-Yarrow et al., 1983) on the development of sensitivity to others' emotions during the second year. In a longitudinal study by Dunn (1988) these changes in understanding, and the changes in family relationships that accompany them have been examined; the findings are clearly relevant to the argument just presented.

First, concerning the relation of emotional experience and cognitive change, the children showed early in their second year remarkably sophisticated understanding of how to annoy, provoke, and comfort other family members — behavior that reflects some awareness of the feelings and goals of the other (Dunn & Munn, 1985). This advanced behavior was shown under the urgent emotional pressure of competition and conflict with sibling or mother. The point at issue, that children use their intelligence on what matters to them, was shown, too, in analyses from observations of the children in their third year, which compared the reasoning offered by the children at 36 months in disputes with thier mothers over different issues (Dunn & Munn, in press). The children marshalled their most mature reasoning in the context of disputes about those issues over which, at 18 and 24 months, they had shown most distress and anger. The investigators argued that in such affectively loaded situations heightened attention, vigilance, and memory effects may all contribute to the learning that occurs, and to the way in which past experience is brought to bear on current functioning (see also Maccoby & Martin, 1983).

Second, consider the issue of verbal discussion and communication over the feelings and intentions of others, concerning the social rules of the family over what is acceptable and what is not. During the second and third year, as has been noted, there is very rapid development in these aspects of social understanding. The longitudinal study of Dunn and colleagues showed that these children were growing up bathed in a continual stream of family discourse on such matters, discourse in which the children were involved from the earliest stage (taking part with head-shaking, nodding, and gesturing even before they were verbal). The frequency with which mothers and siblings engaged the children in such discourse increased over the second year, indicating their increasing expectation for what the children could understand. Not only does it appear likely on common-sense grounds that such explicit articulation of social issues will aid children's developing social understanding, but also, the analyses of individual differences showed correlations over time between both maternal and sibling discussion of feelings and rules, and measures of behavior that reflected relatively sophisticated social understanding by the children (Dunn & Munn, 1986, in press).

People are social creatures, as children, as adolescents, as adults. The findings we have described demonstrate that even young children show particularly advanced behavior on social matters that directly concern them in their family lives. Although growth in this domain may be slow during the second year when compared to the rather abrupt change heralded by the arrival of a sibling, the child's increasing participation in family discourse and the emotional tension created between mother, child, and in some cases a sibling, by the child's growing autonomy and increasing socialization pressure all contribute to the development in understanding of the social world. The arrival of a sibling during this period adds another component to this growing complex of affective and cognitive transactions between the child and his social world.

SUMMARY

The studies we have described of an abrupt, non-age-related change in the social world of young children, and of the more gradual normative developmental changes in social understanding, of the second and third years, highlight several points concerning research on life events and child development.

1. The role of life events in developmental change, whether positive or negative, cannot be usefully addressed without consideration of individual differences. This point is likely to be equally relevant for research on adulthood; strategies that conflate the "weightings" of life events across individuals (as is done in life events scales) are useful only for rather limited questions concerning the average stressfulness of the occurrence.

2. Such changes involve both affective and cognitive experiences; the interconnection between these two is probably deeply significant in the link with developmental change. Although childhood studies have tended to emphasize the latter, studies during adulthood have focused on the former. Some balance needs to be achieved in research at both points of the developmental spectrum.

3. Life events and other changes in the environment that are non-age-related are mediated in part through alterations in family relationships and in discourse about the self, others, and the social world. In trying to understanding how non-normative life events affect development, we must examine the study of changes in relationshpis and in discourse. In studies of the effects of life events on adult development, social support is a variable that is often included and shown to be of importance to the effects of the event. Childhood studies indicate the need for a fine-grained analysis of this variable in terms of social relationships and their mediating role in the impact of life events on development.

4. The preceding point raises an issue of major significance in developmental psychology, concerning the manner in which environmental and other non-age-related influences affect the development of individuals. Developmental behavioral geneticists have drawn our attention to a striking finding: Siblings, individuals who are brought up within the same family who share 50% of their segregating genes, nevertheless differ from one another almost as much as unrelated individuals brought up in separate families (Rowe & Plomin, 1981; Scarr & Grajek, 1982). This research shows that what resemblance there is between siblings is attributable to heredity rather than to the shared family environment. Indeed it is nonshared environmental influence that accounts for the variation between siblings that is attributable to environmental influence (Plomin & Daniels, 1987). Put another way, the research shows that it is differences in experiences within families, rather than between families that contribute in a major way to the development of individual differences. The implication for the preceding point, concerning the mediating role of family relationships in the effects of life events on individuals is this: The same events, such as divorce of parents or death of a family member, are likely to affect different children within the family very differently. This new emphasis in developmental psychology, a focus on within-family rather than between-family differences in experience, has direct importance for our understanding of

the impact on children's development of changes in their social world. Family systems perspectives have underscored the complexity of simultaneous and reciprocal interactions between family members, not just dyads and triads but all members (see, e.g., Hetherington, 1986; Parke, this volume). A life-span approach adds an additional dynamic perspective. It is not just the children in a family who are experiencing change and development but also their parents. Their parents may be experiencing changes in thier own lives as a consequence of their children's development, alterations in relationships with other family members, or in their own life circumstances (see, e.g., Hetherington, 1986; Rossi, 1980). Chapters in this volume by Parke and by Caspi and Elder describe research strategies and findings dealing with the interlocking developmental trajectories of individual family members.

5. The definition of *life event* and its usefulness as a variable of developmental transition requires further examination. Adult developmentalists have not, for example, given this construct either the theoretical or empirical attention that has been given to age-type transitions in early childhood. More attention is needed to the dimensions and properties of events if we are to clarify their developmental role in early childhood (as, e.g., recommended by Brim and Ryff, 1980, for studies of adult personality development or by Danish, Smyer, and Nowak, 1980 for cultural influences). We have attempted in this chapter to show how a fine-grained analysis of an event such as birth of a sibling allows an examination of its role in development of a specific age-related phenomena, social understanding.

6. Careful research that is sensitive to the importance of a naturalistic approach is needed on development in early childhood; we need to attend to particular characteristics of developmental influences — age-relatedness is only one of several — and to attempt to construct the early developmental trajectory of individuals on the basis of interactions — or transactions — between these multiple and multiply based influences. Our conceptions of transitions need to be broadened, and life-span research using a life events model provides one means of doing so.

REFERENCES

Adam, K. S. (1982). Loss, suicide and attachment. In C. Murray-Parkes & J. Stevenson-Hinde (Eds.), *The place of attachment in human behavior* (pp. 987-210). New York: Basic Books.

Brim, O. G., Jr., & Ryff, C. D. (1980). On the properties of life events. In P. Baltes & O. Brim, Jr. (Eds.), *Life-span development and behavior* (Vol. 3, pp. 368–388). New York: Academic Press.

Callahan, E. J., & McCluskey, K. A. (Eds.). (1983). *Life-span developmental psychology: Nonnormative life events.* New York: Academic Press.

Coddington, R. D. (1972a). The significance of life events as etiologic factors in the diseases of children: (I) A survey of professional workers. *Journal of Psychosomatic research, 16,* 7–18.

Coddington, R. D. (1972b). The significance of life events as etiologic factors in the diseases of children: (II) Study of a normal population. *Journal of Psychosomatic Research, 16,* 203–213.

Danish, S. J., Smyer, M. A., & Nowak, C. A. (1980). Developmental intervention: Enhancing life-event processes. In P. B. Baltes & O. G. Brim, Jr. (Eds.), *Life-span behavior and development* (Vol. 3, pp. 340–357). New York: Academic Press.

Dohrenwend, B. S., & Dohrenwend, B. P. (Eds.). (1974). *Stressful life events: Their nature and effects.* New York: Wiley.

Dunn, J. (1985). Stress, development and family interaction. In M. Rutter, C. Izard, & P. Read (Eds.), *Depression in childhood* (pp. 479–489). New York: Plenum Press.

Dunn, J. (1987, January). *Normative life events as a risk factor in childhood.* Paper presented at the Workshop on Risk and Protective Factors in Psychosocial Development, Minster Lovell.

Dunn, J. (1988). *The beginnings of social understanding.* Cambridge: Harvard University Press.

Dunn, J., & Kendrick, C. (1982). *Siblings: Love, envy, and understanding.* Cambridge: Harvard University Press.

Dunn, J., & Munn, P. (1985). Becoming a family member: Family conflict and the development of social understanding. *Child Development, 56,* 764–774.

Dunn, J., & Munn, P. (1986). Sibling quarrels and maternal intervention: Individual differences in understanding and aggression. *Journal of Child Psychology and Psychiatry, 27,* 583–595.

Dunn, J., & Munn, P. (in press). The development of justification in disputes. *Developmental psychology.*

Elizur, J. (1986). The stress of school entry: Parental coping behaviors and children's adjustment to school. *Journal of Child Psychology and Psychiatry, 27,* 625–636.

Field, T. (1984). Separation stress of young children transferring to new schools. *Developmental Psychology, 20,* 786–792.

Herzog, J. G. (1984). *Life events as indices of family stress: Relationships with children's current levels of competence.* Ph.D. dissertation, University of Minnesota.

Hetherington, E. M. (1986). Family relations six years after divorce. In K. Paysley & M. Ihinger-Tollman (Eds.), *Remarriage and stepparenting today: Research and theory.* New York: Guilford Press.

Hetherington, E. M., Cox, M., & Cox, R. (1982). Effects of divorce on parents and children. In M. Lamb (Ed.), *Nontraditional families.* Hillsdale, NJ: Lawrence Erlbaum Associates.

Hetherington, E. M., Cox, M., & Cox, R. (1985). Long-Term Effects of Divorce and Remarriage on the Adjustment of Children. *Journal of the American Academy of Child Psychiatry, 24*(5), 518–530.

Higgins, E. T., & Parsons, J. E. (1983). Social cognition and the social life of the child: Stages as subcultures. In E. Tory Higgins, D. N. Ruble, & W. W. Hartup (Eds.), *Social cognition and social development* (pp. 15–61). Cambridge: Cambridge University Press.

Hinde, R. A., & McGinnis, L. (1977). Some factors influencing the effects of temporary mother-infant separation: Some experiments with rhesus monkeys. *Psychological Medicine, 7,* 197–212.

Hoffman, L. (1979). Maternal employment: 1979. *American Psychologist, 10,* 859–865.

Hughes, M., Pinkerton, G., & Plewis, I. (1979). Children's difficulties on starting infant school. *Journal of Child Psychology and Psychiatry, 20,* 187–196.

Hurme, H. (1978). *Life event research: Findings and methodological problems.* Reports from the department of psychology, University of Jyvaskyla, Finland.

Hurme, H. (1983, July). *Children's life events: Some implications for a life-span view on development.* Paper presented at Meetings of the International Society for the Study of Behavioural Development, Munich.

Maccoby, E. M., & Martin, J. A. (1983). Socialization in the context of the family: parent–child interaction. In E. M. Hetherington (Ed.), *Socialization, personality and social development: Vol. 4. Handbook of Child Psychology* (pp. 1–101). New York: Wiley.

Paykel, E. S. (1978). Contribution of life events to causation of psychiatric illness. *Psychological Medicine, 8,* 245–254.

Plomin, R., & Daniels, D. (1987). Why are two children in the same family so different from one another? *The Behavioural and Brain Sciences, 10* 1–16.

Radke-Yarrow, M., Zahn-Waxler, C., & Chapman, M. (1983). Children's prosocial dispositions and behavior. In P. H. Mussen (Series Ed.) *Handbook of Child Psychology,* Volume IV, E. Mavis Hetherington (Ed.), *Socialization, Personality, and Social Development,* New York: Wiley, pp. 469–546.

Rossi, A. S. (1980). Aging and parenthood in the middle years. In P. B. Baltes & O. G. Brim, Jr. (Ed.), *Life-span development and behaviour* (Vol. 3, pp. 357–367). New York: Academic Press.

Rowe, D. C., & Plomin, R. (1981). The importance on non-shared (E1) environmental influence in behavioural development. *Developmental Psychology, 17,* 517–531.

Rutter, M. (1983). Stress, coping and development: Some issues, and some questions. In N. Garmezy & M. Rutter (Eds.), *Stress, coping and development in children* (pp. 1–41). New York: McGraw-Hill.

Scarr, S., & Grajek, S. (1982). Similarities and differences between siblings. In M. E. Lamb & B. Sutton-Smith (Eds.), *Sibling relationships: Their nature and development throughout the lifespan* (pp. 357–381). Hillsdale, NJ: Lawrence Erlbaum Associates.

Sherrod, L. R. (1983, July). *Child development and life events.* Paper presented at the meetings of the International Society for the Study of Behavioural Development, Munich, Germany.

Sherrod, L. R., & Brim, O. G., Jr. (1986). Epilogue: Retrospective and Prospective Views of Life-Course Research on Human Development. In A. B. Sorensen, F. E. Weinert, L. R. Sherrod (Eds.), *Human development and the life course: Multidisciplinary perspectives* (pp. 557–580). Hillsdale, NJ: Lawrence Erlbaum Associates.

Stillwell, R., & Dunn, J. (1985). Continuities in sibling relationships: Patterns of aggression and friendliness. *Journal of Child Psychology and Psychiatry, 26*(4), 627–637.

Vygotsky, L. S. (1978). *Mind in society: The development of higher mental processes.* Cambridge, MA: Harvard University Press.

Yamamoto, K. (1979). Children's ratings of the stressfulness of experiences. *Developmental Psychology, 15,* 581–582.

Yamamoto, K., & Davis, O. L., Jr. (1982). Views of Japanese and American children concerning stressful experiences. *Journal of Social Psychology, 116,* 163–171.

8 FAMILIES IN LIFE-SPAN PERSPECTIVE:
A Multilevel Developmental Approach

Ross D. Parke
University of Illinois

ABSTRACT

The implication of a life-span viewpoint for understanding how families cope with normative and nonnormative stressful life transitions are examined. A multiple developmental trajectory perspective is presented, which recognizes the utility of multiple levels of analysis in understanding families. Individual developmental trajectories of both children and adults need to be supplemented by an examination of the developmental pathways followed by larger units within the family including dyads (e.g., parent–child; husband–wife and sib–sib relationships), triads (e.g., parent–child–sib; mother–father–child) and families merit consideration as separate units of analysis. It is argued that these units interact across development to produce diverse effects. Historical context—another aspect of a life span approach—is another necessary ingredient in understanding family adaptation to stressful change. These perspectives are illustrated by an examination of the impact of early and late-timed parenthood.

INTRODUCTION

Since the 1970s there has been a resurgence of interest in how families cope with stressful normative and non-normative life transitions. The goal of this chapter is to explore some of the implications of a life-span perspective for research in this area.

A number of features of a life-span approach are relevant to our understanding of these transitions. First, the focus on normative and non-normative events is readily applicable to these issues and considerable attention has already been devoted to these distinctions (Hetherington,

1984; Hetherington & Baltes, this volume; Hetherington & Camara, 1984; Lerner, this volume). Second, the recognition of the embeddedness of individuals and families in a larger network of social systems has been of value for understanding the ways in which individuals and families use social support resources in adapting to stressful change. This viewpoint is widely accepted by advocates of life-span view (Baltes, 1987; Lerner, 1984; Featherman & Lerner, 1985) as well as theorists of other persuasions (Bronfenbrenner, 1979, Bronfenbrenner & Crouter, 1982; Cochran & Brassard, 1979). An extensive literature illustrates the utility of this viewpoint for explaining adaptation to a wide variety of stressors, including divorce, premature birth of an infant, and illness (Hetherington & Camara, 1984; Parke & Anderson, 1987; Parke & Tinsley, 1982; Rutter, 1983). Another facet of families' reactions to stressful transitions that has received less sustained examination is the role of historical or cohort-related changes. As Elder's (1974) classic work on children's reactions to economic hardship in the Depression era has shown, historical contexts are important to consider in understanding stress-related change and the family's response to these events.

THE MANY FACES OF DEVELOPMENT

Other aspects of the life-span perspective have received less attention but nevertheless are of value for understanding stressful change in families. The goal of this chapter is to explore in detail the developmental implications of a life-span viewpoint for our understanding of stress and coping in families. It is argued that there are multiple developmental trajectories within families. Although individual development of children and adults within families is important in order to understand the influence of stressful change, other aspects of development such as the developmental pathway followed by larger units within the family (e.g., the parent–child dyad or the husband–wife dyad) as well as the family unit itself require examination (Sigel & Parke, 1987). Moreover, it is proposed that the concept of multiple developmental trajectories is critical, because it not only recognizes that individuals, dyads, and families may follow disparate developmental pathways but that it is necessary to acknowledge the interplay among these different trajectories in order to understand the effects of stressful change on families. Following the presentation of this general model of multiple developmental trajectories, the value of the model is illustrated by an examination of the impact of early and later timed achievement of parenthood on individuals and families.

The Developing Individual

In prior analyses of the effects of stressful change on families, the developmental perspective is often the individual as the unit of analysis. The particular form that developmental inquiry assumes is often dictated by the disciplinary background and theoretical orientation of the investigator. Therefore for child developmentalists, the focus often has been restricted to the study of changes in the developmental paths of the individual children as a result of various stressful events (e.g., divorce, maternal employment, residence change). In contrast, for sociologists the focus has been generally on changes in the individual adult as a function of stressful shifts and transitions (e.g., onset of parenthood, retirement, divorce). Although life-span theorists have been influential advocates of recognizing the fact that development continues into adulthood, according to a life-span view, these two developmental perspectives cannot be treated independently. Indeed, the developmental pathways of individual children and individual adults need to be considered jointly in order to appreciate the ways in which changes in childrens' development affect or are altered by shifts in the developmental pathways of adults. Following is an examination of the issue of developing individuals—children and adults—from a life-span perspective, including its utility for elucidating the effects of family change.

Individual Children in Developmental Perspective

The ways in which children's reactions to stressful transitions change as a function of development can be viewed from two perspectives: a developmental status perspective and a cultural agenda perspective. First, childrens' cognitive, social, emotional, and biological capabilities will determine their level and quality of understanding of an event, as well as the type of intra-personal resources and coping strategies available to deal with the stressful change. Second, the culturally controlled social agenda that determines the timing of the childs' entry into various social settings such as the transition to elementary school, or junior high school will, in part, shape both the form of the reaction to the stressor and the nature of the coping strategies.

There is a sizable literature that documents the ways in which children react to stressful change as a function of their developmental status. The findings concerning the effects of divorce on children illustrate. Developmental findings from this literature (Hetherington & Camara, 1984) suggest that although children at all ages respond to stressful change, the form of the reactions varies across age. In the work of Wallerstein and Kelly (1980), preschool-age children tend to react by blaming themselves for their parents' divorce, accompanied by fantasies of parental reconciliation. In contrast, children in elementary school are more sympathetic and understanding, less self-blaming, and are able to express anger toward their parents. Adolescents, in turn, are more able to accurately assign responsibility for the divorce and to more realistically assess the set of issues that led to the dissolution. Moreover, the manner of coping shifts as well. In contrast to younger children, about one third of adolescents cope by removing themselves from the family and spend more time in school, the workplace, or the peer group.

The processes underlying these developmentally changing reactions are only poorly understood. From a developmental status perspective, it is likely that shifts in children's ego development, self-control, and social skills as well as changes in children's cognitive understanding and ability to make correct causal attributions for social changes will all contribute to the changing ways in which children of different developmental statuses respond (Dweck & Elliot, 1983; Hetherington, 1984).

Similarly, from a cultural agenda perspective, developmental changes in the organization of children's social networks, particularly their increasing access during adolescence to the school and workplace as sources of social contact and support will determine, in part, the strategies that children utilize to buffer themselves in times of stressful change.

Moreover, these two factors — developmental status and cultural agenda — interact in determining children's reactions to stressful change. Consider the normative transition from elementary to junior high school. A child's attributes, such as temperament, physical appearance, intellectual or athletic abilities may modify the timetable that a child follows. For example, a child of limited academic skill may experience deviations in timing of entry into junior high school or may experience a different classroom climate (e.g., mainstreaming environment) that, in turn, may alter the ways in which the child experiences stressful change events. Although this type of transition is sometimes stressful, the degree of stress is determined, in part, by the types of changes that are taking place in the individual's maturational developmental schedule, particularly the onset of puberty. For example, the degree to which the onset of menarche is associated with the shift from an elementary to a junior high has profound effects on the adjustment of female adolescents (Simmons, Blyth, & McKinney, 1983). It appears that the combination of these two types of changes may have greater impact than either of these shifts alone. Similarly, the imposition of a further stressful transition, such as a non-normative change, (i.e., parental job loss or divorce) may, in turn, yield very different outcomes than if it occurred at another developmental point.

Individual Adults in Developmental Perspective

Not only do children of different ages show varying reactions to stressful change, but adults should be expected to react differently to stress as a function of their development. Although the focus of a life-span perspective largely has been on the elderly, there are changes that occur throughout the course of adult life that merit consideration.

Again, as in the case of children, two perspectives on development are helpful—a developmental status perspective that focuses on changes in social, emotional, physical, and cognitive functioning, as well as a social agenda perspective that focuses on the location of adults along a variety of education, occupational, and social-relational dimensions.

There is a surprising paucity of information concerning normal adult development, especially in the young and middle adulthood years in each of the developmental domains just outlined. In part, this may reflect the assumption that these types of developmental changes are less important in the young and middle adult periods but assume increasing significance during later periods. However, it is clear that developmental status, per se, in terms of cognitive, physical, and social functioning—even in older populations—is not a useful predictor of individual response to transitions, but must be considered in combination with individual adult's position along educational, work, and family trajectories.

Beyond Individual Developmental Trajectories: The Dyad as a Developmental Unit of Analysis

To limit our analysis to individual development, even when both child and adult development are considered, is inadequate. Families are increasingly viewed as composed of sets of interlocking relationships and to understand how families react to change, it is important to recognize the subunits within the family system such as the parent–child, the husband–wife, and the sib–sib relationships (Belsky, 1981; Lerner, 1979; Parke & Tinsley, 1982, 1987).

Parent-Child Dyad.   Mother–child and father–child dyads may follow separate developmental courses that merit examination. These changes are obviously related to the changes that ensue in the individual parent or individual child but are not derivable from a separate examination of either of them. Surprisingly, little is known about the developmental trajectory of dyadic relationships within the family across either childhood or the life course. However, there is substantial documentation that the quality of the relationships between parents and children have a profound impact on children's social and cognitive development (Wachs & Gruen, 1981). More importantly, in the present context, there is substantial evidence that children's reactions to stress are clearly related to the quality of the parent–child relationship (Hetherington, 1984; Rutter, 1983). Moreover, the importance of the parent–child relationship varies across development both as a result of changes in the relationship itself and the extent to which the parent–child relationship is one among other relationships that are available to the individual. For example, in infancy, the relationships that the infant has developed with both mother and father are a better basis for understanding children's responses in a stressful situation than either the mother–infant or father–infant relationship alone. In a study of 1-year-old infants, Main and Weston (1981) identified infants who were securely attached to both parents or to neither parent. They also observed infants who were securely attached to mother and insecurely attached to father and vice versa. Infants who were securely attached to both parents were more responsive to an unfamiliar clown than those who were securely attached to one parent and insecurely attached to the other; the babies who were insecurely attached to both parents were the least sociable with the clown. These results suggest that relationships with both parents are important and underscores the importance of assessing both mother–child and father–child relationships.

How do parent–child relationships shift over time? There is considerable evidence for stability of parent–child relationships over time. A number of studies of infant–parent attachment, for example, have found evidence of considerable stability in the attachment classification from infancy to early elementary school (Sroufe & Fleeson, 1986).

However, stability of parent–child relationships is not inevitable. As Lamb, Thompson, Gardner, Charnov, & Estes (1984) show in their analysis of infant–parent attachment studies, disruptions in family life such as divorce, job loss, and shifts in employment patterns can result in changes in the quality of the infant–parent relationship. For example, some infants show a shift from secure to anxious attachment especially if the level of stress is high; other infants shift toward greater security of attachment over time if the change in family situation is associated with a relief from tension (Thompson, Lamb, & Estes, 1982; Vaughn, Egeland, Waters, & Sroufe, 1979). The findings suggest that the quality of infant–parent attachment relationships are modifiable. As Vaughn et al. (1979) noted, "like any other affectional relationship, infant–mother attachments arise from interaction, they continue to develop even after an affective bond has formed and they are responsive to changes in the behavior of either partners" (p. 975).

Moreover, the importance of the parent–child relationship undergoes change across time and may assume differing degrees of importance at different developmental stages of the child's development. The role of the parent–child relationship as a buffer against stress changes as a consequence of the availability of alternative extra-familial sources of support. During adolescence peer–peer relationships assume increased importance and peer-group ties may serve as an alternative support source in times of stress, such as divorce (Hetherington & Camara, 1984). Similarly, in adulthood, the parent–child relationship changes in a variety of ways as children achieve independence and establish separate households. In times of crisis, such as divorce or the birth of a preterm infant, parents may serve as support figures for their adult children (Hetherington & Camara, 1984; Parke & Anderson, 1987). In older adulthood, the parent–child relationship is likely to undergo further transformations, with the long-standing dependency of the child on the parent reversing itself as parents themselves become dependent on their adult children, especially in times of crisis, such as illness (Hagestad, 1985; Tinsley & Parke, 1984, 1987). Therefore, across development, the relative value and independence of parents and children as sources of support during potentially stressful changes will vary.

Husband–Wife Dyad.   The parent–child relationship is not the only dyad that merits consideration. The quality of the husband–wife relationship is important to consider both in terms of the impact of the relationship on individual's reactions to stressful change and how the nature of the marital relationship changes across development. There is considerable literature that suggests that the quality of the marital relationship is an important determinant of reaction to stressful events (Rutter, 1983). For example, Elder (1974, 1984) has found that the impact of economic hardship varied as a function of the quality of the marital relationship. Dissolution, divorce, and desertion occurred at higher rates in response to hard economic times when marital satisfaction was low.

Less is known concerning the impact of changes in the couple's relationship across the developmental course of marriage on how couples react to stressful events. One might predict that in the early stages of marriage, couples would be more vulnerable to the disruptive impact of stress than at later stages, although an equally persuasive argument could be made for the vulnerability of marriages to the effects of stressful transitions at later stages. For example, a long-standing marriage founded on traditional values may be tested much later when a newly "empty-nested" mother chooses to become employed against her husband's wishes. Similarly, just as there are individual differences in coping style (Lazarus & Folkman, 1984; Moos & Billings, 1982; Moos & Schaefer, 1986), couples may have specific problem-solving or coping strategies that are different than the coping processes of each individual (Krokoff, Gottman, & Roy, 1986). Moreover, these strategies may change across the course of the marital history.

Sib-Sib Dyad.   Another set of familial relationships that merit examination are sibling relations. Sib–sib relationships also vary across development (Dunn & Kendrick, 1982; Lamb & Sutton-Smith, 1982), but until recently little was known about how these relationships serve differentially as buffers to mitigate the impact of stress. In her examination of divorced and stepparent families, Hetherington (1987) has provided an empirical examination of possible effects of stressful marital transitions on sibling relationships:

> Two alternative hypotheses might be offered about siblings experiencing their parents' marital transitions. One would be that siblings will become increasingly rivalrous and hostile as they compete for scarce resources of parental love and attention following their parents divorce and remarriage. . . . An alternative hypotheses would be that siblings in families that have gone through marital transitions will view relationships with adults as unstable, untrustworthy and painful and will turn to each other for sources of solaces, support and alliances. (p. 19)

Some support for both of these viewpoints was found. Siblings in stepfamilies, in contrast to siblings in nondivorced families were viewed as having more difficult sib–sib relationships. The sibling interactions were rated as less positive and more negative by family members. Observations indicated that stepchildren were less warm, more aggressive and rivalrous, and more avoidant than siblings in nondivorced families. Although these findings support the sibling rivalry hypotheses, other findings indicate that children, especially girls in divorced families are warmer, more involved, and less avoidant of their siblings than are children in stepfamilies. These results provide some for support the "sibling as buffer" hypothesis as well. These data illustrate the importance of siblings during times of stressful transition, and indicate the need to consider a variety of dyadic units in understanding stressful change.

Beyond the Dyad: The Triad as a Developmental Unit of Analysis

First, models that limit examination of the effects of interaction patterns to only the father–infant and mother–infant dyads and the direct effects of one individual on another are inadequate for understanding the impact of social interaction patterns in families (Belsky, 1981; Lewis & Feiring, 1981; Parke, Power, & Gottman, 1979; Pedersen, 1980). The full family group must be considered. Second, parents influence their infants indirectly as well as directly. A parent may influence a child through the mediation of another family member's impact (e.g., a father may contribute to the mother's positive affect toward her child by praising her caregiving ability). Another way in which one parent may indirectly influence the child's treatment by other agents is by modifying the infant's behavior. Child behavior patterns that develop as a result of parent–child interaction may in turn affect the child's treatment by other social agents. For example, irritable infant patterns induced by an insensitive and impatient mother may in turn make the infant more difficult for the father to handle and pacify. Thus, patterns developed in interaction with one parent may alter interaction patterns with another caregiver. In larger families, siblings can play a similar mediating role.

Parents have been shown to behave differently when alone with their infant than when interacting with the infant in the presence of the other parent. A sizable body of research has indicated that rates of parent–infant interactive behavior decrease in a triadic in comparison to a dyadic context in both the laboratory (Lamb, 1979; Parke, 1979) and the home (Belsky, 1979; Clarke-Stewart, 1978; Pedersen, Anderson, & Cain, 1980) with infants of varying ages. This difference in quantity of stimulation in a triadic context stems in part from the fact that the infant has two social agents who each provide less input than either would if alone with the infant. Moreover, as Pedersen, Zaslow, Cain, and Anderson (1981) have documented, when the parents are together they have the opportunity to interact with one another, a further condition that generally reduces the levels of focused behavior directed toward the infant.

However, there are significant exceptions (see Schaffer, 1984, for a review). For example, Parke and his colleagues (Parke, Grossman, & Tinsley, 1981; Parke & O'Leary, 1976) have found that certain behaviors increase rather than decrease from dyadic to triadic situations. Specifically, parents expressed more positive affect (smiling) toward their infant and showed a higher level of exploratory behavior in the presence of the spouse. Our hypothesis is that parents verbally stimulate each other by focusing the partner's attention on aspects of the baby's behavior, which in turn stimulates affectionate or exploratory behavior in the partner. It is clear that greater attention should be given to the specification of conditions that are likely to increase as well as decrease parental behavior in the presence of a third person (Parke & Tinsley, 1981; Schaffer, 1984). Overall, these studies indicate that parent–infant interaction cannot be understood by a sole focus on the parent–infant dyad.

Other investigations emphasize the importance of studying the family triad in terms of the impact of the husband–wife relationship on the parent–infant interaction process and the influence of the birth of an at-risk infant on the cohesiveness of the family. In a pioneering investigation, Pedersen (1975) assessed the influence of the husband–wife relationship on the mother–infant interaction in a feeding context. Ratings were made of the quality of the mother–infant relationship in connection with two time-sampling home observations when the infants were 4 weeks old. Of particular interest were the ratings of *feeding competence,* which refers to the appropriateness of the mother in managing feeding. "Mothers rated high are able to pace the feeding well, intersperse feeding and burping without disrupting the baby and seem sensitive to the baby's needs for either stimulation of feeding or brief rest periods during the course of feeding" (Pedersen, 1975, p. 4). When the father was supportive of the mother, she was more competent in feeding the baby.

Further support for the importance of the impact of the marital relationship on parent–infant interaction comes from a recent series of longitudinal studies. In one longitudinal study (Belsky, Gilstrap, & Rovine, 1984), parents and their infants were observed in a family triadic setting at 1, 3, and 9 months after the birth of a first infant. These investigators found that fathers' overall engagement of the infant was reliably and positively related to overall marital engagement at three different times of measurement, whereas maternal engagement was related to the marital relationship only at 1 month of age.

In a second study, mother–infant, father–infant, and husband–wife interaction was observed during three separate naturalistic 1-hour home observations when infants were 1, 3, and 9 months old (Belsky & Volling, 1987). As in the previous study by Belsky and his colleagues, there was a greater degree of relationship between fathering and marital interaction than between mothering and marital interaction. However, this difference is qualified, in part, by the age of the infant, because the patterns are approximately similar at 1 and 3 months, but clearly favoring fathers by 9 months. Further evidence of the differential impact of the quality of the marital relationship on fathers and mothers derives from a further cross-lag analysis. This analysis indicated that marital interaction at 1 month was positively related to father–infant involvement at 3 months. However, the reverse was not true because there was no significant relationship between fathering at 1 month and marital interaction at 3 months. This finding suggests that positive communication between husband and wife about the baby at 1 month promotes stimulating, responsive, and positively affectionate father involvement at 3 months. However, in light of the absence of further evidence that marital communication fosters father involvement at 9 months or maternal involvement at any time, caution needs to be exercised in drawing prematurely firm conclusions about the links between marital and parent–infant relationships.

Other evidence is consistent with these findings. In a recent study of infants 4–8 months old and their parents, Dickie and Matheson (1984) examined the relationship between parental competence and spousal support. Parental competence was based on home observations and involved a variety of components such as emotional consistency, contingent responding, and warmth and pleasure in parenting. Emotional support, a measure of affection, respect, and satisfaction in the husband–wife relationship, and cognitive support, an index or husband–wife agreement in child care, were positively related to maternal competence. Crnic, Greenberg, Ragozin, Robinson, and Basham (1983), in a study of preterm and full-term infants 4 months old, found that support from an intimate (spouse, partner) was strongly and consistently related to a variety of measures of maternal parenting attitudes and behavior. Intimate support was related to satisfaction with parenting, as well as to maternal behavior (a composite index of responsiveness, affection, and gratification from interaction with infant). Moreover, intimate support was related to infants' responsiveness to the parent as well as a cluster of positive infant behaviors during maternal face-to-face interaction. The impact of support on infants was indirect because intimate support modified maternal behavior, which in turn related to infant behavior.

Also, in a cross-cultural study in Japan, Durrett, Otaki, and Richards (1984) found that mothers' perception of emotional support from the father was related to the quality of infant–mother attachment. Specifically, mothers of securely attached infants perceived greater emotional support from the father than mothers of anxiously avoidant infants and anxiously resistant infants. "Even though the husband–wife relationship in Japan likely differs from spousal relationships in America, it is interesting to note that if the mother perceives support from the father, the mother/infant relationships are enhanced" (Durrett et al., 1984, p. 174).

From a life-span perspective, documentation of shifts in the nature of the triads interactions across time would be of interest. For example, do the interaction patterns shift across different stages of life? In infancy, the mother–father alliance may be more important, but may shift at later points when the child can play a more active role. Many questions remain. Are there other important triads such as sibling groups? Are there triadic properties that can be described independently of the interaction patterns of individuals and dyads in various combinations? Are some triads balanced or cohesive? Finally does the triad include all of the family members or are some members excluded? Hetherington (1987), for example, has found that differential treatment of children intensifies aversive sibling relations. Parental alliances with one sibling to the exclusion of another clearly exacerbates family problems. This suggests the need to study larger groupings such as tetrads and to track how these alliances shift across development.

The Family as a Developmental
Unit of Analysis

The consideration of the individual, the dyad, or the triad either alone or in combination is insufficient as a means of assessing the effect of stressful change on families.

Families as units change across development, and respond to change as units. Families develop distinct styles of responding to stressful events and these familial characteristics may change as a result of the developmental history of the family. Reiss (1981) has offered a useful starting point for this analysis by providing a typology of family types. Specifically, Reiss and his colleagues (Reiss, 1981; Reiss & Oliveri, 1980, 1983) have articulated a number of different family paradigms with respect to these issues.

> A paradigm is a set of enduring assumptions about the social world shared by all family members. Although family members may disagree about specific percepts of their social world, their more deeply seated convictions and experiences concerning its safety, equitability and familiarity are shared. Families can be distinguishable from one another by the nature of their paradigms, and three dimensions have been useful in clarifying those differences. Families high on *configuration* believe the social world to be ordered, understandable and through diligent exploration, masterable; families low on this dimension see the world as chaotic, unknown, and dangerous. Families high on *coordination* see the world as treating each member in the same fashion and viewing the family as a single group; families low on the dimension see the world as divided and functioning differently for each member. Finally, families who delay *closure* see the world as novel, exciting, and intriguing; families with early closure see the world as familiar and reminiscent. (Reiss & Oliveri, 1983, p. 81)

These investigators have demonstrated the utility of this level of analysis in a variety of ways. First, the paradigm is useful in predicting the type of pathology or disturbance that an individual might develop in response to a stressful event (Reiss, 1981). For example, families with low configurations and low coordination — families that may be experiencing isolations among family members and pessimism that environmental problems can be solved may, when sufficiently stressed, be at risk for the development of delinquency in children (Reiss, 1981). In contrast, low coordination may also predispose family members to alcoholism if other stresses are sufficiently great (Reiss, 1981). Second, the paradigm may be of value in terms of understanding the type of coping processes in which a family may engage and the targets that are selected to help in terms of stress. For example, Oliveri & Reiss (1981) found that delayed closure was positively associated with the size of the preferred-kin network; families who are open have relationships with a wide range of kin. Coordination was positively related to *shared connection* — the degree to which parents and children in the same family jointly interested in the same subgroupings within the kin network. High configuration families showed low shared connection between the child and his or her parents. It is assumed that families who feel that they can master their social world encourage their children to form their own distinct social ties with their relatives. Similarly, configuration was related positively to the size of the adolescent's network of friends and acquaintances (Reiss, 1981). Finally, coordination was positively related with the degree of inter-connectedness of the kin network (i.e., the extent to which kin know each other).

These family styles would be of varying value for successful adaptation to stress, in part, depending on the type of stressor. For example, in the case of divorce, children might fare best in a high configuration family because they would have strong ties outside the family that could provide support. Similarly, being high on coordination may be beneficial when the stressful event is shared by the family (e.g., an illness, a hurricane) because this would yield support for all family members. On the other hand, low coordination — in which each family member has developed separate social ties may be more beneficial when the stress affects family members differently — as in the case of divorce. Families who maintain similar social ties may suffer due to the necessity of choosing one or other members of the family to support in the crisis.

Other methods of conceptualizing the family as a unit have been suggested; Boss (1980, 1983) has illustrated the utility of the concept of family boundaries. According to this concept, the definition of which members are included in the functional family system has proven useful in determining how families react to stressful changes such as the case of POW father or the alcoholic mother. In the first case, the missing father can be treated as psychologically present but physically absent, which may prolong the family's re-definition of its boundaries excluding the missing member. Alternatively, in the case of the alcoholic mother, the individual is physically present but psychologically absent, which, in turn, produces ambiguity concerning the boundaries of the family unit. The relative utility of various schemes for conceptualizing family units in terms of their value for understanding family reaction to stressful change remains untested.

Many questions remain concerning the utility of this level of analysis. First, little is known yet concerning the ontogenisis of these types of family paradigms. Do these paradigms change over time or are they stable? Although it is clear that there is short-term test–retest reliability, longitudinal studies are necessary to determine the long-term stability or instability of these family paradigms. For example, do these paradigms shift with the developmental levels of the children in the family? Second, these paradigms may not only be useful as a way of characterizing response to stress but can be treated as dependent variables as well. In this case, the shifts along paradigm dimensions would be used as a way of characterizing the reaction to stress.

HISTORICAL CONTEXT: A NEGLECTED
SOURCE OF DEVELOPMENTAL INFLUENCE

A major contribution of the life-span perspective is the reminder that the historical context in which the developmental trajectories of individual dyads and families is important (Elder, 1974; Hareven, 1984). With some notable exceptions (Elder, 1974, 1984), history-graded events have received relatively little attention from researchers of stressful transitions. Viewing stressful transitions from a historical perspective is useful in a number of ways and enhances the understanding of the developmental perspectives previously discussed, by providing a context in which the developmental curves are embedded.

First, the definition of the events that are viewed as stressful may change across historical time. For example, the experience of delivering an infant prematurely in 1936 and in 1986 is a radically different event. Due to the rapid changes and to progress in medical knowledge, the probability of infant survival has increased dramatically. Therefore, the degree of stress associated with this event is likely to be somewhat lessened due to the relative expectation of the viability of a small, sick, preterm infant. At the same time the types of problems shift. In the 1930s or 1950s the child may have died and the ensuing crisis and adaptation focused on the bereavement process. In contrast, the same infant may now survive but the nature of the stress for the family is very different. Extended hospitalization with the accompanying emotional and financial strains followed by long-term physical and mental disability may face families of survivors of the new technology. In this case, both the nature and duration of the stress may change as a result of historical shifts in medical care. For example, Tew, Lawrence, Payne, and Rawnsley (1977) found that parents of surviving spina bifida infants were divorced nine times more often than their age cohort after 5 years, whereas couples whose spina bifida infants were still-born have divorce rates three times as high as their age cohort. These comparisons suggest that the disappointment of bearing and then losing a handicapped child is highly stressful for the couples relationship but that the burden of continuing care has an even more profound impact on the marriage.

The nature of the historical context in which the event occurs may modify the impact of the stressful events as well as the individuals who serve as important support agents (Parke & Tinsley, 1984). A variety of factors need to be considered, including the relative availability of formal support structures, the composition of families, and societal attitudes concerning appropriate sex roles for women and men.

The availability of institutional support systems such as government sponsored agencies or hospital-based programs for families has altered the role of nonfamily agents in assisting with stress-related changes. Second, family household composition has changed since the turn of the century from the extended to nuclear family households. In turn, the availability of extended kin for support may have decreased or its form altered (Tinsley & Parke, 1984). Third, sex-role attitudes have changed, resulting in different family members being affected by change. For example, to the extent that fathers are increasing their level of participation in child care, their availability during times of stressful change is heightened.

To continue our example, fathers of preterm infants increase their involvement in the care of their infants in comparison to fathers of full-term infants, at least in the current era (Yogman, 1982). From a life-span perspective, one might consider whether fathers of earlier cohorts would behave in the same way. Examination of samples in earlier eras would be worthwhile because it is not clear whether these changes would have produced similar shifts in father involvement in another time period. In a different era, characterized by more rigid gender roles for mothers and fathers, the birth of a preterm infant may not necessarily have led to increased paternal involvement. Female members of the family's social network such as friends or relatives (parents or in-laws) may have been called upon to assist the new mother. However, in light of decreased geographical proximity between families and extended kin, family support systems are less often available, which, in turn, increases the likelihood of father involvement. Given that the use of social networks for child care related activity is negatively correlated with the father's involvement in child care (Bloom-Feshbach, 1979), it is suggested that if grandparents and other members of the social network are helping with child care in a situation such as the birth of a preterm infant, there is less impetus and opportunity for the father to be involved in this type of support. In addition, the availability of institution-based programs for training fathers in child-care activities have increased (Parke & Beitel, 1986), which makes it more likely that contemporary fathers will possess the requisite skills to execute these child-related duties. Moreover in our own research, fathers of preterms are more likely to utilize formal support services such as hospital contacts than fathers of full-terms (Parke & Anderson, 1987). Thus, several societal trends converge to create a situation in which fathers are likely to participate more actively in child care than in previous time periods.

TOWARD A PERSPECTIVE OF MULTIPLE DEVELOPMENTAL TRAJECTORIES

Although these levels of analysis—individual, dyadic, triadic, and familial—have been discussed independently, the interplay among these separate developmental trajectories can produce a diverse set of effects on the functioning of the units themselves. In addition, the role that these units play in buffering the impact of stressful change will vary as a result of these interlocking developmental curves. Both the timing and nature of stressful change will be determined by the points at which particular individuals, dyads, triads, or families fall along their respective developmental life courses. Individual families can vary widely in terms of the particular configuration of the life-course trajectories. Consider how the developmental status of the child (individual level) may alter the husband–wife relationship (dyadic level). As Hetherington, Cox, & Cox (1985) found, the stress on the marital relationship in newly remarried parents is greater when the stepdaughter is an adolescent than when the girl is younger. Similarly, the developmental levels of the child and the couple relationship may interact not only in determining the degree to which change is stressful, but in determining the onset of a stressful event. For example, the probability of divorce may increase when children achieve independence and leave home. Individual and dyadic units interact with family levels of analysis. As a couple's relationship changes over time, the associated family paradigm, may, in turn, shift. A marriage that is deteriorating may lead to the family decreasing its level of coordination as the couple begins to view each member separately and not as a single group. The central premise is that the particular configuration of these multiple sets of developmental trajectories need to be considered in order to understand the impact of stressful change on families. Finally, the historical context in which these units are embedded will, in part, determine the nature of the reaction to stressful change.

THE TIMING OF PARENTHOOD: AN APPLICATION OF THE MULTIPLE DEVELOPMENTAL TRAJECTORY PERSPECTIVE

To illustrate the value of adopting this perspective for increasing our understanding of how adults handle potentially stressful change, the timing of the onset of parenthood is examined. In the last 2 decades the timing of parenthood has undergone a set of dramatic shifts: Parenthood is occurring earlier for some and later for others than in prior decades. Two particular patterns can be identified. First, there has been a dramatic increase in the number of adolescent pregnancies during the last 10 years and second there has been a concommitant increase in the number of women postponing childbearing until their 30s and early 40s. What are the implications of these shifts for families and individual family members? And how do these changes become better understood by the application of a life-span perspective?

Early-Timed Parenthood

The most significant aspect of early entry into parenthood is that it is a non-normative event. Achieving parenthood during adolescence can be viewed as an accelerated role transition. What impact does this timing have on individuals, dyads, families and how are these effects modified by historical context?

Individual Level of Analysis

Adolescent childbearing has a variety of implications for the mother, and to a lesser extent the father. The onset of parenthood during adolescence occurs at a time when the individual is not financially, educationally, or emotionally ready to deal with it effectively. In the educational sphere, early childbearing is negatively associated with educational attainment (Card & Wise, 1978). Although females are more severely affected (Card & Wise, 1978), recent evidence indicates that the probability of dropping out of school is higher for males who become fathers while in their teens than for those who delay fathering a child until later (Marsiglio, 1986). Similarly, early onset of parenthood is linked with diminished income and assets as well as poverty, relative to individuals who delay childbearing (Card & Wise, 1978; Furstenberg, Brooks-Gunn, & Morgan, 1987; Presser, 1980); again the effect is particularly severe for women. In turn, this has long-term occupational consequences with early childbearers overrepresented in blue-collar jobs and underrepresented in the professions. For males, early fathering was related to early entry into the labor force but was unrelated to any long-term rate of labor force participation or in the level of income (Card & Wise, 1978). The differences in males and females reflect the fact that females, in most cases, assume greater responsibility than males for rearing their offspring.

In spite of this portrait of the long-term negative impact of early childbearing, there is recent evidence that the developmental pathways of these young parents may be quite diverse and indicative of the non-inevitability of the negative impact of early disruptive life events. Our best evidence of some of the plasticity that individuals show across development comes from the recent follow-up of the effects of teenage childbearing (Furstenberg, Brooks-Gunn, & Morgan, 1987). Teen mothers were followed up 17 years after they gave birth, when they were in their 30s. In terms of education, 30% of the women had received some postsecondary education and 5% had completed college. At the follow-up more than 66% were employed and 66% had not received public assistance in the past 5 years. "In view of the conventional stereotype of the teenage mother, it is surprising to discover that only a minority, albeit a significant one were on welfare and that a quarter had incomes that placed them clearly in the middle class" (Brooks-Gunn & Furstenberg, 1987, p. 14). These findings clearly underscore the importance of viewing early childbearing in a life-span perspective; the diverse life-course trajectories of these women suggests that the individuals can overcome early adversity. The intervening conditions and/or personal characteristics that determine the nature of these developmental outcomes clearly need to be examined.

Infant and Child.   There are a variety of deleterious effects of early childbearing for the offspring. First, there is a greater risk of lower IQ (Broman, 1981; Brooks-Gunn & Furstenberg, 1986), as well as negatively affecting academic achievement and retention in grade (Brooks-Gunn & Furstenberg, 1986; Kinard & Klerman, 1983). Nor are the effects short-lived; they tend to persist throughout the school years (Hoffreth, 1986). The social behavior of children born to teen mothers is modified as well, with several studies indicating that children of teenage parents are at greater risk of social impairment (e.g., under control of anger, feelings of inferiority, fearfulness) and mild behavior disorders (e.g., aggressiveness, rebellious-ness, impulsivity, etc.; Brooks-Gunn & Furstenberg, 1986). Again, not all of the children of teenage mothers suffer these deleterious outcomes. The specification of the factors that permit some children to develop without social or psychological problems under these conditions is an important issue.

Dyadic Level of Analysis

Mother-Father Dyad.   Early childbearing is more likely to be unplanned and to occur outside of marriage and/or a stable relationship. Even if marriage occurs, teenage marriages tend to be highly unstable; separation and/or divorce is two to three times as likely among adolescents than women who are 20 years or older (Baldwin & Cain, 1980). In part, this pattern is due to the fact that the fathers also are often adolescents and as in the case of the teenage mothers often are unprepared financially and emotionally to undertake the responsibilities of parenthood (Parke & Nevelle, 1987; Parke, Power, & Fisher, 1980). However, marriage or cohabitation was closely linked with economic status; women in a stable marriage were more likely to be economically secure and less likely to be on welfare (Furstenberg et al., 1987).

Parent-Child Dyad. What impact do variations in the maternal life course have for child outcomes? The developmental trajectory of teenage mothers' lives are clearly related to the functioning of their children. In a follow-up study, Furstenberg et al. (1987) found a number of features of mothers' lives, such as marital status, welfare status, educational attainment, and the number of children, that were clearly linked with their children's progress. An adolescent with a mother who was unmarried, on welfare, had no school diploma, and had more than three children "increased the likelihood of failure 11 times over a child whose mother did not have these characteristics" (Brooks-Gunn & Furstenberg, 1987, p. 26).

More importantly for our perspective is their finding that the life decisions of mothers are related to their children's development trajectories. Shifts in the mothers' status in a variety of domains—marriage, welfare status, and family size—can be linked to specific effects on the child's behavior. For example, high fertility is a negative predictor of academic performance in preschool but not in adolescence. In contrast, current marital status and educational status influence school performance in adolescence but not in the preschool years. Welfare status influences academic outcomes in both preschool and high school.

Behavior problems show a different pattern. Early, not late welfare expeience influences behavior problems; the early effect is still seen in adolescence because of strong life-course trajectories in behavior problems. In contrast, marital status affects behavior problems in adolescence but not in the preschool period. As Brooks-Gunn and Furstenberg (1987) note:

> Since family support was more available in the early years to young mothers, perhaps not having a father in the household at that time is offset by the presence of other adult relatives (cf. Kellam, Ensminger, & Turner, 1977). By the adolescent years such support is less likely to be forthcoming, so that shared caregiving arrangements are rarer and adolescents in single parent households have fewer adults to which they can turn. (p. 28)

In summary, clear links between the life courses of mother and children are evident and lend support to the argument concerning the utility of tracking the interlocking developmental trajectories of parents and children.

Much less is known about the impact of adolescent fathers on their offspring. In view of the low rates of marriage and high rates of separation and divorce for adolescents, adolescent fathers, in contrast to "on-schedule" fathers have less contact with their offspring. However, it should be noted that contact is not absent, nor is the impact of the contact of father on the young unbeneficial to the children (Brooks-Gunn & Furstenberg, 1987; Furstenberg, 1976). The long-term impact is relatively unexplored.

Family Level of Analysis

The concept of family unit is especially critical in understanding the different developmental pathways followed by adolescent mothers and their offspring in light of the fact that the composition of most family units do not conform to the typical nuclear family constellation. As Hoffreth (1984) has recently demonstrated, families may adopt different forms of organization in response to the onset of adolescent motherhood; Black, one-parent families were more likely to share a household with other extranuclear family members, whereas White, one-parent families were more likely to receive maternal support from outside family members. Moreover, the relative stability of the composition of the family unit varies across family types. Slesinger (1980), in a comparison of extended, two- and one-parent families found that the composition changed in 85% of the one-parent families, 70% of the extended families, and 17% of the two-parent families over an 18-month period. This is of particular importance because adolescent mothers are likely to fall into either single or extended family units. In tracking the residential careers of adolescent mothers, Furstenberg (1980) found that 29% of mothers remained in the family of origin, while 24% moved out at the inception of pregnancy in order to marry, 15% established an independent household, and the remaining 11% returned to their family of origin after marriage or divorce. In terms of family boundaries, it is evident that in a large percentage of cases the distinctiveness of the family unit as a separate entity with its own boundaries is less evident when the onset of parenthood is achieved during adolescence.

There is increasing evidence that the nature of the family unit alters the behavior of adolescent mothers and their offspring. Very often, the maternal grandmother assumes an active caregiving role along with the mother. This type of family constellation has been found to be a protective buffer for the developing child; as Kellam et al. (1977) have shown, children reared in a mother/grandmother, mother/aunt household develop more adequate achievement and social adjustment than children in mother-only or mother-stepfather households.

Similarly, Bolton, MacEachron, Laner, and Gai (1987) found that paternal grandparents can serve a buffering function as well. In this case, the family unit consisted of the adolescent mother and father as well as the father's parents. Levels of inadequate parenting, including child abuse, were lower among adolescent parents who lived in this extended family context.

It is clear that the uniqueness of the family unit needs to be considered in order to understand the unique outcomes for children and adolescents in early-timed parenthood situations. Moreover, as these studies show, the family unit for adolescent parents, in particular, is not a static but a dynamic phenomenon; only by tracking the changing nature of the family context will we be able to understand either the short- or long-term impact of early-timed parenthood.

Historical Effects

Is the experience of achieving parenthood during adolescence different in earlier historical periods than the present? First, as rates of adolescent childbearing rise and the event comes less non-normative or deviant, the social stigma associated with the event may decrease. Second, in combination with increased recognition that adolescent fathers have a legitimate and potentially beneficial role to play, the opportunity for adolescent fathers to participate has probably expanded. Third, the increased availability of social support systems such as special schools, social welfare, intervention programs, and daycare make it somewhat easier for adolescent parents to simultaneously balance educational and occupational demands with parenting demands. It is apparent that the experience of adolescent parenthood is likely to vary across historical periods.

Late-Timed Parenthood

A variety of contrasts exist between becoming a parent in adolescence and initiating parenthood 15 to 20 years later. In contrast to adolescent childbearing, when childbearing is delayed, considerable progress in occupational and educational spheres has potentially already taken place. Education is generally completed and career development is well underway for both males and females.

Individual Level of Analysis

There is clear evidence that the risk of chromosomal abnormality of the infant increases with the mother's age, as well as increased risk of late miscarriage (Baldwin & Nord, 1984). On the male side, there is male infertility which may decrease with age (Anderson, 1975) and some evidence, but not all, suggests that paternal age may be more important than maternal age in some forms of Downs Syndrome (Daniels & Weingarten, 1979).

The relationships between the delayed onset of parenthood and education and career patterns have recently been examined. First, there is a strong association between education level and delayed childbearing and this is particularly true among Japanese and Chinese Americans — groups that place high value on education attainment (Bloom & Trussell, 1984; Taffel, 1984). Second, career and work patterns differ between individuals who began parenthood in their 20s or delayed parenthood until their 30s (Daniels & Weingarten, 1982). These investigators distinguished two patterns of work outside the home and parenting: a simultaneous pattern in which work outside the home and parenting co-exist in the parents' lives and in sequential pattern in which work outside the home and parenthood follow are another. Career and work patterns differed, with the early-timed mothers more likely to follow a sequential pattern, in which career/work involvement was delayed and followed after parenthood was well-established. In contrast, late-timed mothers were more likely to follow a simultaneous pattern in which work outside the home and parenthood coexist in the parent's lives.

What are the consequences of delayed childbearing for father involvement? Again, as for mothers, both early and late timing have advances and drawbacks for fathers. Men who have their children early have more energy for certain types of activities that are central to the father role, such as physical play (Parke & Tinsley, 1981). Similarly, the economic strain that occurs early is offset by avoiding financial problems in retirement due to the fact that children are grown up and independent earlier. In turn, early fathering generally means beginning grandfathering at a younger age, which in turn permits the early-timed father to be a more active grandparent. (For a discussion of these issues, see Tinsley & Parke, 1984, 1987.) In spite of these advantages, when men become fathers early, there are two main disadvantages: financial strain and time strain, due to the competing demands imposed by trying simultaneously to establish a career as well as a family. In contrast, the late-timed father avoids these problems. The late-timed father's career is more settled, permitting more flexibility and freedom in balancing the demands of work and family. Second, patterns of preparental collaboration between the parents may already be established and persist into the parenthood period. In their study, Daniels and Weingarten (1982) found early-timed fathers are less involved in the daily care of a preschool child. According to Daniels and Weingarten, three times as many late-timed fathers, in contrast to their early-timed counterparts, had regular responsibility for some part of the daily care of a preschool child. Possibly, the increase in paternal responsibility assumed by fathers in late-timed families may account for the more optimal mother–infant interaction patterns observed by Ragozin, Bashman, Crnic, Greenberg, and Robinson (1982).

Other evidence is consistent with the finding of greater father involvement when childbearing is delayed. Bloom-Feshbach (1979) reported that the older a father is at the time of his first child's birth, the more he is practically involved with the caretaking of his infant. However, age of father was not associated with expressive-nurturant aspects of the father–child relationship; possibly infant–father attachment, for example, may not be altered by age of the father. Other research suggests one possible mediator of greater father involvement among older fathers. In a recent short-term longitudinal study, Feldman, Nash, and Aschenbrenner (1983) found that one of the predictors of paternal involvement in infant caregiving was low job salience. Although it is possible that older fathers can afford to invest less in their career and therefore low job salience may be tapping a similar dimension, it is possible that time in career and job salience are independent. Assessment of job salience and its relationship to paternal caregiving in early- and late-timed fathers would help clarify this issue.

Dyadic Level of Analysis

Parent–Child Dyad. The patterns of parent–child interaction are affected by the delay in the onset of childbearing as well. Research (Ragozin et al., 1982) indicates that the quality of interaction between mothers and infants differs as a function of the timing of onset of parenthood. Among first-time mothers there was a positive linear relationship between the amount of caretaking responsibility and satisfaction with parenting and maternal age, and a negative linear relationship for social time away from the infant and maternal age. Moreover, the affect expressed to their infant increased with maternal age as well as their social and cognitive teaching skills – as indexed by their success in eliciting vocal and imitative responses from their infants.

The quality of interaction patterns may differ among early and late-timed fathers as well. MacDonald and Parke (1986), in a survey of 390 families, found a negative relationship between paternal age and the amount of time devoted to physical play activities such as wrestling, tossing, and tickling. In addition to confirming this relationship, Nevelle and Parke (1987) found a positive relationship between parental age and participation in board games, musical instruments, and helping with school-related tasks.

Clearly, the social environment provided for the child is likely to be different as a function of having an early versus late-timed father. Other research (MacDonald, 1987; MacDonald & Parke, 1984; Parke, MacDonald, Beitel, & Bhavnagri, 1988) indicates that there are clear relationships between father physical play and peer competence; children with a physically playful father are rated as more competent in their peer relationships. It would be worthwhile to examine the effects of the shifts in play styles of older fathers on their childrens' social development. Together these findings suggest that the quality of the parent–child relationship changes as a result of delayed parenthood.

Husband–Wife Dyad.   The marital relationship varies with the timing of the onset of parenthood. In one recent study, Walter (1986), in a comparison of couples who began childbearing in their early 20s with couples who delayed childbearing until their early 30s, found that the type of marriage differed. The late-timed couples in comparison to the early-timed couples had more equalitarian relationships with their husbands, in which the men participate in child care and household tasks (Daniels & Weingarten, 1982). "For early timed mothers the children are more important than the spouse in this period of child-rearing. There is very little co-operation between spouses; it is almost as if the marital relationship is put on hold" (Walter, 1986, p. 67). This suggests that the type of husband–wife relationship differs as a function of the timing of childbirth. Moreover the kinds of relationships among generations (parents, children, grandparents) differ as well. To explore this issue we turn to the family level of analysis.

Family Level of Analysis

Cross-generational boundaries and relationships differ as a function of the timing of parenthood. Although there are clear boundaries between parents and children in the late-timed families, some evidence suggests that these boundaries are less clear in the case of the early-timed families. Walter (1986) found that the mother–child unit is often stronger than the husband–wife dyad, which, in turn, places the father in a more isolated role within the family. In contrast, within late-timed families, "the generational boundaries between mother and child are preserved, because late timed mothers are better able to differentiate between meeting their own needs and meeting those of their children" (Walter, 1986, p. 67). In summary, the kinds of alliances among family members may differ as a function of the timing of parenthood.

Moreover, the kinds of relationships that evolve with the family of origin differ as well in early- and late-timed families. Although early-timed parents rely heavily on their parents and in-laws for support and advice, late-timed parents show much clearer family boundaries. Walter (1986) found that not only were late-timed parents obviously more likely to have independent households, but reported less frequent visits to their parents and or in-laws. Instead, late-timed parents relied more heavily on non-kin, such as friends than early-timed parents which, in turn, increased their sense of boundaries and distinctiveness from their family of origin.

Historical Effects

Is the experience of postponed parenthood different in past historical periods? Daniels and Weingarten (1982) provide some suggestive findings. These investigators included women from three generations. The oldest cohort, born in the late 1920s and early 1930s had their children between 1945–1955 when early-timed parenthood was the usual pattern. The women in the late-timed parenthood sample were clearly non-normative. The middle-age cohort was born in the late 1930s and began their parenthood careers in the 1955–1970 period. This was a transition sample that contained parents who were following the older pattern of early parenting as well as parents who were delaying the onset of parenting. The youngest cohort was born in the 1950s and their children were born in the 1970s. Late timing was more common and a longer spread between marriage and childbirth was evident.

There were clear cohort effects evident among the late-timed mothers in terms of their patterns of work activity. There is a clear trend across the three cohorts for mothers to move from a sequential pattern in the 1950s to a simultaneous pattern by the 1970s. In the oldest cohort, twice as many late-timed mothers followed a sequential pattern (8 mothers) rather than a simultaneous pattern (4 mothers); in the middle cohort 7 mothers followed the sequential pattern and 5 mothers adopted the simultaneous pattern; and in the youngest cohort the reverse was true, where 7 followed the simultaneous and 5 followed the sequential pattern.

Although these findings require replication, they underscore how various cohorts manage early- and late-timed decisions. For women in the oldest group in which delayed childbearing was non-normative, the compromise involved acceptance of a sequential strategy in which career was temporarily interrupted. In contrast, for women in the youngest cohort the climate of the 1970s with the more liberal attitudes toward maternal employment and more available support systems (e.g., daycare) led to more of these women pursuing both parenthood and careers simultaneously.

STRESSFUL TRANSITIONS AS POINTS OF INTERVENTION

The study of transitions within a life-span perspective has clear implications for intervention. It is assumed that individuals and families that are in a state of disorganization as a result of the stressful encounter will be more susceptible and receptive to intervention aimed at alleviating the stress. At these junctures, it is assumed that families will be more open to information provided by intervention agents than at times when there is no perceived need for assistance or any necessity for change. To cite an example, consider the timing of intervention for father-directed parenting programs. In our work (Parke, Hymel, Power, & Tinsley, 1980), we have chosen to utilize the early postpartum hospital period as a point of intervention for a number of reasons. First, the realities of parenthood are highlighted by the recent birth of the child which, in turn, would result in a assessment of their own limitations and strengths as a potential parent. Second, it is assumed that motivation may be high at this stage. Third, fathers are likely to be available at this point. However, the implications of our development analysis suggest that interventions need to be developmentally sensitive. Interventions vary in their appropriateness as a function of developmental status of the child, for example. Young children with their limited social cognitive skills will be unlikely to benefit, whereas older children and adults may profit from this strategy. Intervention with the parents may be more useful as an intervention strategy that helps the parents cope, which, in turn, may improve the parent–child relationship—the main buffer for younger children. In contrast, increasing peer-group support may be an effective strategy for helping adolescents cope with stressful events. Similarly, the adult developmental level will determine the type of intervention. For an adolescent mother, provision of educational opportunities, financial support and child-care advice may be more appropriate than for the late-timed, but occupationally stable older parent who in turn may profit more from out-of-home care assistance to help balance the demands of home and work.

Following our levels of analysis scheme, the unit (individual, dyad, family) that is the appropriate target of intervention will vary across the type of stressor. For example, in the case of the transition to parenthood, intervention at the couple level is more successful than intervention with either parent alone (Parke & Beitel, 1986). On the other hand, the family as a unit may be a more appropriate target in the case of an ill family member. In the case of a stress-related residence change that was dictated by the husband's employment shift, the wife and children may be more in need of support than the husband who may be integrated into the workplace. Interventions need to be sensitive to the location and type of stress and the unit that is most likely to be the most appropriate point of entry.

CONCLUSIONS

Implications of a life-span perspective for the ways in which individuals and families react to stressful change have been explored. First, it is argued that development can be viewed from two perspectives: developmental status and cultural agenda; these two aspects of development often interact in determining reactions to stress inducing normative and nonnormative events. Second, it is argued that our concept of development needs to be expanded to include adults as well as children. Third, inclusion of different levels of analysis beyond the individual level in our developmental scheme is necessary. Specifically, it is suggested that dyadic, triadic, tetradic, and familial levels of analysis be added to the developmental scenario in order to trace the ways in which these differing units change across development. Tracing these units in combination across development may provide a productive strategy for understanding the ways in which individuals and families respond to stressful change. Finally, a historical perspective on stressful change suggests that the patterns of adaptation to stressful events of individuals and other units of analysis will vary across historical periods. There are a variety of methodological and conceptual issues that merit attention if the potential of this viewpoint is to be realized. First, the analysis of triadic interactions is still poorly understood but some progress is being made (see Barrett & Hinde, 1987; Parke, Power, & Gottman, 1979) in describing these interaction patterns. Second, more attention to the ways in which relationships shift across time is needed. The ways in which changes in one relationship such as the marital dyad affect changes in the sib–sib or parent–child dyad are only poorly understood.

Through recognition of the importance of these multiple levels of analysis and the ways in which they interact across development, our understanding of the ways in which families manage stressful transitions will be increased.

ACKNOWLEDGMENTS

Preparation of this chapter and the research reported were supported in part by National Institute of Child Health and Human Development Grant HD 05951 and by National Institute of Child Health and Human Development Training Grant No. HD 07205. The comments of Mavis Hetherington, Richard Lerner, and especially the detailed and helpful suggestions of Barbara Tinsley on this chapter are appreciated. Finally, thanks to Kathleen Helms and Terry Sturdyvin for their assistance in the preparation of the manuscript.

REFERENCES

Anderson, B. A. (1975). Male age and fertility: Results from Ireland prior to 1911. *Population Index, 41,* 561–567.
Baldwin, W. H., & Cain, V. (1980). The children of teenage parents. *Family Planning Perspectives, 12,* 34–43.

Baldwin, W. H., & Nord, C. W. (1984). Delayed Childbearing in the United States: Facts and Fictions, *Population Bulletin, 39,* 3–42.

Baltes, P. B. (1987). Theoretical propositions of life-span developmental psychology: On the dynamics between growth and decline. *Developmental Psychology,23,* 611–626.

Barrett, J., & Hinde, R. A. (1987, January). *Triadic interactions: Mother-firstborn-secondborn.* Paper presented at Conference on Family relationships, Cambridge University, England.

Belsky, J. (1979). Mother–father–infant interaction: A natualistic observational study. *Developmental Psychology, 15,* 601–607.

Belsky, J. (1981). Early human experience: A family perspective. *Developmental Psychology, 17,* 3–23.

Belsky, J., Gilstrap, B., & Rovine, M. (1984). The Pennsylvania Infant and Family Development Project, I: Stability and change in mother-infant and father-infant interaction in a family setting at one, three and nine months. *Child Development, 55,* 692–705.

Belsky, J., & Volling, B. L. (1987). Mothering, fathering and marital interaction in the family triad: Exploring family systems processes. In P. Berman & F. Pederson (Eds.), *Men's transitions to parenthood: Longitudinal studies of early family experience* (pp. 37–63). Hillsdale, NJ: Lawrence Erlbaum Associates.

Bloom, D. E., & Trussell, J. (1984). What are the determinants of delayed childbearing and permanent childlessness in the United States? *Demography, 21,* 591–610.

Bloom-Feshbach, J. (1979). *The beginnings of fatherhood.* Unpublished doctoral dissertation, Yale University.

Bolton, F. G., MacEachron, A., Laner, R. H., & Gai, D. S. (1987). The adolescent family and child maltreatment: Perspectives on father, mother and child. Unpublished manuscript, Arizona Department of Economic Security.

Boss, P. G. (1980). Normative family stress: Family boundary changes across the life span. *Family Relations, 42,* 541–549.

Boss, P. G. (1983). The marital relationship: Boundaries and ambiguities. In H. I. McCubbin & C. R. Figley (Eds.), *Stress and the family* (Vol. I, pp. 26–40). New York: Bruner/Mazel.

Broman, S. H. (1981). Long-term development of children born to teenagers. In K. Scott, T. M. Field, & E. Robertson (Eds.), *Teenage parents and their offspring* (pp. 194–217). New York: Grune & Stratton.

Bronfenbrenner, U. (1979). *The ecology of human development.* Cambridge, MA: Harvard University Press.

Bronfenbrenner, U., & Crouter, A. (1982). Work and family through time and space. In S. B. Kamerman & C. D. Hayes (Eds.), *Families that work: Children in a changing world* (pp. 39–83). Washington, DC: National Academy Press.

Brooks-Gunn, J., & Furstenberg, F. F. (1986). The children of adolescent mothers: Physical, academic and psychological outcomes. *Developmental Review, 6,* 224–251.

Brooks-Gunn, J., & Furstenberg, F. F. (1987). Continuity and change in the context of poverty: Adolescent mothers and their children. In J. J. Gallagher & C. Ramey (Eds.), *The malleability of children.* Baltimore: Brookes.

Card, J., & Wise, L. (1978). Teenage mothers and teenage fathers: The impact of early childbearing on the parents' personal and professional lives. *Family Planning Perspectives, 10,* 199–205.

Clarke-Stewart, K. A. (1978). And daddy makes three: The father's impact on mother and young child. *Child Development, 49,* 466–478.

Cochran, M. M., & Brassard, J. A. (1979). Child development and personal social networks. *Child Development, 50,* 601–616.

Crnic, K. A., Greenberg, M. T., Ragozin, A. S., Robinson, N. M., & Basham, R. B. (1983). Effects of stress and social support on mothers and premature and full-term infants. *Child Development, 54,* 209–217.

Daniels, P., & Weingarten, K. K. (1979). A new look at the medical risks in late childbearing. *Women and Health, 4,* 17–18.

Daniels, P., & Weingarten, K. (1982). *Sooner or Later: The timing of parenthood in adult lives.* New York: Norton.

Dickie, J. R., & Matheson, P. (1984, August). *Mother-father-infant: Who needs support?* Paper presented at the meeting of the American Psychological Association, Toronto.

Dunn, J., & Kendrick, C. (1982). *Siblings.* Cambridge, MA: Harvard University Press.

Durrett, M. E., Otaki, M., & Richards, P. (1984). Attachment and the mother's perception of support from the father. *International Journal of Behavioral Development, 7,* 167–176.

Dweck, C., & Elliot, E. (1983). Achievement. In E. M. Hetherington (Ed.), *Handbook of child psychology* (Vol. 4, pp. 643–692). New York: Wiley.

Elder, G. H. (1974). *Children of the great depression.* Chicago: University of Chicago Press.

Elder, G. H. (1984). Families, kin and the life course: A sociological perspective. In R. D. Parke, R. N. Emde, H. P. McAdoo, & G. P. Sackett (Eds.), *Review of child development research in the family* (Vol. 7, pp. 80–136). Chicago: University of Chicago Press.

Featherman, D. L., & Lerner, R. M. (1985). Ontogenesis and sociogenesis: Problematics for theory and research about development and socialization across the life span, *American Sociological Review, 50,* 659–676.

Feldman, S. S., Nash, S. C., & Aschenbrenner, B. G. (1983). Antecendents of fathering. *Child Development, 54,* 1628–1636.

Furstenberg, F. F. (1980). Burdens and benefits. The impact of early childbearing on the family. *Journal of Social Issues, 36,* 64–87.

Furstenberg, F. F. (1976). *Unplanned parenthood: The social consequences of teenage child-bearing.* New York: Free Press.

Furstenberg, F. F., Brooks-Gunn, J., & Morgan, S. P. (1987). *Adolescent mothers in later life.* New York: Cambridge University Press.

Hagestad, G. O. (1985). Continuity and connectedness. In V. L. Bengston & J. F. Robertson (Eds.), *Grandparenthood* (pp. 31–34). Beverly Hills, CA: Sage.

Hareven, T. (1984). Themes in the historical development of the family. In R. D. Parke (Ed.), *Review of Child Development Research: The Family* (Vol. 7, p. 137–178). Chicago: University of Chicago Press.

Hetherington, E. M., Cox, M., & Cox, R. (1985). Long-term effects of divorce and remarriage on the adjustment of children. *Journal of the American Academy of Psychiatry, 24,* 578–530.

Hetherington, E. M. (1984). Stress and coping in children and families. In A. Doyle, D. Gold, & D. S. Noskowitz (Eds.), *Children and families under stress* (pp. 7–33). San Francisco: Jossey-Bass.

Hetherington, E. M. (1987, January). *Parents, children and siblings six years after divorce.* Paper presented at conference on family relationships. Cambridge University, England.

Hetherington, E. M., & Camara, K. (1984). In R. D. Parke (Ed.), *Review of child development research, Vol. 7: The family* (pp. 398–439). Chicago: University of Chicago Press.

Hoffreth, S. (1986). The children of teen childbearers. In S. Hoffreth & C. Hayes (Eds.), *Adolescent pregnancy and childbearing* (Vol. 2, pp. 174–206). Washington, DC: National Academy Press.

Hoffreth, S. L. (1984). Kin networks, race and family structure. *Journal of Marriage and the Family, 46,* 791–806.

Kellam, S., Ensminger, M., & Turner, R. J. (1977). Family structure and the mental health of children. *Archives of General Psychiatry, 34,* 1012–1022.

Kinard, E. M., & Klerman, L. (1983). Effects of early parenthood in cognitive development of children. In E. McAnarney (Ed.), *Premature, adolescent pregnancy and parenthood.* New York: Grune & Stratton.

Krokoff, L. J., Gottman, J. M., & Roy, K. R. (1986). Expanding the range of marital interaction research: marital happiness, occupational status and communication orientation effects. Unpublished manuscript, University of Wisconsin, Madison.

Lamb, M. E. (1979). The effects of social context on dyadic social interaction. In M. E. Lamb, S. T. Suomi, & G. R. Stephenson (Eds.), *Social interaction analysis: Methodological issues* (pp. 253–268). Madison: University of Wisconsin Press.

Lamb, M. E., & Sutton-Smith, B. (1982). *Sibling relationships: Their nature & significance across the lifespan.* Hillsdale, NJ: Lawrence Erlbaum Associates.

Lamb, M. E., Thompson, R. A., Gardner, W., Charnov, E. L., & Estes, D. (1984). Security of infantile attachment: Its study and biological interpretation. *Behavioral and Brain Sciences, 7,* 127–147.

Lazarus, R., & Folkman, S. (1984). *Stress, appraisal and coping.* New York: Springer.

Lerner, R. M. (1979). A dynamic interactional concept of individual and social relationship development. In R. M. Lerner & G. Spanier (Eds.), *Social exchange in developing relationships* (pp. 271–305). New York: Academic Press.

Lerner, R. M. (1984). *On the nature of human plasticity.* New York: Cambridge University Press.

Lewis, M., & Feiring, C. (1981). Direct and indirect interactions in social relationships. In L. P. Lipsitt (Ed.), *Advances in infancy research* (Vol. 1). Norwood, NJ: Ablex.

MacDonald, K. (1987). Parent–child physical play with rejected, neglected and popular boys. *Developmental Psychology, 23,* 705–711.

MacDonald, K., & Parke, R. D. (1984). Bridging the gap: Parent-child play interaction and peer interactive competence. *Child Development, 55,* 1265–1277.

MacDonald, K., & Parke, R. D. (1986). Parent-child physical play: The effects of sex and age of children & parents. *Sex Roles, 7–8,* 367–378.

Main, M., & Weston, D. R. (1981). The quality of the toddler's relationship to mother and to father: Related to conflict behavior and the readiness to establish new relationships. *Child Development, 52,* 932–940.

Marsiglio, W. (1986). Teenage fatherhood. High school accreditation and educational attainment. In A. B. Elster & M. E. Lamb (Eds.), *Adolescent fatherhood* (pp. 67–87). Hillsdale, NJ: Lawrence Erlbaum Associates.

Moos, R. H., & Billings, A. (1982). Conceptualizing and measuring coping resources and processes. In L. Goldberger & S. Breznitz (Eds.), *Handbook of stress: Theoretical and clinical aspects* (pp. 3–28). New York: Macmillan.

Moos, R. H., & Schaefer, J. A. (1986). Life transition and crises: A conceptual overview. In R. H. Moos (Ed.), *Coping with life crises.* New York: Plenum.

Nevelle, B., & Parke, R. D. (1987). *Parental age and parent-child play patterns.* Unpublished manuscript, University of Illinois.

Oliveri, M. E., & Reiss, D. (1981). A theory-based empirical classification of family problem-solving behavior. *Family Process, 20,* 409–418.

Parke, R. D. (1979). Perspectives of father-infant interaction. In J. Osofsky (Ed.), *A handbook of infant development* (pp. 549–590). New York: Wiley.

Parke, R. D., & O'Leary, S.E. (1976). Father–mother–infant interaction in the newborn period: Some findings, some observations and some unresolved issues. In K. Riegel & J. Meacham (Eds.), *The developing individual in a changing world* (Vol. 2, pp. 653–663). The Hague: Mouton.

Parke, R. D., & Anderson, E. (1987). Fathers and their at-risk infants: Conceptual and empirical analyses. In P. Berman & F. Pedersen (Eds.), *Men's transitions to parenthood: Longitudinal studies of early family experience* (pp. 197–215). Hillsdale, NJ: Lawrence Erlbaum Associates.

Parke, R.D., & Beitel, A. (1986). Hospital based interventions for fathers. In M. E. Lamb (Ed.), *Fatherhood: Applied perspectives* (pp. 293–323). New York: Wiley.

Parke, R. D., Grossman, K., & Tinsley, B. R. (1981). Father–mother–infant interaction in the newborn period: A German–American comparison. In T. M. Field, A. M. Sostek, P. Vietze, & P. H. Leiderman (Eds.), *Culture and early interactions* (pp. 95–113). Hillsdale, NJ: Lawrence Erlbaum Associates.

Parke, R. D., Hymel, S., Power, T. G., & Tinsley, B. R. (1980). Fathers and risk: A hospital based model intervention. In D. B. Sawin, R. C. Hawkins, L. O. Walker, & J. H. Penticuff (Eds.), *Psychosocial risks in infant-environment transactions* (pp. 174–189). New York: Bruner/Mazel.

Parke, R. D., MacDonald, K., Beitel, A., & Bhavangri, N. (1988). The interrelationships among families, fathers and peers. In R. Dev Peters (Ed.), *New approaches to family research* (pp. XXX–XXX). New York: Bruner/Mazel.

Parke, R. D., & Nevelle, B. (1987). The role of adolescent male in adolescent pregnancy and childbearing. In S. L. Hoffreth & C. D. Hayes (Eds.), *Adolescent pregnancy and childbearing* (Vol. 2, pp. 145–173). Washington, DC: National Academy Press.

Parke, R. D., Power, T. G., & Fisher, T. (1980). The adolescent father's impact on the mother and child. *Journal of Social Issues, 36,* 88–106.

Parke, R. D., Power, T. G., & Gottman, J. M. (1979). Conceptualization and quantifying influence patterns in the family triad. In M. E. Lamb, S. J. Suomi, & G. R. Stephenson (Eds.), *Social interaction analysis: Methodological issues* (pp. 231–253). Madison: University of Wisconsin Press.

Parke, R. D., & Tinsley, B. R. (1981). The father's role in infancy: Determinants of involvement in caregiving and play. In M. E. Lamb (Ed.), *The role of the father in child development* (2nd ed., pp. 429–457). New York: Wiley.

Parke, R. D., & Tinsley, B. R. (1982). The early environment of the at-risk infant: Expanding the social context. In D. Bricker (Ed.), *Intervention with at-risk and handicapped infants: From research to application* (pp. 153–177). Baltimore: University Park Press.

Parke, R. D., & Tinsley, B. R. (1984). Fatherhood: Historical and contemporary perspectives. In K. McCluskey & H. Reese (Eds.), *Life span development: Historical and generational effects* (pp. 203–248). New York: Academic.

Parke, R. D., & Tinsley, B. J. (1987). Family interaction in infancy. In J. Osofsky (Ed.), *Handbook of infancy* (2nd ed., pp. 579–641). New York: Wiley.

Pedersen, F. A. (1975, September). *Mother, father and infant as an interactive system.* Paper presented at the Annual Convention of the American Psychological Association, Chicago.

Pedersen, F. A. (1980). *The father-infant relationship: Observational studies in the family setting.* New York: Praeger.

Pedersen, F. A., Anderson, B. J., & Cain, R. L., Jr. (1980). Parent-infant and husband-wife interactions observed at age five months. In F. A. Pedersen (Ed.), *The father–infant relationship* (pp. 71–86). New York: Praeger.

Pedersen, F. A, Zaslow, M. J., Cain, R. L., & Anderson, B. J. (1981). Caesarean childbirth: Psychological implications of mothers and fathers. *Infant Mental Health Journal, 2,* 257–263.

Presser, H.(1980). Sally's Corner: coping with unmarried motherhood. *Journal of Social Issues, 36,* 107–129.

Ragozin, A. S., Bashman, R. B., Crnic, K. A., Greenberg, M. T., & Robinson, N. M. (1982). Effects of maternal age on parenting role. *Developmental Psychology, 18,* 627–634.

Reiss, D. (1981). *The family's construction of reality.* Cambridge, MA: Harvard University Press.

Reiss, D., & Oliveri, M. E. (1980). Family paradigm and family coping. A proposal for linking the family's intrinsic adaptive capacities to its response to stress. *Family Relations, 29,* 431–444.

Reiss, D., & Oliveri, M. E. (1983). The family's construction of social reality and its ties to its kin network: An exploration of causal direction. *Journal of Marriage and the Family, 45,* 81–91.

Rutter, M. (1983). Stress, coping and development: Some issues and some questions. In N. Garmezy & M. Rutter (Eds.), *Stress, coping and development in children* (pp. 1–41). New York: McGraw-Hill.

Schaffer, H. R. (1984). *The child's entry into a social world.* New York: Academic Press.

Sigel, I.E., & Parke, R. D. (1987). Structural analysis of parent-child research models. *Journal of Applied Developmental Psychology, 8,* 123–137.

Simmons, R. G., Blyth, D. A., & McKinney, K. L. (1983). The social and psychological effects of puberty on white females. In J. Brooks-Gunn & A. C. Petersen (Eds.), *Girls at puberty.* New York: Plenum.

Slesinger, D. P. (1980). Rapid changes in household composition among low income mothers. *Family Relations, 29,* 221–228.

Sroufe, L. A., & Fleeson, J. (1986). Attachment and the construction of relationships. In W. W. Hartup & Z. Rubin (Eds.), *Relationships and development* (pp. 51–72). Hillsdale, NJ: Lawrence Erlbaum Associates.

Taffel, S. (1984). Characteristics of Asian births, United States, 1980. *Monthly Vital Statistics Report.* DHHS Pub. No. (PHS) 8-1120.

Tew, B. J., Lawrence, K. M., Payne, H., & Rawnsley, K. (1977). Marital stability following the birth of a child with spina bifida. *British Journal of Psychiatry, 131,* 79–82.

Thompson, R. A., Lamb, M. E., & Estes, D. (1982). Stability of infant-mother attachment and its relationship to changing life circumstances in an unselected middle-class sample. *Child Development, 53,* 144–148.

Tinsley, B. J., & Parke, R. D. (1984). The contemporary impact of the extended family on the nuclear family: Grandparents as support and socialization agents. In M. Lewis (Ed.), *Beyond the dyad* (pp. 161–194). New York: Plenum.

Tinsley, B. J., & Parke, R. D. (1987). Grandparents as interactive and social support agents for families with young infants. *International Journal of Aging and Human Development, 25,* 261–279.

Vaughn, B., Egeland, B., Waters, E., & Sroufe, L. A. (1979). Individual differences in infant–mother attachment at 12 and 18 months: Stability and change in families under stress. *Child Development, 50,* 971–975.

Wachs, T. D., & Gruen, G. E. (1981). *Early experience and human development.* New York: Plenum.

Wallerstein, J. S., & Kelly, J. B. (1980). *Surviving the breakup: How children and parents cope with divorce.* New York: Basic Books.

Walter, C. A. (1986). *The timing of motherhood.* Lexington, MA: D.C. Heath.

Yogman, M. W. (1982). Development of the father-infant relationship. In H. Fitzgerald, B. Lester, & M. W. Yogman (Eds.), *Theory and research in behavioral pediatrics* (Vol. 1, pp. 221–279). New York: Plenum.

9 COGNITIVE DEVELOPMENT IN LIFE-SPAN PERSPECTIVE:

From Description of Differences to Explanation of Changes

Marion Perlmutter
University of Michigan

ABSTRACT

The purposes of this chapter are to articulate an agenda for cognitive developmentalists and to consider how well it is being met. It is suggested that cognitive developmentalists should be addressing two major questions: What are the ways that cognition changes with age? *and* What are the causes of this change? *An overview of alternative approaches to the study of cognitive development is presented, and an integrative, three tier model, framed within a multidisciplinary perspective is forwarded. It is argued that research on cognitive development has made considerable progress with respect to describing the ways that cognition changes with age but has failed in explaining the causes of age change. Some conceptual reasons for the paucity of such information are discussed, and recommendations are made for the reconceptualization of research design, adoption of a life span perspective, and reassessment of assumptions.*

INTRODUCTION

Cognition is a psychological construct that refers to all of mental life. It includes perception, memory, intelligence, reasoning, judgment, and decision making. It permits humans to represent and to think about the world, to conceptualize experience, to fantasize beyond experience, to maintain a sense of self, and to communicate with others. It expands individual competence and allows us to solve and to circumvent problems. Memory, for example, keeps track of events that have occurred in different times and distant places. Intellectual skills enable us to reflect upon experiences and to attach meaning and significance to them. As individuals, this ability gives us the power to anticipate and plan for the future, to develop strategies, to hypothesize alternatives, and to evaluate consequences. In addition, we can share our perceptions, thoughts, hunches, and interpretations with other people. As a species, this ability gives us the power to profit from a wide variety of skills and a great diversity of experiences. Cognition, then, is of fundamental importance. It underlies all personal adapation and all societal progress.

But cognitive abilities are not fully formed at birth; nor do they remain entirely stable throughout adulthood. All age-related changes in cognition that occur throughout life are referred to as *cognitive development.* These life-span changes in cognition have been studied extensively by basic and applied researchers, by educators, and by clinicians. Some have focused primarily on the changes that occur during childhood and others on the changes that occur during adulthood. Moreover, different subgroups work from alternative theoretical perspectives. Of even greater significance, however, these different subgroups seem to study separate aspects of cognition; they use different methodologies and collect different types of data.

The purposes of this chapter are to articulate an agenda for cognitive developmentalists and to evaluate how well it is being met. In order to do this, major perspectives on cognitive development are reviewed. A conclusion drawn from this review is that current perspectives are largely complementary, rather than competitive. Moreover, it is suggested that child psychologists studying cognitive development generally have limited themselves to a rather restricted portion of this domain. In particular, they have focused almost entirely on description of age-related differences in cognition, and even with respect to this issue, have adopted a rather narrow conceptualization of cognition and confined their investigations mainly to the use of cognition on rather impoverished tasks. It is argued that there should be both a broader conceptualization of cognition and an invigorated focus on causes of age change.

QUESTIONS TO BE ANSWERED
BY COGNITIVE DEVELOPMENTALISTS

A complete statement about cognitive development needs to address two general questions: What are the ways that cognition changes with age? and What are the causes of this change? Some of the underlying issues inherent in each of these questions are discussed here.

What Are the Ways that Cognition Changes with Age?

Observation and description of age differences in cognition have for many years engaged numerous psychologists. Often, a newborn infant triggers interest in this topic (e.g., Darwin, cited in Appelman, 1970; Piaget, 1971), or sometimes the perception of one's own declining cognitive skills catalyzes relatively detailed consideration of cognitive aging (e.g., Hall, 1922; Skinner, 1983). Although much of this fascination has been informal, there also has been considerable progress in systematic documentation of age changes. Indeed, most progress evident in work on cognitive development is relevant to the first question just listed, that is, to description of cognitive change associated with age.

A number of general statements about age differences in cognition across the life span now can be supported by research (see Birren & Schaie, 1985; Flavell & Markman, 1985). Such research has shown, for example, that cognition generally becomes more strategic with age, especially in child-hood, and more sluggish with age, especially in adulthood. Moreover, for some domains rather detailed knowledge about age differences is available. For example, a great deal is known about age differences in infants' visual scanning (e.g., Salapatek, 1975), children's rehearsal (e.g., Ornstein, 1978), adolescents' reasoning (Niemark, 1975, 1979), and adults' intelligence test performance (Horn, 1982). This information might best be viewed as a catalogue of specific performance characteristics of various age groups, although sometimes the pattern of performance across a variety of tasks are taken as evidence about the nature of underlying cognitive mechanisms (e.g., hypothetical constructs).

Although cognitive developmentalists have produced numerous descriptions of differences in performance across age, for the most part they have not attempted to resolve basic issues about the natue of cognition. Although it has been argued that the developmental perspective eventually should enrich understanding about the basic nature of cognition, at present this promise has not been realized. Rather, most cognitive developmentalists adopt assumptions about cognition that are prescribed by some nondevelopmental perspectives. Although these assumptions rarely come to light in the day to day activity of research, they subtly guide decisions about problems that are addressed and types of data that are collected. Some of these assumptions about the nature of cognition relate to: form, generality within individual across situations (intraindividual generality), and generality between individuals in similar situations (interindividual generality).

1. The *form of cognition* refers to whether cognition is assumed to be elemental or holistic. This assumption determines whether cognition is

susceptible to reductionistic analysis, and thus guides research methodology. Because univariate techniques are inadequate for holistic analyses, more sophisticated multivariate techniques are required for grappling with holistic conceptualizations. Although there has been considerable recent progress in the development of multivariate research methods (Nesselroade & Cattell, in press), weaknesses in both holistic conceptualizations and multivariate techniques still limit progress toward a holistic understanding of cognition.

2. *Intraindividual generality* refers to assumptions about generality within an individual across tasks, that is, to whether cognition conforms to general laws and is context independent or is more idiosyncratic and context specific. This assumption determines whether it is possible to adequately understand cognition separate from the context in which it occurs, and thus guides the kinds of situations that must be sampled in research. Because unnatural situations are inadequate for contextual analyses, nonuniversalists are concerned about the situations in which research is carried out. This issue recently has sparked nonuniversalists to argue for increased sensitivity to the ecological validity of research (e.g., Charlesworth, 1976; Jenkins, 1979). In response, some universalists have expressed concern about movement toward an overly particularistic or idiosyncratic science (e.g., Bower, 1977; Crowder, 1977).

3. *Interindividual generality* refers to assumptions about generality across individuals within tasks, that is, to whether all important aspects of cognition are universal or whether some are unique to individuals, chronological ages, cohorts, cultures, subcultures, and/or historical time periods. This assumption determines whether it is possible to generalize across reference groups, and thus guides the subjects that must be sampled in research. Because age, cohort, culture, subcultural, and historical time-period generalizations cannot be made unless universality is assumed, more restrictive interpretation of research is required by nonuniversalists. In general, cognition is now believed to be somewhat specific to age by virtually all cognitive scientists. However, the degree to which there is cohort, cultural, subcultural, or historical time-period specificity still is not agreed upon.

Researchers studying adult development (e.g., Baltes, 1985; Schaie, 1967) have provided persuasive evidence that there are cohort differences in cognition that limit conclusions about generality across historical time periods, and researchers studying cognition in different cultures (e.g., Cole & Scribner, 1976; Stevenson, this volume) have provided persuasive evidence about the cultural relativity of cognition. Nevertheless, both child and adult developmentalists have been fairly insensitive to the cultural specificity of their findings. Moreover, although most cognitive developmentalists have been somewhat sensitized to the cohort specificity of their findings, child developmentalists in particular virtually ignore this issue.

This oversight is a bit surprising, because the field of child development has a strong history of concern about early socialization, which presumably mediates many cohort effects. Still, the dominant view has been consistent with Piaget (1971), and behavioral geneticists (e.g., Scarr-Salapetek, 1976), who have suggested that early life intelligence is biologically canalized. Even if such canalization buffers children some from socially based influences, cohort differences should not be ignored. For example, it is likely that the cohort differences in intelligence test performance that are observed in adulthood (e.g., Baltes, 1985; Schaie, 1967) are largely attributable to cohort differences in children's educational experiences. In addition, there is some evidence that the introduction of "Sesame Street" has contributed to differences in cognitive performance of recent cohorts of young children (Reese, 1974) and a convincing case can be made that profound cohort differences in thinking may occur as a result of the introduction of computers into classrooms (e.g., Papert, 1980; Pea, 1985; Turkle, 1984).

Several issues about the nature of development, that is, about the nature of change that is associated with age, relate to the: form, direction, rate, and endstate of development. In general, particular assumptions about the nature of cognition are more or less compatible with alternative assumptions about the nature of development. Thus, although empirical data could be used to address these issues, typically they are not.

1. The *form of development* concerns whether age change is best characterized as qualitative or quantitative, for example, whether there are magnanimous changes with age (often referred to as *stages*) in the organization, structure, or basic operating characteristics of the system, or only relatively unprofound changes in its efficiency or contents. A holistic view of cognition is most compatible with a qualitative perspective, while an elemental view is most compatible with a quantitative perspective. In actuality, however, the controversy over whether development produces quantitative or qualitative change probably is unresolvable. It is not always clear what data would support a quantitative or qualitative account. In addition, it is possible to formally (e.g., mathematically) simulate quantitative data with qualitative models, and vice versa (see Anderson, 1976).

2. *Direction of development* concerns whether age change is unidirectional or multidirectional, for example, whether within particular portions of the life span all change is characterized by a single developmental trajectory. Traditionally cognitive developmentalists thought all age change during childhood could be characterized by a growth function and all age-related change during adulthood could be characterized by a decline function. More recently, some cognitive developmentalists (e.g., Baltes,

1985; Birren & Cunningham, 1985; Perlmutter, in press) have argued that growth and decline of different aspects of cognitive functioning occur simultaneously at all portions of the life span.

3. *Rate of development* concerns whether the speed of age-related change is susceptible to manipulation, for example, whether there is plasticity in the rate of change and therefore in the ultimate level of functioning. When considering age-related change in cognition during childhood, questions about plasticity or malleability of rate have focused on the possibility of precocious development, that is, on whether development can or should be speeded up. On the one hand, Americans have been accused of unwisely attempting to speed up the natural clock of growth (e.g, Piaget, 1971). On the other hand, some have argued that the amount of time spent in a state of immaturity is inversely related to the ultimate endstate of development, and therefore should not be shortened (e.g., Bruner,1972; Elkind, 1981). When considering age-related change in cognition during adulthood, questions about malleability of rate have focused on the possibility of delaying and slowing decline associated with old age. There has been at least some empirical evidence suggesting that certain life-style factors can contribute to maintenance of functioning in later life (e.g., Schaie, 1984).

4. The *endstate of development* concerns whether development is movement toward a given endstate or is essentially unconstrained, for example, whether there is an open character to the ultimately developed system. Most theoretical perspectives posit no constraints on the endpoint of cognitive development. This position suggests that the cognitive system may be almost infinitely adaptable. However, Piaget (1983) argued that there is an endstate. In particular, he believed that formal operations is the pinnacle of intelligence. At present, evidence of cognitive abilities that do not asymptote or decline in later life is limited. Moreover, although some investigators have begun to search for evidence of post formal forms of thought (see Common, Richards, & Armon, 1984), thus far they have had only modest success.

What Are the Causes
of Cognitive Change Associated with Age?

Most recent research on cognitive development has been rather negligent about *explanation,* that is, about the causes of cognitive development. Although there was considerable early debate about nature versus nurture, much of this debate was poorly framed and the argument became unproductive. Both nature and nurture proved to be important. It is unfortunate that more recent attention has not been give to the causes of age change. As is discussed later, at least some of the neglect may be related to problems in conceptualization of research designs. It is hoped that articulation of these methodological problems will direct attention to explanatory issues and that the multidisciplinary framework presented in a later section is useful in directing such inquiry.

Explanatory study of the causes of age change will have to consider the contribution and mechanisms involved in biological, psychological, and social factors. It will be important, for example, to know about the inevitability of biological constraints. It also will be important to under-stand the systematicity of social influences. Similarly, it will be necessary to grapple with the personal construction and controllability of psychological factors.

MAJOR APPROACHES TO THE STUDY OF COGNITIVE DEVELOPMENT

At present, most scholars considering cognitive development work only loosely within any particular theoretical perspective. In general, the as-sumptions they hold and the overriding issues they attempt to address are at best vaguely specified. Still, each tends to collect types of data that are similar to others working within that perspective but different in important ways from those working within other perspectives. In addition, most researchers mainly notice and address other work from a similar perspec-tive. It appears, in fact, that scientists within each perspective work on fairly separate portions of the cognitive domain. Perhaps for this reason the field has witnessed relatively few major debates.

In the sections that follow four major approaches to the study of cognitive development are discussed. Two of these, the organismic and mechanistic approaches (see also Overton & Reese, 1973; Reese & Overton, 1970), are not particularly focused on developmental issues, but contrast dramatically on the way they view cognition, and thus ultimately predispose adherents to alternative views of cognitive development. A third approach, contextualism, is not so clearly articulated about the nature of cognition, but is well articulated about the nature of development. The fourth approach, psychometrics, is largely empirically driven and atheoretical.

Examples of research on child and adult cognitive development that come from each approach are listed in Table 9.1, along with a summary of characteristics of the approach. It should be noted that classification of scholars and defining characteristics are not so clear as might seem to be suggested. Often the differences between approaches are ones of emphasis rather than absolutes. Moreover, because each approach is represented by numerous scholars who each hold somewhat unique perspectives and subscribe to different subsets of the identifying characteristics, any classification will be somewhat unsatisfying. Still, because these issues seem to underlie much cross talk, their specification should facilitate productive interchange.

Organismic Approach

As is indicated in Table 9.1, the organismic perspective can be characterized as holistic. Cognition is assumed to have emergent properties, that is, to be greater than the sum of its parts. This view is antithetical to reductionist analysis. Moreover, from the organismic perspective, the important aspects of cognition are the universal characteristics that exist across cognitive domains and across individuals. Context is thought to be relatively important. Differences between individuals are hardly acknowledged, and certainly are not considered of interest.

A number of important contemporary cognitive scientists have held an organismic orientation (e.g., Chomsky, 1986; Kohlberg, 1969; Piaget, 1971; Werner, 1948), and one of them, Piaget, is especially well known for his work on cognitive development (e.g., Piaget, 1971; Piaget & Inhelder,

TABLE 9.1
Summary of Assumptions of Alternative Approaches

Assumptions	Alternative Approaches			
	Organismic	*Mechanistic*	*Contextual*	*Psychometric*
Examples of Research				
CHILD	Piaget	Siegler	Vygotsky	Binet
ADULT	Basseches	Salthouse	Baltes	Horn
Nature of Cognition				
FORM	Holistic	Elemental	Holistic	Elemental
INTRA-	Universal	Universal	Specific	Universal
INDIVIDUAL	for	for		for
GENERALITY	Species	Species		Cultures
INTER-	Universal	Universal	Universal	Specific
INDIVIDUAL	for	for	for	
GENERALITY	Species	Species	Cultures	
Nature of Development				
FORM	Qualitative	Quantitative	Qualitative	Quantitative
DIRECTION	Uni-directional	Uni-directional	Multi-directional	Uni-directional
RATE	Fixed	Plastic	Plastic	Plastic
ENDSTATE	Closed	Open	Open	Open

1969). Piaget carried out detailed observations of infants and children and formulated a well-integrated theory of cognitive development. The goal of his inquiry was the specification of species generalized forms of cognition that could be observed to evolve in phylogeny and ontogeny. Evidence for such forms of cognition was derived from consistencies in cognitive performance that could be discerned across domains at various ages. The cognitive performances that Piaget examined included infants' behaviors while engaged in typical interaction with objects in their world and children's reasoning about an assortment of fairly real problems that Piaget (and his collaborators) posed to them. The categories that Piaget used to classify performance were presumed to reflect underlying structures of thought. The age systemicity that was observed in performance was posited to have resulted from stage like development of logico-mathematical cognitive structures. The infant was thought to enter the world with sensorimotor knowing schemes, and eventually, as an adolescent, to development the hypothetico-deductive structures of thought that enable human adults to engage in formal reasoning.

Piaget's ideas about cognitive development currently receive mixed reviews. On the one hand, a strict interpretation of his ideas has not held up to empirical test. A number of cognitive factors that were not viewed as central to reasoning on the Piagetian tasks were found to affect performance. For example, there have been a number of important demonstrations of the ways that attention (e.g., Gelman, 1969) and memory (e.g., Trabasso, 1975) affect performance. In particular, when attention and memory demands are reduced, much more advanced forms of thought than predicted by Piaget are observed in young children. Moreover, numerous violations of the age-related universality across tasks that was implied by Piaget's theory have been noted (see Flavell, 1982). That is, at a single age, contrary to Piaget's view, children are found to use different levels of reasoning on different tasks. Still, anyone who has queried children of a variety of ages on Piagetian tasks must be impressed with the profound differences in reasoning that seem to correspond at least loosely with age. It appears that there is some important age change at least in the predisposition to think in certain ways. However, these changes are unlikely to be attributable solely to shifts in the logico-mathematical structures that Piaget posited.

Piaget also argued that cognitive development, as defined by qualitative shifts in the structure of thought, culminated in adolescence when the stage of formal operations was achieved. Riegel (1973) was the first to question this view. He suggested that there might be further structural development during adulthood. In particular, he hypothesized that during adulthood there is a shift toward dialectic thinking. A few researchers have pursued this idea (e.g., Arlin, 1975; Basseches, 1985; Commons et al., 1984;

Commons, Richards, & Kuhn, 1982), but documentation of truly unique forms of advanced thinking remain scarce.

In summary, the organismic approach views humans as active constructors of knowledge, but also considers biological constraints central in determining both the nature of cognition and the nature of cognitive development. For organismically oriented theorists, human cognition at all ages functions in the same invariant manner as all other biological activity, that is, with the complementary processes of assimilation and accommodation. The basic units of cognition are assumed to be holistic structures that cannot be reduced to constituent parts. These structures of thought are assumed to change systematically across phylogeny and ontogeny. Thus, humans are assumed to move through biologically specified universal stages of cognitive organizations. Cognitive development is conceived of as an ordered sequence of intrinsically guided qualitative transitions in the level of organization of cognitive structures.

Mechanistic Approach

The mechanistic perspective contrasts most clearly with the organismic perspective in its basic world outlook. As is indicated in Table 9.1, the mechanistic perspective can be characterized as elemental. Cognition is assumed to be reducible to independent contents and processes. Progress toward understanding cognition is assumed to be made through the reductionistic processes of componential analysis and experimental isolation of cognitive elements. The mechanistic approach is similar to the organismic approach in its assumption that the proper focus of study is on generalizations about cognition that occur across individuals and across domains, although increasingly there has been recognition that more specific accounts will be needed for various cognitive domains. Moreover, although analysis occurs at the level of generality across individuals, because the contents of cognition are assumed to reflect individual experience, important individual differences are expected in this aspect of cognition.

During the past several decades, American research on cognition has been dominated by the mechanistic approach. This perspective is well represented by behaviorists and neobehaviorists (e.g., Bandura, 1971; Bijou & Baer, 1961, 1965; Skinner, 1983), as well as by those working within the information-processing perspective (e.g., Atkinson & Shiffrin, 1968; Norman, 1976). These experimentalists have been concerned with group similarities in the processing that underlies cognitive performance. Their goal has been to gain a theoretical understanding of the species genral processing involved in intelligent behavior.

The corpus of data collected by mechanistically oriented experimentalists consists of subjects' performance on controlled experimental tasks that are designed according to precise specifications believed to establish the boundaries of processing skill. Often these tasks involve fairly discrete stimuli and simple responses. They are assumed to tap only a restricted number of cognitive processes. For example, subjects may be asked to recognize individual letters in controlled situations designed to exclude extraneous processing, or to learn lists of semantically impoverished stimulus–response pairs constructed in order to eliminate the application of acquired meaning. Aggregating across subjects, comparisons are made of performance under diverse conditions that are assumed to require slightly different cognitive resources. Although it was earlier assumed that general laws of behavior could be discovered, more recently it has been accepted that relatively domain specific analysis is needed.

In general, neither developmental nor interindividual differences have been of interest. Indeed, interindividual differences typically have been treated as measurement errors. Unfortunately, this practice can be misguided because normative descriptions of performance may not be characteristic of anyone. By averaging performance it is possible to mask potentially interesting subgroups that perform substantially above or below the mean. Moreover, this fallacy can extend to modeling of performance. For example, it is possible to develop a model that predicts average performance, but again, if there are different subgroups whose behavior derives from different processes, such a model may reflect only an epiprocess, and not correspond to any real cognitive function.

Although development does not represent a phenomenon of particular interest within the mechanistic approach, many researchers interested in age changes in children's or adults' cognition have worked fruitfully within this framework. Early research focused on associative and mediated processes (e.g., Kendler, 1963; White, 1965). More recently, research has highlighted three fairly distinct aspects of cognition (see Siegler, 1983). These have been referred to in a number of different ways, for example, as *basic mechanisms* (e.g., hardware), *world knowledge* (e.g., data), and *cognitive strategies* (e.g., software). In general, there has been little if any good evidence that the basic mechanisms of cognition differ across life, although their efficiency probably increases during early life and decreases during late life. More importantly, perhaps, throughout life the cognitive system has been found to retain and profit from past experience. There is a continuous age-related increase in world knowledge. In addition, with age the cognitive system gains the capacity to regulate and strategically control itself in potentially adaptive ways.

Because many of the apparently important age-related changes that are observed in cognition seem to derive from experience, some mechanistically oriented researchers presently consider an expertise metaphor of cognitive development promising (e.g., Brown, 1979; Hoyer, 1984). From this perspective, the child is viewed as a relatively universal novice and the older adult is viewed as a relatively universal expert. Many of the domain specific experientially derived changes in problem solving that occur with the acquisition and subsequent automization of expertise seem to parallel general age-related changes in cognition that are observed across the life span.

In summary, although strictly speaking mechanists view humans as basically reactive and assume that knowledge directly reflects the external environment, contemporary mechanistically oriented researchers view humans as reasonably active in their knowing of the world. The mechanistic approach considers the basic units of cognition to be elemental components that can be conceptually decomposed and experimentally isolated. Through time humans are assumed to experience essentially age-irrelevant and entirely open changes in cognition. Thus, cognitive development is conceived of as a environmentally determined quantitiative change in the cognitive system.

Contextual Approach

The contextual approach is not so clearly articulated on a number of issues relevant to the basic nature of cognition. However, it is reasonably clearly articulated on issues relevant to the nature of development. Although contextualism must be considered holistic, emergent properties are conceived of at the level of interaction between organism and environment (e.g., cognition and context), rather than simply in the nature of cognition per se. Therefore, in a strict interpretation of the contextual position, specification of units of cognition may be inappropriate. Cognitive units can be understood only with respect to context.

At present, satisfying conceptualizations of cognitive context units are not available. Therefore, many contextualists focus mainly on the ecology of the organism and refrain from developing models of cognition (e.g., Barker, 1968; Bronfenbrenner, 1979; Charlesworth, 1976; Gibson, 1979; Lewin, 1954). Others who are primarily interested in cognition, but also sympathetic to the assumptions inherent in the contextual approach, rely upon conceptualizations of cognition that have been developed within the organismic or mechanistic perspectives and pay little more than lip service to context (e.g., Baltes, 1985; Jenkins, 1974). Needless to say, contextualists do not search for or expect across-task generality. Thus, domain-specific investigations are prescribed. Moreover, although generalizations are made across individuals, cultural and historical time differences are recognized, in fact, they are emphasized.

The emphasis on both cultural and historical specifity is tied to the view that development is a reciprocal or bidirectional process in which individuals are molded by the social groups that they themselves help to construct. As the individual changes so too does the society. It is interesting that much of the major work coming from a contextual orientation is developmental, and most of the work on cognitive development that has focused on causes of development has come from the contextual approach. It may be that the contextualists' emphasis on change and on interaction between internal (cognition) and external (context) highlights mechanisms of development. However, it also may be that the focus on interaction between cognition and context is limited by impoverished conceptualizations of both cognition and context. For example, Dannefer (1984) has argued that contextualists fail to give adequate attention to either culturally derived capacities or personally constructed choices. Moreover, he argued that the simple recognition of social factors as important underplays the systematicity, multilevel order, and dynamics inherent in social context.

Perhaps the best representation of contextually oriented work on cognitive development comes from dialectic theorists. One important scholar in this tradition was Vygotsky, a Soviet psychologist who has been recognized for his ideas about early cognitive development. Vygotsky (1978) postulated that primitive mental functions are available early in life, but subsequently, with the development of language, there is social transmission of these higher mental functions. The focus of Vygotsky's work was on the social transmission of higher mental functions. Recently, many American child developmentalists have been attracted to this perspective. For example, there now are a substantial number of studies in which either parent, peer, or sibling influences on young children's cognition have been examined (see Azmitia & Perlmutter, in press; Wertsch, 1985).

The developmental perspective typically referred to as the *life-span perspective* (e.g., Baltes & Willis, 1982) also fits well within the contextual orientation (see Featherman & Lerner, 1985). Although Baltes (1985) proposed very mechanistic-like units of cognition (e.g., mechanics and pragmatics of intelligence), his views about the nature of development are quite compatible with the contextualist approach. In particular, his theoretical statements about the life-span perspective emphasize the multidimensionality and multidirectionality of development, as well as its historical and cultural relevance. In addition, his empirical work on cognition in adulthood has focused on plasticity of performance.

In summary, the contextual approach represents an important departure from the other perspectives, particularly in regard to its focus on inputs to development. An important assumption of the contextual approach is that development is a reciprocal or bidirectional process between organism and context. Moreover, in the contextualist perspective social context is given more emphasis than it is afforded in other approaches. Openness in the system is stressed, and diversity in both the nature of cognition and the trajectories of cognitive development are considered of theoretical interest.

Psychometric Approach

The psychometric approach involves an essentially pragmatic and empirically guided endeavour. When first developed, little attention was paid to theoretical understanding of the constructs that were measured. Of central interest were differences between individuals. Indeed, inherent in this approach, which often is described as a *differential approach*, is the belief that important human characteristics will be discovered by examining diversity within the species. That is, it is assumed that by investigating differences between individuals constructs of importance will be highlighed. This perspective contrasts sharply with the approaches discussed previously. Inherent in the organismic and mechanistic approaches is the belief that important human characteristics are derived from examining group similarities, not individual differences.

Psychometric work relevant to cognition is perhaps best reflected by the intelligence testing tradition. This approach originated in attempts to develop measures of individual differences that would predict school success (Binet & Simon, 1905). Attention generally was focused on educational decision making with little concern for the cognitive functions that contributed to performance. Recently, more theoretically oriented psychometric studies of intelligence have been carried out to determine the major dimensions of cognition (e.g., Cattell, 1963; Guilford, 1967; Horn, 1966, 1982). The corpus of data that is collected in such studies is test performance, which is assumed to constitute a representative sample of the behavior of interest. Factor analysis is the predominant analytic technique used to statistically capture patterns of performance across individuals. This more theoretical psychometric tradition has been fruitful, resulting in descriptions of the structure of intellectual abilities. Fluid abilities (Horn & Cattell, 1967) have been found to improve during childhood and probably decline a bit during late adulthood. Crystallized abilities have been found to increase throughout life, although the rate of increase is reduced substantially in adulthood.

Although these psychometrically derived constructs are interesting, they do not provide an account of the processing involved in intelligence. The lack of a model of cognitive processing limits the usefulness of psychometrically derived knowledge, particularly in regard to intervention (i.e., remediation of age-related deficits). In addition, while the reliability of psychometric tests of intelligence tend to be very good, their validity may be questioned, particularly for adults. That is, although intelligence tests for children are reasonably effective in predicting school success, which may be a valid criterion of children's intelligence, it is unclear whether adult intelligence tests differentiate individuals in a meaningful manner. The problem here is that there is no obvious criterion of adult intelligence. Are occupational successes or life adjustments appropriate indicators of adult intelligence? Even if either of these qualities, or some other was considered a good marker, there presently is no consensually adequate means to quantify them.

In summary, the psychometric approach, at least as originally conceived, was largely atheoretical. Few assumptions about the nature of cognition or the nature of development were addressed. Rather, large differential studies of cognitive performance were undertaken. These studies have provided considerable empirical information about cognitive performance across the life span. In particular, they indicate that different cognitive abilities follow different developmental trajectories.

INTEGRATION OF RESEARCH ON COGNITIVE DEVELOPMENT

In the previous section, some of the important assumptions inherent in four approaches to cognition were outlined. In this section, research from these perspectives is integrated. First, findings from alternative approaches are compared. Then, a model of cognition that incorporates these diverse data is presented. Finally, a multidisciplinary framework for considering development is suggested.

Comparison of Findings from Alternative Approaches

Although a detailed review of findings from alternative approaches is beyond the scope of this chapter, a comparison of well-substantiated patterns of results is carried out by examining the cognitive abilities that have been identified as central to each approach. The abilities used for this comparison are summarized in Table 9.2. They include logico-mathematical structures (organismic); basic mechanisms, world knowledge, and cognitive strategies (mechanistic); primary and secondary mental functions (contextual); and fluid and crystallized abilities (psychometric). Although all of these abilities are not uniformly referred to by all adherents of the approaches, they are representative of central constructs. Thus, the abilities simply should be thought of as illustrative. Specification of them is meant to facilitate comparison and integration, even though it is recognized that they will not perfectly conform to everyone's preferred list.

TABLE 9.2

Cognitive Ability	Reference	Stimuli	Analysis of Task Processing	Content	Ascent
Organismic Approach					
Logico-Mathematical Structures	Piaget, 1983	meaningful	complex	impoverished	early childhood
Mechanistic Approach	Siegler, 1983				
Basic Mechanisms		meaningless	simple	improverished	prenatal
World Knowledged		meaningful	simple	improverished	early childhood
Cognitive Strategies		meaningful	complex	improverished	middle childhood
Contextual Approach	Vygotsky, 1978				
Primary Mental Functions		meaningless	simple	rich	prenatal
Secondary Mental Functions		meaingful	complex	rich	middle childhood
Psychometric Approach	Horn, 1980				
Fluid Abilities		meaningless	simple	impoverished	prenatal
Crystalized Abilities		meaningful	simple	impoverished	early childhood

Cognitive Ability	Peak	Descent	Plasticity	Biological Shared	Biological Unique	Environmental Shared	Environmental Unique
Organismic Approach							
Logico-Mathematical Structures	adolescence	none	little			x	
Mechanistic Approach							
Basic Mechanisms	adolescence	late adulthood	little	x			
World Knowledge	late adulthood	none	lots			x	x
Cognitive Strategies	middle adulthood	late adulthood	lots			x	x
Contextual Approach							
Primary Mental Functions	adolescence	late adulthood	little	x		x	
Secondary Mental Functions	none	none	lots				
Psychometric Approach							
Fluid Abilities	early adulthood	late adulthood	little		x		x
Crystalized Abilities	late adulthood	none	lots				

Three factors are considered in the comparison. First, the tasks that have been used to study each cognitive ability are analyzed. It is suggested that cognitive abilities can be usefully classified in terms of the stimulus properties and processing requirements of tasks on which they emerge. Then, the life-span developmental trajectories observed for each ability are examined. It is suggested that the onset, offset, rate, and plasticity of growth and decline of the abilities are important for understanding cognition. Finally, the determinants of development ascribed to each ability are explored. It is suggested that separate cognitive abilities are rooted primarily in biology or experience.

As was indicated earlier, each approach relies upon different types of data to make inferences about cognition and cognitive development. That is, the corpus of data by each approach involves subjects' performance on different types of tasks. The fact that different types of tasks are utilized is critical, because different types of tasks tap different aspects of the cognitive system. Thus, in order to understand and contrast the cognitive abilities identified by each approach it is essential to analyze and compare the tasks on which they have emerged.

At least three distinguishing features can be used to define cognitive tasks. One pertains to stimulus properties. Some tasks involve relatively meaningless stimuli while others utilize meaningful stimuli. A second task factor pertains to processing requirements. Some tasks involve relatively simple processing while others involve complex processing in which the coordination of multiple subprocesses is required. A third task factor pertains to the context in which performance is examined. Some tasks are embedded in rich natural contexts while others are embedded in impoverished, controlled laboratory contexts.

As can be seen in Table 9.2, three types of tasks can be distinguished on the basis of stimulus properties and processing requirements. That is, tasks used to study cognition can be classified as either meaningless and simple, meaningful and simple, or meaningful and complex. Although basic mechanisms (mechanistic), primary mental functions (contextual), and fluid abilities (psychometric) have been developed within different theoretical perspectives, all have emerged in performance on relatively meaningless simple tasks. Analogously, world knowledge (mechanistic) and crystallized abilities (psychometric) have been implicated on meaningful simple tasks, and logico-mathematical structures (organismic), strategies (mechanistic), and secondary mental functions (contextual) have been implicated on meaningful complex tasks.

It is suggested that the cognitive abilities that have been identified on similar tasks represent the same general aspect of cognition, despite the fact that different theoretical views associated with alternative approaches have been attached to them. This analysis implies that there are three types of cognitive abilities, each reflected on different types of tasks. The mechanistic approach, which has used a variety of tasks that include meaningless and meaningful stimuli as well as simple and complex processing, has identified all three of the major types of cognitive abilities. The psychometric approach, which has used tasks involving meaningless and meaningful stimuli that require only limited processing, has identified the two most primitive of these abilities. The contextual approach, which mainly has investigated meaningless simple performance or meaningful complex performance, has identified the most primative and most advanced of the abilities. And the organismic approach, which has examined performance on only meaningful complex tasks, has focused on only the most advanced ability.

Further evidence about the convergence or divergence of cognitive abilities comes from examination of developmental trajectories. As indicated in Table 9.2, basic mechanisms (mechanistic), primary mental functions (contextual), and fluid abilities (psychometric) develop rapidly in early life, then stabilize through most of adulthood, and perhaps decline a bit in late life. As is indicated in Table 9.2, world knowledge (mechanistic) and crystallized abilities (psychometric) have somewhat later onsets and slower rates of development in early life, but seem to maintain at least some continued development through nearly all of life. A third type of ability may encompass logico-mathematical structures (organismic), strategies (mechanistic), and higher mental functions (contextual), although the pattern here is less consistent, at least in part because less relevant data are available. Still, there seems to be some indication that a third type of cognitive ability develops in a somewhat more stage like manner and has greater openness for continued growth in later life.

The final factor to be examined for evidence of convergence or divergence of findings from alternative approaches is the presumed determinant of development, that is, assumptions about whether the abilities are rooted primarily in biology or experience. It should be noted that because causes of age change rarely have been studied directly, assumptions about the determinants of development, rather than substantiated facts, must be considered. As can be seen in Table 9.2, except for the organismic construct (logico-mathematical structures), all of the primitive abilities (basic mechanisms, primary mental abilities, and fluid abilities) are assumed to be rooted in biology and all of the intermediary (world knowledge and crystallized abilities) and advanced (strategies and higher mental functions) abilities are presumed to be rooted in experience. Thus, there is support again for the view that there are at least two general types of cognitive abilities.

Three-Tier Model of Cognition

It is suggested that a three-tier conception of cognition (portrayed in Figure 9.1) incorporates the major cognitive abilities identified by alternative approaches, and has a number of advantages over previously prescribed conceptions. In particular, because this conception is especially sensitive to developmental issues (e.g., developmental trajectories and determinants of development), it highlights important qualities about cognition that are underemphasized in other conceptions. The first tier is believed to be available at birth, the second tier to emerge postnatally, and the third tier probably is not in place until even later in development. In addition, the first tier is believed to be a fairly closed biologically based system in which there is little ontogenetic change, the second tier is thought to be a somewhat more open system rooted in external experience with potential for some ontogenetic growth throughout life, and the third tier is believed to be an extremely open system rooted in internal experience and capable of very substantial ontogenetic change throughout life.

Each overlay tier is believed to give the cognitive system impressive new power. This power is gained because cognition gets filtered through layers that are added postnatally and rooted in experience. That is, starting fairly soon after birth, cognition occurs in a system that has been ontogenetically

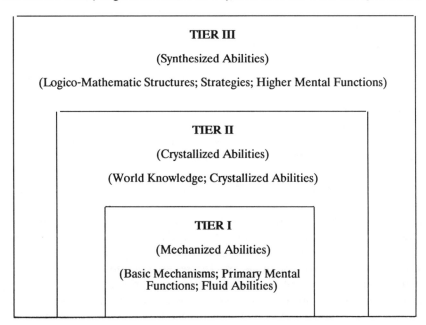

FIGURE 9.1 Three-tier model of cognition.

fine tuned to the subtleties of the environment. Previous modes of operation are not abandoned, but with the addition of environmentally based tiers the cognitive system becomes more effective and more efficient. As with a computer, wherein ultimate utility is very much determined by the data it is fed and the software used with it, the human cognitive system is considerably amplified by ontogenetic additions (e.g., knowledge, strategies). Moreover, with the overlay of new layers slipage in more primitive layers is tolerated. Minor perturbations in lower operations become relatively unimportant in the overall functioning of an ever more powerful system. Still, at some threshold brekdowns in foundation layers disrupt effective operation of the system as a whole.

As previously implied, the first tier is assumed to be the most primitive and to be biologically specified. Although its general structure and function are established at a species level, individual genetic differences result in some diversity. This tier is operable early in life and subsequently gets called into play when an individual faces situations comparable to those experienced in early life, that is, when faced with seemingly meaningless tasks. The developmental course of this tier parallels development of other largely biologically controlled physical systems. Some growth and fine tuning may occur shortly after birth, and some decline, perhaps largely attributable to disease, may occur shortly prior to death. Between very early life and very late life the functional capacity of this tier remains relatively stable. However, the cognitive system as a whole remains open throughout life. Subsequent tiers are added postnatally.

The first tier incorporates what has been identified as basic mechanisms by mechanists, primary mental functions by contextualists, and fluid abilities by psychometricians. Although adherents to each of these approaches have come to the problem in rather different ways, their convergence is encouraging. In particular, it is worth noting that this level of cognition became apparent regardless of whether research focused on group similarities (mechanistic approach) or individual differences (psychometric approach).

The second tier incorporates what has been identified as world knowledge by mechanists and crystallized abilities by psychometricians. It rather passively records external experience, resulting in habituation to unimportant events and anticipation of important events. This tier gives the system the power to operate in an ever more environmentally responsive and adaptive manner. Because many experiences are common to all individuals in a population, much of this second layer is shared with other individuals in the population; however, because some experiences are unique to an individual, part of this second layer is unique to the individual. It may not be surprising, therefore, that this aspect of cognition was identified in both normative (mechanistic) and differential (psychometric) studies. Likewise, because this tier derives from external experience, it should not be surprising that it begins to emerge only after life begins and slows in its rate of growth as newness of experience diminishes.

Although evidence for a third separate tier is less clear, there is at least some support for its inclusion. Such a tier may reflect what mechanists have identified as strategies and contextualists have identified as higher mental functions. It gives humans extensive potential for adaptive modification, and this potential could presumably increase throughout life. The unique aspect of this tier may be that it derives from internal experiences of the cognitive system, that is, it emerges from its own activity. This tier is believed to be especially valuable because it allows the cognitive system to adapt in a way that is not only responsive to the external world but also responsive to its own apparatus (e.g., the first tier). According to this view, while the addition of the second tier primes the cognitive system to operate in an ever more environmentally adaptive manner, the addition of the third tier gives the cognitive system the capacity to actually adjust its modus operandum in a way that can optimize attainment of a specified goal.

Although the second tier seems to emerge out of the organism's activity in the environment, the third tier seems to emerge out of the organism's cognition about its own cognitive activity. The idea here is that if cognition becomes an object of itself it has the power to construct further layers. This process seems similar to what Piaget (1983) described as reflective abstraction and Flavell (1977) articulated as metacognition. Although Piaget suggested that the development of this aspect of cognition is primarily driven by internal mechanisms, Vygotsky (1978) argued that development of higher mental functions is directed by social interaction. Further research should clarify the contribution of both of these factors.

Although the present view postulates only three tiers, it is possible to speculate even further and envision a fourth or possibly fifth cognitive tier. Such layers might derive from the cognitive system's cognition about emotional and biological experience. What is implied here is that as emotional and biological activity are cognitively reflected upon, new cognitive layers could emerge that would result in more adaptive regulation or control of the emotional and biological systems. Indeed, there is some evidence of better integration of affect and cognition in later adulthood (e.g., Labouvie-Vief, 1985). In addition, there is substantial evidence of the potential for at least partial cognitive regulation of physiological processes through biofeedback techiques (e.g., Miller, 1971), and also the suggestion of the potential for some control over biochemical factors that mediate health (e.g., Henry, in press).

In summary, it appears that presently identified cognitive abilities can be incorporated into a three-tier conception. This novel way of viewing cognition is believed to be more powerful than previous conceptions because it incorporates important developmental phenomenon. A first biologically based tier is relatively closed and in place at birth. A second external environmentally based tier is somewhat more open and emerges postnatally. At least one additional infinitely open internal experientially based tier seems to be added during subsequent development.

Multidisciplinary Framework for Considering Development

In this section an admittedly rather simple multidisciplinary framework (see Figure 9.2) for considering development is presented. It is suggested that such a framework can nevertheless facilitate inquiry about causes of development. As can be seen in Figure 9.2, both endogenous and exogenous factors relate to the cognitive system and probably contribute to its development. Biological factors impact Tier I, environmental factors, from both the physical and social world, impact Tier II, and the cognitive system is itself the main impetus for development of Tier III, although the social world may also be important. The main advantage of framing the cognitive system in such a multidisciplinary perspective is that it highlights the diversity of factors that impinge upon cognitive development, and hopefully encourages inquiry about causes of age change. As independent variables from each of these spheres are investigated it is possible that additional aspects of cognition will be illuminated.

CONCLUSIONS

The purposes of this chapter were to articulate an agenda for cognitive developmentalists and to consider how well it is being met. It was suggested that cognitive developmentists should be addressing two major questions: What are the ways that cognition changes with age?, and What are the causes of cognitive changes associated with age? It appears that current research on cognitive development has made considerable progress with respect to describing of the ways that cognition changes with age, but largely has failed to address the explanation of these changes. Some conceptual and methodological reasons for the paucity of information about causes of development are discussed here, along with several recommendations for redirecting research.

First, a reconceptualization of research design is called for. Analysis of extant research points to limitations in both the independent and dependent variables. Because most studies of cognitive development involve cross-sectional designs in which cognitive performance serves as the dependent

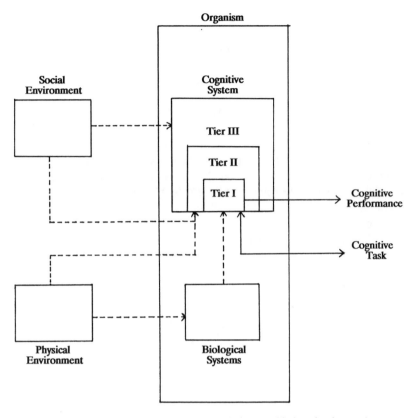

FIGURE 9.2 Multidisciplinary framework for considering development.

variable and age serves as the main independent variable, only descriptions of age differences, not explanations of age changes, are available. Longitudinal studies in which indices of cognitive change, rather than simply cognitive performance, serve as the dependent variable would better address the development of cognition. Cross-sectional studies, although not ideal for studying development, also could provide useful information about causes of age change. However, until now, because cross-sectional studies have incorporated independent variables that are relevant to cognitive performance in a narrow time frame rather than to age change, little information about the causes of age change has been obtained. Cross-sectional studies in which independent variables that are hypothesized to be relevant to age change rather than simply to performance at a specific point in time would provide useful information about development. Optimal studies of cognitive development would examine change in performance rather than performance per se, and thus would be concerned with developmental factors. Rather than simply standard cognitive factors, reformulation of either independent or dependent variables would, however, substantially advance knowledge about the development of cognition.

Second, a life-span (across life) perspective is recommended. The literature on cognitive development indicates that research is almost always carried out with only a relatively narrow age focus. Analysis of the potential value of life-span data suggests that a life-span perspective is most appropriate for understading cognition at all stages of life. It is reasonably obvious that because causal factors can accumulate over time they may become most potent in later life, and at later stages of life there is an increased probability that the time or events needed to trigger latent causes (sleeper effects) may have occurred. It is perhaps less obvious, but still the case, that only with life-span data is it possible to assess the real implications of early life patterns and the full impact of early enriching or depriving factors in development. Scientific evaluation of the relevance of childhood phenomena should no longer be carried out in isolation of other life stages. Rather, each stage of life must be viewed in the perspective of an entire life.

Third, a reassessment of the assumptions of one's approach is suggested. A review of the major perspectives from which cognitive development currently is being addressed indicated that researchers hold different assumptions about the basic nature of cognition and the nature of development. Although these assumptions typically are not explicitly attended to in the day-to-day activity of research, they direct and constrain the questions that are addressed and the types of data that are collected. Some of these assumptions define what are considered to be the interesting aspects of cognition, and others bias one's view about the nature of development. It is unfortunate that these issues rarely get posed as testable hypothesizes. In a number of instances data relevant (e.g., inter- and intraindividual generality) are available. It is no longer defensible to maintain biases that have been refuted by contradicting evidence.

ACKNOWLEDGMENTS

This chapter was written while the author was a fellow at the Institute for Advanced Studies at the Andrus Gerontology Center of the University of Southern California. Thanks are extended to the staff and fellows of the Institute who contributed to an extremely stimulating, productive, and enjoyable time, as well as to the Brookdale Foundation whose National Fellowship Award provided support for it.

REFERENCES

Anderson, J. R.(1976). *Language, memory, and thought.* Hillsdale, NJ: Lawrence Erlbaum Associates.

Appelman, P. (Ed.). (1970). *Darwin: A Norton critical edition.* New York: W. W. Norton.

Arlin, P. K. (1975). Cognitive development in adulthood: A fifth stage? *Developmental Psychology, 11*(5), 602–606.

Atkinson, R., & Shiffrin, R. M. (1968). Human memory: A proposed system and its control processes. In K. W. Spence & J. T. Spence (Eds.), *The psychology of learning and motivation* (Vol. 2, pp. 80–105). New York: Academic Press.

Azmitia, M., & Perlmutter, M. (in press). Social influences on children's cognition: State of the art and future directions. In H. W. Reese (Ed.), *Advances in child development and behavior.* New York: Academic Press.

Baltes, P. B., & Willis, S. L. (1982). Plasticity and enhancement of intellectual functioning. In F. I. M. Craik & S. Trehub (Eds.), *Aging and cognitive processes* (pp. 353–389). New York: Plenum Press.

Baltes, P. B. (1985). *The aging of intelligence: On the dynamics between growth and decline.* Unpublished manuscript.

Bandura, A. (1971). A comparative test of the status envy, social power and secondary reinforcement theories of identificatory learning. In A. Bandura (Ed.), *Psychological modeling: Conflicting theories* (pp. 70–88). Chicago: Aldine-Atherton.

Barker, R. G. (1968). *Ecological psychology: Concepts and methods studying the environment of human behavior.* Stanford, CA: Stanford University Press.

Basseches, M. (1985). *Dialectical thinking and adult development.* Norwood, NJ: Ablex.

Bijou, S. W., & Baer, D. M. (1961). *Child development I: A systematic and empirical theory.* New York: Meredith.

Bijou, S. W., & Baer, D. M. (1965). *Child development II: Universal stage of infancy.* New York: Meredith.

Binet, A., & Simon, T.(1905). Methods nouvelles pour un diagnostic du niveau intellectuel des anormaux. *L'Annee Psychology, 11,* 191–244.

Birren, J., & Cunningham, W. R. (1985). Research on the psychology of aging, concepts and theory. In J. E. Birren & K.W. Schaie (Eds.), *Handbook of the psychology of aging* (pp.3–34). New York: Van Nostrand.

Birren, J. E., & Schaie, K. W. (Eds.). (1985). *Handbook of the psychology of aging.* New York: Van Nostrand.

Bower, G. H. (1977). Discussion at Conference on Developmental and Experimental Perspectives in Memory. Ann Arbor, MI.

Bronfenbrenner, U. (1979). *The ecology of human development.* Cambridge, MA: Harvard University Press.

Brown, A. L. (1979). Theories of memory and the problems of development: Activity, growth, and knowledge. In L. S. Cremak & F. I. M. Craik (Eds.), *Levels of processing in human memory* (pp. 225–258). Hillsdale, NJ: Lawrence Erlbaum Associates.

Bruner, J. S. (1972). The nature and uses of immaturity. *American Psychologist, 27,* 687–708.

Cattell, R. B. (1963). Theory of fluid and crystallized intelligence: A critical experiment. *Journal of Educational Psychology, 54,* 1–22.

Charlesworth, W. (1976). Human intelligence as adaptation: An ethological approach. In L. B. Resnick (Ed.), *The nature of intelligence* (pp. 147–168). Hillsdale, NJ: Lawrence Erlbaum Associates.

Chomsky, N. (1986). *Knowledge of language: Its nature, origins, and use.* New York: Praeger.

Cole, M., & Scribner, S. S. (1976). Theorizing about socialization of cognition. *Ethos, 3,* 250–268.

Commons, M. L., Richards, F. A., & Armon, C. (1984). *Beyond formal operations: Late adolescent and adult cognitive development.* New York: Praeger.

Commons, M. L., Richards, F. A., & Kuhn, D. (1982). Systematic and metasystematic reasoning: A case for levels of reasoning beyond Piaget's stage of formal operations. *Child Development, 53,* 1058–1069.

Crowder, R. (1977). Discussion at Conference on Developmental and Experimental Perspectives in Memory. Ann Arbor, Michigan.

Dannefer, D. (1984). Adult development and social theory: A paradigmatic reappraisal. *American Sociological Review, 49,* 100–116.

Elkind, D. (1981). *The hurried child: Growing up too fast too soon.* Reading, PA: Addison-Wesley.

Featherman, D. L., & Lerner, R. M. (1985). Ontogenesis and sociogenesis: Problematics for theory and research about development and socialization across the lifespan. *American Sociological Review, 50,* 659–676.

Flavell, J. H. (1977). *Cognitive development.* Englewood Cliffs, NJ: Prentice-Hall.

Flavell, J. H. (1982). Structures, stages, and sequences in cognitive development. In W. A. Collins (Ed.), *The concept of development. Minnesota symposium on child psychology* (Vol. 15, pp. 1–28). Hillsdale, NJ: Lawrence Erlbaum Associates.

Flavell, J. H., & Markman, E. M. (Eds.). (1985). *Handbook of child psychology, Vol. 3, Cognitive development.* New York: Wiley.

Gelman, R. (1969). Conservation acquisition: A problem of learning to attend to relevant attributes. *Journal of Experimental Child Psychology, 7,* 167–187.

Gibson, J. J. (1979). *The ecological approach to visual perception.* Boston: Houghton-Mifflin.

Guilford, J. P. (1967). *The nature of human intelligence.* New York: McGraw-Hill.

Hall, G. S.(1922). *Senescence: The last half of life.* New York: D. Appelton.

Henry, S. (in press). The archetypes of power and intimacy and the aging process. In J. E. Birren & V. L. Bengston (Eds.), *Theories of aging: Psychological and social perspectives on time, self, and society.*

Horn, J. L. (1966). Integration of structural and developmental concepts in the theory of fluid and crystallized intelligence. In R. B. Cattell (Ed.), *Handbook of multivariate experimental psychology* (pp. 553–562). Chicago: Rand McNally.

Horn, J. L. (1982). The theory of fluid and crystallized intelligence in relation to concepts of cognitive psychology and aging in adulthood. In F. I. M. Craik & E. E. Trehub (Eds.), *Aging and cognitive processes* (pp. 237–278). New York: Plenum Press.

Horn, J. L., & Cattell, R. B. (1967). Age differences in fluid and crystallized intelligence. *Acta Psychologica, 16,* 107–129.

Hoyer, W. J. (1984). Aging and the development of expert cognition. In T. M. Schlechter & M. P. Toglia (Eds.), *New directions in cognitive science* (pp. 69–87). Norwood, NJ: Ablex.

Jenkins, J. J. (1974). Remember that old theory of memory? Well forget it! *American Psychologist, 29,* 785–795.

Jenkins, J. (1979). Four points to remember: A tetrahedral model of memory experiments. In L. Cermak & F. I. M. Craik (Eds.), *Levels of processing in human memory* (pp. 429–446). Hillsdale, NJ: Lawrence Erlbaum Associates.

Kendler, T. S. (1963). Development of mediating responses in children. In N. C. Wright & J. Kagen (Eds.), *Basic cognitive processes in children. Monographs of the society for research in children development* (Vol. 28, pp. 33–51).

Kohlberg, L. (1969). Stage and sequence: The cognitive developmental approach to socialization. In D. A. Goslin (Ed.), *Handbook of socialization theory and research* (pp. 347–480). New York: Rand McNally.

Labouvie-Vief, G. (1985). Object knowledge, personal knowledge, and processes of equilibration in adult cognition. *Human Development, 28,* 25–39.

Lewin, K. (1954). Behavior and development as a function of the total situation. In L. Carmichael (Ed.), *Manual of child psychology* (2nd ed., pp. 918–983). New York: Wiley.

Miller, N. E. (1971). *Selected papers.* Chicago, IL: Aldine Atherton.

Nesselroade, J., & Cattell, R. (Eds.). (in press). *Handbook of multivariate experimental psychology* (2nd ed.). New York: Rand McNally.

Niemark, E. D. (1975). Intellectual development during adolescence. In F. D. Morowitz (Ed.), *Review of child development research* (Vol. 4, pp. 541–594). Chicago: University of Chicago Press.

Niemark, E. D. (1979). *Human Development, 22,* 60–67.

Norman, D. A. (1976). *Memory and attention: An introduction to human information processing.* (2nd ed.). New York: Wiley.

Ornstein, P. A. (1978). *Memory development in children.* Hillsdale, NJ: Lawrence Erlbaum Associates.

Overton, W. F., & Reese, H. W. (1973). Models of development: Methodological implications. In J. R. Nesselroade & H. W. Reese (Eds.), *Life-span developmental psychology: Methodological issues* (pp. 65–86). New York: Academic Press.

Papert, S. (1980). *Mindstorms.* New York: Basic Books.

Pea, R. D. (1985). Integrating human and computer intelligence. In E. L. Klein (Ed.), New Directions for Child Development: Vol. 28. *Children and computers* (pp. 75–98). San Francisco, CA: Jossey-Bass.

Perlmutter, M. (in press). Cognitive potential throughout life. In J. E. Birren & V. L. Bengtson (Eds.), *Theories of aging: Psychological and social perspectives on time, self, and society.* Hillsdale, NJ: Lawrence Erlbaum Associates.

Piaget, J. (1971). *Biology and knowledge.* Chicago: University of Chicago Press.

Piaget, J. (1983). Piaget's theory. In P. H. Mussen (Ed.), *Handbook of child psychology* (Vol. 1, pp.103–128). New York: Wiley.

Piaget, J., & Inhelder, B. (1969). *The psychology of the child.* New York: Basic Books.

Reese, H. W. (1974). Cohort, age, and imagery in children's paired-associate learning. *Child Development, 45*(4), 1176–1178.

Reese, H. W., & Overton, W. F. (1970). Models of development and theories of development. In L. R. Goulet & P. B. Baltes (Eds.), *Life-span developmental psychology: Theory and research* (pp. 115–145). New York: Associated Press.

Riegel, K. F. (1973). Dialectic operations: The final period of cognitive development. *Human Development, 16,* 346–370.

Salapatek, P. (1975). Pattern perception in early infancy. In L. B. Cohen & P. Salapatek (Eds.), *Infant perception: From sensation to cognition. Basic visual processes* (Vol. I, pp. 133–248). New York: Academic Press.

Scarr-Salapatek, S. (1976). An evolutionary perspective on infant intelligence: Species patterns and individual varieties. In M. Lewis (Ed.), *Origins of intelligence: Infancy and early childhood* (pp. 165–198). New York: Plenum Press.

Schaie, K. W. (1967). Age changes and age differences. *The Gerontologist, 7,* 128–132.

Schaie, K. W. (1984). Midlife influences upon intellectual functioning in old age. *International Journal of Behavioral Development, 7,* 463–478.

Siegler, R. S. (1983). Information processing approaches to development. In P. H. Mussen (Ed.), *Handbook of child psychology* (Vol. 1, pp. 103–128). New York: Wiley.

Skinner, B.F. (1983). Intellectual self-management in old age. *American Psychologist, 38,* 239–244.

Trabasso, T. R. (1975). Representation, memory and reasoning: How do we make transitive inferences? In A. D. Pick (Ed.), *Minnesota symposium on child psychology* (Vol. 9, pp. 135–172). Minneapolis, MN: University of Minnesota Press.

Turkle, S. (1984). *The second self: Computers and the human spirit.* New York: Simon & Schuster.

Vygotsky, L. S.(1978). *Mind in society.* Cambridge, MA: Cambridge University Press.

Werner, H. (1948). *Comparative psychology of mental development.* New York: International Universities Press.

Wertsch, J. V. (1985). *Culture, communication, and cognition.* Cambridge, MA: Cambridge University Press.

White, S. H. (1965). Evidence for a hierarchial arrangement of learning processes. In L. P. Lipsitt & C. C. Spiker (Eds.), *Advances in child development and behavior* (Vol. 2, pp. 187–220). New York: Academic Press.

10 INDIVIDUAL DIFFERENCES IN COGNITIVE DEVELOPMENT:

Does Instruction Make a Difference?

Franz E. Weinert
Andreas Helmke
Max-Planck-Institute for Psychological Research
Munich, F.R.G.

ABSTRACT

There is still a considerable amount of confusion about the real impact of instruction on cognitive development. The goal of this chapter is to illustrate that very different judgments are made depending on different predictors and/or criteria used and the various mechanisms considered.

The first study demonstrates that the impact of school on cognitive development is indeed neglible when the sole criterion utilized is changing individual achievement differences within classrooms. The second study analyzed general, differential, and interactive effects of instruction on various cognitive and motivational outcomes after 1 and 2 years of instruction. The results of this study illustrate that, irrespective of stable individual differences in math achievement within classrooms, instruction has a variety of powerful effects.

INTRODUCTION

There are continual tendencies in scientific communication, as in everyday life, to form stereotypes, which prevail in the face of contradictory experiences because of their simplicity, clarity, endurance, and resistance. Developmental psychology displays two examples of such stereotypes that are directly related to our topic:

1. Individual differences in cognitive competencies stabilize within the course of development so that, after the age of 5, it is possible to predict the performance of adults on intelligence tests with increasing accuracy (Bloom, 1964; Horn & Donaldson, 1980; Wohlwill, 1980). Bornstein and

Sigman (1986) even assume that using the information-processing approach, it is possible to find valid predictor variables in earliest childhood for later performance differences.

2. Schools and individual schooling have only a very minor influence on cognitive development and individual differences. This is true not only for the distribution of intelligence scores in the adult population, but also for academic achievement. Several summary conclusions of rather well-known studies document this pessimistic estimation. Thus, Coleman et al. (1966), in their report on *Equality of Educational Opportunity,* come to the conclusion that "schools bring little influence to bear on a child's achievement that is independent of his background and general social context" (p. 325). Jencks et al. (1972) confirm this conviction "that the character of a school's output depends largely on a single input, namely, the characteristics of the entering children. Everything else — the school's budget, its policies, the characteristics of the teachers — is either secondary or completely irrelevant" (p. 256). And in another passage: "Equalizing the quality of elementary schools would reduce cognitive inequality by 3 percent or less. Equalizing the quality of high schools would reduce cognitive inequality by one percent or less" (p. 109). All these statements are common knowledge; they are being quoted again, because they have been used in many recent publications as secure and generalizable information.

Given these propositions, is it at all worthwhile to reconsider the influence of school on individual differences in cognitive development? It is true that the methods, results, and conclusions in reports by Coleman et al. (1966) and by Jencks et al. (1972) have been questioned repeatedly (Luecke & McGinn, 1975; Mosteller & Moynihan, 1972); and empirical studies completely opposed the skepticism conveyed by Coleman and Jencks: "Teachers *do* make a difference" (Good, Biddle, & Brophy, 1975, p. 7), "School can make a difference" (Brookover, Beady, Flood, Schweitzer, & Wiesenbaker, 1979), "There are important school effects . . . and . . . it is clear that school effects can be very substantial indeed" (Rutter, 1983, p. 13).

It is not, however, the controversy itself that makes this question scientifically interesting, but rather advancements in developmental psychology and various empirical results in the field of educational psychology. A few short notes must suffice to document this notion:

When asking the theoretical question of what it is that actually develops as most cognitive performances improve during the course of childhood, then at present the answers of developmental psychologists concentrate more on structural changes in the knowledge base (Carey, 1985). These changes are evident in the variety, degree of organization, and the accessibility of the individual's available knowledge. Acquisition, comprehension, storage, and application of new information are strongly dependent on this

(Körkel, 1984). In addition to general individual differences in cognitive performances (e.g., Mental Age, IQ), therefore, intraindividual differences in thinking and memory are increasingly the center of scientific attention. It is well-established that the long-term availability of domain-specific knowledge attained in school is less dependent on IQ or other general cognitive characteristics than on the quality of the respective instruction and the further use of this specific knowledge in everyday life or at work. The emphasis on the role of available knowledge for the further acquisition of knowledge and problem solving should, however, not lead to the false conclusion that all children are able to learn anything, provided that instruction is adapted to the individual knowledge base. This is not possible, especially when considering the time restrictions of our schools (Arlin, 1984).

There are numerous indications that length and type of schooling have long-term effects on cognitive development in adulthood, and also on the probability, age of onset, and intensity of intellectual competency decline in old age. This hypothesis may explain not only cohort effects (Baltes & Schaie, 1981), but also differential aging effects (Dixon, Kramer, & Baltes, 1985). It is, however, more of an academic problem to consider the influence of schooling variables on cognitive development in adulthood and old age independently (i.e., wanting to control the effects of varying degrees of schooling that are typically associated with future life and work). Proceeding in this manner could almost lead to an artificial question, because as Willis (1985) stated:

> Education appears to play an interactive role, then, in the maintenance of intellectual functioning. In early stages in the life span, those of higher ability may seek out or be given greater educational opportunities; education serves to foster the development of skills and a knowledge base for future learning. Second, educational level is associated with certain types of lifestyles that foster the maintenance or decline of intellectual abilities. (p. 823)

IQ scores and their individual stability during the school years appear to be less important for lifelong cognitive development than the direct effects of schooling and the indirect influences of different school careers. These lifelong determinants of intellectual development have, until now, hardly been considered in empirical work (acquisition of the knowledge base, development of learning skills, motivation to learn, self-concept, etc.).

Many studies that were theoretically guided, methodically sound, and well controlled, have demonstrated significant effects of specific attributes of schooling on specific aspects of cognitive development (Rutter, 1983; Simpson, 1980; Weinert & Treiber, 1982). It has thus been shown that school influences on child development are, of course, strongly dependent on the type of educational system and its cultural context (Stevenson, Parker, Wilkinson, Bonneveaux, & Gonzalez, 1978). The diverse functions and effects of schooling in different cultures are evident in a comparison of developing and industrial countries, for which the International Association for the Evaluation of Educational Achievement (IEA) studies provide many examples (Walker, 1976). After reviewing the relevant literature, Rutter (1983) concludes that

> the crucial components of effective teaching include a clear focus on academic goals, an appropriate degree of structure, an emphasis on active instruction, a task-focused approach and high achievement expectations. . . . Successful schools seem to vary in how they express academic concerns; however, they are differentiated from unsuccessful schools by this consistent and appropriate emphasis on academic matters and by the fact that this attitude is accompanied by specific actions designated to translate expectations into practice. (p. 20ff)

This is doubtless a very general and abstract summary of the analyses of aggregated data from field studies that may mask varying and partially opposing effects of instruction and other schooling variables. The results of Walberg's (1984) meta-analysis on not less than 3,000 studies makes this especially clear, because it is not possible to extract from this work one single theoretical conclusion on specific teaching–learning relationships.

The dangers of generalized statements become especially evident if one compares them with the results of selected case studies. Pedersen, Faucher, and Eaton (1978), for example, reported on the considerable endurance of the effects that a first-grade teacher had on her pupils. They found that pupils who were instructed by this teacher received above-average grades throughout elementary school and retained a superior status into adult life. The adult status was evaluated on the basis of final educational degree attained, professional position, standard of housing conditions, and personal appearance. Of the former pupils of this special first-grade teacher, 64% achieved a high status, and the remaining 36% achieved a middle status; the corresponding values of former pupils of other first grade teachers were 39% high status, 22% middle, and 39% low status. After several possible explanations for this surprising result had been investigated and rejected, path analyses showed that this teacher had a profound direct effect on school achievement, work efficiency, and student's initiative in the first 2 school years, but the direct influence of the teacher on cognitive development thereafter was negligible. On the other hand, her indirect effects, which led from positive profits at the start to continuous advantages for her pupils in the course of development, were remarkable. Because of the small sample size, the results of this methodologically unusual, but meticulously planned study must be interpreted carefully. Pederson et al. (1978) concluded:

> We do not dispute the fact that regardless of teacher quality, children from privileged background are more likely to achieve high adult status than children from disadvantaged background. But our research does show that the teacher can make a difference, not only to pupils' lives in school, but to their future as well. (p. 307)

But what happens to pupils who constantly fail at school? How does such a predicament influence personality development? A first impression is obtained from a study conducted by Kifer (1975). He compared second-, fourth-, fifth-, and eighth-grade children, who had belonged either to the top or to the bottom 20% of their classes from school entry onward. This quasi-longitudinal study permitted an estimation of the effects of success or failure over an extended period of time. Dramatic differences were demonstrated in children's self-concept of academic ability. Successful students had consistently higher self-concepts across grades. Students with achievement difficulties in second grade indicated relatively positive self-concepts; but in higher grades their self-concept scores dropped consistently, reaching a very low level in the eighth grade. Successful and nonsuccessful pupils had the same initial scores at the scale for intellectual achievement responsibility at the beginning of second grade. Although the successful students showed a sharp increase in scores until the sixth grade, where they reached an asymptote, the scores of the nonsuccessful pupils remained extremely low until the seventh grade, and only then began to rise. The difference between both groups, however, remained significant in the eighth grade.

A study conducted by Rheinberg and Enstrup (1977) supplemented these findings. They consistently found that students who attended a special school for slow learners showed a lower level of test anxiety and displayed a higher self-concept of ability than did students with a comparable level of intelligence attending normal schools. The investigators explained the differences as a reference group effect: Accumulative experiences of failure and constant perception of oneself as having an inferior position in the social group of the classroom lead to reactions that might be described as a kind of learned helplessness.

In order to be able to model the influences of school in general and instruction in particular on cognitive development in a life-span perspective, much further research is required. Longitudinal studies are of particular value by enabling measurement of short-term and long-term influences of instruction on various criteria of student development simultaneously. In the following, results of two empirical studies are reported, which were planned in order to describe and try to explain such effects. On the one hand, they deal with the reduction of individual performance differences within classrooms through mastery learning; on the other hand, they deal with the impact of specific instructional variables on diverse academic achievements and motivational tendencies of students. These two studies are supposed to show that differences in instruction may have important consequences for students' cognitive and motivational development, without simultaneously altering stable achievement differences within classrooms.

QUALITY OF INSTRUCTION, LEARNING PROGRESS, AND ACHIEVEMENT DIFFERENCES

The goal of this study (see Treiber & Weinert, 1985; Treiber, Weinert, & Groeben, 1976, 1982) was to describe and explain cognitive performance differences of pupils within elementary school classrooms, differences between school classes and their changes in the course of instruction. Seventy-seven fifth-grade math teachers and their classrooms took part in this study. Using elaborate mathematic achievement tests, standardized methods of classroom observation, aptitude tests, questionnaires and interviews, 2,200 students from elementary schools in the Heidelberg area were studied. Additionally, teachers and parents were questioned. The study extended over 1 year and included three waves. The planned analysis of various postulated effects on the basis of various theoretical assumptions led to the multilevel design shown in Table 10.1. For purposes of brevity, we confine ourselves to the most important points of the investigation and its results.

Many classes could be identified in which a reduction of individual differences in mathematic achievements within the classroom took place as

TABLE 10.1
Multilevel Description and Explanation of Reducing Achievement Differences Within Classrooms by Different Aspects of Instructional Quality

Level of Analysis	Descriptive Indicators	Explanation Models
Classes of students	Change of dispersion measures of classroom achievement scores	Organizing classroom activities for mastery learning
Groups of students	Differences of mean achievement scores of successful and poor students	Direct instruction
Single students	Intraindividual changes of achievement scores	Proactive individualized teacher–student interaction

a result of instruction (i.e., after controlling alternative explanatory variables), whereas in another group of classes, the achievement differences remained the same or increased during that year.

Learning conditions unrelated to instruction proved to be especially explicative, no matter which level of explanation was chosen. Students' cognitive abilities (combined intelligence test scores), along with parental support of the learning activities, accounted for approximately 40% of the variance between school classes regarding the reduction of individual differences in mathematic achievements.

Characteristics of the teacher's instructional behavior determined the following percentages of variance in the reduction of performance differences reached in mathematics:

at the *class* level (through variables of mastery-oriented organization of teaching–learning processes; measured by a teacher questionnaire in 58 classrooms): about 28% of the differences between school classes;

at the level of *student groups* within classes (measured by process variables of direct instruction in $N = 8$ classrooms): approximately 20% in the group of above-average students (upper third of intelligence; $N = 96$) and only 10% in the group of below-average students (lower third of intelligence; $N = 95$);

at the *individual student* level (through variables of observed proactive teacher–student interaction in eight classrooms): about 37% for above-average students, but only 21% for below-average students.

The most important result of the study was the fact, contrary to expectations, that in all classes where a reduction in differences of mathematic performance took place, it was not to the advantage of the poorer students, but to the disadvantage of the good students. It could be shown that the performance of good students in classes with reduced performance variance decreased between the first and second mathematics test relative to the performance in other classes, without a simultaneous performance increase by poorer students. In classes with large performance differences, even highly intelligent pupils were fully fostered, whereas the less intelligent children in these classes performed as well as the comparison group in homogeneous classes. Figure 10.1 presents the corresponding data.

Consistent with the reported results, performance differences among the students within classrooms remained the same or increased during a school year when teachers oriented themselves on the concept of mastery learning,

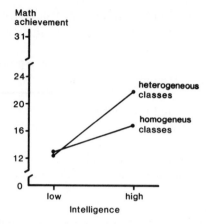

Math achievement

FIGURE 10.1 Math achievement of students with low versus high intelligence in homogeneous and heterogeneous classes.
Note. From *Gute Schulleistungen für alle?* (p. 118) by D. Treiber and F. E. Weinert, 1985, Münster: Aschendorff. Reprinted by permission.

applied to a direct instruction approach, and organized individualized teacher–student interactions predominantly proactively. Contrary to the model propagated by Bloom (1971) and deviating from the theoretical assumptions of Brophy and Good (1974), it was shown that highly effective forms of instruction particularly favor successful students without putting the weaker students at a disadvantage and, on the whole, do not lessen achievement differences in the class, but are more likely to increase them.

In classes with reduced performance variance, not only is teaching relatively ineffective, but also the average level of attention of students is rather low. Particularly poorer students use available learning time in school insufficiently. Although the performance requirements in the homogeneous classes are low, students evaluate their teachers as well as the quality of instruction less positively than do students in classes with larger performance differences.

In summary, the interindividual differences in mathematics in many of the classes we studied changed during the course of the school year. Contrary to theoretical expectations, effective instruction leads to equal or increased performance differences between students within a classroom. A reduction in variance was only observed under the condition of ineffective instruction and brought poor students no achievement advantages, but instead disadvantaged successful students. Individual achievement differences proved to be very persistent in the age group studied. This pattern of results agrees with findings reported in a study on German high schools (Baumert, Roeder, Sang, & Schmitz, 1985, 1986) and corresponds to the conclusions drawn by Arlin (1984) on the grounds of a literature review on the value of the mastery model under the condition of normal school instruction:

> I submit that many educators find themselves in the uncomfortable dilemma related to the "time-achievement-equality dilemma" . . . But educators, and

particularly teachers, are faced daily with individual differences among students. Not only do these differences remain stable . . ., but they often seem to increase with each year of schooling. . . . Mastery theorists suggest an equilibrium of high and equal achievement accompanied by low and equal learning time. But equality of learning time and of achievement appear to be mutually exclusive. If equal learning time is desired, as in many current forms of schooling, the inequalities of achievement outcome appear to be an inevitable concomitant. If equality of achievement outcome is chosen as an end, as in mastery learning, then inequality of time seems necessary as a means. (p. 82f)

Considering the reported results, many studies present a paradox. Increases in time given for presenting and using new content knowledge very much resemble instructional investments with rapidly diminishing returns. Slow learners reach a plateau beyond which substantial changes in cognitive competencies become unlikely. Even when controlling entry knowledge, students display striking intra- and interindividual differences in their use of instructional opportunities for acquiring new knowledge. Ruling out measurement errors, poor optimal instructional, and motivational states as alternative explanations to account for these phenomena, we have as yet only a poor understanding of both internal and external conditions, mechanisms, and correlates of acquisition of knowledge and cognitive skills—that is to say, how individuals with different aptitudes encode, organize, and represent new knowledge into their already existing knowledge system.

It could be speculated that low aptitudes and abilities act as constraints for specific learning processes. According to our observations, children with poor mathematical abilities produce few, rigid and nonabstract hypotheses in solving word problems. Data to test this theoretical assumption are, however, still missing. Thus, microanalytic studies are necessary for better understanding the learning processes of students with varying abilities and/or differing previous knowledge, and under different conditions of instruction.

QUALITY OF INSTRUCTION
AND LEARNING OUTCOMES

Does the stability of interindividual achievement differences mean that instruction has extremely little or even no effect on students, as has often been maintained in the literature? Does it make any difference if teachers instruct well or poorly? Are the results of the empirical studies perhaps applicable only over a short duration? Are there different effects of instruction when considering various achievement criteria and diverse aspects of motivation? These are some of the questions that were central to a second longitudinal study (Helmke, Schneider, & Weinert, 1986; Helmke & Schrader, 1987; Weinert & Helmke, 1987). The study is the German contribution to the IEA Classroom Environment Study: Teaching for Learning (Ryan & Anderson, 1984; Ryan & Shapiro, in press).

The major goal of the Classroom Environment Study (CES) was to investigate which instructional quality and classroom management variables are important predictors of student outcomes. The core of the CES consisted of a follow-up measurement of students' cognitive and affective entry characteristics, enriched by an intensive classroom observation study. The German contribution to the study expanded this design and carried out a longitudinal study with 5 measurement points between the beginning of fifth grade and the end of sixth grade. Also, the classroom observation was complemented by a classroom rating device. Additionally, special emphasis was given to student motivational variables, particularly facets of student self-concept, achievement-related attitudes, test anxiety, and motivation to learn.

Study participants were 39 fifth-grade classrooms from German primary schools. All students were selected from rural and urban schools in the Munich area. The sample of 39 teachers consisted of the regular classroom and mathematics teachers for these classes.

The subject matter of the study was mathematics. To ensure the content validity of the math test, items were specially developed to cover the curriculum of fifth- and sixth-grade classroom mathematics instruction, namely arithmetic skills and word problems in the fifth grade, and understanding of the "fraction" concept and operations with fractions and decimals in the sixth grade. This curriculum is obligatory for mathematics teachers; only minor variations with regard to the sequence of the topics are permissible. Thus, the curriculum and the opportunity to learn in the 39 classrooms were highly comparable.

General Effects of Instruction on Classroom Achievement Outcomes

Classrooms with the highest achievement gains were characterized by a systematic pattern of management and instruction variables that is similar to the concept of direct instruction. Teachers who produced substantial achievement gains in their classrooms showed the following three main characteristics: (a) their classroom management was highly efficient and the rate of student misbehavior was very low; (b) they maintained a strong academic focus and used the time intensively for covering content rather than for procedural activities, nonacademic social contacts, and so on; and

(c) their management of seatwork consisted of actively monitoring and supervising the work of individual students by correcting errors, diagnosing the reasons for errors made, offering help, and inspecting individual papers (rather than merely walking around the classroom or sitting at the desk, correcting tests, etc.).

In contrast, other frequently claimed indicators of instructional quality, such as the frequency of teachers' structuring cues and directives, as measured by the low-inference observational system, turned out to be irrelevant for achievement outcomes.

The positive impact of direct instruction on student achievement is by now a well-established phenomenon, at least for pupils in the lower grades. In contrast, the results concerning typical indicators of instructional quality were puzzling, but only at first glance. For example, as far as instructional cues are concerned, it is probably not maximal but optimal provision of cues that is important. The low-inference observational system, however, could not detect aspects like optimal timing, appropriateness and other qualitative aspects of instructional cues.

Interactional Effects of Classroom Instruction and Teacher Diagnostic Competence on Achievement

We argued that teacher diagnostic sensitivity might be a crucial prerequisite for giving appropriate cues, that is, matching the difficulty level of cues with the achievement level of the addressed student. This interpretation is supported by a recent study of Helmke and Schrader (1987). Diagnostic sensitivity was measured as teachers' accuracy of predicting the rank order of their students' math posttest results. Using residualized posttest achievement scores as criterion, there was a significant disordinal effect between teacher diagnostic sensitivity and teachers' use of structuring cues (Figure 10.2).

In other words, neither diagnostic sensitivity nor the mere frequency of structuring cues alone appear to affect cognitive growth. Rather, diagnostic sensitivity can be regarded as a necessary precondition for the successful use of structuring cues. It provides for the fine tuning of instructional activities. Particularly, components of adaptive teaching, such as exact timing; appropriate pacing; and matching the difficulty of tasks and questions with learners' knowledge base, require a minimum of diagnostic sensitivity on the teacher's part. In contrast, cognitive growth is extremely limited for the combination of high-diagnostic sensitivity and low frequency of cues: When accurate knowledge about students' actual achievement competence is rarely transformed into cues—for whatever reasons—there is a strong negative impact on achievement growth.

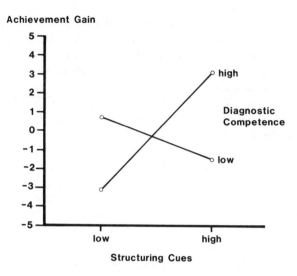

FIGURE 10.2   The interactive effect of teacher diagnostic competency and frequency of structuring cues on classroom achievement gain. *Note.* From "Interactional Effects of Instructional Quality and Teacher Judgement Accuracy on Achievement" by A. Helmke and F. W. Schrader, 1987, *Teaching and Education, 3,* p. 96. Reprinted by permission.

Differential Effects of Classroom Instruction on Achievement Depending on Students' Cognitive Prerequisites

It is well established that prior knowledge and general intelligence are the strongest predictors of academic achievement outcomes (Walberg, 1984). However, systematic comparisons of the two predictors show that domain-specific knowledge outperforms intelligence.

This is not a surprising finding, considering the fact that individual differences in prior knowledge encompass and confound two indicators of cognitive prerequisites. First, prior knowledge is directly relevant to learning in that it is a necessary or (at least) facilitating component in the acquisition of new knowledge. Second, when learning histories are similar, individual differences in prior knowledge are indicators of aptitudes, which as such are more accurate predictors of academic achievement than general intelligence. Our results are in accordance with these expectations (see Table 10.2).

However, it remains unclear what impact various instructional styles may have depending on students' cognitive entry characteristics. To clarify this aspect, the growth of achievement of eight groups of students was studied. These groups were set up by dichotomizing the pretest and intelligence distribution (on individual level) and instructional quality (on classroom

TABLE 10.2
Correlation Between Students' Cognitive Prerequisites
and Math Achievement

	Predictors			
Criteria	Prior Knowledge	(1)	Intelligence	(2)
Achievement (after 1 year)				
• total	.74	.66	.48	.18
• arithmetic skills	.65	.58	.37	.02
• word problems	.71	.59	.53	.32
Achievement (after 2 years)				
• total	.66	.59	.45	.19
• fraction concept	.56	.44	.35	.26
• computation with fractions and integers	.61	.55	.46	.08

Note: (1) after controlling for intelligence scores
(2) after controlling for pretest scores

level) and then combining low/high prior knowledge and low/high intelligence. Efficiency of instructional management (low/high) was used as an indicator of instructional quality. Figure 10.3 shows the impact of these variables on math achievement 2 years later (that is, at the end of Grade 6). Both the outstanding role of prior knowledge as well as the (less important) role of general intelligence on math achievement are obvious. It should be noted that the predicted achievements concerned a content area that was largely unrelated to the tasks set in the math pretest. Thus, our analysis provides a comparison of general intelligence and specific mathematical aptitudes. Surprisingly, the quality of instruction (management efficiency) had a substantially stronger effect on the more difficult task (computation with fractions and decimals) than on the easier criterion task (concept of fraction). The ANOVA confirmed the impression given by Figure 10.3. The main effects of prior knowledge, general intelligence, and instructional quality (except for the fraction concept test), were highly significant but no significant interaction effects emerged.

Compensatory Effects of Student Self-Concept and Instructional Style on Academic Achievement

The achievement-fostering effect of direct instruction is mainly due to the fact that external direction of student-learning activities forms behavior patterns in all students, which are normally displayed only by highly

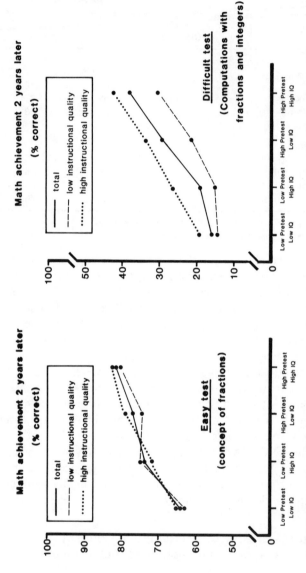

FIGURE 10.3 Differential effects of classroom instruction on math achievement 2 years later, depending on students' cognitive prerequisites.

motivated students with good study habits and adequate cognitive competencies.

Insofar as this view is valid, the role of the individual motivation level as a determinant of performance may depend on the extent to which the direct instruction method is actually effective. Thus, when students have greater freedom during instruction, and when their learning activities are less controlled, the impact of individual levels of motivation on achievement should increase. This simple hypothesis needs qualification. Direct instruction encompasses many widely different components. Our hypothesis emphasizes the role of the individual support component within direct instruction as a main determinant in a system in which teaching compensates for deficient motivation. In contrast, we do not think that the management component of direct instruction will have a compensatory effect. The latter aspect, indicating merely the avoidance of classroom disturbances and the successful management of instructional time by the teacher, is not sufficient for guiding and controlling the learning behavior of students. As a consequence, instruction can only compensate for motivational deficits if students' learning behavior is guided by individualized supportive contacts.

The central motivational aspect chosen for this study was the self-concept of ability. This construct has recently gained importance in theories of achievement motivation. We regard the self-concept of academic ability as a decisive determinant of individual learning behavior and learning outcomes. It is assumed that students with a high self-concept can manage their task-related behavior more effectively. That is, they set their own standards (rather than taking over the goals set by their teachers), calculate efforts needed to arrive at these goals, and do not give up easily in the face of difficulties. Furthermore, their performance is more efficiently shielded from impairing worry-cognitions in achievement-related situations during instruction as well as during the test situation itself. We hypothesize that self-regulated autonomous learning activities become less significant when instruction provides a high degree of individualized supportive contact. As a consequence, correlations between students' self-concept of ability and their achievement should decrease. Thus, we assume a mechanism of functional compensation.

In order to form subgroups of classrooms according to the intensity of the two instructional variables, the 39 classes were split into thirds (each containing 13 classrooms) of low, medium, and high intensity for (a) teachers' individualized supportive contact and (b) teachers' use of instructional time. Separately for each of the six groups previously described, the tool of multiple regression was used to calculate the variance in math achievement scores that could be explained by indicators of students' self-concept of ability (for details, see Weinert & Helmke, 1987).

Figure 10.4 presents the results concerning our central hypothesis. The pattern of results concerning the role of teachers' individualized supportive contact clearly supports our hypothesis. Instruction characterized by this feature has the effect of dramatically decreasing the predictability of achievement from students' academic self-concept measured the previous year. The coefficient of the group "high support" was significantly higher than the coefficients of the groups "medium support" ($z = 2.45, p < .010$) and "low support" ($z = 3.15, p > .001$). In summary, it may be said that the pattern of results provides convincing evidence of a compensatory impact of the support component of direct instruction. Somewhat oversimplifying the case, one might say that in classes characterized by intensive individualized supportive contact, self-concept of ability was relatively unrelated to achievement.

Conversely, the results concerning the role of teachers' use of instructional time show no significant trend with regard to the predictive power of students' self-concept for math achievement under different levels of teachers' use of instructional time (i.e., the management component of direct instruction).

Similar, although weaker, results are to be expected if one disregards the determination of achievement in mathematics by students' self-concept and teachers' supportive contact (as measured by correlation coefficients), and analyzes instead the influences of these two variables on the level of academic achievement. The results in Table 10.3 (supplemented by Scheffé-tests for differences between group means) depict that for students with a low self-concept of ability in classrooms with little individual supportive

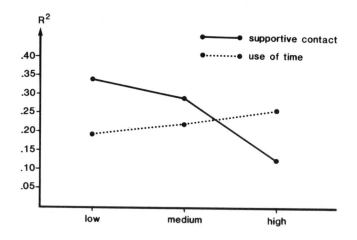

FIGURE 10.4   Level of the instructional variables.

TABLE 10.3
Mean Math Achievement Dependent on Teachers' Intensity of Individual Supportive Contact and Students' Self-Concept of Ability in Mathematics

	M	M_{adj}	SD	N
Low student self-concept				
Low supportive contact	38.41	45.63	12.11	73
High supportive contact	44.87	50.28	13.15	71
High student self-concept				
Low supportive contact	56.43	52.87	13.15	71
High supportive contact	54.52	51.43	14.23	68

contact by the teachers, performance in mathematics is especially poor. Under the same instructional conditions, students with a high self-concept of ability clearly perform better.

For the group of students with high self-concept of ability, the intensity of teacher supportive contact makes no difference for achievement. In contrast, students with a low self-concept of ability achieve definitely higher in classrooms with high supportive contact than in classrooms with low supportive contact. This result is also in accordance with our basic assumptions. Furthermore, Table 10.3 shows that the pattern of results is similar (but weaker) when the regular posttest scores are replaced by posttest scores adjusted for the influence of the pretest (by means of analyses of covariance).

These differences become more easily understood when learning behavior of students with different levels of self-concept of own ability in classrooms with low versus high supportive contact is compared (see Table 10.4).

Table 10.4 illustrates that students' learning behavior in classrooms with low versus high supportive contact can be distinguished as a function of

TABLE 10.4
Indicators of Students' Learning Behavior Dependent of Teachers' Intensity of Supportive Contact and Students' Self-Concept of Ability

	Students' active engagement during instruction (teacher rating)		Students' effort spent for school (self-report)	
	M	SD	M	SD
Low student self-concept				
Low supportive contact	2.33	1.04	4.79	1.80
High supportive contact	2.65	1.10	5.16	1.51
High student self-concept				
Low supportive contact	3.54	0.97	5.53	1.24
High supportive contact	3.25	1.25	5.52	1.41

students' self-concept. The differences in attentional behavior, as well as in effort between students with low versus high self-concept of ability are rather expansive in classrooms with low support, whereas the differences tend to level out in classrooms with high supportive contact. Thus, the functional compensation between self-concept and instructional variables becomes apparent not only in the determination of math achievement, but also in its effect on the attained achievement level. The threshold at which such functional compensations between motivation and instruction can be expected, is presently unclear. On the basis of the meta-analyses available, Walberg (1984) concluded that the essential factors of academic achievement "appear to substitute, compensate, or trade-off for one another at diminishing rates of return" (p.22).

Short-Term and Long-Term Effects of Instruction on Achievement and Motivation

When the impact of instruction is under consideration, short-term performance effects as well as long-term effects on student motivational development should be emphasized. Does direct instruction make students in this long-term perspective increasingly dependent on external learning guides? Do students become more passive, and will there be increasing deficits in building up motives to learn and to achieve? Or is the opposite effect to be expected, namely an improvement in individual motivation as a result of instructionally caused increases in actual competence, which in turn affects subjective perceived competence? Both assumptions emerge in the literature, but without adequate empirical evidence. The interrelationships, however, seem to be more complicated, and the course of motivational development is certainly more differentiated than such simple contentions suggest (see Table 10.5).

We found that direct instruction had a positive effect not only on growth of achievement, but also on students' self-concept of ability. Furthermore, it led to a reduction of test anxiety after 2 years. At the same time, however, attitudes toward school and mathematics significantly declined. Does this mean that strict external direction of students' learning activities by the teacher, at the expense of self-regulatory tendencies and competencies, lead not only to an improvement in academic achievement, but also to an increase in the expectancy components in the area of learning and academic motivation, while the value components of motivation (e.g., the enjoyment of classroom activities and intrinsic interest) are reduced? Presently, this question cannot be satisfactorily answered on an empirical basis.

CONCLUDING REMARKS

"Instruction does make a difference" and "instruction does not make a difference" appear to be two completely opposite convictions concerning

TABLE 10.5
Zero-Order Correlations Between Observational Measures of Direct Instruction and Classroom Cognitive and Motivational Outcomes after 1 Year ("Short-Term") and 2 Years ("Long-Term") of Previous Instruction; $N = 39$ Classrooms

Classroom Outcome	Management	Use of Time	Indiv. Support	Clarity
Short-term consequences				
Math achievement				
Arithmetic skills	.49	.35	.22	.33
Word problems	.52	.29	.33	.22
Motivation				
Self-concept of ability	.43	.24	.04	.13
Positive attitude				
toward school	.12	−.08	−.29	.05
Positive attitude				
toward math	.01	.11	−.18	.27
Long-term consequences				
Math achievement				
Mastery of the				
fraction concept	.38	.40	.36	.38
Computation with				
fractions and integers	.29	.25	.16	.37
Motivation				
Self-concept of ability	.19	.35	.00	.41
Positive attitude				
toward school	−.39	−.32	−.35	−.17
Positive attitude				
toward math	−.27	.04	−.22	.08

the importance of instruction for cognitive development. However, there is evidence supporting both suppositions. If the reduction of interindividual differences within classrooms (e.g., of IQ, aptitudes, or achievements) is the sole criterion, then school does contribute little. It is quite a different case when the influence of instruction of the growth of academic achievement and on changes in achievement-related motives and attitudes is considered. Here, powerful instructional effects are found. However, simple effects are not to be expected. Academic achievements are altogether overdetermined. In order to attain a specific achievement level, different patterns of conditions may be sufficient, but only a portion of these conditions is necessary. Consequently, many (simultaneous) compensatory effects, and many (successive) cumulative effects have to be taken into account. This fact often makes the results of cross-sectional research designs desolate. The level of student aptitudes motivation, and study habits on the one hand, and teacher expectancies, instructional quality, peer norms, and parental support on the other hand produce complex effects. These effects are often inconsistent with regard to their influence on different criteria of individual development. Nevertheless, there are empirical regularities that make theoretical sense. Good examples of this were found in the reported results of the Munich study.

REFERENCES

Arlin, M. (1984). Time, equality, and mastery learning. *Review of Educational Research, 54,* 65–86.

Baltes, P. B., & Schaie, K. W. (1981). Aging and intelligence. In H. J. Wershow (Ed.), *Controversial issues in gerontology* (pp. 63–76). New York: Springer.

Baumert, J., Roeder, P. M., Sang, F., & Schmitz, B. (1985). Leistungsentwicklung und Ausgleich von Leistungsunterschieden in Gymnasialklassen [Growth of achievement and equalizing within-classroom differences in high schools]. *Beiträge aus dem Forschungsbereich Schule und Unterricht,* Nr. *12,* Berlin: Max-Planck-Institut für Bildungsforschung.

Baumert, J., Roeder, P. M., Sang, F., & Schmitz, B. (1986). Chancenausgleich - ein latentes Problem des Gymnasiums? [Equalizing of individual achievement differences within classrooms—A latent problem of high schools?].In U. Steffens (Ed.), *Qualität von Schule.* Wiesbaden: Hessisches Institut für Bildungsplanung und Schulentwicklung (HIBS).

Bloom, B. S. (1964). *Stability and change in human characteristics.* New York: Wiley.

Bloom, B. S. (1971). Learning for master. In B. S. Bloom, J. T. Hasting, & G. F. Madaus (Eds.), *Handbook on formative and summative evaluation of student learning* (chap. 3). New York: McGraw-Hill.

Bornstein, M. H., & Sigman, M. D. (1986). Continuity in mental development from infancy. *Child Development, 57,* 251–274.

Brookover, W., Beady, C., Flood, P., Schweitzer, J., & Wiesenbaker, J. (1979). *School social systems and student achievement. Schools can make a difference.* New York: Praeger.

Brophy, J. E., & Good, T. L. (1974). *Teacher-student relationships.* New York: Holt, Rinehart, & Winston.

Carey, S. (1985). *Conceptual change in childhood.* Cambridge, MA: MIT Press.

Coleman, J.S., Campbell, E. R., Hobson, C. J., McPartland, J., Mood, A. M., Weingold, F. D., & York, R. L. (1966). *Equality of educational opportunity.* Washington, DC: U.S. Government Printing Office.

Dixon, R. A., Kramer, D. A., & Baltes, P. B. (1985). Intelligence: A life-span developmental perspective. In B. B. Wolman (Ed.), *Handbook of intelligence: Theories, measurement, and applications* (pp. 301–350). New York: Wiley.

Good, T. L., Biddle, B. J., & Brophy, J. E. (1975). *Teachers make a difference.* New York: Holt, Rinehart & Winston.

Helmke, A., Schneider, W., & Weinert, F. E. (1986). Quality of instruction and classroom learning outcomes: The German contribution to the IEA Classroom Environment Study. *Teaching and Teacher Education, 1,* 1–31.

Helmke, A., & Schrader, F. W. (1987). Interactional effects of instructional quality and teacher judgment accuracy on achievement. *Teaching and Education, 3,* 91–98.

Horn, J. L., & Donaldson, A. (1980). Cognitive development in adulthood. In O. G. Brim, Jr., & J. Kagan (Eds.), *Constancy and change in human development* (pp. 445–529). Cambridge, MA: Harvard University Press.

Jencks, C., Smith, M., Acland, H., Bane, M. J., Cohen, D., Gintis, H., Heyns, B., & Michelson, S. (1972). *Inequality: A reassessment of the effect of family and schooling in America.* New York: Basic Books.

Kifer, E. (1975). Relationships between academic achievement and personality characteristics: A quasi-longitudinal study. *American Educational Research Journal, 12,* 191–210.

Körkel, J. (1984). *Die Entwicklung von Gedächtnis- und Metagedächtnisleistungen in Abhängigkeit von bereichsspezifischen Vorkenntnissen.* Unpublished doctoral dissertation, Universität Heidelberg.

Luecke, D. E., & McGinn, N. F. (1975). Regression analyses and education production functions: Can they be trusted? *Harvard Educational Review, 45,* 325–350.

Mosteller, F., & Moynihan, D. P. (Eds.). (1972). *On equality of educational opportunity.* New York: Vintage.

Pedersen, E., Faucher, T. A., & Eaton, W. W. (1978). A new perspective on the effects of first-grade teachers on children's subsequent adult status. *Harvard Educational Review, 48,* 1–31.

Rheinberg, F., & Enstrup, B. (1977). Selbstkonzept der Begabung bei Normal- und Sonderschülern gleicher Intelligenz: ein Bezugsgruppeneffekt. *Zeitschrift für Entwicklungspsychologie und Pädagogische Psychologie, 9,* 171–180.

Rutter, M. (1983). School effects on pupil progress: Research findings and policy implications. *Child Development, 54,* 1–29.

Ryan, D. W., & Anderson, L. (1984). The IEA Classroom Environment Study: Promises and pitfalls. *Evaluation in Education, 8,* 87–93.

Ryan, D., & Shapiro, B. (Eds.). (in press). *The Classroom Environment Study: Teaching for learning.* Oxford: Pergamon Press.

Simpson, M. (1980). The sociology of cognitive development: *Annual Review of Sociology, 6,* 287–313.

Stevenson, H. W., Parker, T., Wilkinson, A., Bonneveux, B., & Gonzalez, M. (1978). Schooling, environment, and cognitive development: A cross-cultural study. *Monographs of the Society for Research in Child Development, 43* (Serial No. 178).

Treiber, B., Weinert, F. E. (1985). *Gute Schulleistungen für alle?* [Success in school for all students?]. Münster: Aschendorff.

Treiber, B., Weinert, F. E., & Groeben, N. (1976). Bedingungen individuellen unterrichtserfolges. *Zeitschrift für Pädagogik, 22* (pp. 153–179).

Treiber, D., Weinert, F. E., & Groeben, N. (1982). Unterrichtsqualität, Leistungsniveau von Schulklassen und individueller Lernfortschritt. *Zeitschrift für Pädagogik, 27,* 563–576.

Walberg, H. J. (1984). Improving the productivity of America's schools. *Educational Leadership, 41,* 19–30.

Walker, D. A. (1976). *The six-subject survey: International studies in evaluation—An empirical study of education in twenty-one countries.* New York: Wiley.

Weinert, F. E., & Helmke, A. (1987). Compensatory effects of student self-concept and instructional quality on academic achievement. In F. Halisch & J. Kuhl (Eds.), *Motivation, intention, and volition* (pp. 233–247). Berlin: Springer.

Weinert, F. E., & Treiber, B. (1982). School socialization and cognitive development. In W. W. Hartup (Ed.), *Review of child development research* (Vol. 6, pp. 704–758). Chicago: The University of Chicago Press.

Willis, S. L. (1985). Towards an educational psychology of the older adult learner. Intellectual and cognitive bases. In J. E. Birren & K. W. Schaie (Eds.), *Handbook of the psychology of aging* (pp. 818–847). New York: Van Nostrand.

Wohlwill, J. F. (1980). Cognitive development in childhood. In O. G. Brim, Jr. & J. Kagan (Eds.), *Constancy and change in human development* (pp. 359–444). Cambridge, MA: Harvard University Press.

11 CULTURE AND SCHOOLING:
Influences on Cognitive Development

Harold W. Stevenson
University of Michigan

ABSTRACT

This chapter reviews the findings of two cross-cultural studies of the influence of schooling on the cognitive development of children. The first study involves a comparison of Chinese, Japanese, and American elementary school children. The second study involves Quechua-speaking Indian children who live in Peruvian villages or cities. Both studies focus on the influence of parental beliefs and academic experiences on scholastic achievement and cognitive development in elementary school children.

INTRODUCTION

In our research on the influence of schooling on the cognitive development of children, we have studied children in several very diverse cultures: urban children in Taiwan, Japan, and the United States, and Quechua-speaking Indian children who reside in cities and villages in Peru. Individual studies have been designed for a variety of purposes, but all have included some consideration of how parental beliefs influence the scholastic achievement and cognitive development of young elementary school children.

The evidence concerning the relation of schooling and cognitive abilities seems clear. Attending school improves children's skill in the types of activities and material that are taught in school, and also results in improved performance on cognitive tasks that require information and abilities that are not directly taught to the children (Rogoff, 1981;

Stevenson, 1982). The argument that is made in this chapter is that the degree to which children's academic and cognitive abilities are improved by schooling is dependent on parental beliefs about such fundamental phenomena as human malleability, parental responsibility, and the future. These beliefs influence both parental involvement with their children and the degree to which they expect a society to emphasize the role of schooling in children's development.

The first section of this chapter describes some of the data we have obtained in our cross-cultural studies of Chinese, Japanese, and American elementary school children. The second section is devoted to a description of some of our findings from Peru.

COMPARATIVE STUDIES OF CHINESE, JAPANESE, AND AMERICAN CHILDREN

Our initial purpose in studying Asian and American elementary school children was to investigate the role of orthography in reading. The Chinese, Japanese, and English written languages use different orthographic systems, and some writers have suggested that reading achievement in Chinese and Japanese is aided by the use of distinctive, whole characters and a more regular relation between grapheme and phoneme than occurs in English (e.g., Rozin & Gleitman, 1977). Very quickly, however, it became apparent that the major cognitive differences among children from these three cultures were not in their reading ability, but in their ability in mathematics and other cognitive domains. These differences can be illustrated by describing the performance of kindergarten, first, and fifth graders in three tasks: mathematics, general information, and vocabulary. Although other cognitive tasks were given to the kindergarten and elementary school children, the structure of the other tasks differed at the different age levels, thereby precluding comparisons of developmental changes in their performance.

The Samples

The samples for these studies were obtained from three urban settings: the Minneapolis metropolitan area; Taipei, Taiwan; and Sendai, Japan. With the cooperation of school authorities, we were able to select representative, random samples of 24 kindergarten classrooms, and 20 first- and 20 fifth-grade classrooms in each of the three cities. From each class we then randomly chose 6 boys and 6 girls for intensive study. This procedure yielded samples of 288 kindergarten children, 240 first-graders, and 240 fifth-graders in each city. The children were given achievement and cognitive tasks, their mothers and teachers were interviewed, and extensive observations were conducted in the children's classrooms.

The Tasks

Our first step in constructing the mathematics test was to analyze the content of the kindergarten and elementary school textbook series used in each city. A list was compiled of each concept and skill introduced, and the grade and semester in which it first appeared. Items were constructed to tap concepts and skills introduced in the textbooks used in each culture. Both computational and word problems were included. Items were constructed for each grade level from kindergarten through sixth grade, and the tests developed for each culture were identical except for language. All tests were individually administered. Word problems were read to the child to avoid the possibility that failure to solve the problems was due to poor reading ability. The test for elementary school children included 70 items. These were supplemented by simpler questions tapping basic numerical and mathematical concepts in a 30-question test for kindergarteners.

The general information test was similar to those used in standardized tests of intelligence. Children were asked questions tapping common knowledge. A distinction was made between questions requiring inferential reasoning and those dependent on factual knowledge. It was decided to minimize the number of the first type because the purpose of the test was to assess the amount of common knowledge the child had acquired through everyday experience. The procedure for developing items involved reviewing the Japanese, Chinese, and American versions of the Wechsler Intelligence Scale for Children (Revised; WISC-R), reading popular books and materials written for children in each country, and discussing possible questions with native speakers of each language. After reviewing a larger number of questions and obtaining agreement that the questions were culturally appropriate, a final list of 26 questions was selected for the kindergarten children. Questions were of the types: "What is bigger, an elephant or a horse?"; "From what direction does the sun rise?"; and "Why can't people live under water?" The test for the elementary school children also contained 26 items, but some of the easy items were eliminated and more difficult items were substituted. The more difficult items were ones such as "What causes an eclipse?" and "Why do blankets keep us warm?"

A vocabulary test similar to those contained in many tests of children's intelligence also was constructed. Children were asked to define words. The words were obtained from many different sources: the lexicon of all words contained in the readers used in the elementary schools of the three cities, popular books and magazines for children from each culture, and the Japanese, Chinese, and American versions of the WISC-R. Words were reviewed by native speakers of each language who also were skilled in at least one of the other languages. The final list contained 25 words that were judged to be of equal difficulty in the three languages, were considered to have preciseldy the same meaning in the three languages, and could be scored reliably. Typical words included in the test were "bicycle," "mud," "museum," and "banish." The kindergarten test contained 31 items, 13 in a picture vocabulary test, 8 in a test of prepositions within sentences, and 10 that involved defining words selected from among those used in the elementary school test.

Scores on all three tests increased, of course, through the elementary school years. More interesting, however, is the question of whether the developmental changes in the three cultures were comparable. To illustrate the relative degree of cross-national change, standard (z) scores were computed at each grade level. For example, scores of all 864 kindergarten children on the mathematics test were combined into a single distribution and a z score for each child was computed. Scores were then recombined by country and the mean z scores were determined for each country. The same procedure was followed for each task at each grade level. If children in each country were equally successful in mathematics, the three mean z scores would be 0. The degree to which the mean z scores depart from 0 indicates how well, or how poorly, the children in one country did relative to those in the other two countries.

Mathematics.   Scores for the mathematics test appear in Figure 11.1. American children's scores declined across the elementary school years in relation to those of the Japanese and Chinese children, the scores of the Chinese children increased, and those of the Japanese children remained high from kindergarten through the fifth grade. The poor performance of American children in mathematics is not an unusual finding, for other studies have reported that during the middle- and high-school years American students do much less well in mathematics than their Japanese peers (e.g., McKnight et al., 1987). What is so startling about our results is that the difference is evident as early as kindergarten.

As we have reported, the poor performance of the first- and fifth-grade American children on the mathematics test is related to many factors, such as less frequent instruction in mathematics, less homework, and a less demanding curriculum in mathematics (Stevenson, Lee, & Stigler, 1986; Stigler, Lee, Lucker, & Stevenson, 1982). For example, we have estimated that the American first-grade teachers spent approximately 11 hours a week and that fifth-grade teachers spent approximately 8 hours a week on language arts (Stevenson et al., 1986). In contrast, the American teachers spent an average of only 3 hours a week on mathematics at both first and fifth grades. Japanese teachers, on the other hand, devoted more similar

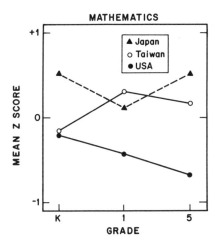

FIGURE 11.1 Chinese, Japanese, and American children's performance on the mathematics test.

amounts of classroom time to language arts and mathematics at both first (8.7 vs. 5.8 hours) and fifth (8.0 vs. 7.8 hours) grades. Values for the Chinese teachers were very similar to those for the Japanese teachers.

Why should there be such great differences in the amount of time American teachers devote to instruction in reading and mathematics? For some reason—possibly related to the diversity of languages spoken by immigrants to America—Americans have a strong belief that skill in reading English is a more important accomplishment during the elementary school years than is skill in mathematics. Evidence for such a belief appeared in the data from the interviews held with the children's mothers. Despite the large amount of time spent on instruction in reading, nearly half of the American mothers of fifth graders who suggested that academic improvements should be made in their children's schooling mentioned reading. Only 5% mentioned mathematics.

Responses of the children also revealed different perceptions of the roles of reading and mathematics in the three cultures. For example, the fifth-graders were asked to rate their abilities in mathematics and reading (e.g., "How good at math are you?") and their own brightness (i.e., "If you were to rank all the students in your class from the brightest to the most stupid, where would you put yourself?"). American children's self-perceptions of their brightness were strongly related to their evaluations of their reading ability; Chinese and Japanese children were more likely to consider themselves to be bright if they perceived themselves as being skilled in mathematics. The correlation between the self-ratings of brightness and of reading ability was .47 for the American children, but was .29 for the Chinese children, and .16 for the Japanese children. When the self-ratings of brightness and of mathematics ability were computed, however, the correlation was .37 in Taiwan and .46 in Japan. For the American children, the correlation was .20. Beliefs about the importance of mathematics and reading appear to determine the time and effort that members of the three cultures are willing to devote to instruction during the elementary school years.

Another, more basic set of beliefs also appears to play an important role in determining the outcomes of schooling. We (Stevenson et al., 1986) and others (e.g., Azuma, Kashiwagi, & Hess, 1981), have found that Japanese mothers place greater emphasis on the value of effort than do American mothers, and that American mothers, in turn, place greater emphasis on ability than do Japanese mothers in their explanations of successful performance in school. The dedication of students, parents, and teachers to children's schooling is dependent on the degree to which there is acceptance of the belief that this devotion will yield important benefits to the children. Such a belief is closely related to theories of human behavior long espoused in Asian philosophies.

The malleability of human behavior has often been described in Chinese writings (Munro, 1977). Uniformity in human nature is assumed; differences that arise among people are believed to be primarily a result of life experiences rather than an expression of innate differences among individuals. Emphasis is placed, therefore, on the virtue of effort as the avenue for improvement and accomplishment. A similar theme is found in Japanese philosophy, where individual differences in potential are de-emphasized and great importance is placed on the role of effort in modifying the course of human development. Effort and self-discipline are considered by Japanese to be essential bases for accomplishment. Lack of achievement is attributed to the failure to work hard, rather than to a lack of ability or to personal or environmental obstacles.

Cultural differences in these beliefs were demonstrated in several ways. For example, clear differences were found when mothers were asked to evaluate the role of effort, ability, and other factors in achievement. The mothers were told:

> Many factors contribute to children's academic performance in school, such as the child's effort, the child's natural ability, the difficulty of the schoolwork, and luck or chance. Which of these do you think is most important in determining a child's performance in school? Which is next in importance? Next?

After the mother had made the four choices the interviewer continued:

> Let's say you give 1 point to (the item ranked lowest by the mother) according to its importance in determining children's performance in school. Now say

you had a total of 10 points you could give. How many points do you think you would give (next lowest item)? To (item ranked second?)

The mean number of points assigned to each of the items appears in Figure 11.2. American mothers assigned fewer points to effort than did the Chinese and Japanese mothers, but assigned more points to ability.

Other data lead to similar conclusions about the relation of ability to achievement. Mothers were asked to rate their child's intelligence and academic potential. In a country such as the United States, where mothers emphasize the role of ability in determining academic success, there should be a closer relation between the ratings of intelligence and academic potential than in a country such as Japan, where less emphasis is given to ability. In other words, the degree to which mothers believe intelligence and academic potential are related should differ among the three countries. This is what was found. Correlations between the ratings of intelligence and academic potential were .70 and .65 for the ratings made by American mothers of first- and fifth-graders. The correlations were .54 and .45 for the

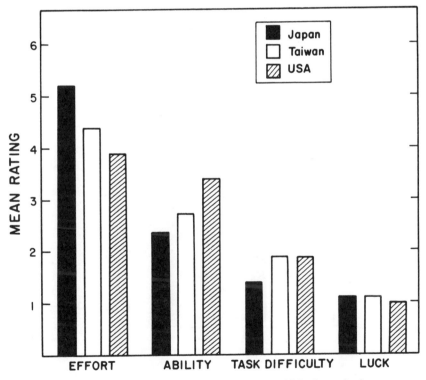

FIGURE 11.2 Mothers' ratings of factors contributing to children's academic success.

ratings made by the Chinese mothers, and .50 and .43 for the ratings made by the Japanese mothers. Differences between the American and both the Chinese and Japanese correlations at fifth grade were statistically significant, and between the American and Japanese correlations at Grade 1.

This pattern of beliefs about effort and ability also appeared in the responses of the children. The fifth-graders were asked to rate a series of statements on a 7-point scale with alternatives ranging from strongly disagree to strongly agree. For statements such as "People tend to have the same amount of math ability," and "Any student can be good at math if he/she works hard enough,"American fifth-graders showed the greatest amount of disagreement. These data are presented in Figure 11.3. On the other hand, for a statement such as, "The tests you take can show how much or how little natural ability you have," American children showed the greatest degree of agreement. Their mean rating for their degree of agreement was 4.7; the means for the Chinese and Japanese children were 3.9 and 2.8.

To the degree that parents and children believe success depends on ability rather than effort, they are less likely to foster participation in activities, such as doing homework, attending afterschool classes, and assisting their children with their mathematics, that would elicit strong effort toward

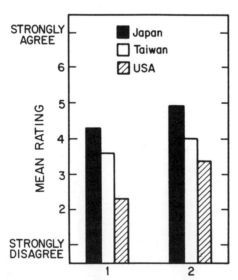

1 People tend to have same amount of math ability
2 Any student can be good at math if he/she works hard enough

FIGURE 11.3 Children's ratings of beliefs about mathematics.

learning by their children. These activities, in fact, are not ones used with great frequency by American parents as means for improving their children's scholastic performance. Thus, the lower emphasis given to mathematics as an academic subject and to effort as a means of accomplishment seem to be important variables underlying the American children's lower accomplishments in mathematics in elementary school. Why should mathematics be emphasized in school if the route to demonstrating achievement is through reading well, and why should the child who receives average or below average grades in mathematics study hard when innate ability is believed to be such an important determinant of achievement?

General Information and Vocabulary. The mean z scores for the general information test appear in Figure 11.4, and the scores for the vocabulary test appear in Figure 11.5. Developmental changes in the relative performance of the children from the three countries are even more dramatic than were the changes in the mathematics scores. American kindergarten children received remarkably high scores on the general information test. Their mean score was nearly one standard deviation above the mean for kindergarten children from all three countries. In contrast, the average score for the Chinese kindergarteners was nearly half of a standard deviation below the overall mean. The changes in relative status after kindergarten were so great that by the fifth grade the mean scores for the children from the three countries did not differ significantly from each other. Scores for the American children had declined; scores for the Chinese children had improved; and scores for the Japanese children remained more stable.

The pattern was similar for the vocabulary test, except that the relative decline for the American children occurred between first and fifth grades. There was a decline in the relative status of the Japanese children between kindergarten and first grade, and again the scores for the Chinese children increased after kindergarten.

These results were unexpected. We had no a priori basis for assuming that attendance at school would be accompanied by such differential effects on the scores of the children on these two tests. An obvious interpretation is that these differences could be due to a bias in the items used at different ages or in the scoring of the tests. We reject these possibilities because professionals in each country, including psychologists and teachers, evaluated all of the items for their appropriateness, and each item was scored independently by two native speakers from each country. Any differences in scores assigned by these two persons were resolved through group discussion by the persons from all three countries who were scoring the tests. The

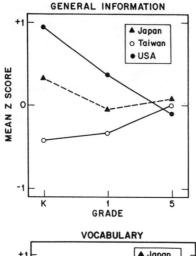

FIGURE 11.4 Children's performance on the test of general information.

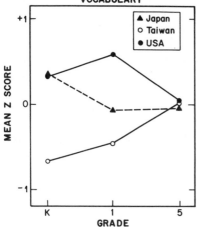

FIGURE 11.5 Children's performance on the vocabulary test.gure

interpretation is more complex and depends on cultural beliefs about the roles of general experience and schooling on child development. These beliefs differ greatly between Asian and American cultures.

The preschool years are considered to be a very special time in the lives of Chinese and Japanese children. Children are highly valued in each culture and until the child enters school, the child is the recipient of great indulgence on the part of parents and other adults. Azuma (1986) has described the period for Japanese children in the following way:

Many foreign observers, ranging from sixteenth century Jesuit missionaries to contemporary American anthropologists, have noted that young children in Japan, though "indulged," are, nevertheless, well behaved. Hara and Wagatsuma (1974) report that in many parts of Japan people used to believe that, because a child came from another world and was not yet deeply settled in this world until age 6 or 7, he or she had to be treated with indulgence and tenderness up to then. Otherwise, it was said, the child would soon go back to the other world. (p. 8–9)

This view is very different from that espoused by American parents. Rather than seeing the preschool years as a period for indulgence, American parents appear to see this as a time when they are especially important in helping the child develop cognitive skills. American parents spend a great deal of time with their kindergarten children and are more likely to engage them in intellectually stimulating activities than are Chinese and Japanese parents. For example, 98% of the American mothers said they read to their kindergarten children, compared to 84% of the Japanese mothers and 76% of the Chinese mothers. The frequency with which parents of kindergarten children reported taking their children on outings to such places as museums, parks, and theaters was much higher among American parents than among Chinese and Japanese parents. American mothers reported that they, their husbands, or they and their husbands together took their child on an average of 8.6 outings during the month preceding the interview. The mean for Chinese parents was 4.8, and for Japanese parents, 1.1. American mothers also reported that they spent more time with their kindergarten children than did Chinese and Japanese mothers. On a typical weekday, for example, the American mothers said they interacted with or were available to their kindergarten children an average of 9.2 hours a day. The values for the Chinese and Japanese mothers were 6.9 and 6.7 hours a day.

The situation changes markedly after the child enters elementary school. American parents appear to assume that the education of their children is now the school's business and are likely to become less involved with their child's intellectual development and school activities than they were before the child entered first grade. Chinese and Japanese mothers, on the other hand, consider entrance to school as the time when their interaction with their children begins to become especially important. They mobilize themselves, their child, and other members of the family to foster the child's education. This is the time of the Japanese *kyoiku mama,* the educational mom who plays such an important role supervising the child's educational progress, and a time in the Chinese family when all members—parents, siblings, and grandparents—become available to assist children with their schoolwork. Both Chinese and Japanese children were provided more assistance with their homework, for example, than were American children. Among mothers of first-graders, American mothers estimated that someone—usually themselves—assisted their child with homework an average of 14 minutes a day. The averages for Taiwan and Japan were 27 and 23 minutes a day.

Another indication of the devotion of families to the child's schoolwork appears in the willingness of Chinese and Japanese mothers to reduce children's responsibility for daily chores around the home. Among the elementary school children, 23% of the Chinese children and 73% of the Japanese children were assigned chores. Among American children, 93% had daily chores. Few American children, but 14% of the Japanese children avoided doing their daily chores. Why were so few Chinese children required to do chores? Among first-graders, the main reason was that they were too young. Among fifth-graders, it was because they were too busy. One Chinese mother summed the feelings of many mothers when she said it would break her heart to ask her child to do chores. When asked why, she replied that it was because chores would take her child from his homework. Although 73% of the Japanese children had chores, they were ones, the mothers often explained, that would help the child by instilling a sense of responsibility or by teaching the child good habits, rather than because doing the chores would be helpful to the family.

The emphasis on academic pursuits is evident in the amount of time children spent doing homework and reading for pleasure each week. Mothers were asked to estimate the amount of time their child spent on homework during weekdays and on weekends doing homework and in reading for pleasure. The results for the first-graders illustrate the cross-national differences that exist. The average estimates for homework were 71, 490, and 230 minutes per week for the American, Chinese, and Japanese children, respectively. The respective estimates for reading for pleasure each week were 188, 235, and 296 minutes per week. The lesser progress of the American children cannot be unrelated to the fact that they spend less than half as much time each week during the elementary school years as the Chinese and Japanese children in activities that have the potential for enhancing cognitive development.

Cross-national differences in relative scores on the general information and vocabulary tests appear to be strongly related, therefore, to the different beliefs and expectations parents have about early and later childhood. In all three cultures, entrance into elementary school is an important point in the child's life. In Chinese and Japanese families it is the time when hard work, both in the family and at school, begins. Children are expected to dedicate themelves to their academic studies and members of the family begin to assume greater responsibility for helping the children make progress. As a result, there is rapid improvement, not only in academic tasks, but also in other cognitive domains, such as possessing a greater fund of common knowledge and knowing definitions for a larger number of words. The transition from preschool to elementary school appears to follow a different course for many American children. During their preschool years, parents assume responsibility for their child's cognitive development, but the child's entrance into elementary school is a cue for many parents to abdicate some of these responsibilities. Academically relevant activities occupy a modest portion of the child's time at home and parents offer little daily support for such activities. As a result, academic achievement and cognitive development do not maintain the rate of development that occurred during the preschool years.

COMPARATIVE STUDIES OF
QUECHUA-SPEAKING INDIAN CHILDREN

Our work in Peru suggests other variables that have an important influence on cognitive development. We began this research because in Peru, as in many other developing countries, a large proportion — perhaps 50% — of school-age children do not attend school. Differences exist between families that send their children to school and those that do not (Stevenson, 1982). Children who attend school come from families where, compared to the families of children who do not attend school, parents have a higher level of education, where there is greater evidence of modernity, as reflected in possessing such items as a radio or books, and where efforts are made to teach the children such fundamental things as colors and the seasons of the year. Even after the influence of these and other variables are removed statistically in the prediction of the influence of schooling on cognitive development, significant effects of schooling remain. These conclusions are based on the results of over 20 tasks that were given to the children. Here, however, only the results of two tasks, mathematics and general information, are discussed.

The Samples

The children lived in one of three areas in Peru: shanty towns (*barriadas*) in the outskirts of Lima; Andahuaylas, a remote part of the highlands; and Lamas, a region in the northeast rain forest. Access to many of the villages in Andahuaylas and Lamas is only by foot. All of the children in the groups discussed were from Quechua-speaking families, who in the immediate or distant past resided in the Peruvian highlands. The children were from 9 to 12 years old. Some children in each location had never been to school; others were enrolled in the first, second, or third grade. Approximately 60 children were included in each of the groups, making a total of over 700 children.

The Tasks

Tests were constructed in the same manner as those for the study of Chinese, Japanese, and American children. The mathematics test was based on the types of problems that appear in Peruvian mathematics textbooks. Problems ranged from ones involving counting and reading numbers to oral word problems and written calculations. The general information test relied on items of common knowledge that Peruvian children might be expected to know, such as how many paws a dog has, what pumps blood through our bodies, and the colors of the Peruvian flag.

Test Results

As can be seen in Figure 11.6, the greater the amount of schooling, the higher were the scores in mathematics. The effects were not equivalent, however, in the three locations. Children in Lamas showed less improvement from successive years of schooling than did the children in Andahuaylas and Lima. The high scores of the Lima and Lamas children who did not attend school can be explained by children's daily experiences in contributing to the family income. In Lima, older elementary school children are expected to provide some income to the family, and to do so by selling items in downtown areas or collecting materials, such as glass, which they sell. In Lamas, children are more fluent in Spanish than are their parents. Because the economy is controlled by Spanish-speaking mestizos, the children assist their parents in bartering or selling their farm products. In each case, children are required to become skilled in basic arithmetical concepts and skills in order to carry out their daily tasks. Children are not called upon to play these roles in the Quechua-speaking highlands communities. Commerce is carried on in Quechua, and children are not needed as translators. Children assist their parents in farming rather than in attempting to earn money through selling.

Scores on the general information test also reflected less rapid development in Lamas. Although there was a greater difference between first-graders and the children who did not attend school in Lamas than in Andahuaylas and Lima, the contribution of successive years of schooling was notably smaller in Lamas than in either of the other two locations. The increase between the scores of first- and third-graders on the general information test was 11 points in Lima and 15 points in Andahuaylas, but only 6 points in Lamas. The mean percentages of correct response appear in Table 11.1.

Interpretation

The slower development of children in Lamas is undoubtedly due to many factors, including less frequent attendance at school; greater poverty; a lower level of parental education; and more limited access to radios, books, and other sources of information. A more basic factor, however, is the typical villager's orientation in time. For residents of Lamas, time seems to

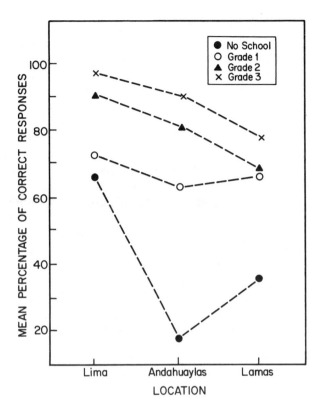

FIGURE 11.6 Peruvian children's performance on the mathematics test.

TABLE 11.1
Mean Percentage of Correct Response

Schooling	Lima	Andahuaylas	Lamas
None	45	44	28
Grade 1	46	43	36
Grade 2	54	54	35
Grade 3	57	58	42

consist of the present and the past. In Lima and Andahuaylas, however, there is also a clear sense of the future. Answering questions about the future was easy for adults in the latter two locations, but often resulted in hesitant, vague responses on the part of the villagers of Lamas. With only a dim sense of the future, it was more difficult for adults in Lamas to comprehend the value of school attendance.

Residents of Lamas conceive of the future as a continuation of the present. Thinking or planning for the future is of less importance than making sure that the present is productive. Their children, they proposed, would be farmers and herdsmen when they grew up, following the occupations they and their families before them had followed. Even though the primary occupation of persons in both Andahuaylas and Lamas were farming and herding, only 21% of the parents in Andahuaylas, but 79% of the parents in Lamas, said their children would follow these occupations. No parent in Lamas, but 24% of the parents in Andahuaylas proposed that their children would become professionals. Going beyond the most fundamental aspects of schooling would be of little value for the future farmer of a small jungle plot. On the other hand, becoming a professional requires intense dedication to schooling. The strong motivation of Lima parents for their children's schooling is evident in the expectation — obviously unrealistic — that 56% of the children would become professionals.

Why do residents of Lamas not look forward to the future? Probably because they reside in one of the poorest areas of Peru and are minority members of a mestizo-dominated culture. The barter economy of Lamas has been stable for centuries. Only recently, with the construction of new roads and the creation of new jobs in the cocaine trade, has there been visible improvement in the economic status of families within the lifetime of any individual. These changes may lead to more consideration by the residents of Lamas of how academic preparation in the present may lead to greater opportunties for their children in the future.

CONCLUSION

What, then, is the influence of attending school on cognitive development? Many experiences in school contribute to improved performance on cognitive tasks such as those included in these studies. Children learn to attend to adult directions, have practice in answering formal questions, develop strategies for analyzing problems and remembering materials, become more fluent in formulating answers, and develop means of representing the world in abstract rather than concrete terms. Other studies have pointed to the importance of these variables. Research would be incomplete, however, unless efforts were made to understand the belief systems of the families in which the children live. What children experience at school as well as at home are dependent on these beliefs, and both sources of experience have important effects on cognitive development.

The research that has been described delineates the possible roles of several types of belief on children's performance. If parents do not believe strongly in the importance of a particular type of skill, it is unlikely that the child will be given the experience, assistance, and psychological support necessary for rapid development of the skill. This appeared to be the case for American parents and their children's performance in mathematics. The lack of attention given to mathematics by American parents is in marked contrast to the attention given by parents in Asian cultures, such as in Japan and Taiwan. Without a stronger belief among American parents that mathematics is an important skill to be acquired, it is unlikely that teachers will devote more time to mathematics, that the curriculum will become more demanding, or that children will be motivated to spend the time necessary to master fundamental mathematical knowledge and skills.

Perhaps even more important than parents' belief in the importance of particular skills is the degree to which they believe that effort on the part of their child is an important determinant of successful performance. When this belief is shared by the child, both the parent and child have a reason for dedicating the time and effort necessary for the child's academic achievement. The importance of hard work is diminished to the degree that parents believe that native ability is a basis for accomplishment. Holding this belief has many possible negative consequences. It provides an excuse for offering some children less challenging curricula and making fewer demands for their mastery of the material. Even worse, it fosters the belief in some children, especially those who have lower levels of prior achievement, that expenditure of effort is useless in the face of low ability. Belief in the importance of hard work, coupled with the belief that this should occur in elementary school, appears to be one of the most important bases for the rapid cognitive development of Chinese and Japanese children during the elementary school years.

Asian and American mothers appear to differ greatly in their beliefs about the obligations of parents during the preschool and elementary school years. Many American mothers appear to believe that the time in which they are primarily responsible for fostering their child's development is during the preschool years. Japanese and Chinese mothers, in contrast, appear to give less stress to providing their children with a stimulating environment before they enter school, but mobilize themselves and other members of their families to aid the children after this. Cognitive development of both schooled and nonschooled children must depend, in part, on the types of experiences and opportunities provided by their families outside of school.

Finally, the emphasis that schooling receives in a culture also appears to depend on the degree to which parents are able to contemplate the importance of present events for the child's later life. If the future is not seen as a time in which improvement in the life situation is possible, parents find little utility in regular or extended attendance at school. This appeared to be the case in Lamas. Parents who attended only a few years of school themselves were unenthusiastic about their children's academic experiences. Attendance at school was not accompanied by the same types of cognitive development as occurred in other Peruvian communities, where parents believed that investment in schooling during the child's early years could pay off in greater opportunities in adulthood.

The purpose in this chapter has been to discuss how development in childhood is related to what occurs in other phases of the life span, in this case, the relation of cognitive development and parental beliefs. Unless we understand how child development and development through the life span are interrelated, we cannot fully comprehend either. Moreover, our understanding cannot be complete unless we investigate the manner in which these two factors are interrelated in cultures other than our own.

ACKNOWLEDGMENTS

The research reported in this chapter was supported by grants from the National Science Foundation, the National Institute of Mental Health, and the William T. Grant Foundation. It was conducted in collaboration with many persons, including Shinying Lee, James Stigler, Max Lummis, and Alexander Wilkinson.

REFERENCES

Azuma, H. (1986). Why study child development in Japan? In H. W. Stevenson, H. Azuma, & K. Hakuta (Eds.), *Child development and education in Japan* (pp. 3–12). New York: W. H. Freeman.

Azuma, H., Kashiwagi, K., & Hess, R. D. (1981). *Hahaoya no taido koudo to kodomo no chiteki hattatsu.* [The effect of mother's attitude and behavior on the cognitive development of the child: A U.S.-Japan comparison] Tokyo: University of Tokyo Press.

McKnight, C. C., Crosswhite, F. J., Dossey, J. A., Kifer, E., Swafford, J. O., Travers, K. J., & Cooney, T. J. (1987). *The underachieving curriculum: Assessing U.S. school mathematics from an international perspective.* Champaign, IL: Stites Publishing.

Munro, D. J. (1977). *The concept of man in contemporary China.* Ann Arbor, MI: University of Michigan Press.

Rogoff, B. (1981). Schooling and the development of cognitive skills. In H.C. Triandis & A. Heron (Eds.), *Handbook of cross-cultural psychology. Developmental psychology* (Vol. 4, pp. 233–294). Boston: Allyn & Bacon.

Rozin, P., & Gleitman, L. R. (1977). The structure and acquisition of reading II: The reading process and the acquisition of the alphabetic principle. In A. S. Reber & D. L. Scarborough (Eds.), *Toward a psychology of reading* (pp. 1–53). Hillsdale, NJ: Lawrence Erlbaum Associates.

Stevenson, H. W. (1982). Influences of schooling on cognitive development. In D. Wagner & H. W. Stevenson (Eds.), *Cross-cultural studies of child development* (pp. 208–224). San Francisco: W. H. Freeman.

Stevenson, H. W., Lee, S. Y., & Stigler, J. W. (1986). Mathematics achievement of Chinese, Japanese, and American children. *Science, 231,* 693–699.

Stevenson, H. W., Stigler, J. W., Lucker, G. W., Lee, S. Y., Hsu, C. C., & Kitamura, S. (1986). Classroom behavior and achievement of Japanese, Chinese, and American children. In R. Glaser (Ed.), *Advances in instructional psychology,* (Vol. 3, pp. 153–204). Hillsdale, NJ: Lawrence Erlbaum Associates.

Stigler, J. W., Lee, S. Y., Lucker, G. W., & Stevenson, H. W. (1982). Curriculum and achievement in mathematics: A study of elementary school children in Japan, Taiwan, and the United States. *Journal of Educational Psychology, 74,* 315–322.

12 LESSONS FROM THE LIFE SPAN:

What Theorists of Intellectual Development Among Children Can Learn from Their Counterparts Studying Adults

Robert J. Sternberg
Yale University

ABSTRACT

Although thus far the study of adult intelligence has been influenced by the study of the intelligence of children the reverse has not been true. In this chapter it is proposed that those studying intelligence in children could benefit from a consideration of the perspectives and assumptions found in theorists of adult intelligence. Ten lessons are presented that child psychologists studying intelligence can learn from those studying adult intelligence.

INTRODUCTION

Human development comprises two fields, *de facto* if not *de jure*. The first field is that of child development; the second field is that of adult development. The first field concerns itself with people roughly through the age of later adolescence, and the second field picks up from there. The first field deals with relatively few years in the life of the person — at most, 20 or so — whereas the second field deals with more than three times as many years — roughly, 70. Each field has its own specialized society: the Society for Research in Child Development, in the first case, and the Gerontological Society, in the second case. The first field has its own division of the American Psychological Association (APA), called the "Division of Developmental Psychology," but lest there be any mistake about its purview, there is also a separate division for the second field called the "Division of Adult Development and Aging": The membership of the two divisions shows only modest overlap, as do the kinds of papers presented in their purview at meetings of the American Psychological Association. The first field has its own prestigious journals, such as *Child Development,* the *Journal of Experimental Child Psychology,* and *Developmental Psychology.* For many years, the last of these journals published occasional articles about adult development, but with the institution of the new APA journal, *Psychology and Aging,* one can expect the division to be complete. Prestigious journals such as *Gerontology* and the *Journal of Gerontology* concentrate on adult development, and only a couple of journals, such as *Developmental Review* and *Human Development*, regularly contain articles about both child and adult development. Even here, the former journal specializes more in child development and the latter in adult development.

More important than the separation into specialized societies, APA divisions, and journals, is the separation into different points of view about human development, in general, and, from the standpoint of this chapter, intellectual development, in particular. Psychologists in the two camps approach intellectual development, and questions about it, with rather different perspectives. In the field of intellectual development, the study of children has the longer history than the study of adults, and more importantly, the study of adults has been heavily influenced by the study of children, but not vice versa. The thesis of this chapter is that there is a need for the study of children to be more heavily influenced by the study of adults—that assumptions and predilections commonplace among theorists of adult intelligence need at least to be examined by those studying intelligence in children. In particular, I delineate 10 lessons I believe child psychologists studying intelligence can and should learn from those studying intelligence among adults.

LESSON #1: INTELLECTUAL DEVELOPMENT DOES NOT END IN ADOLESCENCE

The tradition in the field of child psychology is that intellectual development more or less ends in adolescence. After all, the field ends there, and what could there be after the end of the world? This tradition is not limited to any one perspective. The traditional Stanford–Binet, and tests like it, used ages only up to about 15 years, 6 months, or 16 years, as the denominator for the intelligence quotient. If higher chronological ages were used, IQs dropped precipitously. Even more recent tests, providing norms in the form of deviation rather than ratio IQs, often end their norms in upper adolescence, and like the Stanford-Binet, recommend the use of those norms for adults, sometimes with a correction factor. Piaget's (1972) theory of intelligence, of course, ends with the period of formal operations, which suggests the culmination of intellectual development in the early teens, unless one takes the more sound point of view that formal operations continue to develop throughout adulthood. Even from this point of view, however, further change in intelligence is solely quantitative, not qualitative. Most information-processing theorists of intellectual development in children also end their theorizing at the age of adolescence (see Sternberg, 1984). In the field of childhood intellectual development, one is very much reminded of the ending to so many good fairy tales: "And they lived happily ever after."

Unfortunately, the view that intellectual development ends in adolescence is a fairy tale. Those who have chosen seriously to study intellectual development over the life span disagree as to what happens to the course of intelligence over the life span, but they agree that the story does not end in adolescence. Horn (1968) has suggested that fluid ability (as measured by tests such as abstract analogies and letter series) continues to increase at a decreasing rate throughout early adulthood, and then starts to decrease; crystallized ability continues to increase throughout the adult life span (short of possible senility), although at a decreasing rate. Schaie (1979; Baltes & Schaie, 1976) has questioned this view, suggesting that, for the most part, all aspects of intelligence show increase or at least stability throughout most of the life span. Baltes, Dittmann-Kohli, and Dixon (1984) have argued that there is much more plasticity, multidimensionality, multidirectionality, and interindividual variability in intelligence over the life span than previous views have recognized. If different positions have all seemed to have some merit, according to these authors, it is because they all do so for at least a subset of adults.

The view of intellectual development continuing beyond adolescence has obvious implications for the study of adult intelligence, and it has implications for the study of intelligence in children as well. First, it suggests that adolescent intelligence is part of a dynamic and ongoing process of intellectual development, not the end of it. Second, it suggests that whatever it is that we have studied as intelligence in children is not necessarily the whole story of intelligence, and we might want to look at adult intelligence in order to determine whether there is anything we have missed in concentrating upon children in the construction of both theories and tests. Third, it acknowledges that just as there are changes in life requirements from infancy to early childhoood and from early to later childhood that render necessary some changes in what it is we should test when we test intelligence, so might there be changes in life requirements from adolescence to adulthood that would render necessary changes in adult tests. Finally, it suggests that what adolescents can do mentally is not necessarily the pinnacle of mental accomplishment, and that just as we traditionally asked what preoperational children cannot do that concrete-operational children can do, and what concrete-operational children cannot do that formal-operational children can do, we should ask what formal-operational children cannot do that postformal-operational adults can do. For those who prefer theories other than Piaget's, the same set of questions remains, with different terminology.

In some of our own research (Wagner & Sternberg, 1985), we have investigated practical intelligence as a function of levels of development in two specific domains — academic psychology and business. Our particular thrust was to investigate *tacit knowledge,* or the tricks of the trade one needs to know in order to succeed that one is not explicitly taught. We found that both quantity and quality of tacit knowledge increase over levels of expertise among adults. We interpret these data as indicating that what might be viewed as one aspect of crystallized intelligence (Cattell, 1971), tacit knowledge, continues to increase throughout the professional life span.

In some research in a different vein, Sternberg and Downing (1982) tested college students in the development of their ability to comprehend third-order relations in analogical reasoning. The students had to perceive analogies between analogies. We found that the ability to understand third-order relations continues to increase during the college years, and the pattern of development recapitulates development of second-order analogical reasoning. In other words, development of a higher order extends well past the 16-year-old level. Even into the early 20s, students are increasing in their ability to solve problems of a difficulty level greater than that of traditional intelligence tests.

LESSON #2: ADOLESCENCE IS NOT THE PINNACLE OF INTELLIGENCE EITHER

Traditional views have been of adult intelligence as a long road downhill culminating in relative stupidity, and then death. For example, the Stanford-Binet norms traditionally employed a correction factor in calculating IQs so that adults would not look too stupid relative to children. The Horn (1968) view allows for increases in adulthood in crystallized intelligence — what is known — but for decreases in the core of intelligence, fluid intelligence — the ability to learn and reason. One can easily imagine older adults as bit collectors of facts who, once they have collected the facts, do not know quite what to do with them.

Recent theory and research have suggested that this view is wrong in spirit as well as in detail. Three lines of research are particularly relevant.

The first line of research in cognitive psychology suggests that the possession, and more importantly, the organization of knowledge are much more important to intelligence than we had previously realized (see, e.g., Chase & Simon, 1973; Chi, Glaser, & Rees, 1982; Lesgold, 1984). Expertise of all kinds, including intellectual expertise, is critically dependent on both the availability and the accessibility of knowledge to thought. Of course, knowledge is useless in the absence of mental processes to organize and operate upon it, but the mental processes are also useless unless they have something to which they can apply.

The second line of research is that on wisdom and its relation to intelligence (Clayton, 1982; Dittmann-Kohli & Baltes, in press; Sternberg, 1985b). People argue as to the extent to which intelligence is dependent on experience; no one seems to argue as to the extent to which wisdom is dependent on experience. Wisdom evolves through the accumulation and sorting out of experiences, and seems almost to be distinctively characteristic of older individuals. There just do not seem to be many wise adolescents walking around. We may well want to look for precursors of wisdom in children, and indeed, such looking would be one way in which the study of adult intellectual development can inform the study of childhood intellectual development. But we cannot understand the development of wisdom if we look at adolescence as the end of the story of intellectual development.

The third line of research is on the development of creativity and intellectual giftedness, more generally (Amabile, 1983; Gruber, 1980, 1982; Simonton, 1984; Sternberg, 1985b; see also Sternberg, in press; Sternberg & Davidson, 1986). It has become clear that our attempts to understand intellectual giftedness in children have often been rather sterile, and limited by our rather sterile, perhaps even puerile, notions of puerile giftedness. The great contributions of adults to the world are not through their scores on conventional intelligence tests, and do not even seem to be much reflected in their scores on such tests. The talents of great artists, politicians, writers, scientists, and the like continue to develop in adulthood, and to develop in ways that seem to represent something more than the mere incremental accumulation of facts. Adult giftedness is clearly something so much more interesting than high IQ that one cannot help but wonder whether we should not greatly expand our study of childhood giftedness. Feldman (1987), in his studies of prodigies, has done just that. But there are highly creative and talented children who are not prodigies, and who could expand our notions and studies of giftedness in ways that would help us realize there is more to intellectual giftedness than high IQ.

In my work with Janet Davidson (Davidson & Sternberg, 1984; Sternberg & Davidson, 1983), we have pursued the notion that a particularly important aspect of giftedness is insight ability. We have found that scores on our various measures of insight are only moderately correlated with scores on conventional measures of intelligence (in the mid-.60s). Moreover, many students classified by the schools as *gifted* are not particularly insightful, whereas many students who are insightful are not classified as gifted. In the extreme case, schools may find insightful children to be "pains in the neck," and actually select them out of gifted programs because of their being perceived as behavior problems.

LESSON #3: INTELLIGENCE IS MUCH MORE MULTIFACETED THAN TRADITIONALLY THOUGHT

To traditional theorists of intelligence, a multifaceted view of intelligence was any view that contrasted with Spearman's (1972) view of intelligence as dominated by a general factor. The Cattell–Horn theory of fluid and crystallized abilities (Cattell, 1971; Horn, 1968), Thurstone's (1938) theory of primary mental abilities, and Guilford's (1967) theory of the structure of intellect are all placed in the multifaceted camp. Contemporary views of intelligence, however, derived in large part from the study of adults, have suggested that with the possible exception of Guilford, these views were all narrower than we should like. Gardner (1983) has suggested that there exist multiple intelligences that are much broader in scope than intelligence as it has traditionally been conceived; Gardner includes within this scope talents such as musical and bodily-kinesthetic ones. Baltes, Dittmann-Kohli, and Dixon (1984), Charlesworth (1976), Neisser (1976), and Sternberg (1985a) have all suggested that there exists a practical side to intelligence that goes beyond the academic and more formal one. Labouvie-Vief (1982) has suggested that adult intelligence may even differ in kind from the intelligence of children.

A multifaceted view of intelligence suggests that we have relied too heavily upon the IQ as our primary measure of intellectual functioning. There are just too many intellectual skills of interest in a child that are not captured by IQ. We know that the predictive validity of an IQ test decreases after school age, perhaps in part because the criteria become less reliable, but also because IQ matters less to most on-the-job kinds of performance than it does to school grades. One interpretation of this fact is that IQ is more relevant for children than for adults, and in at least one sense, this is true: School grades do matter more for children than for adults. But we need to recognize that there is more to real-world childhood intelligence than school grades indicate. Schools tend to reward socially conforming behavior; some bright children are not socially conforming. Schools tend to reward good memory and analytic skills; some bright children are noteworthy for their synthetic skills, which may actually be perceived by teachers as a threat. Schools tend to reward children who know how to play the school game; some bright children do not want to play the school game. But this is not to say that the ability at least to learn what the school game is, is not part of intelligence. To the contrary, this is part of what constitutes the adaptive, or practical side, of childhood intelligence.

In my own triarchic theory of intelligence (Sternberg, 1985a), intelligence is conceived of as having three aspects: its relation to the internal world of the individual, its relation to the external world of the individual, and its relation to experience. The first part of the theory, relating intelligence to the internal world, specifies the mental processes, strategies, and representations underlying intelligent performance. For example, the theory specifies three kinds of processes — metacomponents, or executive processes used to plan, monitor, and evaluate one's problem solving; performance components, used to execute the plans of the metacomponents; and knowledge-acquisition components, used to learn how to solve problems in the first place. The second part of the theory, relating intelligence to the external world, specifies three functions of the processes of intelligence in real-world contexts: adaptation to existing environments, selection of new environments, and shaping of existing environments to turn them into new environments. The third part of the theory, relating intelligence to experience, specifies that the processes of intelligence are particularly important in intellectual functioning when applied in real-world contexts that require coping with novel kinds of tasks and situations, or when they are in the process of becoming automatized.

LESSON #4:
INFORMAL KNOWLEDGE
CAN BE AS IMPORTANT TO INTELLIGENCE
AS IS FORMAL KNOWLEDGE

Wagner and Sternberg (1985) found that level of tacit knowledge is only trivially related to IQ, but is significantly related to on-the-job performances. Wendy Williams and I are currently studying tacit knowledge in college students, seeking to discover the tricks of the trade that matter for success in undergraduate school. Cynthia Berg is now extending the study of tacit knowledge to younger children, recognizing that children, like adults, need to know tricks of the trade, in school and elsewhere, in order to perform well. In studying tacit knowledge in children, we borrow on the theory and research designs for adults, thereby extending the breadth of our conceptualization of intelligence in children.

Current cognitive research on intelligence and expertise is placing ever-increasing stress on the importance of knowledge, and such a stress is important. But the literature overwhelmingly emphasizes formal knowledge, such as that used by physicists, mathematicians, policymakers, chess players, or whatever. I would argue that informal, or tacit knowledge is at least as important to adult functioning as is formal knowledge, and to the functioning of children as well. In school, in church-related activities, at home, and in countless other settings, children need to learn the rules of the game. They may not act upon them, or may even deliberately violate them (as may adults). But in stressing only formal knowledge, we may be missing a really important focus of intellectual functioning. We need to study informal knowledge and its intelligent use with at least the diligence we have devoted to studying formal knowledge. We also need to recognize that academic and practical forms of intelligence are quite different, and can occur in varying amounts in different people.

LESSON #5: INTELLECTUAL DEVELOPMENT IS NOT A SUBSET OF COGNITIVE DEVELOPMENT NARROWLY DEFINED

The field of intellectual development has often been defined rather narrowly—as a subset of an already often narrowly defined field, namely, cognitive development. Even the broadest theory of intellectual development available, Piaget's (1972), seems to have a lot more to say about scientific and logical reasoning than it does about the intelligence that leads someone to be a great literary critic, historian, or politician. It is not an accident that Wagner and I (1985) published our studies of tacit knowledge in the *Journal of Personality and Social Psychology,* or that Amabile, Simonton, and I have published most of our studies of creativity in the same journal, or ones like it. The field of cognitive psychology, including cognitive development, has traditionally been defined in such a narrow way that topics and research paradigms that diverge even modestly from the prototype for the field are often viewed as outside the field.

In studying adults, it has become clear that variables such as life goals, plans, and purpose (Gruber, 1982; Pascual-Leone, 1983); attitudes toward the nature and use of the intellect (Berg & Sternberg, 1985a, 1985c); and attitude toward as well as ability to cope with novelty (Berg & Sternberg, 1985b) all affect the utilization of one's intelligence, if not the intelligence itself. Conceiving of intelligence narrowly drains from the construct much of what makes it most interesting. In studying children, it has always been much easier to conceive of intelligence narrowly, because their life path—at least in our society—tends to be so circumscribed. Such narrowness is more difficult in the study of adults, and hence studies of intelligence in adults have broadened out. The spreading activation of this broadened conceptualization of intelligence to the study of intellectual development in childhood is, I believe, all to the good. We need to get away from the monolithic notions we often have about intelligence as wholly school-like because children spend so much time in school.

Sternberg and Suben (1986) have reviewed the work of various ethnographers interested in the interface between intelligence and the environment, and have concluded that in order to understand how intelligence develops, one must first understand its relation to the surrounding context. They report, for example, on the work of Heath (1983), who found that what is considered to be "intelligent" differs markedly in different subcultures within the United States. Sternberg and Suben conclude that intelligence is "socialized" in different ways in different environments. Parents generally want their children to be smart; but what constitutes "smart" differs across sets of parents. Unfortunately, only a small subset of the parental notions correspond to what the schools consider to be smart. As a result, there can be a mismatch between the abilities that are placed at a premium by schools versus parents. Children who adapt well in home environments may therefore not adapt well in school environments, and be labeled as *unintelligent* by the schools.

LESSON #6: THE TRADITIONAL EVALUATIVE CRITERIA FOR THEORIES AND TESTS OF INTELLIGENCE ARE TOO NARROW

It is important, of course, to validate theories and measures of intelligence externally as well as internally. One could propose a theory of intelligence, or a theory of anything else, that is internally consistent, but that has no relation to any thought or behavior that takes place in the real world. Sternberg (1977) argued for the equal importance of both internal and external validation of theories of intelligence.

At the same time, the external criteria against which we have validated and developed our theories and measures of intelligence have been narrow, almost pitifully so. The most common external criteria against which new tests of intelligence are evaluated are old tests of intelligence. Small wonder that our measurement of intelligence has not progressed far in the last century. The other common criteria are achievement tests and school grades. Is it any wonder that our notion of intelligence, in general, has become almost indistinguishable from our notion of academic intelligence, in particular, and that one often has to fight hard to convince people that there is intelligence beyond the school house? Conventional IQ scores, school grades, and achievement test scores are so easily obtainable from children's files, and seem to be so right as external criteria for tests of intelligence, that we have been lulled into complacency in our assessments.

Fortunately, things are not so easy with adults. School grades are a trivial part, or no part at all, of adult functioning. As a result, investigators of adult intelligence need to be creative in discovering or devising criteria against which to assess theories and tests of adult intelligence. The level of creativity demonstrated to date has not been mind boggling: Standard criteria are things like socioeconomic class, years of education, grades in adult education courses, IQ test scores, and the like. Wagner and Sternberg (1985) used standard measures of professional advancement, such as citation and productivity rates for university professors, and merit raises and performance ratings for business executives, but these criteria are also, of course, far from perfect. Indeed, no one criterion can ever be perfect, so it is necessary to use a multiplicity of criteria against which to assess any theory or test.

Wagner and I have been taken to task (orally, although not in writing, to my knowledge), for the use of value-laden criteria. After all, not everyone wants to produce the most papers possible, or win the largest possible merit raises. There is more to life, we are told, than academic productivity and merit raises. Of course, we wholeheartedly agree. As previously noted, no criterion is perfect. What many people seem not to realize is that the criteria used for assessing theories and tests used for children are just as value-laden as the criteria used for adults. Test scores, achievement test scores, and school grades all reflect the society's values as to what is important for academic success in childhood. Many societies do not have any of these indicators, and some of those societies would not be interested even in the possibility of having them. I am amazed when people complain about our criteria for adults, but feel comfortable with using school grades as criteria for children: Both criteria — all criteria — are value-laden.

One direction that Wagner and I believe deserves further exploration is the use of idiosyncratic criteria for measurements. In our new work, we are asking adults what they believe to be important criteria of success, and, then to evaluate themselves in terms of how well they have fulfilled their own criteria. Ultimately, it might be possible to obtain objective measures on these criteria. The idea is that we need not use criteria that are uniform across all individuals. Rather, we should consider the possibility of measuring the extent to which people have achieved their own life goals.

LESSON #7: INTELLIGENCE IS IN PART IN THE EYE OF THE BEHOLDER

Intelligence is partly in the eye of the beholder, that is, something we invent. This point of view has been argued forcefully by Neisser (1979), who has claimed that *"intelligent person"* is a prototype-organized Roschian concept. Our confidence that a person deserves to be called "intelligent" depends on that person's overall similarity to an imagined prototype, just as our confidence that some object is to be called "chair" depends on its similarity to prototypical chairs. There are no definitive criteria of intelligence, just as there are none for chairness; it is a fuzzy-edged concept to which many features are relevant. (p. 185)

There exist many differences in people's conceptions of intelligence as a function of the target population about which the question is asked, and of who is asked. One kind of difference is cross-cultural. Wober (1974), for example, found that the Baganda tribe tended to associate intelligence with mental order, whereas the Batoro associated it with some degree of mental turmoil. A second kind of difference is developmental: Siegler and Richards (1982) found differences in what adults conceived of intelligence to be at different ages in childhood; Yussen and Kane (1983) found differences in what children of different ages conceived intelligence to be; and Berg and Sternberg (1985a) found differences in conceptions of intelligence as a function of both age of adult raters and age of hypothetical individuals to be rated. Sternberg, Conway, Ketron, and Bernstein (1981) even found differences in conceptualizations across different groups of adults, such as people entering a supermarket (mostly housewives) as opposed to people entering a train station during rush hour (mostly business commuters). We define certain patterns of behavior as intelligent, and then judge people in terms of their conformity to these patterns. The greater the conformity to one or more of these stereotypes, the greater is the judged intelligence of the individual.

It is easy to see the effects of conceptions of intelligence in adulthood: What is expected of an intelligent lawyer, for example, is quite different from what is expected of an intelligent business executive, and this is in turn quite different from what is expected of an intelligent college professor — or plumber. But because children tend more to adhere to a single track in the activities we plan for them — the school track — it is often harder to see the effects of people's conceptions of intelligence among children. Yet, Fry (1984) studied teachers' conceptions of intelligence for teachers of children of different ages, and found that teachers emphasized different things for different levels of advancement: Social skills counted more at the elementary level, verbal skills at the secondary level, and abstract-reasoning skills at the college level. Children who are intelligent in ways other than those teachers may be looking for can be at a substantial disadvantage when compared to their agemates.

Of course, intelligence is not wholly in the eyes of the beholder. Consider a person who is totally unable to solve problems, or to cope with novelty, or to render certain kinds of cognitive processing automatic. Such a person would be unintelligent in any environment because of a severe inability to adapt to that environment. Attempts to understand the cognitive mechanisms underlying problem solving, coping with novelty, or automatization need not therefore be viewed as hopelessly culturally limited. At the same time, the behavioral instantiations of these skills are likely to be culturally limited. In other words, the mechanisms of cognition do not differ from one culture to another, but the problems that need to be solved do differ, as does what is considered novel. And this last point brings us to the eighth lesson.

LESSON #8: WHAT IS NOVEL OR FAMILIAR FOR CHILDREN IN ONE ENVIRONMENT IS NOT NECESSARILY NOVEL OR FAMILIAR FOR THOSE IN ANOTHER ENVIRONMENT

No one would think of judging the intelligence of a lawyer by measuring his or her skill in designing physics experiments; conversely, no one would think of judging the intelligence of a physicist by measuring his or her skills in drawing upon legal precedents and putting them together to argue for the innocence of a client. The person in one profession does not have the knowledge of the person in another profession, and cannot be fairly assessed on the basis of knowledge he or she does not have; this person could not be expected to have comparable background in another profession to his or her own. One could even argue that the kind of thinking required of a lawyer is of only marginal relevance for a physicist, and vice versa.

Yet, the same assumptions that are obvious in our thinking about adults have never been obvious in our thinking about children. We somehow expect children to have a uniformity of background that they do not have. Children are socialized in radically different ways, and in particular, they are socialized to be intelligent in ways that result in intelligence taking different forms (Sternberg & Suben, 1986). Heath (1983), for example, found an emphasis on nonverbal communication in Black families that did not exist in White families, and an emphasis on verbal communication in White families that did not exist in Black families. Children from both environments had been socialized to be intelligent in ways that made sense in their environmental milieus, but the socialization experiences were not equally helpful when the children found themselves in a standard, White, middle-class schooling environment. There are now scores of studies that show that children (and adults) from nonstandard backgrounds can perform the very same tasks with familiar materials that they are unable to perform with unfamiliar ones (see, e.g., Laboratory of Comparative Human Cognition, 1982).

Many theorists believe that the ability to cope with relative novelty is an important part of intelligence (e.g., Piaget, 1972; Raaheim, 1974; Sternberg, 1985a). But what is novel for one youngster can be familiar for another, and vice versa. The contents and processes that are the stock in trade of IQ tests are differentially familiar to children, and hence do not measure intelligence equally or even fairly for all of them. Some children have seen abstract analogy items so often that they can solve them without even reading the directions; other children, unfamiliar with such items, may be uncertain of what to do even after reading the instructions for the first time. The point to be made, of course, is that we must be as conscientious in our concerns about age- and culture-relevance for children as we are for adults. There is no one path in life for children, any more than there is for adults. This fact motivates our next lesson.

LESSON #9: INTELLIGENCE RESIDES IN THE INTERACTION BETWEEN THE INDIVIDUAL AND THE ENVIRONMENT

This point, argued forcefully by Valsiner (1984), takes into account not only the individual and the context in which that individual resides, but the effects of the context on the individual (adapation to the environment) and the effects of the individual on the context (shaping of the environment).

Reading the traditional psychometric literature, or even the more recent information-processing literature, one might come to the conclusion that intelligence is wholly an organismic property—that an individual would be equally intelligent, regardless of the place or time of birth, or of the circumstances of his or her growth and development. But this is not so. It is interesting to watch the reputations of individuals in occupations that place high demands upon their intelligence, such as scholarly activity, go up and down. We tend to create organismic interpretations of what has happened: The person has burned out, or has lost interest, or lost ideas, or given up. Often, however, the person has not changed at all, but rather, the environment has. The Zeitgeist in the field of scholarly activity may change, so that abilities that once were important no longer are, whereas new abilities become more important. Consider the abilities needed to succeed in cognitive psychology, for example, in the Gestalt era, versus the mathematical-modeling era, versus the computer-modeling era. They are somewhat different, and a person who might thrive in one era might falter in another. The same is true for children. How many "late-bloomers" are really not late-bloomers at all, but rather children who finally found the right teacher, or the right setting, to cultivate and allow their potential to bloom? In my own checkered school career, I was an above-average but not exceptional student—until the fourth grade. Perhaps I was a late-bloomer. But could it have been a coincidence that in the fourth grade I had the first supportive, warm, and caring teacher that I had encountered during my elementary-school years? My intelligence probably did not change, but my interactions with the environment certainly did.

Reading the writings of certain contextualists, one might come to think that context is everything (Berry, 1974; Rogoff, Gauvain, & Ellis, 1984). It isn't. Although context determines the manifestations of intelligence, and the forms intelligent behavior is averred to take, there must be something to interact with the context—something that is not wholly contextually determined. The individual is more than the sum of his or her contexts. Both individual and contextual change, as well as changes in their interaction, need to be taken into account in understanding intelligence. The changes in context form the basis for the tenth and last lesson.

In the triarchic theory of human intelligence (Sternberg, 1985a), the components of intelligence are viewed as universal. In any culture, one needs to recognize problems when they exist, define their nature, plan ways to solve them, and so on. Thus, the basic cognitive apparatus is seen as fixed across time and space. What differs cross-culturally is the contextual instantiations of this cognitive apparatus. The very innovative ideas that might be seen as intelligent in one culture might be seen as culture-threatening, and not very intelligent, in another culture.

LESSON #10: COHORT EFFECTS APPLY TO CHILDREN AS WELL AS TO ADULTS

Life-span researchers are exquisitely sensitive to cohort effects. Indeed, it is impossible to read widely in the life-span literature without coming across disquisitions on cohort effects, and how they affect our interpretations of psychological phenomena. For example, much of the debate regarding relative stability versus decline of intellectual functioning over the life span hinges on the nature of cohort effects upon existing data bases.

Cohort effects apply to children as well as to adults, but mention of such effects is almost totally absent from the literature of child psychology, including the psychology of intellectual development in children. Nutrition changes; the norms of parent–child relationships change; schooling practices change; the levels at which textbooks are written, and the kinds of subject matter considered appropriate for textbooks, change. Indeed, the whole culture changes: I went to college during the last throes of the hippie era; my (older) brother went to college 4 years earlier, before the hippie era;

and if I had a younger brother who differed in age as my brother and I do (about 4 years), he would have gone to college after the hippie era. Each of us would have received quite a different style of education in quite a different milieu. To me, the life of a college student today seems very different from the life of a college student in the late 1960s and early 1970s. We need to recognize that our theories of intellectual development in children bear the same potential limitations as our theories of intellectual development in adults. To the extent that context matters — and it does — we should realize that only some of what we say can possibly be for keeps. There will always be the need for new theories and research on intellectual development, because, to some extent, such development is always changing: Intellectual development, like so many other things in life, is a moving target.

CONCLUSION

To conclude, I have argued that the study of intellectual development among adults, based on a life-span perspective, holds valuable lessons for the study of intellectual development among children. Some of the lessons are unheeded; most seem scarcely even to be recognized. But their importance is not diminished by their lack of recognition. Many of us hope to see the day when the study of human development is better characterized as a single field than as a dual one. In the meantime, though, the two fields would do better to learn from than to ignore each other.

ACKNOWLEDGMENT

Preparation of this chapter was supported by Contract MDA90385K0305 from the Army Research Institute.

REFERENCES

Amabile, T. M. (1983). *The social psychology of creativity*. New York: Springer.
Baltes, P. B., Dittmann-Kohli, F., & Dixon, R. A. (1984). New perspectives on the development of intelligence in adulthood: Toward a dual-process conception and a model of selective optimization with compensation. In P. B. Baltes & O. G. Brim, Jr. (Eds.), *Life-span development and behavior* (Vol. 6, pp. 33–76). New York: Academic Press.
Baltes, P. B., & Schaie, K. W. (1976). On the plasticity of intelligence in adulthood and old age: Where Horn and Donaldson fail. *American Psychologist, 31,* 720–725.
Berg, C. A., & Sternberg, R. J. (1985a). *Implicit theories of intelligence across the adult life span*. Manuscript submitted for publication.

Berg, C. A., & Sternberg, R. J. (1985b). Response to novelty: Continuity versus discontinuity in the developmental course of intelligence. In H. Reese (Eds.), *Advances in child development and behavior* (pp.2–47). New York: Academic Press.

Berg, C. A., & Sternberg, R. J. (1985c). A triarchic theory of intellectual development during adulthood. *Developmental Review, 5,* 334–370.

Berry, J. W. (1974). Radical cultural relativism and the concept of intelligence. In J. W. Berry & P. R. Dasen (Eds.), *Culture and cognition: Readings in cross-cultural psychology* (pp. 225–229). London: Methuen.

Cattell, R. B. (1971). *Abilities: Their structure, growth, and action.* Boston: Houghton Mifflin.

Charlesworth, W. R. (1976). Human intelligence as adaptation: An ethological approach. In L. B. Resnick (Ed.), *The nature of intelligence* (pp. 147–168). Hillsdale, NJ: Lawrence Erlbaum Associates.

Chase, W. R., & Simon, H. A. (1973). The mind's eye in chess. In W. G. Chase (Ed.), *Visual information processing* (pp. 215–281). New York: Academic Press.

Chi, M. T. H., Glaser, R., & Rees, E. (1982). Expertise in problem solving. In R. J. Sternberg (Ed.), *Advances in the psychology of human intelligence* (Vol. 1, pp. 7–75). Hillsdale, NJ: Lawrence Erlbaum Associates.

Clayton, V. (1982). Wisdom and intelligence: The nature and function of knowledge in the later years. In S. Brent (Ed.), *Aging and wisdom: Individual development and social function.* New York: Springer.

Davidson, J. E., & Sternberg, R. J. (1984). The role of insight in intellectual giftedness. *Gifted Child Quarterly, 28,* 58–64.

Dittmann-Kohli, F., & Baltes, P. B. (in press). Towards an action-theoretical and pragmatic conception of intelligence during adulthood and old age. In C. N. Alexander & E. Langer (Eds.), *Beyond formal operations: Alternative endpoints to human development.* New York: Oxford University Press.

Feldman, D. (1987). *Nature's gambit.* New York: Basic Books.

Fry, P. S. (1984). Teachers' conceptions of students' intelligence and intelligent functioning: A cross-sectional study of elementary, secondary, and tertiary level teachers. In P. S. Fry (Ed.), *Changing conceptions of intelligence and intellectual functioning: Current theory and research* (pp. 157–174). Amsterdam: North-Holland.

Gardner, H. (1983). *Frames of mind: The theory of multiple intelligences.* New York: Basic Books.

Gruber, H. (1980). The evolving systems approach to creativity. In S. Modgil & C. Modgil (Eds.), *Toward a theory of psychological development* (pp. 269–299). Windsor, England: NFER Publishing.

Gruber, H. (1982). On the hypothesized relation between giftedness and creativity. In D. H. Feldman (Ed.), *Developmental approaches to giftedness and creativity.* San Francisco: Jossey-Bass.

Guilford, J. P. (1967). *The nature of human intelligence.* New York: McGraw-Hill.

Heath, S. (1983). *Ways with words.* New York: Cambridge University Press.

Horn, J. L. (1968). Organization of abilities and the development of intelligence. *Psychological Review, 75,* 242–259.

Laboratory of Comparative Human Cognition (1982). Culture and intelligence. In R. J. Sternberg (Ed.), *Handbook of human intelligence* (pp. 642–719). New York: Cambridge University Press.

Labouvie-Vief, G. (1982). Dynamic development and mature autonomy. *Human Development, 25,* 161–191.

Lesgold, A. (1984). Acquiring expertise. In J. Anderson & S. Kosslyn (Eds.), *Tutorials in learning and memory* (pp. 31–60). New York: Freeman.

Neisser, U. (1976). *Cognition and reality: Principles and implications of cognitive psychology.* San Francisco: Freeman.

Neisser, U. (1979). The concept of intelligence. *Intelligence, 3,* 217–227.

Pascual-Leone, J. (1983). Growing into human maturity: Toward a metasubjective theory of adulthood stages. In P. B. Baltes & O. G. Brim (Eds.), *Life-span development and behavior* (Vol. 5, pp. 118–156). New York: Academic Press.

Piaget, J. (1972). *The psychology of intelligence.* Totowa, NJ: Littlefield Adams.

Raaheim, K. (1974). *Problem solving and intelligence.* Oslo: Universitetsforlaget.

Rogoff, B., Gauvain, M., & Ellis, S. (1984). Development viewed in its cultural context. In M. H. Bornstein & M. E. Lamb (Eds.), *Developmental psychology* (pp. 533–571). Hillsdale, NJ: Lawrence Erlbaum Associates.

Schaie, K. W. (1979). The Primary Mental Abilities in adulthood: An exploration in the development of psychometric intelligence. In P. B. Baltes & O. G. Brim, Jr. (Eds.), *Life-span development and behavior* (Vol. 2, pp. 67–115). New York: Academic Press.

Siegler, R. S., & Richards, D. D. (1982). The development of intelligence. In R. J. Sternberg (Ed.), *Handbook of human intelligence* (pp. 897–971). New York: Cambridge University Press.

Simonton, D. (1984). *Genius, creativity, and leadership.* Cambridge, MA: Harvard University Press.

Spearman, C. (1927). *The abilities of man.* New York: Macmillan.

Sternberg, R. J. (1977). *Intelligence, information processing, and analogical reasoning: The componential analysis of human abilities.* Hillsdale, NJ: Lawrence Erlbaum Associates.

Sternberg, R. J. (Ed.). (1984). *Mechanisms of cognitive development.* New York: Freeman.

Sternberg, R. J. (1985a). *Beyond IQ: A triarchic theory of human intelligence.* New York: Cambridge University Press.

Sternberg, R. J. (1985b). Implicit theories of intelligence, creativity, and wisdom. *Journal of Personality and Social Psychology, 49,* 607–627.

Sternberg, R. J. (Ed.). (in press). *The nature of creativity.* New York: Cambridge University Press.

Sternberg, R. J., Conway, B. E., Ketron, J. L., & Bernstein, M. (1981). People's conceptions of intelligence. *Journal of Personality and Social Psychology, 41,* 37–55.

Sternberg, R. J., & Davidson, J. E. (1983). Insight in the gifted. *Educational Psychologist, 18,* 51–57.

Sternberg, R. J., & Davidson, J. E. (Eds.). (1986). *Conceptions of giftedness.* New York: Cambridge University Press.

Sternberg, R. J., & Downing, C. J. (1982). The development of higher-order reasoning in adolescence. *Child Development, 53,* 209–221.

Sternberg, R. J., & Suben, J. (1986). The socialization of intelligence. In M. Perlmutter (Ed.), *Perspectives on intellectual development: Minnesota symposia on child psychology* (Vol. 19, pp. 201–235). Hillsdale, NJ: Lawrence Erlbaum Associates.

Thurstone, L. L. (1938). *Primary mental abilities.* Chicago: University of Chicago Press.

Valsiner, J. (1984). Conceptualizing intelligence: from an internal static attribution to the study of the process structure of organism-environment relationships. In P. Fry (Ed.), *Changing conceptions of intelligence and intellectual functioning: current theory and research* (pp. 63–89). Amsterdam: North-Holland.

Wagner, R. K., & Sternberg, R. J. (1985). Practical intelligence in real-world prusuits: The role of tacit knowledge. *Journal of Personality and Social Psychology, 49,* 436–458.

Wober, M. (1974). Towards an understanding of the Kiganda concept of intelligence. In J. W. Berry & P. R. Dasen (Eds.), *Culture and cognition: Readings in cross-cultural psychology* (pp. 261–280). London: Methuen.

Yussen, S. R., & Kane, P. T. (1983). Children's ideas about intellectual ability. In R. Leahy (Ed.), *The child's construction of social inequality* (pp. 109–133). New York: Academic Press.

13 THE LIFE-SPAN INTERVENTION CUBE

Orville G. Brim, Jr.
Vero Beach, Florida

Deborah A. Phillips
University of Virginia

ABSTRACT

Three elements of life-span development theory are selected for their special relevance to the planning of social policies to aid human development. Their influence should be expressed in planning and decision-making about when, where, and with whom to intervene; about specific ages, behavioral domains, and social populations as selected targets of intervention. These ideas are presented graphically in the life-span intervention cube. An analysis is made of current social policies for children, and certain policies are displayed within the cube along the three dimensions of age, population, and domain. The failures to fully utilize the life-span development theory and research are described and illustrated. The realities of the political process of policy formation are reviewed and analysis is carried out of the basic conflicts between life-span development theory and the realities of politics.

INTRODUCTION

Social policies to improve human development are based in part on assumptions about the nature of development. Presumed links between old age and dependency, and the persistent faith in early intervention, for example, guide the timing and targeting of some of our nation's major social intervention programs. In this chapter we describe the implications of life-span development theory for the design and assessment of these social policies. We present an analytical tool—the "life-span intervention cube"; use it to examine current policies for children; then consider how efforts to use new facts and theory about human development might fare in the real political world of policy formation.

277

Child Development and Social Policy

The origins of child development research in the United States are in activist, policy-oriented research institutes (Sears, 1975; Senn, 1975; Smuts & Hagen, 1986), but the concern about social policy and uses of research findings faded out for the 25 years following World War II. Since the 1970s, policy issues have regained the attention of the child development community. Organizations have been established to link research to policy. For example, the Society for Research in Child Development has established a Washington office, formed a Committee on Child Development and Social Policy, launched the Congressional Science Fellowship Program, and initiated a monograph series on child development and social policy (Stevenson & Siegel, 1984). Training programs in child development and social policy have proliferated in recent years (Masters, 1983) to meet the need for child development scholars who are conversant with policy issues. Conference proceedings and publications in developmental psychology also indicate the growing policy emphasis in the field (Zigler, 1980).

Concerns about the relation of developmental research and social policy have moved on from argument about whether research can or should influence policy decisions, to discussion that assumes research and policymaking are inextricably linked and focuses on how to have a more effective collaboration (Hayes, 1983; National Research Council, 1978; Takanishi, DeLeon, & Pallak, 1983). The contemporary challenge is to match pressing policy issues with current theory and research evidence. One aspect of this challenge, addressed here, concerns the application of relatively new knowledge about developmental processes to issues of the timing, targeting, and patterning of social interventions.

Three Elements of
Life-Span Development Theory

Other chapters in this volume describe the main assumptions, concepts, and propositions of life-span theory, and the ways in which it integrates some previously diverse strands from child psychology, studies of old age, and the neglected middle years of life. It spans disciplines that otherwise would stand as separate perspectives; it stitches together what we know about human development at different ages.

Three elements of this theory are of particular relevance to social interventions. The first is its optimistic emphasis on malleability of the human and the possibility of modifying the effects of early experience throughout development. The developmental timing of interventions thus emerges as a key issue in policy planning. The second element calls attention to the considerable heterogeneity that characterizes any age group and suggests that age-linked eligibility criteria may not serve as adequate indicators of need. The third notes that distinct behavioral domains have different rates and features of developmental change, thus requiring domain specificity in the design and timing of interventions.

The Life-Span Intervention Cube

Once it is acknowledged that the course of development can be altered throughout the life span and that age alone may not be an adequate criterion for the targeting of interventions, the question of when and with whom to intervene becomes quite complex. When answers to this question must be tailored to specific behavioral goals (e.g., literacy, good health, stable employment), the complexity of designing interventions is further increased.

The life-span intervention cube is a tool for planning and analyzing human development policies from a variety of perspectives. The dimensions of the cube — age, social population, and behavioral domain — express the significant contributions to policy thinking that emerge from life-span theory and its intellectual antecedents. These dimensions define the basic elements of social interventions: developmental timing, eligibility criteria, and behavioral goals. The cube has the specific value of letting us assess the goodness of fit between optimum life-span development policies and our current policies for children. It also aids in understanding the competing pressures on the allocation of public resources. These are the central issues discussed in this chapter.

Realities of Politics

Optimum timing and targeting of interventions to benefit human development are ideals. Actual decisions about when, where, and with whom to intervene are influenced by political pressures that often are quite different from the rational calculus guiding optimal intervention strategies. Among scientists in child and life-span development, both optimism and skepticism exist about the feasibility of applying research and theory to policy formation. Some say that scientists have a responsibility to bring their knowledge to bear on political debates (Bronfenbrenner, 1974; Miller, 1969). Others have been frustrated by experiences with a political process they view as characterized by fragmentation of issues, quick fix approaches to major social problems and misuses of research (Atkinson, 1977; Maccoby, Kahn, & Everett, 1983). In the last section of this chapter we bring into confrontation our conception of the ideal decision-making process and political realities surrounding intervention programs. We examine the arguments that are likely to predominate as federal program priorities are established and "need for benefits" is assessed. We then analyze the degree of fit between these arguments and life-span development theory.

LIFE-SPAN DEVELOPMENT THEORY
AND INTERVENTION

The Possibility of Change

The life-span perspective on development is notable for its assertion that the course of development is more open than many have believed. Malleability is no longer viewed as the special reserve of childhood, but is increasingly understood to characterize all stages of development.

Research on a diverse range of adverse conditions shows that the consequences of the events of early childhood are continually transformed by later experiences (Garmezy, 1983; Hetherington, Cox, & Cox, 1982; Sameroff, Seifer, & Zax, 1982; Werner & Smith, 1977). Even the seemingly permanent effects of pre- and postnatal malnutrition on brain development are potentially reversible if subsequent development occurs in a nutrition-rich, stimulating environment (McKay, Sinisterra, McKay, Gomez, & Floreda, 1978; Morgan & Winick, 1980; Richardson, 1976a; Winick, 1980).

Plasticity is not limitless, however. More intensive interventions of longer duration seem necessary to produce change beyond sensitive growth periods (Bateson, 1979; Henderson, 1980; Immelmann & Suomi, 1981). For example, studies consistently reveal that children adopted in infancy ultimately attain higher IQs than later adopted children, even when selection factors are controlled (Scarr & Weinberg, 1976; Tizard, 1978). Thus, far from trivializing the importance of early experience, evidence of diminishing responsivity to environmental inputs implies that a prevention strategy aimed at the young may be considerably less expensive than interventions aimed at adults (Brim & Kagan, 1980; Lerner, 1984).

A central controversy in the developmental sciences, in fact, concerns the identification of periods when organisms are most responsive to environmental influence. We know that in childhood there are periods of biological development marked by optimum ages for certain changes such as learning to walk, to read, or to understand number concepts.

Virtually unstudied at this time is the idea of optimum periods for change after the childhood years. Recent work on the treatment of mental retardation in adolescents has suggested that, under some conditions, interventions initiated later in life may be optimally timed (Feuerstein, Rand, Hoffman, & Miller, 1980; Hobbs & Robinson, 1982). Thus, although human malleability may not remain at a constant level across the life span, the alternative view that constraints necessarily increase with age is also not warranted. A more justifiable position is that the life span is dotted with a great number and variety of times that are optimal for introducing interventions or planned efforts by individuals on their own behalf (Sherrod & Brim, 1986).

A critical policy issue, therefore, is to designate the optimal timing of interventions. Beneficial changes in an individual's circumstances that are initiated in middle childhood, adulthood, or even during the elderly years can produce major gains in functioning. Life-span development theory directs that the current emphasis of most intervention programs on the early years can be balanced with explicit consideration of interventions directed to later stages of life.

Individual and Group Diversity Within Age Categories

Research on development has started serious questioning of the predictive value of chronological age for such policy-relevant characteristics as functional capacity and social status. In life-span studies, emphasis is placed on the considerable diversity that characterizes each age group, rather than on efforts to identify common themes associated with age. Accordingly, some life-span theorists have suggested that age, considered in isolation from other characteristics, is irrelevant to determinations of risk or dependency on the one hand, or likely effectiveness of interventions, on the other (Featherman, 1980).

Social class and gender have surfaced in the empirical literature as two major moderators of age effects. For example, perinatal complications have markedly distinct effects on subsequent childhood development that vary with the sex of the child and socioeconomic status of the infant's family (Werner & Smith, 1977). The literature on the developmental effects of divorce has provided similar evidence that boys and girls show different responses at different stages following divorce of their parents (Hetherington, Cox, & Cox, 1982; Wallerstein, 1983). And, Richardson's (1976b) review of the Dutch Famine research suggests that the effects of prenatal malnutrition varied with the pre-war nutritional status of the mother.

In each case, the effects of an environmental insult affecting a single stage of development varied with other characteristics of the affected population. Taking this argument one step farther, within people of similar ages and populations striking individual differences are evident. One of the most challenging empirical issues facing developmentalists today is deciphering why some individuals succumb to adverse experiences—or respond to interventions—whereas others of similar age and background recover quickly and may even benefit from adversity.

Decisions about targeting and associated concerns about "who can benefit most" are integral to intervention policies. Determination of "need" is necessarily a central point of debate. The contribution of current developmental knowledge is to question whether and when chronological age, as compared to other factors such as social class and family structure, is an appropriate basis for determining program eligibility.

Domain Specificity

We have said that periods of plasticity and periods of resistance to change are interwoven throughout development. Periods of plasticity, of course, would appear to offer optimal points of entry for social interventions.

These multiple entry points across the life span occur at different times in different domains of behavior. The optimal timing of interventions will vary with the developmental goal of the intervention, such as literacy, health maintenance, or nutrition. Initiated with the early work on maturational readiness, more recent research in areas ranging from primatology (Sackett, Sameroff, Cairns, & Suomi, 1981) to cognitive development (Wachs & Gruen, 1982) has called attention to domain-specific effects of both deprivation and stimulation.

From a policy perspective, domain specificity further complicates the task of selecting the "right" time to intervene because the time will vary with the behavioral target of the intervention. Moreover, what used to be relatively predictable status transitions—from school to work, or from marriage to parenthood—are increasingly occurring off-time. Consider the prevalence of both delayed and teenaged childbearing, job retraining necessitated by major economic shifts, and prolonged disability in the young adult years associated with Acquired Immune Deficiency Syndrome (AIDS).

In summary, neither developmental nor social needs are predictably tied to specific age periods. Most social programs and benefits incorporate relatively static assumptions about the timing and sequencing of developmental changes and life events. More attention to domain specificity as a central variable in policy planning should produce policies that fit the timing of interventions to the specific problem being addressed.

THE LIFE-SPAN INTERVENTION CUBE

The life-span intervention cube is defined by chronological age, other population characteristics such as income and family structure, and domain of behavior such as health, education, and social welfare. Although the age dimension is continuous, social population and domain are categorical dimensions. As seen in Figure 13.1, the smallest unit of policy analysis can be thought of as an *intervention cell*. When a program addressing a discrete behavioral goal for a specific age group is targeted by income, functional status, or some other population dimension, a single cell is produced. Each cell in the cube thus represents an opportunity space: the interaction of a single age group, one social population, and one domain. An example is the Head Start Program, which provides early education to preschool-age children from low-income families.

By mapping various programs and benefits onto the cube, different geometric shapes appear—plugs, bars, slices, blocks, as well as the single cells. The shapes illustrate the pattern of social investment and social neglect that characterizes our social interventions for different age groups, populations, and domains.

Chronological Age

The age dimension involves the issue of the developmental timing of interventions. It aids evaluation of the extent to which existing policies reflect current knowledge about the potential effectiveness of interventions across the life span. We can see whether filled cells (that is, cells in which some service or benefit is provided) congregate around discrete age groups or whether they are dispersed across the age range.

The age dimension also illustrates whether policies in a given domain, such as nutrition, provide continuity of care across adjacent age groups. When programs are designed to provide continuity, entire or partial plugs appear in the cube, extending from top (Old Elderly) to bottom (Prenatal) for a specific population. Figure 13.2 illustrates continuity of care in nutrition programs. In the absence of efforts to integrate programs across ages the cube would be dominated by single cells and bars.

Social Population

The population dimension involves the issue of diversity within age categories. To the extent that great variability characterizes every group defined by age, consideration of functional and more refined indicators of need for public assistance are required. Among the elderly, for instance, assumptions about their inherent dependence are being challenged by increasing reliance on functional measures of individual capacity. Several alternative criteria have been or could be used to determine program eligibility. When programs are available to all persons of a given age, ignoring their social characteristics, a horizontal bar is produced in the cube

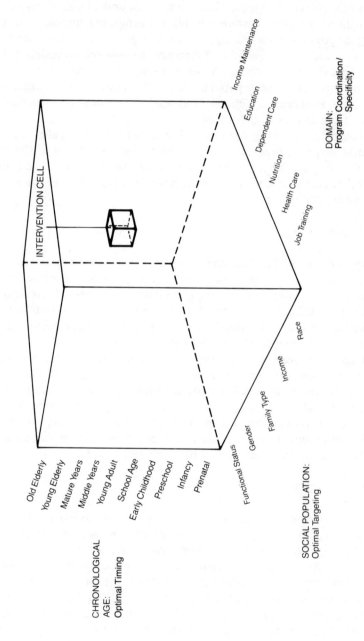

FIGURE 13.1 Generic cube.

284

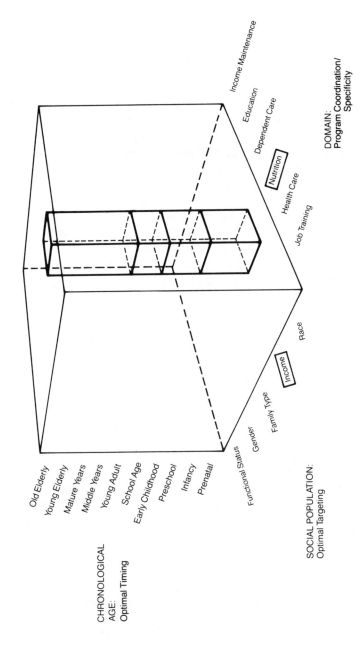

FIGURE 13.2 Nutrition policy: A plug.

CHRONOLOGICAL
AGE:
Optimal Timing

Old Elderly
Young Elderly
Mature Years
Middle Years
Young Adult
School Age
Early Childhood
Preschool
Infancy
Prenatal

Functional Status
Gender
Family Type

SOCIAL POPULATION:
Optimal Targeting

Income

Race

Job Training
Health Care
Nutrition
Dependent Care
Education
Income Maintenance

DOMAIN:
Program Coordination/
Specificity

spanning functional status, gender, family type, income, and race. Figure 13.3 illustrates this kind of policy with reference to a variety of benefits for the elderly. Alternatively, when programs addressing single domains are targeted by social characteristics, either single cells or plugs emerge depending on the number of age groups served.

Behavioral Domain

The domain dimension involves familiar questions of coordination of programs aimed at different areas such as health, education, or employment. It directs our attention to what is often referred to as *domain specificity;* an old idea but recently given increased attention. It also aids examination of indirect benefits, and unanticipated consequences, of policies that cross over into nontargeted domains.

When policies are coordinated across different domains, the cube reveals horizontal bars and blocks, depending on the number of age groups and populations served. Figure 13.4 illustrates Social Security disability benefits that provide income support payments; vocational rehabilitation and job training; Medicare (and sometimes Medicaid) health coverage; and, in the case of low-income disabled persons, supplemental income and Food Stamp benefits.

Domain specificity states that distinct optimal periods exist for the introduction of interventions with differing behavioral goals. Some goals are served best by early intervention; others are better addressed in mid- or late-life. Still others may be amenable to intervention at multiple points or may require on-going interventions, particularly in the case of basic survival needs such as health, shelter, and nutrition. It is only in the crudest formulation of a policy that planners can make a choice of when to intervene without simultaneous and studious attention to the behavioral focus of the intervention.

Domain specificity would be illustrated in the cube by variation along the age dimension in the spacing and length of cells and plugs for different domains. In the extreme, inattention to domain specificity would be illustrated by vertical plugs covering all age groups for each policy domain, or more likely, plugs that span the same subset of age groups for each domain.

Competition for Resources

In addition to identifying gaps, overlaps, and discontinuities in services, the cube depicts the competing demands that affect political decisions on resource allocation. Conflict is likely between criteria that distribute benefits by age group or by domain. Should social policies emphasize

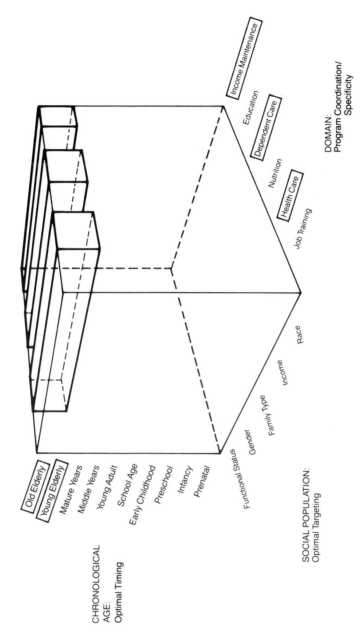

FIGURE 13.3 Benefits for the elderly: 3 bars.

CHRONOLOGICAL
AGE:
Optimal Timing

Old Elderly
Young Elderly
Mature Years
Middle Years
Young Adult
School Age
Early Childhood
Preschool
Infancy
Prenatal

Functional Status
Gender
Family Type
Income
Race

SOCIAL POPULATION:
Optimal Targeting

Job Training
Health Care
Nutrition
Dependent Care
Education
Income Maintenance

DOMAIN:
Program Coordination/
Specificity

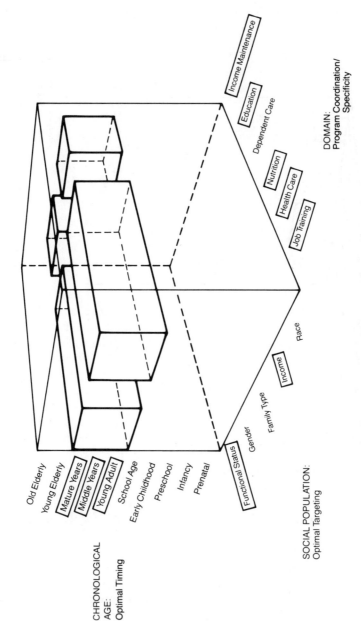

FIGURE 13.4 Coordinated disability benefits: 2 broken bars.

investment in a coherent set of problems across the life span or offer a comprehensive array of programs to a single age group?

The first strategy is approximated in the area of nutrition policy, in which the Women, Infants, and Children Supplemental Feeding Program (WIC) is targeted on the prenatal and infancy years, the Child Care Food Program serves some preschool-age children, the School Lunch program serves school-age children, Food Stamps are available to low-income adults, and Meals on Wheels provides nutritional food to the elderly. The plug in Figure 13.2 represents this.

The strategy of offering comprehensive services to a single age group is most closely followed for the elderly who benefit from income maintenance (Social Security), dependent care (tax credit and Medicare), health (Medicare), and nutrition (Meals on Wheels) programs, with only the nutrition benefits restricted by income. Figure 13.3 illustrates this composite of benefits for the elderly, showing three bars. (The single cell for nutrition is excluded for ease of illustration.)

Adding the population dimension creates an even more complex, but more realistic, portrayal of the conflicts inherent in the allocation of public resources. The policy issue most evident today is that of age versus functional need (Neugarten & Neugarten, 1986). The debate is whether policies should distinguish among members of an age category who vary in their need for services, or whether the services should be provided to all persons of the same age regardless of demonstrated need. For example, the Meals on Wheels program for the elderly is targeted by income, whereas Social Security benefits are provided to all elderly individuals who have contributed to the program.

In fact, both age and income serve as proxies for "need." To simplify the distribution of resources, eligibility formulas rely on these easily verified population characteristics rather than on more precise — but cumbersome — determinations of need for specific benefits. Neugarten (1982) and Featherman (1980) have suggested that life-span research be used to push society toward an age-irrelevant benefit structure, in which need is defined as a characteristic of individuals, rather than of age groups. Brim (1983) has further suggested that age may be a good indicator of need in the very early years of life when development shows less individual diversity, but less effective during the adult years when increased heterogeneity, the impact of social class, gender, poverty, and other forces attenuate the correlation between age and need for assistance.

As the timing and sequencing of major life status passages become increasingly less correlated with age, arguments now are made for expanding access to benefits to all age groups and using within-age eligibility criteria for purposes of targeting. For example, why not offer education and job training benefits to individuals across the life span and, perhaps, across social populations? The resulting slice is illustrated in Figure 13.5.

Spaces in the Cube:
A Comparative View

The cube can give a sharp graphic comparison of policies in public and private sectors of society, in different levels of government in the United States, in different countries, and in different historical periods. Our illustrations are drawn from current United States policies. If a similar analysis were to be made in Sweden, or in Germany, the forms and patterns that would appear in the cube would be quite different.

We expect that social programs encompassing complete slices of the cube are more frequent in countries other than the United States given basic differences in political philosophy and resource bases. Similarly, we expect cubes portraying the various levels of government would show differing degrees of investment in different domains (e.g., education vs. income support) attributable to different funding bases. And cubes illustrating private policies may have relatively more single cell interventions compared to those illustrating public policies, given differences in the size and diversity of private versus public constituencies.

Differences in wealth, in knowledge about how to improve the quality of life, as well as in population demography and the types of human development problems that characterize different nations, will influence what configuration appears — what cells are filled in the cube. Actual, as well as optimal, policies will differ depending on history, culture, and region.

THE CURRENT STATUS OF SOCIAL POLICIES
FOR CHILDREN

Even a cursory examination of federal programs for children reveals that contemporary developments in life-span theory and its associated disciplines have not been incorporated into the assumptions that affect policy. Instead, interventions and benefits characterized by illogical gaps in coverage, contradictory goals, and poor coordination have proliferated (Phillips, 1984). Among the reasons for this state of affairs is a reluctance to trade in prior assumptions about development for new ideas.

The assumptions about development that bolstered the political reforms of the 1960s, most notably the deterministic nature of early experience, continue to underlie contemporary policies focused on the childhood years. Despite growing evident of the continuous and malleable nature of human

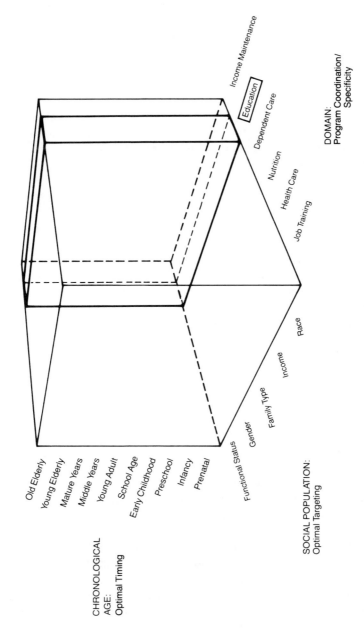

FIGURE 13.5 Hypothetical education benefits: A slice.

CHRONOLOGICAL
AGE:
Optimal Timing

Old Elderly
Young Elderly
Mature Years
Middle Years
Young Adult
School Age
Early Childhood
Preschool
Infancy
Prenatal

SOCIAL POPULATION:
Optimal Targeting

Functional Status
Gender
Family Type
Income
Race

Job Training
Health Care
Nutrition
Dependent Care
Education
Income Maintenance

DOMAIN:
Program Coordination/
Specificity

development, social policy debates are still dominated by a "vaccination approach" to human development. The resulting array of social programs is characterized by one-shot interventions for very young children premised on promises of long-term effects, and by caretaking programs for the elderly that fail to acknowledge enduring opportunities for change in the advanced stages of life.

Even within the childhood population, younger children are the focus of a more diverse (and less controversial) range of services than are older children, and in particular, than are adolescents. Although we are far from specifying domain-specific optimal periods when interventions are most likely to be effective, the current clustering of childhood interventions in the infancy and preschool years to the relative neglect of middle childhood and adolescence implies that little attention has been paid to these issues in policy debates.

The appeal of providing services to very young children is self-evident. This is when dependency is greatest and the costs of inattention to basic needs are often highest. Accordingly, WIC benefits that are technically available to children as old as 5 years of age are in practice provided almost exclusively to pregnant and nursing women and their infants under 1 year of age. Similarly, young children's health services enjoy tremendous popular support, so one finds both voluntary and publicly legislated programs focusing on this cell of young children's health. In contrast, policies that would provide adequate care and health education for adolescents generally provoke controversy. To the extent that benefits are provided to older children, they adopt the treatment strategies that characterize many adult programs rather than the prevention approach of early interventions. Head Start, for example, is characterized as *early education,* whereas Chapter I elementary and secondary school programs are referred to as *remedial education.*

The assortment of federal programs designed to provide assistance from the prenatal period through adolescence is also characterized by striking discontinuities in the continuum of services for children as they advance in age. For example, there are no policies to assure that children who have attended Head Start will receive Chapter I compensatory education services when they enter elementary school despite documentation that sustained benefits require follow-up services (Rescorla, Provence, & Naylor, 1982; Rutter, 1979; Seitz, Rosenbaum, & Apfel, 1985). A similar discontinuity at a critical junction is found in the Aid to Families with Dependent children income-support program. Recent budget cuts have forced the elimination of 18- to 21-year-olds from the program in many states (Washington, 1984), thus eliminating aid to a group of children who may require basic assistance to make the transition from high school to college or employment.

With regard to issues of population targeting, children's programs tend to rely on more specific eligibility criteria than programs that serve other age groups. In contrast to programs for the elderly, where age alone often determines eligibility, family income has joined age as a major determinant of eligibility for programs targeted on children. The majority of children's services—Head Start, Chapter I, School Lunch, Aid to Families with Dependent Children, Medicaid—are restricted to children in poor families. The Women, Infants, and Children Supplemental Feeding program provides an example of even more specific targeting. Benefits are provided exclusively to low-income women who have been certified by a health professional to be at nutritional risk. This situation is illustrated in Figure 13.6, which is characterized by blocks concentrated in the family income row—as contrasted with the bars in Figure 13.3—for a variety of children's programs.

In summary, the failure to articulate a coherent, logical intervention strategy for children from the prenatal to the teen years has produced a haphazard collection of programs, concentrated on the youngest age groups, largely targeted by income, and bolstered by an undue concern about the irreversibility and costs of later problems. This state of affairs is not, however, merely a reflection of outmoded knowledge. It also derives from a much more general conflict between prevailing political pressures and the implications of a life-span approach to intervention.

LIFE-SPAN DEVELOPMENT THEORY
AND THE REALITIES OF POLITICS

The fiscal pressures to maximize cost-effectiveness result in (a) efforts to limit eligible populations for services to those most likely to benefit; and (b) the provision of services when they are most likely to remediate problems and promote self-sufficiency. Issues of prevention are particularly prominent, as illustrated by the successful funding in 1986 of a "Children's Initiative." Only programs with evaluation data demonstrating effective remediation or enhancement of development were included in the legislation (U.S. Congress, 1985). In instances like these, political and empirical goals appear quite compatible with the interests of researchers in identifying opportunities for change that represent optimal entry points for intervention, and in examining individual differences in responsiveness to interventions.

Nevertheless, the guidelines for policy-making derived from life-span development theory are mostly incompatible with the familiar political pressures. As a first instance, the timeframe for problem-solving is set to a large extent by 2-, 4-, and 6-year election cycles. The immediacy of reelection pressures combined with the multitude of issues on the political

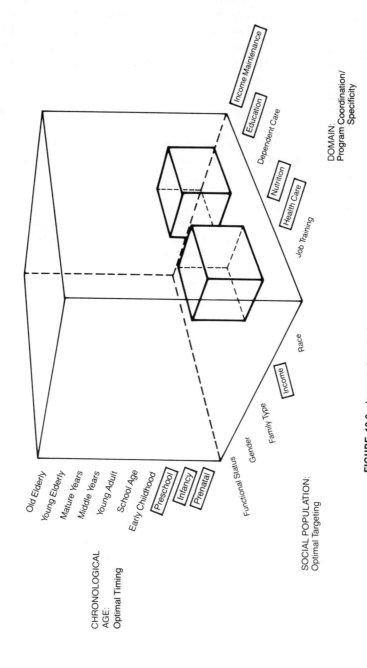

FIGURE 13.6 Income targeted programs for children: 2 blocks.

agenda promotes an episodic rather than a long-range perspective on policy development. There is a fundamental contradiction between a political system that seeks closure on issues and a theory about human development that advances a long-term perspective on intervention. But, the bright side of this process is that social issues constantly resurface, and policy responses to major issues such as tax and welfare reform are often several years in the making, thereby creating frequent opportunities for utilizing new knowledge and changing the prior policies.

A second incompatiblity between the life-span approach to intervention and prevailing political incentives is in the determination of eligibility for federal benefits. Two aspects are important. First, relatively static assumptions about the timing and sequencing of life events predominate in eligibility criteria. Even at the most basic level of estimating eligible populations static demographic profiles are used, instead of the longitudinal perspective suggested by life-span scholars. The sharply differing consequences for policy planning are illustrated by comparing 1984 figures that placed the percentage of children under 18 years old living with only one parent at 23%, and time series estimates (Glick, 1979) that nearly 60% of all children born in 1984 will live in a single-parent family at some time prior to age 18.

The other aspect of this second point is that politicians prefer to base eligibility criteria on relatively noncontroversial indicators of need. This explains the predominance of age-linked eligibility standards. Age provides a clear-cut proxy for "need" and avoids the controversy that accompanies eligibility based on income, family structure, functional status, and other more subjective, value-laden criteria. Despite evidence of vast heterogeneity within age groups and increasing variability in major life transitions, politicians are unlikely to abandon chronological age as a major element of social policy precisely because it is relatively neutral. People do not say that having more or less of it is better; and most people experience all "variations" on age. Moreover, age has a nonintrusive, low-cost of appraisal compared to other criteria.

A third incompatibility is between the emphasis of worthwhile interventions at all ages of the life span — a central element in life-span theory — and interest group politics and public perceptions of "acceptable" uses of tax dollars. Political responses to social problems represent bargains that are struck among competing demands, values, and priorities. Issues, populations, and age groups have differential draws on politicians' time, interest, and money.

For example, young children and the elderly are viewed as legitimately dependent populations, thus there is greater political support for social interventions aimed at the beginning and end of life. Age groups in mid-life bear the burden of proof the self-sufficiency is clearly impaired before a consensus can be reached that public benefits are warranted. Thus, controversy does not surround benefits to disabled adults, but is endemic to adult poverty programs.

Similarly, some social programs are greeted with greater support than others. Early education, given its target population of young children and its documented long-term benefits, is more popular than child care, which is often portrayed as a support program for low-income adults (Phillips & Zigler, in press). Health programs, particularly for pregnant women, terminally ill adults, and the elderly also generate strong support, in contrast to income-support programs. Even within the domain of health, mental health is at a decided disadvantage when placed alongside prenatal care, cancer research, and long-term nursing care for the elderly, as evidenced by the rapid decline in expenditures on community mental health relative to other health programs.

In summary, decision making about human development policy occurs in the context of powerful constraints established by political realities. The contribution of life-span development theory, therefore, becomes one of introducing new questions about the timing, targeting, and patterning of social interventions. The degree of influence these questions will have in shaping future social interventions will depend on the persuasiveness of the scientific community and the compatability of its arguments with the central concerns of politicians.

CONCLUSIONS

We are left, then, with the question of how to make choices about when, where, and with whom to intervene, given the new ideas generated by contemporary research and the pressures placed on them by political constraints. Each dimension identifies important issues for consideration.

The age dimension identifies optimal timing of interventions across the life span as a goal to approximate. Early intervention remains a sound principle, but only in the context of adequate follow-up services and equal attention to problems that are most appropriately addressed later in life.

The population dimension competes with age insofar as it emphasizes the multiple determinants of need that affect individuals regardless of their age. Poverty, poor health, and illiteracy are obvious candidates for this role, but there are many additional indicators that warrant attention. The aim is to identify the most precise match between benefit and need, and often, multiple population factors would be incorporated in eligibility criteria.

The domain dimension brings attention to program coordination and also raises the issue of domain specificity. The policy challenge is one of identifying age-appropriate interventions that are tailored to the particular aspect of development in question (e.g., reading skills, physical health, employability)—a task that is much more complex than identifying a sensitive period of development and directing all interventions to that period.

The life-span intervention cube directs our attention to the necessity of simultaneous consideration of all three dimensions. Like Rubik's Cube, the solution—in this case optimal timing and targeting of interventions—entails simultaneous manipulation of all three dimensions represented in the faces of the cube. Any change in one of these changes the configuration of all three, a concentrated focus on one dimension is fated to be an unsuccessful strategy. This approach to social policies for human development acknowledges that an optimal and realistic intervention strategy is necessarily the endproduct of a process of trade-off's and compromises, given limited resources and many other constraints on the ideal manipulation of each dimension.

REFERENCES

Atkinson, R. C. (1977). Reflections on psychology's past and concerns about its future. *American Psychologist, 32,* 205–210.

Bateson, P. P.G. (1979). How do sensitive periods arise and what are they for? *Animal Behavior, 27,* 470–477.

Brim, O. G., Jr. (1983, August). *The policies and politics of life-span development.* Paper presented at the biennial meetings of the Internaltiona Society for the Study of Behavioral Development, Munich.

Brim, O. G., Jr., & Kagan, J. (1980). *Constancy and change in human development.* Cambridge, MA: Harvard University Press.

Bronfenbrenner, U. (1974). Developmental research, public policy, and the ecology of childhood. *Child Development, 45,* 1–5.

Featherman, D. (1980). The life-span perspective in social science research. In O. G. Brim & J. Kagan (Eds.), *Constancy and change in human development* (pp. 675–738). Cambridge, MA: Harvard University Press.

Feuerstein, R., Rand, Y., Hoffman, M. B., & Miller, R. (1980). *Instrumental enrichment: An intervention program for cognitive modifiability.* Baltimore, MD: University Park Press.

Garmezy, N. (1983). Stressors of childhood. In N. Garmezy & M. Rutter (Eds.), *Stress, coping, and development in children* (pp. 43–84). New York: McGraw-Hill.

Glick, P. C. (1979). Children of divorced parents in demographic perspective. *Journal of Social Issues, 35,* 112–125.

Hayes, C. D. (Ed.). (1983). *Making policies for children: A study of the federal process.* Washington, DC: National Academy Press.

Henderson, N. D. (1980). Effects of early experience upon the behavior of animals: The second twenty-five years of research. In E. C. Simmel (Ed.), *Early experiences and early behavior: Implications for social development* (pp. 45–78). New York: Academic Press.

Hetherington, E. M., Cox, M., & Cox, R. (1982). The aftermath of divorce. In M. Lamb (Ed.), *Nontraditional families* (pp. 233–288). Hillsdale, NJ: Lawrence Erlbaum Associates.

Hobbs, N., & Robinson, S. (1982). Adolescent development and public policy. *American Psychologist, 37,* 212.

Immelmann, K., & Suomi, S. (1981). Sensitive phases in development. In K. Immelmann, G. Barlow, L. Petrovitch, & M. Main (Eds.), *Behavioral development* (pp. 395–431). New York: Cambridge University Press.

Lerner, R. M. (1984). *On the nature of plasticity.* New York: Cambridge University Press.

Maccoby, E. E., Kahn, A. J., & Everett, B. A. (1983). The role of psychological research in the formation of policies affecting children. *American Psychologist, 38,* 80–84.

Masters, J. (1983). Models for training and research in child development and social policy. In G. Whitehurst (Ed.), *Annals of child development* (Vol. 1, pp. 263–301). Greenwich, CT: JAI Press.

McKay, H., Sinisterra, L., McKay, A., Gomez, H., & Floreda, P. (1978). Improving cognitive ability in chronically deprived children. *Science, 200,* 270–278.

Miller, G. A. (1969). Psychology as a means of promoting human welfare. *American Psychologist, 24,* 1063–1075.

Morgan, B. L. G., & Winick, M. (1980). Effects of environmental stimulation on brain N-acetylneuraminic acid content and behavior. *Journal of Nutrition, 110,* 425–432.

National Research Council. (1978). *The federal investment in knowledge of social problems (Vol. 1): Study project report.* Washington, DC: National Academy Press.

Neugarten, B. L. (1982). *Age or need? Public policies for older people.* Beverly Hills, CA: Sage.

Neugarten, B. L., & Neugarten, D. A. (1986). Age in the aging society. *Daedalus, 115,* 31–50.

Phillips, D. (1984). Continuity of care: Theory, evidence, and policy applications. In D. Phillips (Ed.), Continuity of care: A guide for social programs [Special issue]. *International Journal of Mental Health, 12*(4), 5–21.

Phillips, D., & Zigler, E. (in press). The checkered history of federal child care regulation. In E. Rothkopf (Ed.), *Review of research in education* (Vol. 14). New York: Columbia University Press.

Rescorla, L. A., Provence, S., & Naylor, A. (1982). The Yale Child Welfare Research Program: Description and results. In E. Zigler & E. W. Gordon (Eds.), *Daycare: Scientific and social policy issues* (pp. 183–199). Boston: Auburn.

Richardson, S. A. (1976a). The relation of severe malnutrition in infancy to the intelligence of school children with different histories. *Pediatric Research, 10,* 51–58.

Richardson, S. A. (1976b). Review. *Contemporary Sociology, 5*(5), 663–665.

Rutter, M. (1979). Maternal deprivation, 1972–1978: New findings, new concepts, new approaches. *Child Development, 50,* 283–294.

Sackett, G. P., Sameroff, A. J., Cairns, R. B., & Suomi, S. J. (1981). Continuity in behavioral development: Theoretical and empirical issues. In K. Immelmann, G. Barlow, L. Petrovitch, & M. Main (Eds.), *Behavioral development: The Bielefeld interdisciplinary project* (pp. 23–57). Cambridge, MA: Cambridge University Press.

Sameroff, A. J., Seifer, R., & Zax, M. (1982). Early development of children at risk for emotional disorder. *Monographs of the Society for Research in Child Development, 47* (7, Serial No. 199).

Scarr, S., & Weinberg, R. A. (1976). IQ test performance of black children adopted by white families. *American Psychologist, 31,* 726–734.

Sears, R. R. (1975). Your ancients revisited: A history of child development. In E. M. Hetherington (Ed.), J. W. Hagen, R. Kron, & A. H. Stein (Associate Eds.), *Review of child development research* (Vol. 5, pp. 1–74). Chicago: University of Chicago Press.

Seitz, V., Rosenbaum, L. K., & Apfel, N. H. (1985). Effects of family support intervention: A ten-year follow-up. *Child Development, 56,* 376–391.

Senn, M. J. E. (1975). Insights on the child development movement in United States. *Monographs of the Society for Research in Child Development, 40* (3–4, Serial No. 161).

Sherrod, L. R., & Brim, O. G., Jr. (1986). Epilogue: Retrospective and prospective views of life course research on human development. In A. B. Sorenson, F. E. Weinert, & L. R.

Sherrod (Eds.), *Human development and the life course: Multidisciplinary perspectives* (pp. 557–580). Hillsdale, NJ: Lawrence Erlbaum Associates.

Smuts, A. B., & Hagen, J. W. (Eds.). (1986). History and research in child development. *Monographs of the Society for Research in Child Development, 50* (4–5, Serial No. 211).

Stevenson, H., & Siegal, A. (Eds.). (1984). *Child development research and social policy* (Vol. 1). Chicago: University of Chicago Press.

Takanishi, R., DeLeon, P., & Pallak, M. (1983). Psychology and public policy affecting children, youth and families. *American Psychologist, 38,* 67–69.

Tizard, B. (1978). *Adoption: A second chance.* New York: The Free Press.

U.S. Congress, Select Committee on Children, Youth, and Families (1985). *Opportunities for success: Cost-effective programs for children.* Washington, DC: Government Printing Office.

Wachs, T. D., & Gruen, G. E. (1982). *Early experience and human development.* New York: Plenum.

Wallerstein, J. S. (1983). Children of divorce: Stress and developmental tasks. In N. Garmezy & M. Rutter (Eds.), *Stress, coping, and development in children* (pp. 265–302). New York: McGraw-Hill.

Washington, V. (1984). Support for dependent children—Continuity of care in the AFDC program. In D. Phillips (Ed.), Continuity of care: A guide for social programs. *International Journal of Mental Health, 12,* 59–77.

Werner, E. E., & Smith, R. S. (1977). *Kauai's children come of age.* Honolulu: University of Hawaii Press.

Winick, M. (1980). Nutrition and brain development. *Natural History, 89,* 6–13.

Zigler, E. (1980). Welcoming a new journal. *Journal of Applied Developmental Psychology, 1,* 1–16.

Author Index

A

Abramson, L. Y., 91, 92, 94, 100, 109, *110, 111, 113*
Acland, H., 220, *238*
Adam, K. S., 151, *155*
Allen, L., 125, 132, *141*
Allen, V. L., 22, 39, 40, 41, *44*
Alloy, L. B., 100, 109, *113*
Allport, G. W., 23, *42*
Alwin, D., 68, 86–87, *88*
Amabile, T. M., 263, *273*
Ames, R., 41, *42*
Anderson, B. A., 179, *185*
Anderson, B. J., 167, *189*
Anderson, E., 160, 165, 173, *188*
Anderson, J. R., 195, *214*
Anderson, L., 228, *239*
Anderson, P., 49, *64*
Anisman, H., 93, 105, *114*
Apfel, N. H., 292, *298*
Appelman, J. R., 193, *214*
Aries, P., 50, *64*
Arlin, M., 221, 226–227, *238*
Arlin P. K., 199, *215*
Armon, C., 196, 199, *215*
Arnett, J., 9, *17*
Arnold, A. P., 26, *45*
Arsenian, J., 122, *139*
Arsenian, J. M., 122, *139*

B

Aschenbrenner, B. G., 180, *181*
Asher, S. J., 11, *16*
Atkinson, J. W., 92, *110, 112*
Atkinson, R., 200, *215*
Atkinson, R. C., 279, *297*
Azmitia, M., 203, *215*
Azuma, H., 246, 250, *258*

Baer, D. M., 200, *215*
Baldwin, J. M., 2, 8, *16*
Baldwin, W., 176, *185, 186*
Baldwin, W. H., 179, *185, 186*
Baltes, P. B., 2, 4*n*, 6, 7, 8, 9, 11, 13, 14, *16,* 22, 28, 29, 36, 40, *42, 45,* 68, *88,* 95, 96, 97, 98, *110, 111,* 160, *186,* 194, 195, 196, 202, 203, *215,* 221, *238,* 261, 263, 264, *273, 274*
Bandura, A., 200, *215*
Bane, M. J., 220, *238*
Barker, R. G., 121, *139,* 202, *215*
Barrett, J., *186*
Bartrop, R. W., 93, *111*
Bashman, R. B., 169, 180, 181, *189*
Basseches, M., 199, *215*
Bates, J. E., 29, *42*
Bateson, P., 138, *140*
Bateson, P. P. G., 280, *297*

Baumert, J., 226, *238*
Beady, C., 220, *238*
Beitel, A., 173, 184, *189*
Bell, D., 49, 51, 52, 61, *64*
Bell, R. Q., 34, *42*
Bellah, R., 61, 62, *64*
Belsky, J., 6, *16,* 163, 166, 167, 168, *186*
Bem, D. J., 133, *140*
Bengston, V. L., 23, *42*
Bennett, E. L., 30, *43*
Benson, H., 93, *112*
Berg, C. A., 266, 269, 272, *273*
Bernstein, M., 269, *275*
Berry, J. W., 272, *274*
Biddle, B. J., 220, *238*
Bijou, S. W., 200, *215*
Billings, A., 165, *188*
Binet, A., 204, *215*
Birren, J. E., 13, *16,* 193, 196, *215*
Blau, P. M., 70, 71, *88*
Block, J., 22, 28, 28, *42,* 80, *88,* 118, 121, 122,
    123, 136, 138–139, *139, 140*
Block, J. H., 121, 122, *139, 140*
Bloom, B. L., 11, *16*
Bloom, B. S., 219, 226, *238*
Bloom, D. E., 180, *186*
Bloom-Feshbach, J., 173, 181, *186*
Blyth, D. A., 39, *46,* 162, *190*
Boli, J., 49, 50, 51, 53, *64, 65*
Boli-Bennett, J., 49, *64*
Bolton, F. G., 178, *186*
Bonner, J., 30, *46*
Bonneveaux, B., 222, *239*
Bornstein, M. H., 219–220, *238*
Borysenko, J. Z., 93, *112*
Borysenko, M., 93, *112*
Boss, P. G., 171, *186*
Bourdieu, P., 72, *88*
Bower, G. H., 194, *215*
Bower, T. G. R., 7, *16*
Bowles, S., 58, *64,* 74, *88*
Bradley, R., 5, *16*
Brassard, J. A., 160, *186*
Brim, O. G., Jr., 3, 8, 13, *16,* 22, 27, 33, 40,
    43, 85, *88,* 96, *111,* 144, *155, 157,* 280,
    281, 289, *297*
Broman, S. H., 176, *186*
Bronfenbrenner, U., 9, 12, *16,* 36, *43,* 68, 81,
    88, 89, 160, *186,* 202, *215,* 279
Brookover, W., 220, *238*
Brooks-Gunn, J., 40, *43,* 175, 177, 178, *187*

Brophy, J. E., 220, 226, *238*
Brown, A. L., 202, *215*
Brown, G. H., 100, *111*
Bruner, J. S., 196, *215*
Buell, S. J., 27, *43*
Burns, M., 109, *111*
Busch-Rossnagel, N. A., 33, *44*
Bush, E. S., 99, *111*
Buss, A. H., 131, *140*

C

Cain, R. L., Jr., 167, *189*
Cain, V., 176, *185*
Cairns, R. B., 2, *16,* 282
Caldwell, B., 5, *16*
California Achievement Test, 102
Call, V., 75, *90*
Callahan, E. J., 144, *155*
Camara, C., 10, *17,* 69, 85, *89*
Camara, K. A., 10, 11, *17,* 160, 161, 165, *187*
Campbell, E. R., 220, *238*
Canter, A., 93, *111*
Card, J., 175, *186*
Carey, S., 220, *238*
Carlton-Ford, S. L., 39, *46*
Caspi, A., 124, 133, *140*
Castellon, C., 95, *113*
CAT (*See* California Achievement Test)
Cattell, R. B., 23, *43,* 123, *140,* 204, *215,* 262,
    264, *274*
Chandler, M. J., 8, *18*
Chapman, M., 150, 152
Chapman, R., 93, *112*
Charlesworth, W., 194, *215,* 202
Charlesworth, W. R., 264, *274, 278*
Charnov, E. L., 164, *188*
Chase, W. R., 263, *274*
Chess, S., 29, 36, 38, *43, 45*
Chi, M. T. H., 263, *274*
Chomsky, N., 198, *215*
Clark, R. W., 92, *112*
Clarke-Stewart, K. A., 167, *185*
Clayton, V., 263, *274*
Cluff, L. E., 93, *111*
Cochran, M. M., 160, *186*
Coddington, R. D., 144, *155, 156*
Cohen, D., 220, *238*
Cole, M., 194, *215*
Coleman, J. S., 220, *238*

Coleman, P. D., 27, *43*
College Entrance Examination board, 102, *111*
Commons, M. L., 196, 199–200, *215*
Conley, J. J., 118, *140*
Conway, B. E., 269, *275*
Cook, T. D., 23, *44*
Cooney, T. J., 244
Cornelius, S. W., 68, *88*
Costa, P. C., Jr., 116, *141*
Costa, P. T., 22, 118, 119, *140*
Cowan, C. P., 6, *16*
Cowan, P. A., 6, *16*
Cox, M., 6, 9, 10, *17*, 144, 151, *156*, 174, *187*, 280, 281, *297*
Cox, R., 6, 9, 10, *17*, 144, 151, *156*, 174, *187*, 280, 281, *297*
Crandall, V. C., 93, *111*
Crandall, V. J., 93, *111*
Crnic, K. A., 169, 180, 181, *186, 189*
Crockett, L. J., 41, *43*
Crosswhite, F. J., 244, *258*
Crouter, A., 160, *186*
Crowder, R., 194, *215*
Cunningham, W., 13, *16*, 196, *215*

D

Daniels, D., 154, *157*
Daniels, P., 180, 182, 183, *187*
Danish, S. J., *156*
Dannefer, D., 9, *16*, 203, *215*
Datan, N., 96, *112*
Davidson, J. E., 263, *274, 275*
Davis, O. L., Jr., 143, *157*
DeLeon, P., 278, *299*
Dickie, J. R., 168, *187*
Dictionary of Occupational Titles, 122, *140*
Diener, C. I., 92, 93, *111*
Dittmann-Kohli, F., 261, 263, 264, *273, 274*
Dixon, R. A., 221, *238*, 261, 264, 278
Dodge, K., 136, *140*
Dohrenwend, B. P., 144, *156*
Dohrenwend, B. S., 144, *156*
Donaldson, A., 219, *238*
Dossey, J. A., 244, *258*
Downing, C. J., 262, *275*
Drugan, R. C., 93, *112*
Duncan, G., 82, *89*
Duncan, O. D., 70, 71, *88, 89*

Dunn, J., 143, 146, 147, 148, 149–150, 150, 152, 153, *156, 157,* 166, *187*
Durrett, M. E., 169, *187*
Dweck, C., 162, *187*
Dweck, C. S., 92, 93, 96, 99, 101, 101–102, *111*
Dwyer, J., 107, *112*

E

East, P., 38, *43*
East, P. L., 36, 38, *44*
Eaton, W. W., 222–223, *239*
Educational Research Service, 102–103, *111*
Egeland, B., 164, *190*
Eichorn, D. H., 125, *140*
Elder, G. H., 10, 69, 85, *89,* 93, 96, 97, 109, *111, 113,* 160, 165, 172, *187*
Elder, G. H., Jr., 2, 10, *17,* 29, *43,* 120, 124, 133, *140*
Elizur, J., 143, *156*
Elkind, D., 196, *215*
Elliot, E., 162, *187*
Ellis, S., 272, *275*
Emmerich, W., 23, 24, 27, 30, 31–32, *43*
Ensminger, M., 177, 178, *187*
Enstrup, B., 223, *239*
Epstein, S., 22, *43,* 58, *64,* 118, 123, *140*
Erikson, E. H., 23, 24, 27, *43, 89,* 119, *140*
Erikson, R., 71, 74, *89*
Estes, D., 164, *188, 190*
Evans, A. S., 93, *112*
Everett, B. A., 279, *298*

F

Faucher, T. A., 222–223, *239*
Featherman, D. L., 2, 9, 12, 14, *17,* 25, 26, 27, 28, 29, *43,* 69, 74–75, 75, 77, 81, 82, 84, 85, 86, 87, *89,* 160, *187,* 203, *215,* 281, 289, *297*
Feiring, C., 166, *188*
Feldman, D., 263, *274*
Feldman, S. S., 181, *187*
Feuerstein, R., 280, *297*
Fiala, R., 57, *64*
Field, T., 143, *156*
Fisher, T., 176, *189*
Flavell, J. H., 193, 199, 211, *215*
Fleeson, J., 164, *190*

Flood, P., 220, *238*
Floreda, P., 280, *298*
Folkman, S., 165, *188*
Foner, A.,, 10, 11, *18,* 120, *141*
Ford, D. H., 23, 31, *45*
Fox, B. H., 93, *111*
Freud, S., 23, 24, *43*
Fry, P. S., 269, *274*
Furstenberg, F. F., 9, *17,* 175, 177, 178, *187*

G

Gai, D. S., 178, *186*
Gangestad, S., 137, *140*
Garcia, C., 131, *140*
Gardner, H., 264, *274*
Gardner, W., 164, *188*
Garmezy, N., 280, *297*
Gauvain, M., 272, *275*
Gecas, V., 68, *89*
Gelman, R., 199, *215*
Gibson, J. J., 202, *215*
Giddens, A., 70, 72, *89*
Gilliard, D., 99, *111*
Gilstrap, B., 168, *186*
Gintis, H., 58, *64,* 74, 220, *238*
Girgus, J. S., 102, 110, *112*
Glaser, R., 263, *274*
Gleitman, L. R., 242, *258*
Glick, P. C., 295, *297*
Goetz, T. E., 92, 99, *111*
Goldthorpe, J. H., 71, 72, 74, *89*
Gomez, H., 280, *298*
Gonzalez, M., 222, *239*
Good, T. L., 220, 226, *238*
Gordon, C., 23, *42*
Gottlieb, G., 7, *17*
Gottman, J. M., 165, 166, 185, *189*
Gould, S. J., 25, 26, 34, *43*
Grajek, S., 154, 157
Green, A. W., 122, *140*
Green, E. J., 26, *43*
Greenberg, M. T., 169, 180, 181, *186*
Greenough, W. T., 26, *43*
Greer, S., 106, *111*
Groeben, N., 224, *239*
Grossman, K., 167, *188*
Grouse, L. D., 30–31, *43*
Gruber, H., 263, 266, *274*
Gruen, G. E., 5, 19, 164, *190,* 282, *299*
Guilford, J. P., 204, *215,* 264, *274*

H

Hagen, J. W., 278, *299*
Hagestad, G. O., 9, *17,* 120, *140,* 165, *187*
Haggarty, R. J., 93, *112*
Hall, C. S., 24, *43*
Hall, G. S., 193, *215*
Hall, J., 49, *64*
Hamilton, E. W., 109, *111*
Hamilton, G., 60, *64*
Hannan, M. T., 87, *90*
Hareven, T., 172, *187*
Harper, L. V., 34, *42*
Harris, T. J., 100, *111*
Hartup, W. W., 7, *17*
Hauser, R. M., 82, *89*
Hayes, C. D., 278, *297*
Heath, S., 267, 270, *274*
Helmke, A., 228, 229, 233, *238, 239*
Helson, R., 120, *140*
Henderson, N. D., 280, *297*
Henry, S., 211, *215*
Hernandez, D., 68, *89*
Herzog, J. G., 144, *156*
Hess, R. D., 246, *258*
Hetherington, E. M., 6, 9, 10, 11, *17,* 40, *43, 44,* 69, 85, *89,* 144, 149, 151, 155, *156,* 159–160, 160, 161, 162, 164, 165, 166, 169, 174, *187,* 280, 281, *297*
Heyns, B., 220, *238*
Higgins, E. T., 145, *156*
Hinde, R. A., 138, *140,* 151, *156, 186*
Hirsch, J., 30, 31, *44*
Hobbs, N., 280, *297*
Hobson, C. J., 220, *238*
Hochschild, A., 62, *64*
Hoffman, L., 144, *156*
Hoffman, M. B., 280, *297*
Hoffreth, S., 176, *187*
Hoffreth, S. L., 178, *187*
Hogan, D. P., 75, *89,* 133, *141*
Hollier, A., 9, *17*
Honzik, M. P., 125, 132, *141*
Hood, K. E., 2, *16*
Hooker, K., 37, *46*
Horn, J. L., 6, *17,* 193, 204, *215,* 219, *238,* 261, 262, 264, *274*
Houts, A. C., 23, *44*
Hoyer, W. J., 202, *215*
Hsu, C. C., 244, 245, *258*
Hughes, M., 143, *156*

Hurme, H., 144, *156, 157*
Hymel, S., 184, *189*
Hyson, R. L., 93, *112*

I

Ickes, W., 23, 31, 34, *46,* 121, *142*
Iker, H. P., 93, *113*
Imboden, J. B., 93, *111*
Immelmann, K., 280, *298*
Inhelder, B., 198–199, *216*
Inkeles, A., 48, *64*

J

Jackman, M., 70, *89*
Jackman, R., 70, *89*
Jaworski, B. J., 97, *111*
Jemmott, J. B., III, 93, *112*
Jencks, C., 220, *238*
Jenkins, J., 194
Jenkins, J. J., 202, *215*
Johnson, M., 10, 11, *18,* 120, *141*
Jones, M. C., 41, *44*

K

Kagan, J., 3, 8, 13, *16,* 22, 23, 27, 40, *43, 44,* 57, *64,* 68, *89,* 131, *140,* 280
Kahn, A. J., 279, *298*
Kamen, L. P., 103, 107, *112*
Kane, P. T., 269, *275*
Kaplan, B., 2, *17*
Kashiwagi, K., 246, *258*
Kasl, S. V., 93, *112*
Kaslow, N. J., 100, 109, *113*
Katkovsky, W., 93, *111*
Kauffman, M. B., 8, 11, 12, *18,* 34, *45*
Keasy, D. B., 100, *112*
Keith, J., 120, *141*
Kellam, S., 177, 178, *187*
Keller, S. E., 93, *113*
Kelly, J. B., 161
Kendler, T. S., 12, *17,* 201, *215*
Kendrick, C., 146, 149–150, *156,* 166, *187*
Kertzer, D., 120, *141*
Ketron, J. L., 269, *275*
Kifer, E., 223, *238,* 244, *258*
Kiloh, L. G., 93, *111*
Kinard, 176

Kitamura, S., 244, 245, *258*
Klerman, 176
Kluckhohn, C., 23, 24, *44,* 116, *141*
Kohlberg, L., 198, *215*
Kohn, M. L., 58, *64,* 68, 69, 70, 73, 81, 84, 85, 87, *89, 90*
Körkel, J., 221, *239*
Kornhauser, W., 48, *65*
Kramer, D. A., 221, *238*
Krokoff, L. J., 165, *187*
Kucher, J. S., 38, *44*
Kuhn, D., 200, *215*
Kurdek, L. A., 11, *18*

L

Laboratory of Comparative Human Cognition, 271, *274*
Labouvie, E., 118, *141*
Labouvie-Vief, G., 211, *215,* 264
Lamb, M. E., 164, 166, 167, *188, 190*
Laner, R. H., 178, *186*
Lanford, A., 57, *64*
Langlois, J. H., 38, *43*
Lasch, C., 52, 61, *64*
Laudenslager, M. L., 93, *112*
Lawrence, K. M., 172, *190*
Lazarus, L., 93, *111*
Lazarus, R., 165, *188*
Lee, S. Y., 244, 246, *258*
Lenerz, K., 36, *38, 44*
Lerner, J. V., 36, 38, *43, 44, 46*
Lerner, R. M., 2, 6, 7, 8, 9, 11, 12, 13, *17, 18,* 22, 23, 24, 25, 26, 27, 30, 31, 32, 33, 34, 36, 38, 41, *43, 44, 45, 46,* 160, 163, *187, 188,* 203, *215,* 280, *298*
Lesgold, A., 263, *274*
LeShan, L., 93, *112*
LeVine, R. A., 116, 120, *141*
Levy, S. M., 93, 105, *112*
Lewin, K., 202, *215*
Lewis, M., 33, *45,* 166, *188*
Licht, B., 92, 96, 99, *111*
Liker, J. K.. 96, 97, *111,* 165
Linden, C., 5, *18*
Lindzey, G., 24, *43*
Lipsitt, L. P., 28, 36, 40, *42,* 95, 96, 97, 98, *111*
Locke, S. E., 93, *112*
Lockwood, D., 71, *90*

Lowe, J. W., 120, *141*
Lowell, E. L., 92, *112*
Luborsky, L., 95, *113*
Lucker, G. W., 244, 245, *258*
Luckhurst, C., 93, *111*
Luecke, D. E., 220, *238*
Lunt, P. S., 70, *90*

M

Maccoby, E. E., 279, 298
Maccoby, E. M., 153, *157*
MacDonald, K., 181, *188, 189*
MacEachron, A., 178, *186*
Macfarlane, J. W., 125, 132, *141*
Madsen, R., 61, 62, *64*
Magnusson, D., 22, 39, 40, *45,* 121, *141*
Maier, S. F., 93, *112*
Main, M., 164, *188*
Mann, M., 49, *65*
Markman, E. M., 193, *215*
Marsiglio, W., 175, *188*
Martin, J. A., 153, *157*
Masters, J., 278, *298*
Matheson, P., 168, *187*
Mayer, K., 48, *65*
McCall, R. B., 5, 7, *18*
McCandless, B., 99, *112*
McCartney, K., 7, *18,* 31, 33, *45,* 124, 137, *141*
McClearn, G. E., 30, *45*
McClelland, D. C., 92, 93, *112*
McCluskey, K. A., 144, *155*
McCrae, R. R., 22, *43,* 116, 118, 119, *140, 141*
McGinn, N. F., 220, *239*
McGinnis, L., 151, *156*
McKay, A., 280, *298*
McKay, H., 280, *298*
McKinney, K. L., 162, *190*
McKnight, C. C., 244, *258*
McPartland, J., 220, *238*
Mead, G., 48, *65*
Mendez, O., 38, *46*
Metalsky, G. I., 94, *113*
Meyer, D., 93, *112*
Meyer, J., 48, 50, 51, 53, *64, 65,* 93, 112
Michelson, S., 220, *238*
Miller, G. A., 279, *298*
Miller, J., 69, 70, 73, 81, 84, 85, 87, *89, 90*

Miller, K. A., 69, 70, 73, 81, 84, 85, 87, *89*
Miller, N. E., 211, *215*
Miller, R., 280, *297*
Mischel, W., 22, *45,* 57, 58, *65,* 117, 118, *141*
Mitchell, V., 120, *140*
Moane, G., 120, *140*
Mood, A. M., 220, *238*
Moore, J., 120, *141*
Moos, R. H., 165, *188*
Morgan, 175, 177, *187*
Morgan, B. L. G., 280, *298*
Morris, T., 106, *111*
Mortimer, J. T., 81, *90*
Moss, H. A., 22, 23, *27, 44, 45*
Mosteller, F., 220, *239*
Moulton, R. W., 92, 112
Moynihan, D. P., 220, *239*
Mueller, W., 48, *65,* 68, *90*
Munn, P., 152, 153, *156*
Munro, D. J., 246, *258*
Murphy, G., 24, *45*
Murphy, T., 5, *18*
Murray, H., 23, 24, *44*
Murray, H. A., 116, *141*
Mussen, P. H., 41, *44*

N

Nash, S. C., 181, *187*
National Research Council, 278, *298*
Naylor, A., 292, *298*
Neisser, U., 264, 268, *274*
Nelson, P. G., 30–31, *43*
Nesselroade, J. R., 9, *16,* 22, 23, 24, 29, 31, 32, *42, 45,* 68, *88, 96, 110,* 194, *215*
Neugarten, B., 120, *140, 141*
Neugarten, B. L., 96, *112, 140,* 289, *298*
Neugarten, D. A., 289, *298*
Nevelle, B., 176, 181, *189*
Nicholls, J. G., 98, *112*
Niederman, J. C., 93, *112*
Niemark, E. D., 193, *215, 216*
Nolen-Hoeksema, S., 98–99, 100, 101, 102, 110, *112*
Nord, C. W., 179, *186*
Nordeen, E. J., 26, *45*
Nordeen, K. W., 26, *45*
Norman, D. A., 200, *216*
Nowak, C. A., *156*

O

O'Leary, S. E., 167, *188*
Oliveri, M. E., 170, *188,* 189
O'Connor, S., 53, *65*
Oppenheimer, R., 73, *90*
Ornstein, P. A., 193, *216*
Otaki, M., 169, *187*
Otto, L. B., 75, *90*
Overton, W. F., 11, 12, *18,* 197, *216*

P

Pallak, M., 278, *299*
Papert, S., 195, *216*
Parcell, T. L., 68, *90*
Parke, R. D., 33, *45,* 160, 163, 165, 166, 167, 173, 176, 180, 181, 184, 185, *188, 189, 190*
Parker, T., 222, *239*
Parkin, F., 71, 72, *90*
Parsons, J. E., 98, *112, 113,* 145, *156*
Pascual-Leone, J., 266, *275*
Patterson, G. R., 124, *141*
Paykel, E. S., 144, *157*
Payne, H., 172, *190*
Pea, R. D., 195, *216*
Peake, P. K., 22, *45,* 118, *141*
Pearlin, L. I., 69, *90*
Pedersen, E., 222–223, *239*
Pedersen, F. A., 166, 167, 167–168, *189*
Peirce, C. S., 101, *113*
Penny, R., 93, *111*
Perlmutter, M., 196, 203, *215, 216*
Persons, J. B., 109, *113*
Pervin, L. A., 121, *141*
Petersen, A. C., 39, 41, *43, 45*
Peterson, C., 91, 92, 94, 95, 100, 108, 109, *113*
Pettingale, K. W., 106, *111*
Phillips, D., 290, 296, *298*
Piaget, J., 136, *141,* 193, 195, 196, 198–199, 211, *216,* 260, 266, 271, *275*
Pinkerton, G., 143, *156*
Plewis, I., 143, *156*
Plomin, R., 5, *18,* 31, *45,* 131, 154, *157*
Portocarero, L., 71, 74, *89*
Poulton, E. B., 2, 8, *16*
Power, T. G., 166, 176, 184, 185, *189*
Presser, H., 175, *189*
Provence, S., 292, *298*

R

Raaheim, K., 271, *275*
Raber, S. M., 96, *113*
Radke-Yarrow, M., 150, 152, *157*
Ragozin, A. S., 169, 180, 181, *186, 189*
Ramirez, F., 49, 50, 51, 53, *64, 65*
Ramsy, N. R., 75, *90*
Rand, Y., 280, *297*
Rao, P. A., 109, *113*
Rawnsley, K., 172, *190*
Reedy, M. N., 23, *42*
Rees, E., 263, *274, 278*
Reese, H. W., 2, 12, *16, 18,* 22, 28, 36, 40, *42,* 95, 96, 97, 98, *111,* 195, 197, *216*
Reiss, D., 170, 171, *188, 189*
Reppucci, N. D., 92, 99, 101, *111*
Rescorla, L. A., 292, *298*
Reznick, J. S., 131, *140*
Rheinberg, F., 223, *239*
Rholes, W. S., 98, *113*
Richards, D. D., 269, *275*
Richards, F. A., 196, 199–200, *215*
Richards, P., 169, *187*
Richardson, S. A., 280, 281, *298*
Riegel, K. F., 12, *18,* 199, *216*
Riley, M. W., 10, 11, *18,* 74, *90,* 120, *141*
Roberts, A., 99, *112*
Robins, L. N., 124, *141*
Robinson, N. M., 169, 180, 181, *186, 189*
Robinson, S., 280, *297*
Rockwell, R. C., 10, *17*
Rodin, J., 107, *112*
Roeder, P. M., 226, *238*
Rogoff, B., 241, 272, *275*
Rogosa, D., 87, *90*
Rosenbaum, L. K., 292, *298*
Rosenblum, L. A., 33, *45*
Rosenzweig, M. R., 30, *43*
Ross, J., 98, *113*
Rossi, A. S., 155, *157*
Rotenberg, K. J., 98, *113*
Rovine, M., 168, *186*
Rowe, D. C., 154, *157*
Rozin, P., 242, *258*
Rubin, K. H., 137, *141*
Ruble, D. N., 98, *112, 113*
Rutter, M., 10, *18,* 73, *90,* 125, *141,* 144, 149, *157,* 160, 164, 165, *190,* 220, 221, 222, *239,* 292, *297*
Ryan, D. W., 228, *239*

Ryan, S. M., 93, *112*
Ryder, N. B., 11, *18*
Ryff, C. D., 85, *88,* 96, *111, 155*

S

Sackett, G. P., 282, *298*
Salapatek, P., 193, *216*
Sameroff, A. J., 8, *18,* 280, 282, *298*
Sang, F., 226, *238*
Scarr, S., 2, 7, 7–8, *18,* 31, 33, *45,* 116, 117, 124, 137, *141,* 154, 280, *298*
Scarr-Salapatek, S., *157,* 195, *216*
Schaefer, J. A., 165, *188*
Schaffer, H. R., 167, *190*
Schaie, K. W., 11, *19,* 96, *113,* 193, 194, 195, 196, *215, 216,* 221, *238,* 261, *275*
Schleifer, S. J., 93, *113*
Schmale, A. H., 93, *113*
Schmitz, B., 226, *238*
Schneider, W., 228, *238*
Schneirla, T. C., 27, 33, 36, *45*
Schoenbach, C., 69, 70, 73, 81, 84, 85, 87, *89*
Schoenberg, R., 69, 70, 73, 81, 84, 85, 87, *89*
Schooler, C., 58, *64,* 69, 70, 73, 81, 84, 85, 87, *89*
Schrader, F. W., 228, 229, *238*
Schrier, B. K., 30–31, *43*
Schulman, P., 95, 104, *113*
Schultz, R., 97, *113*
Schweitzer, J., 220, *238*
Scribner, S. S., 194, *215*
Sears, R. R., 278, *298*
Seifer, R., 280, *298*
Seitz, V., 292, *298*
Seligman, M. E. P., 91, 92, 93, 94, 95, 100, 102, 103, 104, 107, 108, 109, *110, 112, 113, 114*
Semmel, A., 94, *113*
Sengelaub, D. R., 26, *45*
Senn, M. J. E., 278, *298*
Sewell, W. H., 68, *90*
Shadish, W. R., 23, *44*
Shapiro, B., 228, *239*
Sherrod, L. R., 144, *157,* 281, *298*
Shiffrin, R. M., 200, *215*
Shipman, W. G., 41, *46*
Siegal, A., 278, *299*
Siegler, R. S., 201, *216,* 269, *275*
Sigel, I. E., 160, *190*
Sigman, M. D., 219–220, *238*

Sillen, J., 38, *46*
Simmel, G., 48, *65*
Simmons, R. G., 39, *46,* 81, *90,* 162, *190*
Simon, H. A., 263, *274*
Simon, T., 204, *215*
Simonton, D., 263, *275*
Simpson, M., 221, *239*
Sinisterra, L., 280, *298*
Skinner, B. F., 193, 200, *216*
Sklar, L. S., 93, 105, *114*
Slesinger, D. P., 178, *190*
Slomczynski, K. M., 81, *90*
Smith, D., 48, *64*
Smith, M., 220, *238*
Smith, M. B., 138, *141*
Smith, R. S., 8, *19,* 280, 281, *299*
Smuts, A. B., 278, *299*
Smyer, M. A., *156*
Snyder, M., 23, 31, 34, *46,* 121, 137, *140, 142*
Sofer, C., 120, *142*
Søorensen, A. B., 75
Sorokin, P. A., 71, *90*
Spanier, G. B., 41, *45*
Spearman, 264, *275*
Spenner, K. I., 74, 74–75, 75, 81, 82, 84, 86, *89, 90*
Starnes, T., 99, *112*
Stattin, H., 39, 40, 41, *44*
Stein, M., 93, *113*
Stephan, C. W., 38, *44*
Sternberg, R. J., 261, 262, 263, 265, 267, 267–268, 269, 271, 272, *273, 274, 275*
Stevenson, H. W., 222, *239,* 242, 244, 246, 253, *258, 273, 299*
Stigler, J. W., 244, 246, *258*
Stillwell, R., 147, 148, *157*
Sroufe, L. A., *142,* 164, *190*
Suben, J., 267, 270, *275*
Sullivan, W., 61, 62, *64*
Suomi, S. J., 280, 282, *298*
Susman, E. J., 22, 23, *45*
Sutton, J., 60, *64*
Sutton-Smith, B., 166, *188*
Swafford, J. O., 244, *258*
Swindler, A., 61, 62, *64*

T

Taffel, S., 180, *190*
Takanishi, 278, *299*
Tanenbaum, R. L., 100, 109, *113*

Taylor, B., 39, 41, *45*
Teasdale, J. D., 91, 92, *110*
Tew, B. J., 172, *190*
Thomas, A., 29, 36, 38, *43, 46*
Thomas, G., 50, *65*
Thomas, W. I., 116, *142*
Thompson, L., 5, *18*
Thompson, R. A., 164, *188, 190*
Thurstone, L. L., 264, *275*
Tinsley, B. J., 163, 165, 173, 180, *189, 190*
Tinsley, B. R., 160, 167, 180, 184, *189*
Tipton, S., 61, 62, *64*
Tizard, B., 280, *299*
Tobach, E., 36, *46*
Trabasso, T. R., 199, *216*
Travers, K. J., 244, *258*
Treiber, B., 221, 224, *239*
Trussell, J., 180, *186*
Tuma, N. B., 87, *90*
Turkle, S., 195, *216*
Turner, R. H., 123, *142*
Turner, R. J., 177, 178

U

U.S. Congress, 293, *299*
Uphouse, L. L., 30, *46*

V

Valsiner, J., 271, *275*
Vaughn, B., 164, *190*
Visintainer, M. A., 93, *114*
Volling, B. L., 168, *186*
Volpicelli, J. R., 93, *114*
von Baeyer, C., 94, *113*
Vygotsky, L. S., 151, *157,* 203, 211, *216*

W

Wachs, T. D., 5, *19,* 164, *190,* 282, *299*
Wachtel, P., 34, *46,* 124, 136, *142*
Waddington, C. H., 7, *19*
Wagner, R. K., 262, 265, 266, 268, *275*
Walberg, H. J., 222, 230, 236, *239*

Walker, D. A., 222, *239*
Wallerstein, J. S., 161, *189,* 281, *299*
Walter, C. A., 182, *189*
Warner, W. L., 70, *90*
Washington, V., 292, *299*
Waters, E., 164, *190*
Weber, M., 49, *65*
Weinberg, R. A., 280, *298*
Weinert, F. E., 221, 224, 228, 233, *238, 239*
Weingarten, K. K., 180, 182, 183, *186, 187*
Weingold, F. D., 220, *238*
Weisz, J. R., 96, 98, *113, 114*
Werner, E. E., 8, *19,* 280, 281, *299*
Werner, H., 8, *19,* 198, *216*
Wertsch, J. V., 203, *216*
West, S. G., 22, 34, *46*
Weston, D. R., 164, *188*
White, S. H., 201, *216*
White, S. W., 11, *16*
Wiesenbaker, J., 220, *238*
Wiggins, J. S., 22, *46*
Wilkinson, A., 222, *239*
Willis, S. L., 203, *215,* 221, *239*
Windle, M., 31, 36, *46*
Winick, M., 280, *299*
Wise, L., 175, *186*
Wober, M., 269, *275*
Wohlwill, J. F., 27, *46,* 119, *142,* 219, *239*
Wortman, C. B., 92, 93, 101, *111*
Wright, E. O., 70, 71, 72, *90*

Y

Yamamoto, K., 143, *157*
Yogman, M. W., 173, *189*
York, R. L., 220, *238*
Yussen, S. R., 269, *275*

Z

Zabski, S., 36, *44*
Zahn-Waxler, C., 150, 152
Zaslow, M. J., 167
Zax, M., 280, 292
Zigler, E., 296, 278, *298, 299*
Znaniecki, F., 116, *142*

Subject Index

A

Achievement, 101–105
  in adults in workplace, 104–105
  in children, 101–102
  compensatory effects on, 231–236
  explanatory style link with, 92–93
  instructional effects on
    differential, 230–231
    general, 228–229
    interactional, 229–230
    long-term, 236
    short-term, 236
  outcomes, 228–229
  in students
    cognitive prerequisites and, 230–231
    instructional style and, 231–236
    self-concept and, 231–236
    teacher characteristics and, 228–229
    teacher diagnostic sensitivity and, 229–230
  in young adults in college, 102–104
    freshmen, 103
    upperclassmen, 103–104
Adolescence, psychosocial functioning in, 38–40
Adult feedback, role of, 99
ASQ. See Attributional Style Questionnaire
Attributional Style Questionnaire (ASQ), 94–95

B

Behavior
  explosive, 125–131
  marked changes in, 149
  withdrawn, 131–135
Bounded control system, 54–55

C

CAVE. See Content Analysis of Verbatim Explanations
Child(ren). See also Child psychology
  achievement in, 101–102
  analysis of, 176
  birth of sibling and, 146–148
  class and socialization of, 67–88
  class mobility of, 76–80
  comparative studies of, 242–252
    Asian and American, 242–252
    conclusion on, 256–257
    general information on, 248–252
    mathematics, 244–248
    Quechua-speaking Indian, 252–256
    samples for, 242, 253
    tasks in, 242–252, 253
    test results, 253–255
    vocabulary, 248–252
  explosive, 125–131
  gifted, 263

individual, in developmental perspective, 161–163
  social lives of, 143–146
    implications for study of changes in, 149–151
  social policies for, 290–293
  social understanding in, 143–146, 151–153
  withdrawn, 131–135
Child development, 259–260
  and social policy, 278
Childhood. *See* Child(ren)
Child psychology
  conclusions on, 63–64
  emergent perspectives in, 55–59
  implications for research in, 63–64
  and life-span development, 1–15
  public attention to, 47–50
    perspectives on, 48–49
  normative implications in, 60–61
  social construction of, 47–64
  social structural implications in, 61–63
Class
  categories of, 71–72
  and child socialization, 85–88
  description of, 69, 70
  mobility
    influence of, 80–85
    patterns of, 76–80
  schema for capitalist economies, 74–76
  social, 70–74
    socialization, tendencies of, 68–69
    structuration, 72–73
Cognition. *See also* Cognitive development
  changes in, with age, 193–196
    causes of, 196–197
  description of, 191–192
  form of, 193–194
  three-tier model of, 209–212
Cognitive development, 192. *See also* Cognition; Intellectucal development
  conclusions on, 212–214
  cultural influence on, 241–258
  individual differences in, 219–238
  schooling influence on, 241–258
  research on, 205–208
    findings in, comparison of, 205–208
  study of, approaches to, 197–205
    contextual, 202–204
    mechanistic, 200–202
    organismic, 198–200
    psychometric, 204–205
Communications, changes in, 150–151

Competence, 54–55
Construct, definition of, 22
Content Analysis of Verbatim Explanations (CAVE), 95
Continuity
  cumulative, 124–125, 137–138
  interactional, 124, 136–137
Control, 55

D

Development
  adult, 259–260
  advance in, 149–150
  changes in, 150
  cognitive. *See* Cognitive development
  concept of, 6–9
  direction of, 195–196
  endstate of, 196
  faces of, 160–171
  form of, 195
  influences on
    age-graded, 9–11
    class mobility, 80–85
    historical, 172–173
    history-graded, 9–11
    non-normative, 9–11
  intellectual, 260–262
  levels of
    dyadic, 163–166, 176–177
    familial, 169–171, 177–178
    individual, 161–163, 175–176
    multiple, 173–183
    triadic, 166–169
  as life-long process, 3–6
  personality, 21–41
  rate of, 196
  in social understanding, 151–153
Differences. *See* Individual differences

E

Environment
  adaptation to, 271–272
  intelligence and, 266–267, 270–271
Explanatory style
  achievement and, 92–93
  across the life span, 91–110
  continuity of, 109–110
  first major trauma influence on, 100
  health and, 93–94, 107–109

intergenerational transmission of, 100
life-span development and, 95–98
measurement of, 94–95
origins of, 98–101
role of adult feedback in, 99
stability of, 109–110
Explosive behavior. *See* Behavior, explosive

F

Family(ies)
analysis of, in early parenthood, 169–171, 182
as developmental unit of analysis, 169–171
in life-span perspective, 159–185
relationships, 169–171
Father-child relationship. *See* parent–child relationship

H

Health, 105–109
explanatory style and, 93–94, 107–109
Helplessness and health, 106–107
Hopelessness and health, 106–107
Husband-wife relationship, 165

I

Individual. *See also* Self
development of, 161
differences, 219–238
in achievement, 224–236
institutional character of, 52–55
structure, definition of, 27
Infant, analysis of, 176
Institutional boundaries, 55
Institutional structure, 50–52
individualism and, 52–55
organizational changes in, 53
Intellectual development, 260–262. *See also* Intelligence
definition of, 266
theories on, 272
Intelligence. *See also* Intellectual development
adult, views of
traditional, 262
multifaceted, 263–264
conceptions of, 268–269
environment and, 266–267, 270–271

knowledge and, 265
measures of, 267–268
theories of, 267–268
triarchic, 264–265
wisdom and, 262–263
IQ, 221, 264, 267
Irritability, 33

L

Life course
behavior in, measurement of, 122–124
childhood precursors of, 115–139
early personality and, 135–138
institutional structure and, 50–52
pattern(s) of, 120–121
of explosive children, 125–131
of withdrawn children, 131–135
personality in, 138–139
analysis of, 120–124
coherence of, 117–124
situation measurements of, 119
study of, 117–124
time measurements of, 119
situations in, 121–122
structure of, 120–121
subjective side of, 51
Life disorganization, early personality and, 124–135
Life-span. *See also* Life-span development
explanatory style across, 91–110
ideas, 59–60
lessons from, 259–273
perspective
class and child socialization in, 85–88
cognitive development in, 191–214
families in, 159–185
stressful transitions in, 183–184
research, forms of, 1–3
Life-span development, 1–15. *See also* Life-span
change and, 280–281.
child psychology and, 1–15
diversity in, 281–282
domain specificity in, 282
explanatory style and, 95–98
intervention cube, 279, 282–290, 291, 294
behavioral domain, 286, 288
chronological age, 283, 285
generic, 284
resource competition, 286, 289–290

social population, 283, 286, 287
  spaces in, comparative view of, 290
interventions, 13–14, 280–282
  political realities and, 279–280
political realities and, 293–296
propositions in, 3–12
theory, elements of, 278–279

M

Mental age, 221, 264, 267
Mother–child relationship. *See* Parent–child relationship
Motivation, effects of instruction on, 236
Motives, 54

P

Parent–child relationship, 163–165, 176–177, 181
Parenthood
  historical effects on, 179, 182–183
  levels of analysis in
    dyadic, 176–177, 181–182
    family, 177–179, 182
    individual, 175–176, 179–181
  timing of, 174–183
    early, 175–179
    late, 179–183
PEATS. *See* Pennsylvania Early Adolescent Transitions Study
Pennsylvania Early Adolescent Transition Study (PEATS), 37–38
Perception, 54
Personality
  in age-graded life course, 126
  coherence of, 117–124
  components of
    generic, 24–27
    idiographic, 30–32
    universal, 24–27
  definition of, 23–24
    debates about, 22–23
    differences of, 22
  early
    and life course, 135–138
    and life disorganization, 124–135
  function of, 23
  "how" of, 36–37
  structure of, 23
  study of, framework for, 117–124

Personality development, 21–41
  adolescent psychosocial functioning and, 38–40
  approaches to
    ipsative, 30–32
    nomothetic-differential, 27–30
  components of
    generic, 24–27
    idiographic, 30–32
    universal, 24–27
  conclusions on, 41
  life-span model of, 32–40
  pubertal maturation and, 38–40
  social context of, 38–40
  subgroup commonalities in, 27–30
Psychology of childhood. *See* Child psychology

R

Relationships
  husband-wife, 165, 181–182
  marked changes in, 149
  parent-child, 163–165, 176–177, 181
  sibling-sibling, 166

S

Self. *See also* Individual
  as actor, 54–55
  definition of, elements of, 57–58
  economy of, 54
  polity of, 55
  technological capability structure of, 54–55
Sibling birth, 146–148
  immediate impact of, 146–147
Sibling-sibling relationships, 166
Social class, 69, 70–74
  influence of, 80–85
Social status, 70
Status, 70
  description of, 69, 70

T

Tantrums. *See* Behavior, explosive
Temper tantrums. *See* Behavior, explosive
Trauma, first major, 100

W

Wife–husband relationship, 165
Withdrawn behavior. *See* Behavior, withdrawn